ISRAELI EXCEPTIONALISM

PRAISE FOR THE BOOK

"M. Shahid Alam's...book...is a fascinating historical analysis, densely detailed and referenced, of the nature and trajectory of Jewish nationalism. It is bracingly honest, dispensing with the usual Western pieties to describe three elements of what Edward Said called Israel's 'ideology of difference.' These are, firstly, the notion of Jewish chosenness and divine right to Palestine; secondly, the 'miraculous' creation and survival of the state; and thirdly, the uniquely tragic history of the Jewish people.

Israeli Exceptionalism is nearly the best introduction to Zionism there is, but not quite. It feels slightly improvised....Alam's central arguments, his insistence—against the grain for the traditional left—on bringing culture into the equation, and the wealth of fresh information in this fascinating book, make it essential and provocative reading for any serious student of the conflict."

—Robin Yassin-Kassab, author of *The Road from Damascus* (Penguin),
in *Holy Land Studies* (forthcoming)

"For those unfamiliar with the extraordinary evolution of Israeli exceptionalism emanating from its Zionist narrative and assuring Israel's incredible success as a colonial settler state, M. Shahid Alam's book is the one to read. He has recorded a compelling, uniquely comprehensive and enlightening historical analysis of the inherently destabilizing dynamic of Zionism."

—Elaine Hagopian, Professor Emerita of Sociology at Simmons College, in *Pulse*

"*Israeli Exceptionalism* is not only a must read, it is a must-think-about book.

[Alam] does a fascinating job of creating a repository of references on Zionism by way of narrative and footnotes. Although I think of myself as well read on the topic, I attest that I learned much from *Israeli Exceptionalism*, not only in terms of identifying new references, but also in terms of analysis and context."

—Sam Bahour, commentator, in *Arab News*

...many will consider the book to be controversial, and most will consider it provocative. Nobody will think it is uninteresting or irrelevant. It is novel in insights, keen in analysis, and sharp in language. The dominant discourse in the West, certainly in the US, about the Arab-Israeli conflict is usually simplistic, often cowardly, and almost always tendentious. Alam's counter-narrative, in spite of its indignant tone and grim prognosis, is a brave and bracing antidote to much mainstream blather on the subject."

—Ahrar Ahmad, Professor of political science at
Black Hills State University, in *Informed Comment*

"Alam demonstrates clearly, through voluminous evidence and a carefully argued analysis, that Zionism was never benign, never good—that from the very beginning, it operated according to a 'cold logic' and, per Rumi, had 'no humanity.' Except perhaps for Jews, which is where Israel's and Zionism's exceptionalism comes in.

This is a critically important book. It enhances and expands on the groundbreaking message of Shlomo Sand's work. If Sand shows that Jews were not 'a people' until Zionism created them as such, Alam shows this also and goes well beyond to show how Zionism and its manufactured 'nation' went about dispossessing and replacing the Palestinians and winning all-important Western support for Israel and its now 60-year-old 'exclusionary colonialism.'"

—Kathleen Christison, author of *Perceptions of Palestine*
and the *Wound of Dispossession*, in *CounterPunch*.

ISRAELI EXCEPTIONALISM

THE DESTABILIZING LOGIC OF ZIONISM

M. Shahid Alam

ISRAELI EXCEPTIONALISM
Copyright © M. Shahid Alam, 2009.

First published in 2009 by PALGRAVE MACMILLAN® in the United States—a division of
St. Martin's Press LLC, 175 Fifth Avenue, New York, NY 10010

Where this book is distributed in the UK, Europe and the rest of the world, this is by Palgrave
Macmillan, a division of Macmillan Publishers Limited, registered in England, company
number 785998, of Houndmills, Basingstoke, Hampshire RG21 6XS.

Palgrave Macmillan is the global academic imprint of the above companies and has companies
and representatives throughout the world.

Palgrave® and Macmillan® are registered trademarks in the United States, the United
Kingdom, Europe and other countries.

ISBN: 978-0-230-61998-2

Library of Congress Cataloging-in-Publication Data

Alam, M. Shahid (Mohammad Shahid), 1950-
   Israeli exceptionalism : the destabilizing logic of Zionism / M. Shahid Alam.
       p. cm.
   ISBN: 978-0-230-61998-2 (alk. paper)
   1. Zionism—Israel—History. 2. Israel—Politics and government. I. Title.

DS149.5.I75A53 2010
320.54095694—dc22   2009008817

A catalogue record of the book is available from the British Library.

Design by Scribe Inc.

First PALGRAVE MACMILLAN paperback edition: September 2010

10 9 8 7 6 5 4 3 2 1

Printed in the United States of America.

Transferred to Digital Printing in 2010.

You have the light, but you have no humanity. Seek humanity, for that is
the goal.

—Rumi

CONTENTS

PREFACE

Why is an economist writing a book on the geopolitics of Zionism? This is easily explained. I could have written a book about the economics of Zionism, the Israeli economy, or the economy of the West Bank and Gaza, but how would any of that have helped me to understand the cold logic and the deep passions that have driven Zionism?

Zionism is a historic movement that emerges from the guts of Europe's turbulent history. It is propelled by the dialectical interactions between two intertwined streams of Western civilization, the Jewish and Christian. And, as it has unfolded, Zionism has brought both these Western streams into a dangerous collision with the Islamicate. It would not be easy squeezing this tragic history into an economic model or a set of econometric estimations.

In my capacity as an "economist" too, Zionism, at its core—as an exclusionary settler colonialism—was scarcely a strange beast. I began grappling with colonialism as a graduate student. In one of the three essays that I wrote for my PhD dissertation, I used the tools of economics to explain why the free trade that the British imposed on India in the nineteenth century had led to its pauperization. A decade later, after I had secured "citizenship" in the department of economics at Northeastern University, I returned to this subject again. In several articles, leading to a book, *Poverty from the Wealth of Nations*, I examined the theory, history, and evidence on the connections between colonialism and backwardness in the global economy that emerged during the nineteenth century.

Zionism has always piqued my interest because of the cleverness that it brought to the defense of its aims. I had my first encounter with a Zionist in 1974 when I was a student at the University of Indiana at Bloomington. When my interlocutor discovered my opposition to Zionism, the conversation quickly took an eerie turn. In anger, assuming that I was an Arab, he placed the blame for the Holocaust on the Arabs. If the Arabs had not resisted the entry of Jews into Palestine, there would have been no Jews in

Europe for the Nazis to exterminate; they would all be in Palestine. This was my first taste of the self-righteous rhetoric of Zionism.

I first began writing about Zionism when I was persuaded by the attacks of 9/11 to enter into the public discourse on the "clash of civilizations," a brilliantly executed ideologization of the Zionist onslaught against the Arabs. At this time, I first began asking myself, why had Zionism achieved such dramatic success during a phase of global capitalism when all overt imperialist intrusions into the periphery were being rolled back and terminated? My early jabs at this question produced a few essays that became part of my previous book, *Challenging the New Orientalism*. I will let the reader decide if the book in hand, the result of three years' labor, has produced a more definitive explanation.

Writing about Zionism has not been easy. The history of Zionism is history gone wrong, and not only for the Palestinians. The tragedy for the Palestinians is obvious, although blinded by racism and the Zionist bias of their media, Westerners only recently have begun to see this tragedy for what it is. It has been a tragedy for the Jewish people too, who were co-opted by the Zionists to place their energy, their talent, and their hopes on a project they should never have undertaken, and whose only chance of success lay in obliterating the hopes of another people. The more trapped this project becomes in its own logic, the greater the destruction it becomes willing to wreak. It chooses destruction in order to delay coming to terms with, and making amends for, the tragedy it has spawned.

Thankfully, during my encounters with Zionism, I have received warm support from a few good friends. They stood by me when my writings provoked the ire of Zionists and some of their overzealous acolytes. Critics of Zionism have never been safe from reprisals in the United States; after 9/11, their position became more precarious. Alone, I could not have faced the special attention I was receiving from this band of zealots. For their warm support, friendship, and counsel in these difficult times, I am grateful to Elaine Hagopian, Syed Shakeel, Ken Barney, Paul de Rooij, Lawrence Davidson, Frank Naarendorp, Kamal Ahmed, Susan Barney, Nazim Ali, Agha Sayeed, Teepu Siddique, Amr Fahmi, and Muhammad Idrees Ahmad. I could not have asked for more supportive friends on my difficult journeys in Zionist territory.

Two of my friends deserve my special thanks. Very generously, Elaine and Ken provided extensive comments on an earlier draft of this book, which proved very helpful in revisions of the manuscript. I hasten to add that these friends do not agree with all the particulars of the case that I present in this book. Indeed, my differences with Ken produced at least one very lively exchange of opposing viewpoints about the part played by secular Jewish messianism in the creation of Israel.

I would be remiss if I did not acknowledge a more personal debt to Farzana, Junaid, and Noor—my wife and sons—for putting up, during the past three years, with the more than usual dose of my dour prose about all that is wrong with the world. Now that this book is behind us, I promise there will be more sweetness and light, more Rumi and Ghalib, more Iqbal and Faiz.

I will close with words borrowed from al-Beruni's *Kitäb al-Hind*: "We ask God to pardon us for every statement of ours which is not true. We ask Him to help us that we may adhere to that which yields Him satisfaction. We ask Him to lead us to a proper insight into the nature of that which is false and idle, that we may sift it so as to distinguish the chaff from the wheat. All good comes from Him, and it is He who is clement towards His slaves. Praise be to God, the Lord of the worlds, and His blessings be upon the prophet Muhammad and his whole family!"

PART I

ISRAELI EXCEPTIONALISM

Israel is unique in the world for the excuses made on its behalf.
—Edward Said[1]

Chapter 1

Varieties of Exceptionalism

Israel is not another example of the species nation; it is the only example of the species Israel.

—Martin Buber

Only Israel lives in, and constitutes, God's kingdom.

—Jacob Neusner

For me the supreme morality is that the Jewish people has a right to exist. Without that there is no morality in the world.

—Golda Meier, 1967[2]

IN AUGUST 1897, THE FOUNDERS OF ZIONISM proposed a novel plan for the "liberation" of a nation that did not yet exist. They called for the liberation of *European* Jews in Palestine, not in Europe.[3] A colonial plan so ambitious, daring, even quixotic, would have to be defended by myths that could match the ambitions of the Zionists.

There is no dearth of histories, analyses, and psychoanalyses of Zionism and its founders; they could easily fill a sizable library.[4] This book will overlap with this literature, but it also brings a different focus to the Zionist question. We focus on the germ of the Zionist idea, its core ambition—clearly discernible at its launching—to create a Jewish state in the Middle East by displacing the natives. This *exclusionary* colonialism would unleash a deeply destabilizing logic, if it were to succeed.[5] It could advance only by creating and promoting conflicts between the West and the Islamicate.[6] Since its creation, this primordial logic has driven the Jewish state to deepen this conflict. Overweening ambition launched Zionism, but the destabilizing logic of this idea has advanced and sustained it. This is our primary theme.

The Zionists proposed to lead the Jews—who had been for millennia a global religious community—into Palestine and turn them into a nation with a land and state of their own.[7] In the early years of the movement, most Jews dismissed Zionism as utopian adventurism, since the Jews lacked the basic prerequisites of a nation state.[8] They were not a nation, as commonly understood; nor did they possess a national territory. In order to overcome these grave deficiencies, the Zionists would have to find a surrogate mother country, seize Palestine, persuade Western Jews to colonize this land, and empty Palestine of its native population. The Zionists were not lacking in ambition.

So ambitious, so egregious a nationalist project demanded a prodigious and sustained effort at mythmaking. The Zionist ideologues would have to justify their violent mission, glorify it, and eventually place it beyond criticism. They would have to convince the diverse and scattered Jewish communities in the West that they are a nation, descended from the ancient Hebrews. They would have to motivate Jewish communities in the West, who were mostly satisfied with their lives and prospects, to become pioneers in Palestine. They would have to divert Jewish migrants, fleeing anti-Semitic persecution in Eastern Europe, away from their preferred Western destinations to the risks of colonizing a backward land. They would have to construct legal and moral alibis for their territorial conquests in the Middle East. In order to engage in repeated ethnic cleansing of the Palestinians, they would have to deny that their victims had any rights to their lands or that they had ever existed as a people.

The Zionists could *not* take possession of Palestine on their own. They would have to recruit one or more of the great powers to do it for them. This would be a first in history. Some great power would have to engage in "altruistic" colonialism, seize a territory, and give it over to another people for colonization. Such altruistic colonialism appeared even less credible because the Jews had no ethnic or religious affinity to any of the great Western powers who could do their bidding. The Zionists faced another more daunting task: they would have to persuade one or more great powers to act *against* their own national interests.

There is no arguing that the tasks before the Zionists were formidable. In order to mobilize the Jews behind these nearly impossible goals, the Zionist ideologues would have to forge a nationalism that evoked both deep fears and lofty ambitions. They would constantly remind the Jews that they are an ancient people, divinely favored, uniquely talented, racially superior, and undefeatable, who deserved more than any other people to make history as a great nation. The Zionists would have to construct an ideology of Jewish exceptionalism. They would have to endow their project, the Jews and the state they proposed to create, with a nearly inexhaustible repertoire of exceptional qualities. Nothing less would serve to prop and propel this utopian project into reality.

The Zionists have met this ideological challenge with admirable success. Few nationalists have shown more cunning, brought more energy, or been more successful at asserting their exceptionalist claims than the Zionists. These exceptionalist claims are diverse and they concern Judaism, Jews, and Israel—overlapping categories, for the most part. It was easy enough to assert the exceptionalism of Judaism and the Jews, which had roots in the Jewish Bible. In addition, the Zionists launched new claims of exceptionalism about their "liberation" movement, the long history of Jewish suffering, the Jewish ability to outlive their enemies, their signal contributions to human civilization, and their spectacular victories against Arab armies. At the same time, they created negative exceptionalisms too that depicted Israel as a small country, under siege by hostile Arab armies, whose existence was constantly under threat and whose right to exist was denied by its enemies.

These exceptionalist claims now form an integral part of the self-image of most Israelis and Jews. It is a rare partisan of Zionism who does not claim that Israel is in some ways special, anomalous, superior, miraculous, rare, exceptional, *sui generis*, unique, even amazingly unique. In Zionist writings, all too often Israel enters the world's stage decked in the full regalia of exceptionalist claims. Moreover, as one Israeli academic emphasizes, "it is the duty of Jews to preserve that uniqueness and to 'dwell apart.'"[9]

Some of the rhetoric about Israeli and Jewish exceptionalism is merely conceited, a defect of piquant patriotism, or a paroxysm of high-spirited partisanship. This banal exceptionalism is not the issue here. Israeli exceptionalism stirs our curiosity only when it is ideological, when it enters the vocabulary of maleficent Zionist advocacy, when Israel recruits this language to rescind the rights of Palestinians. This exceptionalism provokes our interest because it seeks to obfuscate Israel's colonialist character, to elevate it above historical analysis, and to tear it from the historical category of colonialism to which it belongs. Israel uses its exceptionalist claims to smear its Palestinian victims, to whitewash its segregated society as the only democracy in the Middle East, to justify its settler colonialism as a well-deserved denouement to the long history of Jewish "exile." In Edward Said's apt phrase, we have chosen to engage with Israeli exceptionalism because it is an "ideology of difference."[10]

Israeli exceptionalism is overweening in its ambition. This rhetorical projection of its power seeks nothing less than to exempt Israel from the censure of world conscience, and, no less, the scrutiny of Jewish ethics. For six decades, it has succeeded in placing Israel above the sanction of international laws, legitimizing its expansionist policies, and exempting its crimes from the world's moral and legal sanctions. Protected by the baneful language of exceptionalism, Israel claims the right to mangle millions of lives, to persist in violence, start new wars, and, more recently, to threaten its neighbors with nuclear holocaust.

The ideological project of Israeli exceptionalism has been orchestrated and staffed by brilliantly clever impresarios. It has been promoted by a legion of handlers and hacks: shamelessly partisan anchors, editors, columnists, film producers, novelists, and historians. They have invented a new language, with its peculiar vocabulary, grammar, manuals, and literature. They unremittingly spin their narratives of exceptionalism. They are ever ready to invent new species of exceptionalisms, and put old ones to new uses, as world conscience slowly ratchets its moral reading on Israel. This project has recruited archaeologists as well as geneticists to support its atavistic claims.[11]

Israeli exceptionalism has taken three principal forms. An important branch of this exceptionalism, rooted in the Jewish doctrine of chosenness, invokes the "divine right" of the Jewish people to nullify the historical and legal rights of Palestinians to their homeland. Implicitly, this gives the long-suffering Jews the right to expel or exterminate the Palestinians if they do not recognize the superior Jewish rights to their land. A second branch marshals Israeli achievements—and some of these do appear exceptional at first sight—to build the morale of the flock and win support for Israel in the West. It also serves to justify *ex post facto* the dispossession of the "inferior" Palestinians by the "superior" Jews. A third species of exceptionalism claims for the Jews a uniquely tragic history and portrays Israel as a uniquely vulnerable country. In order to secure itself against these "unique" threats to its existence, Israel claims exemption from the demands of international laws.

· · ·

No single idea has played a stronger supportive role in mobilizing both Jewish and Christian support for Zionism than the doctrine of divine election or chosenness.[12]

This doctrine was not the original driving force behind Zionism. The founding fathers of Zionism were mostly secular Jews who sought a solution to the "Jewish problem" by creating a Jewish state—in the sense of a state of, for, and by the Jewish people—in Palestine. Nevertheless, by deciding to *locate* their state in Palestine, the early Zionists were also choosing to harness the mythic power of Palestine as the "promised land" and the ancient homeland of the Jewish people. Eminently secular though he was, Theodore Herzl too understood the lure of this mythic power.

"Palestine is our ever-memorable historic home," he wrote in 1896. "The very name of Palestine would attract our people with a force of marvellous potency."[13] Over time, because of this choice, the doctrine of divine election would become one of the central pillars in the edifice of Israeli exceptionalism.[14] Ironically, but unavoidably, political Zionism would both seek and gain traction as an eschatological movement to create the world's only eschatological state—the embodiment of divine promises and prophecies.

When it was first proposed, political Zionism had little to recommend itself apart from the allure of the "promised land," the ancient Jewish belief that their divinely appointed destiny, their earthly salvation and glory, were tied to Palestine. Some Jews greeted the Zionist project with consternation; they worried that any plan for the creation of a Jewish state would give an impetus to anti-Semitism in Europe. Others regarded it with derision, because they saw this as a fantastic utopia with little chance of success. The success of the Zionist plan depended on fulfilling three apparently unattainable conditions: persuading Jews to abandon their present homes, in Europe and the Americas, for the hazards of colonizing a backward land; wresting control of Palestine from its Ottoman sovereign; and disappearing the Palestinians from their lands. Some very real hurdles blocked the Zionists from creating these conditions.

There was another hitch. Political Zionism lacked the religious sanction to work for the restoration of Jews to Palestine. According to traditional readings of the Jewish Bible, Orthodox Jews believed that their "restoration" would be the work of the Jewish Messiah, who would appear as part of God's plan for the culmination of history.[15] Moreover, starting in the nineteenth century, a growing number of assimilated Jews had come to invest the "return to Zion" with symbolic meaning that could be pursued even in exile. Overcoming the opposition of Orthodox Jews or the skepticism of assimilated Jews would not be easy.

The early Zionists treated these objections with disdain. Indeed, when their adversaries described their plans as quixotic or insane, they took these as compliments. "It is the Zionists' good fortune," Chaim Weizmann declared at a public meeting in 1914, "that they are considered mad; if we were normal, we would not consider going to Palestine but stay put like all normal people."[16] Apart from their sober hopes of ending Jewish persecution and the Jewish "exile," the visions of reconstituting Jewish power that animated some of the leading early Zionists were quite heady. Taking the cue from biblical accounts of Davidic splendor, they spoke of establishing Jewish power on a scale that the Israelites could not attain in ancient times.

Zionism dared a handful of ambitious Jews to engage in a Nietzschean enterprise, to create their eschatological state *without* the intervention of a Jewish Messiah. In an entry in his diary on September 3, 1897, just a few days after the first World Zionist Congress in Basel, Theodore Herzl wrote in his diary, "At Basel, I founded the Jewish State. If I said this out loud today, I would be answered by universal laughter. Perhaps in five years, certainly in fifty, everyone will know it." Herzl best captures the early Zionist chutzpah in the epigraph to his novel, *Altneuland*, written in 1902: "If you will it, it is no fable."[17] In time, this epigram gained wide circulation as an inspirational Zionist slogan. In 1909, in a lecture to the London University Zionist Society, Chaim Weizmann, struck the same Nietzschean note when he declared, "We have to create our title out of our wish to go to Palestine."[18]

Once the practical and moral difficulties of their plan became clearer, the Zionists would find the doctrine of Jewish chosenness handy. "One need only imagine what would happen in the world," Nahum Goldmann wrote in 1978, "if all the peoples who lost their states centuries or millennia ago . . . were to reclaim their land."[19] In other words, how were the Zionists going to justify the theft of land from the Palestinians? One argument claimed that since the Palestinians were not a people—on the specious ground that Palestine was not a sovereign state—they had no juridical rights over their lands.[20] With greater malice, another claimed that most of the Arabs living in Palestine at the end of the British mandate were not natives; they were recent immigrants from neighboring Arab countries, attracted to Palestine by the growing demand for labor induced by Jewish colonization.[21] A third argument was simpler. The Zionists contended that Palestine was *terra nullius*, an empty land: quite simply, the Palestinians just did not exist.

The biblical doctrine of chosenness was enough to clinch the validity of Zionist claims to Palestine.[22] The Zionists had little difficulty convincing their Jewish and Christian audiences—the only ones that mattered—that seizing Palestine was not a theft. Populations raised on biblical myths believed that God had promised Palestine to the Jews; it was their eternal inheritance. Accidents of earthly history—such as the absence of the owners—could not annul ownership rights that were divinely ordained. Zionism was a messianic movement to restore Palestine to its divinely appointed Jewish owners. Once this quaint narrative was accepted, the Jewish colonists could claim that they were only "redeeming" their lands. Conversely, the Palestinian, whether his ancestors were the ancient Canaanites or Hebrews, would forfeit all rights to his lands; he had become a usurper.

Jewish sacred history supported the Zionists on another important matter: the creation of a Jewish majority in Palestine, preferably by driving out the native population.[23] At first, the Zionists gave little thought to the Arab presence in Palestinian. They pretended that the Palestinians were vagrants, without any love for their land or homes, who could be persuaded to leave with a little bribe.[24] When the Palestinians did not oblige, the Zionists prepared to evict them by force, under the fog of war. That opportunity arrived all too soon, following the approval of the UN partition plan in November 1947. Starting in December 1947, the Jewish colons expelled some 800,000 Palestinians, destroyed their towns and villages, and made sure that they would never return to their homes in what had now become the Jewish state of Israel. This ethnic cleansing of Palestinians may have troubled some secular Jews; but a new generation of more religious Zionists, better acquainted with the conquest narratives of the Torah, would argue that Yahweh had urged rather more extreme measures when the ancient Israelites were taking possession of Canaan.[25] In comparison to their legendary forebears, the Zionists had been kind to the Palestinians.

When the Zionists became more expansive in their territorial ambitions, once again, they found support in the Torah. The Lord's promise to the Israelites was not restricted to Canaan. In a more generous vein, He had redrawn the borders of the Jewish inheritance to include all the lands between the Nile and Euphrates.[26] In terms of present-day borders, this expansive Israeli empire would include Egypt, Palestine, Jordan, Syria, Lebanon, Iraq, and perhaps the northern parts of Saudi Arabia. If the Zionists could use the Bible to claim Palestine, they could invoke the same divine authority to claim the rest of the Arab Middle East as well. On the third day of Suez War in 1956, Ben-Gurion told the Knesset—according to an account of it given by Israel Shahak—"that the real reason for it is 'the restoration of the kingdom of David and Solomon' to its biblical borders. At this point in his speech, almost every Knesset member spontaneously rose and sang the Israeli national anthem."[27]

The doctrine of election did not merely set the Jews apart from other nations: it set them *above* these nations.[28] "Jewish religion," according to Yehezkel Dror, "sees the Jewish people and Israel as *radically unique in their essential nature* and in their existential justification, as both a fact and a norm" (emphasis added).[29] Over time, this growing emphasis on the "radical uniqueness" of Israel would give rise to racist tendencies. Since the Jews were the chosen instruments of God's intervention on earth, some Jewish thinkers took this to mean that Jews were not subject to the laws of nature and society.[30] In other words, as long as the Jews believed that they were acting as instruments of God's will, they did not have to place themselves under the laws of Gentile nations. As Israelis have moved to the religious right, a shift propelled by the logic and experience of Zionism itself, Zionist advocates have shown an increasing willingness to justify their human rights abuses as a Jewish prerogative.[31] As its victims continue to resist the advance of Zionism, the "chosen people" slowly but surely take on the hues of a "master race" with the capacity to legitimize their actions by merely willing them into existence.

       .   .   .

The Zionist rhetoric of divine election would carry little conviction if they could not achieve unexpected victories that would be seen as "divine favors." In the event, Zionist achievements, before and after the creation of Israel, exceeded even their own sober expectations. The Zionist ideologues would now burnish these achievements so that they could carry the weight of the exceptional, unique, and even miraculous. We turn now to the invention of these more mundane Israeli exceptionalisms.

The creation of Israel—ostensibly, against the heaviest odds—is often offered as proof of Israeli exceptionalism. Unfailingly, the words, miracle or miraculous can be found in close proximity to any mention of the creation of Israel.[32] Speaking in Washington to the American Jewish Committee, on the fiftieth anniversary of the creation of Israel, Prime Minister Netanyahu claimed that the creation of Israel was "a miracle with no parallel in history." He argued that only one people, the Jews, lost their state, were scattered, and then, some nineteen hundred years later, returned to reestablish their state on its original site.[33] It is a claim that Zionists repeat frequently without recognizing its irony. Of European colonial-settler states, there has been no dearth in recent centuries. Only Israel, however, advertises itself as the restoration of a state that had ceased to exist in antiquity. Most people would be grateful that such oddities have been rare, that Israel remains an anomaly, the only member of a very numerous class of extinct states that has emerged in a new incarnation through ethnic cleansing.

All too often, Israel's military victories too are described as "miraculous." In the Zionist narrative, the contest between Israel and the Arabs is nearly always unequal, with the odds stacked against Israel. It is always "tiny" Israel defending itself against the entire Arab world; or the Israeli army, beleaguered, alone, faces the combined might of multiple Arab armies. Israel always enters the scene as a Jewish David battling an Arab Goliath. Israel's victories, therefore, are seen as validating biblical prophecies. Alternatively, they demonstrate its exceptional leadership, military, and fighting skills, in a stunning reversal of the perennial role of Jews as the victims of anti-Semitic hatred. One avid Zionist described Israel's victory in the War of June 1967 as the "most overwhelming victory in the annals of warfare."[34] Israel's repeated victories, its capacity to attack Arabs at will, are trumpeted as proofs of Israeli exceptionalism, the unique ability of this small country to defeat an entire civilization.

In war and peace alike, Israelis claim moral uniqueness for their actions in their domestic and foreign relations. "It is a grave error," wrote Rabbi Kook, "to be insensitive to the distinctive unity of the Jewish spirit, to imagine that the Divine stuff which uniquely characterizes Israel is comparable to the spiritual content of all the other national civilizations."[35] Likewise, Ben-Gurion spoke of Israel's "unique moral mission." Zionists seeking to place Israel's "special relationship" with the United States above the tug of international politics, argue that "America supports Israel because as nations they share a unique moral character."[36] In August 1995, when an Israeli general revealed that the Haganah had killed Egyptian prisoners of war in the Suez War, Prime Minister Yitzhak Rabin denounced the general for shining the light on a rogue event. He protested that "the IDF achieved its start as a humanitarian army, whose soldiers were blessed with a unique ethical standard. The exceptions teach nothing about the general rule."[37]

Some claims of Israeli exceptionalism work only by carefully restricting the comparisons to countries in the Middle East. Thus, Israeli leaders and their Zionist acolytes in the West never tire of reminding Western audiences that Israel is the only democracy in the Middle East. Israel alone holds up the beacon of freedom in this benighted corner of the world, held in the vise-grip of monarchs and dictators. Similarly, Israel draws attention to its "miraculous growth" since 1948, its high standard of living, education levels, and technology, which make it an outlier, an exceptional society in the Middle East.[38] In these cases, as in some others, Israel makes the claim to singularity by locating itself in the Middle East. It uses geography to conceal the fact that it is a European outpost in the Middle East, a colonial-settler state that has continued to draw upon the financial resources, skills and technology of the most advanced Western societies.

Israel is also America's "most valuable strategic asset" in the Middle East. Since June 1967, when it inflicted a stunning military defeat on the two leading Arab nationalist states, Egypt and Syria, Israel has endlessly claimed the status of America's most valuable and most reliable ally in the Middle East. During the Cold War, Israel was the West's bulwark against Arab nationalism and Soviet domination of the Middle East. Since the end of the Cold War, it has claimed that it is the best defense against the Islamist threat to Western interests in the Middle East. Israel is America's "aircraft carrier," its "fortress" in the Middle East. In his speech to the American Jewish Committee in May 1998, Prime Minister Netanyahu claimed that "the single most important factor in the Middle East itself that prevented Soviet domination of that area was Israel."[39] Israel also asserts—as one more proof of its indispensability to the United States—that it is one of a small handful of countries that have always voted with the United States in the UN General Assembly. They forget to add that the other members of this elite club are Tuvalu, Nauru, and Marshall Islands.

.   .   .

A third species of exceptionalism makes claims about a unique history of Jewish suffering. It focuses on the adversities endured by Jews—their legal disabilities, persecutions, and expulsions—while passing over periods of tolerance, given the norms of the age, during which they prospered and made many signal contributions both to Jewish culture and to the economy, knowledge, and culture of Gentile societies.

It appears that this "lachrymose historiography" of a uniquely suffering Jewish people emerged during the nineteenth century; it was expected to compensate increasingly secularized Jews for their loss of faith and rituals.[40] Since the creation of Israel—and following the Holocaust—this approach to Jewish historiography has become more pervasive, making it nearly impossible, in some circles, to conceive of Jews playing any role in European history other than that of victims. In recent decades, a few Jewish historians have been busy extending this lachrymose approach to the history of the Jews in the Middle East, a region that has historically treated its religious minorities more humanely than Christian Europe. This revisionist rewriting of Jewish history in the Middle East is determined to document, exclusively and obsessively, every discrimination, every injury, and every slight endured by Middle Eastern Jews.[41]

The hatred that has produced and produces the uniquely Jewish suffering is also unique. Directed only against Jews, this unique species of hatred is irrational, enduring, universal, and boundless in its malicious intent. "Hatred of Jews has been humanity's greatest hatred," write Dennis Prager and Joseph Telushkin in their widely acclaimed book, *Why the Jews?* "While hatred of other groups has always existed, no hatred has been as universal, as deep, or as permanent as anti-Semitism."[42] Anti-Semitism is unique because it hates Jews not because of what they *do*, but because of *who* they *are*. This historiography lifts anti-Semitism out of history; the hatred of Jews exists outside the matrix of causation, independently of the flux of material, social, and political conditions; it does not arise from ethnic rivalries and jealousies; it is unrelated to the divisive politics of the ruling classes. In other words, anti-Semitism is a primal, immanent characteristic of the Gentile world. So pervasive is this canonical understanding of anti-Semitism that many Jews and Westerners now equate any hostility toward the Jews—even that of their Palestinian or Arab victims—with anti-Semitism. Indeed, any criticism of Israel is denounced as anti-Semitic.

No human tragedy—in Zionist historiography—can even begin to match the horror of the Holocaust. It stands in a class by itself. Never before were humans exterminated by these cold, industrial methods; never before have so many humans been exterminated in so ghastly a fashion; never before, and never since, has one group of humans sought the complete annihilation of another. The Zionists were describing anti-Semitism as a uniquely perverse hatred even before it erupted in the industrial insanity of the Holocaust. Only Jew hatred could produce the most unimaginable crime ever perpetrated against any people.[43] The Holocaust was the natural terminus of a hatred that was as boundless, enduring, and unprovoked as anti-Semitism.

Zionists have spilled a vast quantity of polemical ink to establish, argue, and defend the uniqueness of the Holocaust. As soon as one claim to its uniqueness is contested, new ones are discovered. Its uniqueness sacralizes the Holocaust; to compare it to any other genocide, other crimes against humanity, is to degrade it, desacralize it. It is as if history could have "chosen" no one but the Jews for this unimaginable suffering. In effect, this means that the Holocaust is the renewal in historical time of the original covenant between God and the Jewish people, now sealed in the incineration chambers of Auschwitz. God has once again *chosen* the Jews by making them—and them alone—suffer death by incineration. To question the uniqueness of the Holocaust, to compare it to the extermination of the Native Americans, the Tasmanians, the Hereros, the Congolese, the Gypsies, the Cambodians, or the Tutsis, is to dishonor this covenant, to question the uniqueness of the Jewish people.

Although anti-Semitism has waned since the Holocaust among Western Christians, a new form of anti-Semitism—so the Zionists insist—has taken its place in the Islamicate. This new Islamic anti-Semitism, with its roots in the Qur'an and the Traditions of the Prophet, has arisen to target both Israel and Jews in the Western world. According to the Zionist narrative, this new anti-Semitism greeted the Jewish settlers even as they began arriving in Palestine to reclaim their "promised land." Driven by their "ancient" hatred of Jews, the Arabs began organizing attacks against the earliest Jewish settlers in Palestine even though they had brought "prosperity" to their Arab neighbors. In May 1948, Arab hatred of Jews led to the concerted invasion by five Arab armies of the fledgling state of Israel. Indeed, Israel's Arab neighbors and its own Palestinian population have never ceased to threaten Israel: they have never given up their resolve to destroy the world's only Jewish state through wars, economic blockade, and terrorist attacks.

The Zionists claim that Israel's neighbors, driven by their hatred of Jews, pose a unique threat to its national security, unlike any faced by other countries in the world. Israel—they argue—is the only country in the world whose right to exist is not recognized by its enemies, whose very existence is threatened by its enemies, and whose defeat in a war will lead to the complete destruction of its population. In other words, having already suffered the Holocaust, Israel daily faces the imminent possibility of yet another genocide. Since Israel faces the threat of total annihilation, the world should not demand restraint from Israel. Israel cannot take any risks in the pursuit of peace, or make any compromises with the Palestinians or Arabs.

This Israeli myth of "national security exceptionalism" emerged very soon after Israel's creation.[44] In September 1949, a little over a year after the creation of Israel, David Ben-Gurion declared that Israel's national security problem was "utterly unique and [without] parallel among the nations." In August 1952, he repeated that Israel's security problem was a "one of a kind problem, much as [Jews] are one of a kind people."[45] Over time, writes Gil Merom, "notions of national security exceptionalism percolated so deeply into Israeli society that they became integrated into the discourse of society's most critical minds. Indeed, exceptionalist argumentation can be found in the writings of distinguished scholars and independent opinion makers that were deeply critical of Israel's foreign policy and rhetoric."[46] In this, as in so many other instances, some of the brightest Zionists and Israelis begin to believe in the myths of their own construction.

·   ·   ·

Critics of Zionism and Israel—including a few Israelis—have charted an inverse exceptionalism, which describes an Israel that is aberrant, violates international norms with near impunity, engages in systematic abuse of human rights, wages wars at will, and has expanded its territories through conquest. This is not the place to offer an exhaustive list of these negative Israeli exceptionalisms, but we will list a few that are more egregious.

As an exclusionary settler colony, Israel does not stand alone in the history of European expansion overseas: but it is the only one of its kind in the twentieth and twenty-first centuries.[47] Since the sixteenth century Europeans have established exclusionary settler colonies in the Americas, Australia, and New Zealand—among other places—whose white colons displaced or nearly exterminated the indigenous population to create new societies in the image of those they had left behind. By the late nineteenth century, however, this genocidal European expansion was running out of steam, in large part, because there remained few surviving Neolithic societies that white colons could exterminate with ease; in tropical Africa and Asia, the climate and the pathogens were not particularly kind to European settlers.

The Zionist decision in 1897 to establish an exclusionary colonial settler state in Palestine marked a departure from this trend. In 1948, some fifty years later, the Jewish colons from the West would create the only state in the twentieth century founded on conquest and ethnic cleansing.[48] Israel is also the only exclusionary colonial-settler state established by the modern Europeans anywhere in the Old World.

In Israel, moreover, settler colonialism is not something that belongs to its past. After their victory in the June War of 1967, the Israelis decided to extend their colonial settler project to the West Bank, Gaza, Sinai, and the Golan Heights. In recent decades, the demand for another massive round of ethnic cleansing of Palestinians in the Occupied Territories—and even inside Israel's pre-1967 borders—has moved from the extremist fringes of the Israeli Right to the mainstream of Israeli politics.

Israel is most likely the only country in the world that insists on defining citizenship independently of geography. On the one hand, it has continued to deny the right of return—and hence rights of citizenship—to millions of Palestinians who or whose parents and grandparents were expelled from Palestine in two massive rounds of ethnic cleansing since 1948.[49] At the same time, under its Law of Return, Israel, automatically and instantly, grants citizenship to applicants who are Jews, persons of Jewish parentage, or Jewish converts. Under this law, as Mazin Qumsiyeh puts it succinctly, "no Jew emigrates to Israel; Jews (including converts) 'return' (hence the name of the law)."[50] In addition, the Jewish immigrants receive generous support from the state upon their arrival in Israel. In other words, Israel turns internationally recognized rights of residence and citizenship on their head, denying these rights to those who have earned them by birth, while granting them freely to those who claim them because of ancient religious myths.

In recent years, critics have increasingly charged Israel with practicing legal discrimination against Palestinians. Such discrimination is massive and blatant in the Occupied Territories where Israel has established Jewish-only settlements, connected to pre-1967 Israel by Jewish-only roads. Since June 1967, the Palestinians in these territories have suffered under a system of military occupation, which shows even less regard for their human rights than South Africa's apartheid. A former U.S. president, Jimmy Carter, recently dared to acknowledge the existence of apartheid in the Occupied Territories in the title of his new book, *Palestine: Peace Not Apartheid.*[51] Instantly, America's mainstream media—led by Zionist censors—began savagely attacking President Carter for mentioning the unmentionable. Not a few political and academic careers in the United States have met a premature end for lesser offenses.[52] Jimmy Carter, the octogenarian former president, had little to lose.

Inside its pre-1967 borders too, Israel has allocated rights based on ethnicity. Until 1966, Palestinians in Israel were governed under martial law, which severely restricted their civil and political rights, including their right to free movement, to establish their own media, and to protest or form political parties.[53] Since its founding, Israel has openly tied its immigration policy to Jewish ethnicity. Israeli law defines land to be a property of the Jewish people, owned on their behalf by the Jewish National Fund (JNF), a quasi-governmental organization. Israel nationalized all the lands belonging to the Palestinians it expelled in 1948, and it has continued to expropriate Palestinian lands under a variety of arbitrary measures. As a result, the JNF today owns 93 percent of all the lands in pre-1967 Israel.[54] Yet, even in his moment of daring, President Carter shrank from addressing the presence of apartheid inside pre-1967 Israel.

Israel is the only country in the world that refuses to define its borders. Its *de facto* borders have shifted with impressive frequency. At first, the armistice line of 1948 served as Israel's borders; but they expanded outward in 1956, 1967, and 1982 because of wars and conquests. On a few occasions, Israel had to retract from the territories it had invaded: from the Sinai in 1957, from the Sinai again in 1978, from Southern Lebanon in May 2000, and from Southern Lebanon again in August 2006. In addition, since the Oslo Accord of 1993, Israel has defined a new set of internal "borders" inside the West Bank to contain and neutralize the Palestinian resistance inside a set of regulated Bantustans.

If Israel has not yet reached or exceeded the borders of David's mythic Kingdom, it is not because of any lack of ambition. The constraint is demographic. In order to expand beyond its present borders, Israel would need a more ample supply of Jewish colons willing to assume the risks of colonization. Fortunately for the Arabs, these colons are in short supply, as they were before the rise of the Nazis in Germany. Had Israel succeeded in attracting five million Jewish colons after 1967, the Sinai would still be under Israeli occupation, and its borders in the north would extend to the Litani River and across the Jordan River in the east. Luckily for the Arabs, Israeli expansionism has been stalled by the poverty of Jewish demography. That could change very quickly, however, if Israel decides to soften the requirements for conversion to Judaism. Millions of Jewish converts from the poorest countries in the world, attracted by the promise of a better life, could start pouring into Israel under its Law of Return. Clearly, the Zionists have weighed this option, but, so far, they have rejected it: not because of the objections of Orthodox Jews, but because the gains it will bring now are likely to be offset by its longer-term risks. It would appear that Israel's demographic constraints are binding: and these constraints may well determine the ultimate destiny of this exclusionary colonialism.

Chapter 2

Sources of Exceptionalism

We do not fit the general pattern of humanity.
—David Ben-Gurion

Only God could have created a people so special as the Jewish people.
—Gideon Ezra[1]

The fecundity of the Zionist project in producing claims of exceptionalism is not in doubt. Anyone who scans the voluminous Zionist literature will be suitably impressed by its repeated resort to claims of Jewish and Israeli exceptionalism. There is scarcely any aspect of Israeli or Jewish history that has not been embellished with some claim to uniqueness.

Israeli exceptionalism has many uses. It defends, obscures, explains away the "abnormal" character of the Zionist nationalist project. When the Irish sought national liberation, their goal was straightforward. They wanted to regain national control over their lives and their country from a foreign power. No one had to convince the Irish that they are descended from the gods, that they possessed a unique essence that set them apart from all other peoples, or that their history, religion, race, language, morality, or culture set them *above* their colonial masters. Occasionally, driven by exuberance or hubris, nationalists have advanced exceptionalist claims, but the success of their movement has not depended on their acceptance. The Irish claimed sovereignty because they *knew* that they are a nation with their own territory. To create their own state, they did not have to establish that they are exceptional.

The Zionists confronted two handicaps that Irish nationalists did not face. The diverse and scattered Jewish communities of Europe—and even more so, the world—did not constitute a *single* people. Instead, the Jews of the world were loosely united by their religious heritage, *but* they shared their languages, cultures, and genes with their neighboring communities. Moreover, no Jewish community had its own country, a substantial and contiguous territory where it formed a majority of the population. Despite these twin Jewish deficits—the absence of a nation and a national territory—the Zionists were determined to "liberate" the Jews of Europe and endow them with their own state.

The Zionists would remedy the first deficit by denying its existence. They knew that the Jews were not a nation, but it would be unwise to begin their "nationalist" movement with the admission that a Jewish nation did not yet exist. They also did not think that this deficit was a serious hindrance to their movement. With help from anti-Semites, whose attacks had been growing in recent decades, the Zionists were convinced that they could quickly convince enough frightened Jews that they are a nation. Instead of constructing a nationalism based on a common religion, however, the Zionists chose to cultivate a racial basis for Jewish nationalism. They embraced the anti-Semitic accusation that Jews of Europe are an alien race—*not* Germans or Russians—descended from the ancient Hebrews.

A racial identity offered the best hope of inculcating nationalism in ethnically diverse Jewish communities. Only an identity, based on the myth of a common descent, could unite peoples who were as different ethnically and culturally as the Jews of Portugal, Britain, Germany, Greece, and Russia. Only the myth of racial unity, only the conviction that they are a single family, descended from Abraham and Jacob, could unite orthodox, conservative, and Reform Jews into a nation. Once the Jews were convinced of their racial identity, preserved over hundreds of generations in exile, this would also endow them with pride in their ancient pedigree and their unique ability to survive and preserve their racial purity through difficult conditions. This was sure to engender a strong sense of their distinctiveness, superiority, and destiny, rooted in Jewish traditions and the Jewish Bible. With confidence, the Jews could see themselves as a unique nation, both ancient and divinely blessed.

The Zionists were more candid about their land deficit; this was not something they could fudge. Indeed, their land deficit defined the "abnormal" condition of Jews; they were an abnormal people because they did not have a country they could call their own. Conceptually, the land deficit was easier to fix. The Jews only had to stake a claim to Palestine as their country: and there were two ways of doing this. Jews of secular persuasion could claim that they had a historical right to Palestine, since they were descended from the ancient Israelites. In addition, it would be easy to reclaim this land because—according to early Zionist rhetoric—"this was a land without a people." No one had claimed Palestine during their absence. The religious Jews had a simpler and—for them—more irrefutable claim. Their God had promised the land to their ancestors for keeps. All they had to do was invoke their divine right to this promised land.

It turns out, after all, that the Jews are a *people* with their own *land*. Once the Zionists had made their case, there would be nothing abnormal about their national project. This was the official rhetoric of the Zionist project of national liberation for the Jewish people. On the back of this rhetoric, the Zionists would succeed in convincing the Western world to support their exclusionary colonial project in the Middle East.

The Zionist leaders were not deceived by their own rhetoric. They were keenly aware of their twin deficits, and they directed all their energies to removing them. In a manner of speaking, their rhetorical flourishes were stopgap measures that bought them time, support, and resources to create new facts on the ground in Palestine. They would use the rhetoric of a Jewish race and of divine election to gain control of Palestine, where they would establish a Jewish majority through ethnic cleansing. Once the Jews would start colonizing Palestine, they would seek to forge, out of the diverse ethnicities from which the colons were drawn, a new Jewish nation.

In 1948, the Zionists had taken the first significant steps toward overcoming their land deficit; but they were not yet a Jewish nation. In April 1950, David Ben-Gurion—the chief architect of Israel—in a speech to the High Command of the Israeli army, said, "we are still not a nation, and we still do not have a land. A land 90 per cent desolate, arid, and empty is not a land; and a population in which one person does not understand the language of his neighbor, a population which is not aware of the culture of the nation and has no knowledge of the land, and is not attached and committed to the nation's culture and outlook, is not a nation capable of facing its enemies and its problems in time of need."[2] It was not yet time to retire the myths of racial purity and divine election.

The Zionists were convinced that locating their Jewish state in Palestine would remedy their twin deficits in one stroke. This is why they turned down, in 1903, the British offer to give the Jews territory in East Africa; again, in 1912, they turned down a Portuguese offer to colonize Angola.[3] The Zionists rejected these offers even though their efforts to acquire Palestine had met with little success; and they would not succeed in these efforts until late 1917. It is true that some Zionists coveted Palestine for religious reasons, but there were few religious zealots in the ranks of the Zionists at this early date. Practical considerations weighed more heavily in their rejection of alternatives. The Zionists knew that their best chance of mobilizing Jewish support for their colonial project lay in harnessing their myths, messianic hopes, and memories. Only a Jewish state in Palestine could do this; hence their insistence on tying their project to Palestine.

Political Zionism faced tough competition for the support of Europe's Jews. It had to compete with assimilationism, several Jewish autonomy movements, and, most importantly, the radical political movements that had been gaining ground especially in Eastern Europe.[4] Indeed, most Jews did not see Zionism as a viable solution to the Jewish problem. The prospects of Zionism appeared dim at this time. Palestine was still a part of the Ottoman Empire; and the Zionists had failed to persuade the Ottoman Sultan to cede control over this territory, sacred to Muslims, to European Jews. Instinctively, to combat these secular competitors, the Zionists appealed to the messianic hopes of Jews, but with a twist. They argued that Zionism was a pragmatic alternative to divine redemption. The rationale for political Zionism had been prepared in the previous decades by Rabbi Alkali and Rabbi Kalischer, who maintained—in the words of Arthur Hertzberg—that "self-help was a necessary preamble to the miraculous days of the Messiah rather than a rebellion against heaven."[5]

While the Zionists claimed that the creation of a Jewish state would inaugurate an era of "normalcy" for Jews, they also emphasized that this state would have a special mission among the nations of the world. Israel would not be an Albania or Slovakia. The Jews must persist in their divine mission of serving as a "light unto nations." In order to retain their distinctness as God's "chosen people," the Jews—to use the words of Arthur Hertzberg—"must aspire to the role of the mentor of the Middle East, or the most blessedly modern small state, or the richest of the reviving national languages, or the most ideologically correct socialism."[6] This was an attempt to translate into modern, secular terms the ancient Jewish doctrine of divine election. In the words of an Israeli academic, "the justification of Zionism and, indeed, of the perpetuation of the Jewish people as a separate and unique entity, lies in their potential for additional radically creative contributions to humankind, all the more so as humanity urgently needs another Axial Age."[7]

A deeper irony surrounded the Zionist project. It proposed to end Jewish "abnormalcy" in Europe by creating an "abnormal" Jewish state in Palestine. Palestine was not *terra nullius*. In order to create an overwhelming Jewish majority in Palestine, the Zionists would have to expel the natives. In other words, the Zionists were proposing to create an exclusionary colonial settler state in Palestine. It was unlikely that the Palestinians, Arabs, or Muslims would regard this invasion of their lands as a normal, acceptable, or friendly act. If a Jewish state could be established in Palestine, it would face neighbors who would view its existence as an outrage that would not be easily forgotten or forgiven. Clearly, the Zionists were proposing to trade one "abnormalcy" for a greater, more ominous one.

This abnormality of the Zionist project—seeking nationhood for the Jews on someone else's land—has driven, and continues to drive, the ever-proliferating variants of Israeli exceptionalism. The Zionists had to find ways to rationalize their claim to Palestine, a land overwhelmingly populated by Arabs for more than a thousand years. The ancient Jewish myth of chosenness provided one rationale. Palestine is Jewish because Yahweh had promised it to them, to be theirs forever. Once the Western world accepted the doctrine of the promised land, they would see the Palestinians as squatters, and the Jews—the divine title-holders—could evict them whenever they chose to exercise their irrevocable right of ownership. In Palestine, the Zionists would use their military superiority to demonstrate that mythical land claims can take precedence over centuries of ownership rights.

The Europeans had justified their exploitation of the colonies of occupation by claiming that they were civilizing the natives. In the exclusionary colonies of settlement, where they sought to exterminate the natives, they spoke of *improving* the land; the natives were part of the wild fauna that had to be eliminated. In the early years of their colonizing project—when Palestine was still a part of the Ottoman Empire—the Zionists often argued that their presence in Palestine would improve the Palestinians. The earliest Jewish colons had described the Palestinians as savages, asserting that they were in dire need of improvement.[8] When Palestine came under British occupation, however, the Zionists changed tack: they spoke more often now of all the ways in which they were improving the *land* of Palestine, making the deserts bloom with their toil and technology. After 1948, when the Jewish colons had expelled most Palestinians from their lands, they would justify their displacement of Palestinians by pointing to the incomparably superior civilization they were building in their place.[9] These Israeli claims of superiority would carry more weight if they could be couched in the language of exceptionalism. If Western audiences could view Israeli achievements as miraculous, unique, one of a kind, *sui generis*, they would find it easier to dismiss the pain of Palestinians as a small sacrifice made in a greater cause.

Claims of the uniqueness of the Holocaust have served the same purpose. In this case, the Zionists invoke the enormity of a European crime against Jews to make Palestinian lives expendable. Since Israel alone—claim the Zionists—provides an ironclad guarantee against a repeat of the Holocaust, the expulsion of Palestinians becomes an acceptable sacrifice. In the scale of morality, besides, the expulsion of Palestinians does not bear comparison with what the Jews had endured at the hands of the Nazis. The Jewish colons had expelled the Palestinians, not exterminated them.

The Jews' unique suffering also gives them unique entitlements. As Jacob Neusner puts it, the Holocaust not only sets Jews apart from others, it gives them a "claim upon those others."[10] The Holocaust survivors have the right to demand that the Palestinians sacrifice their long-held rights in recognition of the incomparably greater calamities endured by Jews. By establishing the "*peculiar distinctiveness* of the Jews," according to Nathan Glazer, the Holocaust gave Jews "the right to consider themselves specially threatened and specially worthy of whatever efforts were necessary for survival" (emphasis in original).[11] Indeed, the Zionists have deployed Holocaust "uniqueness" to gain complete immunity for Israel from any critical examination. By conflating Israel with Holocaust survivors, they have argued that only those who are incorrigibly anti-Semitic would dare to accuse Israel of any wrongdoing against the Palestinians. Only anti-Semitic hatred could inspire such calumny against the Jews.

Some forms of Israeli exceptionalism are designed to secure Western support for Israel. To this day, Israel depends heavily on the military, financial, and diplomatic support of the United States. Indeed, so great is this dependence on the United States, the Zionists maintain a vast, multilayered lobbying apparatus to ensure that there is no drop in American support for Israel. The many battalions of the Israel lobby work indefatigably to burnish Israel's image.[12] In order to win Western sympathy, the Zionists have cultivated an image of Israel as a beleaguered Western outpost in the Islamic heartland, the only "democracy" in the Middle East, a small heroic country constantly forced to defend itself against terrorist attacks by Muslims. These carefully cultivated images of Israeli exceptionalism have helped Americans to identify with Israel, to see it as one of *our* kind, to take pride in it, and, therefore, to support it politically.

Israeli exceptionalism not only seeks to rationalize—and to disguise—the fundamental "abnormality" of the Zionist project. It invokes Jewish uniqueness as the only hope for the survival of Israel. Only a truly exceptional people, fully committed to Israel's unique mission to the world, could face the difficult challenges of an "abnormal" state. The Israelis have no choice but to believe in their "uniqueness" if they are to survive. Only this gives hope that they will outlive their adversaries. In the words of Yehezkel Dror, loss of their "sense of uniqueness" would "propel [Israeli] decline because of external and internal attrition processes, diminished high-energy levels that are needed for long-range survival in the Middle East, and added decay processes that are very dangerous to Israel's geo-strategic situation."[13] In short, only Israeli exceptionalism can exempt Israel from the law that unravels extremist projects.

PART II

THE DESTABILIZING LOGIC OF ZIONISM

The state of Israel has had explosives—the grievances of hundreds of thousands of displaced Arabs—built into its very foundations.
                                        —Isaac Deutscher, 1954[1]

CHAPTER 3

A VIOLENT HISTORY

Will those [Palestinians] evicted really hold their peace and calmly accept what was done to them? Will they not in the end rise up to take back what was taken from them by the power of gold . . . And who knows, if they will not then be both prosecutors and judges.
—Yitzhak Epstein, 1907[2]

As to the war against the Jews in Palestine . . . it was evident twenty years ago that the day would come when the Arabs would stand up against us.
—Ahad Ha'am, 1911[3]

The question is, do we want to conquer Palestine now as Joshua did in his day—with fire and sword?
—Judah L. Magnes, 1929[4]

Historical logic points to the eventual dissolution of the Jewish state. The powers around us are so great. There is such a strong will to annihilate us that the odds look very poor.
—Benny Morris, 2008[5]

FEW ZIONISTS WOULD DENY THE ESCALATING VIOLENCE that has attended the insertion of Jewish colons into the Middle East. Mostly, however, the Zionists draw attention to the Arabs as the source of this violence and blame it on their rejection of Israel. Moreover, they maintain that Arab rejection of Israel is rooted in their ancient and religiously inspired hostility toward Jews.

The Zionist movement in Palestine has generated endemic violence between Jewish settlers and Palestinians. Since 1948, this violence has repeatedly pitted Israel against the Palestinians and its Arab neighbors. It has dragged Western societies, especially the United States, into ever widening and deepening conflicts with the Islamicate. It is the thesis of this chapter, and, indeed, this book, that the history of these ever-expanding circles of conflict and instability was contained in the Zionist idea itself.

Instability and violence are integral to Zionism: they have flowed from its inner logic. They are not incidental to it.

In their private musings, a few of the early Zionists warned of the destabilizing consequences of their colonial project. This is scarcely surprising. They could not ignore the grave risks inherent in the Zionist project once the Palestinians began to resist the colonization of their lands; and this began early. Nevertheless, the Zionists preferred to shelve these concerns, convinced that the "natives" lacked the will, organization, and resources to derail their plans. While the Zionists engaged in voluminous and intense discussions about their colonial project, about how to make it succeed, they never developed a coherent "Arab doctrine," one that offered an objective appraisal of the unfolding Arab response to Zionism or how to deal with it. In part, they may have felt that this was unnecessary. "It is a disgrace that, to date," wrote Yitzhak Epstein in 1907, *"nothing whatsoever has been done in this regard* [the question of Jewish attitude toward Arabs], that so far not even one Jew has devoted himself to this topic, so that we are complete *illiterates in anything concerning the Arabs*, and all of our knowledge about them is folk wisdom."[6] After all, the earliest Zionists—according to Ahad Ha'am, writing in 1891— believed that "the Arabs are all savages who live like animals and do not understand what is happening around them."[7] Why worry about these "savages"? Surely, they would be swept away by the inexorable advance of civilization that the Jewish settlers were introducing into the region. On other occasions, when the Zionists took note of the incipient Arab resistance, they preferred to dismiss their concerns with wishful thinking. The resistance of the Palestinians would be fleeting, they reasoned. Once they would begin to reap the benefits of Jewish colonization—in rising land prices and new employment opportunities—they would welcome the settlers with open arms.[8]

In general, the Zionists wanted to believe that the Palestinians were not a people; they had no attachment to their land, no national identity, no national aspirations. If *they* are not a people, then we can take away their land from them. The irony in all this is palpable. The Jews—who were not yet a people, because they had no land they could call their own—asserted that the Palestinians, who had their own land, were *not* a people. This not-so-clever deception had only one end: so that one people without a land could steal it from another people who had it.

The Zionists tried the diplomatic approach to overcome the Palestinian resistance. They sought help from the nascent pan-Arab nationalists who were dreaming of recovering their glorious heritage of the Abbasid era. In return for their advocacy of the pan-Arab cause, in the councils of the great powers, the Zionists invited the Arab nationalists to sacrifice

Palestine. It would be a small sacrifice for a higher objective, the creation of an Arab kingdom stretching from Morocco to Iraq. The historic centers of Arab civilization—the Zionists explained helpfully—lay in Baghdad, Damascus, and Cairo, not in Jerusalem. Why should the Arabs grudge the loss of Jerusalem if this would advance their dream of restoring the ancient Arab empire?[9] The Zionists met with some initial success in these efforts. In 1919, at the Conference of Versailles, Chaim Weizmann persuaded Emir Faisal, a key leader of the putative Arab revolt against the Ottomans, to cede Palestine to the Zionists. When he had to confront Arab anger at this surrender of Islamicate lands, Emir Faisal made his agreement with the Zionists conditional on the creation of the Arab kingdom that he and his family sought.[10] This conditional agreement too was short-lived. Under Arab nationalist pressure, the Emir repudiated his deal with the Zionists.

The Zionists could not long uphold their fiction of creating a Jewish state in Palestine without violence. The first to challenge their complacency was the right wing of the Zionist movement. In an essay that laid the foundations of Revisionist Zionism in 1923, Ze'ev Jabotinsky rejected the fiction that the Palestinians would voluntarily surrender their historical rights to Palestine. He wrote that the Arabs would "resist alien settlers as long as . . . they possess a gleam of hope that they can prevent 'Palestine' from becoming the Land of Israel." Jabotinsky argued that a change in the avowed Zionist strategy was imperative: in order to succeed, the Zionists would have to extinguish the Arab's "gleam of hope." If the Zionists could not buy the Arabs' acquiescence, they would have to be defeated and crushed. Settlement would proceed, in the words of Jabotinsky, "under the protection of force that is not dependent on the local population, behind an iron wall which they will be powerless to break down."[11] Jabotinsky had forced into the open what was always implicit in the Zionist idea—and, indeed, in the thinking of the Zionist leadership. Despite their public stance, they had always known what Jabotinsky now challenged them to acknowledge and confront openly.

The use of violence against the Palestinians was not the Zionist's fallback plan. Privately, they knew that this was the only option that had a chance of succeeding. Openly and covertly, with or without British support, the Zionists had always prepared for a showdown against the Palestinians; they had prepared well, too. When the showdown came in 1948, the Zionists achieved their goals almost in their entirety. They defeated the armies of five Arab proto-states and created a Jewish state in 78 percent of Palestine after driving out most of its Arab population. In October 1956, taking advantage of British and French plans to capture the Suez Canal, Israel occupied the Sinai in a lightning strike. Next, less than twenty years after its creation, in the June War of 1967, Israel proceeded to deal a crushing defeat on three Arab armies, occupied the rest of Palestine, the Sinai, and the Golan Heights—and, in the process, quadrupled its territories. Most importantly, however, they had dealt a stinging blow to the appeal and promise of Arab nationalism, then supposedly at the height of its power. Arab nationalists would never recover from this ignominy.

Yet, despite these spectacular successes, Israel has failed to attain normalcy. Alternatively, is it the case that Israelis have not pursued normalcy because this does not serve their interests?

Many Israelis now openly acknowledge that something has gone awry. The Israelis have engaged in two massive rounds of ethnic cleansings in 1948 and 1967. They have repeatedly defeated the Arabs—in 1948, 1956, 1967, and 1973—in military encounters. The Jewish population of Israel has increased more than eightfold since the founding of Israel in 1948. They have demonstrated their ability to attack Arab targets in the West Bank, Gaza, Iraq, Syria, Lebanon and Tunisia with impunity. They have secured nearly unconditional U.S. backing for their colonization of the West Bank and Gaza; and they continue to strangulate the Palestinians in these territories.[12] They have engineered the largest ongoing financial and military transfer from one country to another in history. They command one of the most powerful armies in the world, with state-of-the-art weaponry from the U.S. arsenal; they command nuclear weapons; and they have a fleet of submarines capable of launching nuclear missiles. They have the unconditional support of the Jewish diaspora, more powerful and better organized than ever before. For many years now, Israel has pushed the Arabs into a corner where they are ready to recognize Israel and sue for peace. Yet, the Zionists have repeatedly spurned the offer. Despite the vast advantages they have accumulated over the Arabs, the Israelis want more. They want Israel to be the only state with a military capability in the region. It appears that Israelis will never feel secure unless the Arabs disband the military arm of their states.

Much more than wars, the Israelis fear the prospect of peace with the Arabs, since this would undermine decades of their work to prove that they are a "strategic asset" to the United States. The Israelis do not feel secure in what they had dreamed would be a safe haven for the world's Jews. Israel has yet to break away from its dependence on Western powers. Despite their strangulation of Palestinians, they have failed to extinguish the Palestinian's "gleam of hope." When the Israelis co-opted the secularist Palestine Liberation Organization and assigned them to police the West Bank and Gaza, the more radical Hamas took up the Palestinian struggle.

Groups that are more militant than Hamas wait in the wings, ready to replace Hamas should their resolve weaken under the Israeli siege. As a result, the Israelis do not see an end in sight to their state of abnormalcy. Their future remains insecure.

Why have Israel's triumphs—and no one would question the magnitude of these achievements—failed to inspire confidence in its ability to survive in the longer-term? Why do Arab societies continue to deny Israel the "right to exist"?

More than six decades after its creation—six decades of impressive military, territorial, demographic and economic gains—Israel is still engaged in destroying its neighborhood. Israel continues to improve its destructive advantage, apparently, in the name of creating an ironclad security; but its real objective is to snuff out the last pockets of resistance to its hegemony. Israel is still committed to redrawing the map of the Middle East, intent on carving the existing states into ineffectual microstates, more dependent than the existing oligarchies on Israel and the Western powers for their survival. After defeating nearly all its Arab adversaries, after a successful campaign to push the United States to invade and occupy Iraq, after devastating Lebanon in a new war in July 2006, Israel is now goading the United States to unleash its war machine against Iran, to use nuclear weapons if necessary to destroy its nuclear facilities. Israel persists in its policy of ethnic cleansing against Palestinians, in slow motion, all the while preparing to launch a final round of ethnic cleansing to finish the job it had begun in 1948. Barring the United States, people everywhere view Israel as an oppressive, racist state, the world's only apartheid. The Jews had acquired their own state—as Hugo Bergmann, a young Jewish philosopher from Prague had feared in 1919—only by betraying Jewish ideals.[13]

In short, the creation of Israel has not solved the "Jewish question"; this has only changed its location, shape, and name. The Europeans had long wrestled with what they called the "Jewish question." Unwittingly, perhaps, the Nazis and the Zionists have succeeded in transforming the "Jewish question" into the "Zionist question." By virtue of this transmutation, a *global* "Zionist question" has now replaced the European "Jewish question." Anxiously, the world now waits for Israel to make its next significant move. Anxiously, the world hopes against hope that its next significant move will be motivated by magnanimity, not driven by megalomania; that it will recognize the rights of all Palestinians; that it will redress the wrongs done to them in the same spirit that Jews have sought and received redress for the wrongs done to them by the Nazis. Yet, no one—based on sober appraisal of the Israeli record—expects that Israel, any time soon, will be ready to make the kind of historic compromises that dismantled the apartheid in South Africa, and has since carried the blacks and whites in that country toward reconciliation and peace. Some would argue that Israel has moved past the point where it can make such deep compromises: that it has trapped itself too inextricably in its dream-turned-nightmare to reach out toward any resolution of its problems other than by the use of massive force. Only time will tell whether hope prevails or despair, whether Israel chooses the course of reason or blunders on the path to wars.

CHAPTER 4

ZIONISM IN NUCE

Two important phenomena, of the same nature, but opposed, are emerging at this moment in Asiatic Turkey. They are the awakening of the Arab nation and the latent effort of the Jews to reconstitute on a very large scale the ancient kingdom of Israel. These movements are destined to fight each other continually until one of them wins.

—Najib Azouri, 1905

It is all bad and I told Balfour so. They are making [the Middle East] a breeding place for future war.

—Col. Edward Mandell House, 1917

It is our destiny to be in a state of continued war with the Arabs.

—Arthur Rupin, 1936

The day we lick the Arabs, that is the day, I think, when we shall be sowing the seeds of an eternal hatred of such dimensions that Jews will not be able to live in that part of the world for centuries to come.

—Judah L. Magnes, 1947[1]

A SPECTER HAUNTS THE MIDDLE EAST TODAY: the specter of a terrible conflict that pits Israel, its Western sponsors, and their Middle Eastern client regimes against Islamicate societies.

The project that initiated this conflict was proposed at a rare meeting in Basel that brought together two hundred Jewish delegates from seventeen countries. In August 1897, these delegates met under the leadership of Theodore Herzl, a Jewish journalist, to create a new organization—henceforth known as the World Zionist Organization—that would spearhead the Zionist movement. The aim of this movement—contained in the declaration made at the end of this meeting, and known as the Basel Program—was simple. "Zionism strives," the Program declared in euphemisms, "for the establishment of a publicly and legally secured home in Palestine for the Jewish people."[2]

Stripped of euphemisms, the Jewish delegates in Basel declared their resolve to create an exclusive Jewish colonial settler state in Palestine. At the time, Palestine was a province of the Ottoman Empire and populated, for more than a thousand years, by Muslim and Christian Arabs. In some ways, the intent of the Basel Program was not radical. During much of the nineteenth century, especially its last three decades, various European nations had seized different parts of Africa, established them as colonies, and opened them to white settlers. The Zionists too wanted to seize Palestine and open it to Jewish settlers. However, the Zionist plan was more ambitious: they only wanted the land in Palestine, without the natives or their labor.

The Zionist plan suffered from a deficiency that would have normally proved fatal.[3] It lacked an enforcement mechanism; there was no Jewish mother country to back their colonial project. The Jews did not have a state of their own, which could seize Palestine and throw it open to Jewish colonization. That was the Zionist challenge. How would they create a Jewish colonial settler state in Palestine when they did not possess the military power to seize and hold the territory? Nevertheless, they succeeded brilliantly. In 1948, some fifty-one years later, they had created their colonial settler state in Palestine. It was overwhelmingly Jewish too, exactly as the Zionists had wanted it to be.

Israel has also survived, the only settler colony established in the century before World War II to manage this feat. In the second wave of colonization, beginning in the first decades of the nineteenth century, the Western powers established many colonies of occupation in Africa and Asia. By the early decades of the twentieth century, several of these colonies, especially those in Africa, had attracted sizable numbers of white colons, some of whom began dreaming of creating their own states. In most cases, indigenous liberation movements aborted their dreams. In the era of decolonization heralded by the end of World War II, all but three of these settler colonies were dismantled. Only in South Africa, Palestine, and Southern Rhodesia, the white settlers broke away from their mother country to create their own states. The settler state in Southern Rhodesia was short lived; founded in 1964, it was dismantled in 1980. The whites-only state in South Africa lasted quite a bit longer; it broke away from Britain in 1910 and did not yield power to black South Africans until 1994. Only Israel, established in 1948 by Jewish settlers in what was Palestine, endures to this day.

Israel's creation and survival are anomalies. Its birth was oddly timed, emerging just as the world was entering an era of radical decolonization. In addition, Zionism was a pure settler colonialism. It was the intent of the Jewish colons to exclude the natives, by one means or another, from their Jewish state. They nearly achieved this goal too, shortly after the creation of Israel, through massacres and ethnic cleansing of the Palestinians. Instead of withering away, moreover, this exclusive colonial state has done quite well. In June 1967, Israel dramatically extended its territories, and its Jewish population has increased more than eightfold in the sixty years since its creation.

Israel faces another anomaly. Settler colonies that cleansed their territory of the indigenous population—such as the United States, Canada, Australia, and New Zealand—have never again faced a native problem. Israel has not been so lucky. While the Jewish settlers engaged in massive ethnic cleansing, they could not exterminate the natives. As a result, the Palestinians continue to disturb the Zionists' dream. Although heavily outgunned, betrayed by nearly every Arab state, constantly under siege, and repeatedly subjected to devastating attacks, arrests, humiliation, and torture, the Palestinians refuse to surrender, and continue undaunted in their struggle, ready to throw up new cohorts of resistance as earlier cohorts are defeated or co-opted. Over time, the Zionist's native problem has gotten worse.

Unctuously, the Zionists offer the creation of Israel and its repeated military victories as proofs of the tenacity and heroism of the Jewish people, their ability to rise in triumph from the ashes of the Holocaust. These Zionist claims make no mention of the manifold and overwhelming advantages the Jewish colons have always brought to their confrontation with the Palestinians. Once we recognize the immense disparity in power between the Jews and Palestinians, the Israeli "miracles" present themselves mostly as demonstrations of superior power. On the other hand, the refusal of the Palestinian resistance to bow before the superior power of the Jewish colons affirms the resilience of the human spirit in the face of overwhelming odds.

It is tempting to celebrate the creation of Israel as a great triumph, perhaps the greatest in Jewish history. Indeed, the history of Israel has often been read in the West as the heroic saga of a people marked for extinction, who emerged from Nazi death camps—from Auschwitz, Belzec, and Treblinka—to establish their own state in 1948, a Jewish haven and a democracy that has prospered even as it has stood up valiantly against Arab threats, boycotts, wars, and terrorist attacks. Without taking away anything from the sufferings of European Jews, we insist that this way of thinking about Israel—apart from its demonstration of the mythmaking prowess of Zionists—has merit only as a partisan narrative. It seeks to insulate Israel against the charge of a devastating colonization by falsifying history, by camouflaging the imperialist dynamics that brought it into existence, and diverting attention from the perilous wars into which it now seeks to drag the West, the Islamicate, and especially the Jews.

When we examine the consequences that have flowed from the creation of Israel, when we contemplate the greater horrors that may yet flow from the logic of Zionism, Israeli triumphs appear in a different light. We are forced to examine these triumphs with growing dread and incredulity. Israel's early triumphs, though real enough from a Zionist standpoint, have slowly mutated by a fateful process into ever-widening circles of conflict that now threaten to escalate into major wars between the West and the Islamicate. Although this conflict has its provenance in a specific colonial ambition, the dialectics driving this ambition has slowly endowed it with the characteristics of a civilizational war: and perhaps worse, a religious war.

The tragedy of Israel is not fortuitous. Driven by history, chance, and cunning, the Zionists wedged themselves between two historical adversaries, the West and Islam, and by harnessing the strength of the first against the second, they have produced a conflict that can only grow deeper over time. In this conflict, Israel's triumphs are temporary, are indeed illusory, since they evoke a deeper, wider response from the societies that suffer the devastation of its triumphs. In the long run, in the time scale of history, by relentlessly pressing its advantages, Israel only ensures that its adversaries will slowly build the defenses that will eventually rise to match Israel's military might and its expansionist ambitions.

Zionist historiography claims tirelessly that the emergence of a Jewish state in Palestine marks a triumph over Europe's centuries-old anti-Semitism, and, in particular, over its twentieth-century manifestation, the demonic, industrial plan of the Nazis to stamp out the existence of the Jewish people. However, this is a tendentious reading of Zionist history. It obscures the historic offer Zionism made to the West—the offer to rid the West of its Jews, to lead them out of Christendom into the Islamicate heartland. In offering to "cleanse" the West of the "hated Jews," the Zionists were working *with* the anti-Semites, not against them. Quite early on, Theodore Herzl pointed to this complementarity as the bedrock of Zionism; in order to succeed, the Zionists would have to harness Europe's anti-Semitic energy, the repulsion it harbored against Jews.[4] It did not matter that Jews and anti-Semites had been historical adversaries, that Jews have been the victims of Europe's religious vendetta since Rome first embraced Christianity. Zionism would change this relationship. Jews and anti-Semites would now enter into a new relationship that would work to the advantage of Jews.

Inserting the Zionist idea into Western politics has worked a sea change in the relationship between Western Jews and Gentiles. In order to succeed in their colonial enterprise, the Zionists would have to create an adversary, common to the West and the Jews. The Zionists had chosen to colonize Palestine because a Jewish state in any other territory—in Uganda or Argentina—would be entirely deficient in the mythos, which the Zionists knew they would need to persuade Western Jews to embrace their colonial enterprise. Palestine had other advantages, too. In choosing Palestine, the Zionists were also acquiring the adversary that would deepen their partnership with the West. Only a Jewish state waging wars in the Middle East could energize the West's crusader mentality, its evangelical zeal, its dreams of end-times, its imperial ambitions; a Jewish state in Africa or Latin America was unlikely to evoke any of these tendencies. In time, the rise of Arab—and later Islamicate—resistance to a Jewish state in the Islamicate heartland would create the common adversary that would continue to justify and deepen the Jewish-Gentile partnership. Those who protest that this dialectics was no part of Zionist ambitions can scarcely deny that this has been the inevitable outcome of Zionist success.

Israel, then, was the product of a historic partnership that seems unlikely at first blush, between Western Jews and Western Christendom, in particular, the Anglo-Saxon faction of the Western world, which has been most directly involved with the promotion of the Zionist movement.[5] It is the powerful alchemy of the Zionist idea that created this partnership. The Zionist project to create a Jewish state in Palestine possessed the unique power to convert two historical antagonists, Jews and Gentiles, into allies united in a common imperialist enterprise against the Islamicate world. The Zionists harnessed the negative energies of the Western world—its anti-Semitism, its Crusading nostalgia, its anti-Islamic bigotry, its deep racism, its imperialism—and focused them on a new colonial project, the creation of a surrogate Western state in the Islamicate heartland. To the West's imperialist ambitions, this new colonial project *appeared* to offer a variety of strategic advantages. Israel would be located in the heart of the Islamicate; it would sit astride the junction of Asia, Africa, and Europe; it would guard Europe's gateway to the Indian Ocean; and it could monitor developments in the Persian Gulf with its vast reserves of oil. It did not matter that these advantages were temporary, that they were mostly illusory, since they would be more than offset by the strategic costs of the alliance between the Zionists and the Western powers. It did not matter because the Zionists could manipulate the domestic politics of key Western societies to override their strategic interests.

The partnership the Zionists were projecting, between the Western powers and Western Jews, was a stroke of brilliance. The Zionists were going to leverage Western power in their cause. As the Zionist plan would unfold, inflicting pain on the Islamicate and evoking Islamicate anger against the West and Jews, the complementarities between the two would deepen. In time, new complementarities would be discovered, or created, between the two rival but interwoven strains of Western history, Christian and Jewish. In the United States, the Zionist movement would give encouragement to evangelical Protestants—who looked upon the birth of Israel as a sign of the imminence of the end time—and convert them into fanatic partisans of Zionism. In addition, the modern West, which had hitherto traced its central ideas and institutions to Rome and Athens—*via* the Renaissance and Enlightenment—would be repackaged as a Judeo-Christian civilization. This reframing not only underscores the Jewish roots of the Western world, it also makes a point of emphasizing that Islam is the outsider, the adversary.

Zionism owes its success entirely to this improbable partnership. On their own, the ship of the Zionist enterprise could not have sailed from European shores and docked in Palestine. The Zionists could not have created Israel by bribing or coercing the Ottomans into granting them a charter to colonize Palestine. Despite his offers of loans, investments, technology, and diplomatic expertise, Theodore Herzl was repeatedly rebuffed by the Ottoman Sultan. It is even less likely that the Zionists, at any time, could have mobilized a Jewish army in Europe to invade and occupy Palestine, against Ottoman and Arab opposition to the creation of a Jewish state on Islamicate lands.

The West-Zionist partnership was indispensable for the creation of a Jewish state. This partnership was also fateful. It produced a powerful new dialectic, which has encouraged Israel, as the political center of the Jewish Diaspora and the chief outpost of the West in the heart of the Islamicate, to become ever more daring in its designs against the Islamicate and beyond. In turn, a wounded and humiliated Islamicate, more resentful after every defeat suffered at the hands of Israel and the United States, has become more determined to recover its dignity, its autonomy and power—and to seek to advance this recovery on the strength of Islamic ideas. In addition, the humiliation of the Islamicate has also given rise to radical factions—their numbers still miniscule—who have decided to use violence to achieve their political ends. This destabilizing dialectic has now brought the West itself into direct confrontation against the Islamicate. We are now staring into the precipice. Yet, there is little appreciation in the West of the scale of this impending disaster: or the will to pull back from it.

The remaining chapters in Part II will describe more amply the workings of Zionism, painted so far only in broad brushstrokes. Primarily, this means that we have to acquire the clearest understanding of the goals of political Zionism. We can look for this in the public statements, the aims and actions of Zionist organizations, their circumlocutions, and the private musings of Zionists. Once we have identified these goals, or a hierarchy of goals, that Zionism set for itself, we can begin to read the history of the Zionist movement, the methods and tools it employed, as flowing from these goals. We can identify the allies the Zionists would seek, the enemies they would create, the hatreds they would incite, the deceptions they would practice, and the substitutes they would explore if one set of actions or tools were unavailable or lost their efficacy.

It is the principal theme of this book that once we identify the goals of Zionism, understand the commitment of the founding Zionists to these goals, form a reasonable estimate of the resources that Zionists will eventually command from Jewish communities in the West, and pin down the forces in Western societies that Zionism can mobilize, then we can map the general course that Zionism will take. Familiarity with the history of Zionism will confirm that this predicted trajectory is very close to the course it has actually taken.

Admittedly, the Holocaust could not have been predicted. Nevertheless, despite Zionist claims that the creation of Israel flowed from this catastrophe, this anachronistic claim cannot survive examination. Knowledge about the Holocaust became widely known only *after* World War II, but the infrastructure of the Jewish state in Palestine was already in place by the mid-1930s. "Zionism," an Israeli historian reminds us, "was not the invention of desperate refugees from Nazi persecution—it was well on its way to achieving its goals *before* the Holocaust, in which most of its potential citizens were murdered" (emphasis added).[6]

Zionism was no ordinary nationalism. This book is dedicated to exploring all the ways in which the abnormality—or uniqueness—of this nationalist movement has determined the course that it has taken, the deep conflicts it has created, the wars that have marked its history, and the new wars that it strives even now to deliver, wars that will pit the United States, Israel, and their Western allies against the Islamicate world. These consequences are neither arbitrary nor accidental. The tragedy of Zionism is written into its design; its end is contained in its beginning.

CHAPTER 5

THE ARABS HATE US

God forbid that we should harm any people, much less a great people whose hatred is most dangerous to us.

—Yitzhak Epstein, 1907

The Western form of anti-Semitism—the cosmic, satanic version of Jew hatred—provided solace to wounded [Arab] feelings.

—Bernard Lewis, 2006

Why should the Arabs make peace? If I were an Arab leader I would never make terms with Israel. That is natural: we have taken their country.

—David Ben-Gurion, 1956[1]

THE ZIONISTS BLAME THE VIOLENT BIRTH OF Israel, and its increasingly violent aftermath, on the Palestinians and Arabs. Notwithstanding what they might admit in private, there is no admission of Jewish guilt, of any wrong done to the Palestinians or Arabs. It is the Jews, not Arabs, who are the aggrieved party.

In order to mask its colonial character, the Zionists dress their movement in the language of national liberation: a concept purloined from the discourse of colonized peoples in the twentieth century. This apologia makes no mention of who the Jews are or how they came to be in Palestine. It *begins* with the Jews already *in* Palestine, enduring hardships, defending their communes, villages, and towns against vicious Arab attacks, and struggling against great odds to gain their independence. The British make cameo appearances in this narrative, as partisans of the Palestinians, delaying or obstructing the creation of a Jewish state in Palestine. In this narrative, the Arabs are the anti-Semites. Their opposition to the Jewish state stems from villainy; they oppose Zionism because they hate Jews. In May 1948, driven by anti-Semitic bile, just when the state of Israel announced its birth, the Palestinians and the neighboring Arabs banded together and invaded the fledgling state of Israel, to destroy it at the very moment of its birth, and drive the Jews into the sea.

Of all the *new* states that emerged in the postwar era—the Zionists claim—Israel alone confronted invading armies at its birth. The Arabs threatened the new state with extinction and the Jews with genocide. Although Israel defeated the invading Arab armies in 1948, and again in 1967 and 1973, the Arabs have never given up their dream of destroying the Jewish state. They continue to prepare for new wars, they mount terrorist attacks against Israelis at home and abroad, they impose economic boycotts, and constantly threaten its very existence. Israel is the only state in the world that faces threats to its very existence. The security threats Israel faces are unique.

A more sophisticated version of this narrative is also available. It incorporates a bit more history. It claims that the Jews are a unique people with an ancient history and a special destiny; they are God's chosen people, returning, under His divine plan, to the land promised in antiquity to their forebears. Once the Jews are identified as the "chosen people" of the Jewish Bible—for many Jews and Protestant Christians, a part of their religious beliefs—the Arabs in Palestine become interlopers, regardless of how long they have lived there. With greater malice, some Zionists go farther in their delegitimization of the Palestinians. They have argued that most of the Arabs had entered Palestine only recently, attracted by the employment opportunities created by the arrival of Jewish colons in the late nineteenth century.[2] In insisting on their legal and national rights to Palestine, the Arabs are acting against God's plans: and this bravado, this perversity can only stem from a deep hatred of the Jews. The Arab failure to recognize the superior rights of Jews, their failure to restore the Jewish patrimony to its rightful owners, is the new anti-Semitism. The Arabs are the new enemy of the Jews.

The Zionists offer at least two accounts of the origins of Arab anti-Semitism. The first maintains that the Muslims have always harbored a deep anti-Semitism, only slightly less virulent than its Christian counterpart. In recent years, a few Zionist writers have been constructing a new historiography of Islamic anti-Semitism that seeks to trace its roots to the Qur'an and the Traditions of Prophet Muhammad.[3] In addition, they are rewriting the history of Jewish and Christian communities under Islamicate rule; nearly all Western historians, including those who bring an Orientalist approach to their subject, acknowledge that Christian and Jewish minorities under Islam generally enjoyed more rights than Jewish or Muslim minorities in Christendom.[4] These revisionists are working to replace the existing historiography with a selective focus on those aspects of Islamic law and practice, which fall short of *modern* Western professions

of equal civil and political rights for all citizens. These revisionists make
their case by selectively stringing together examples of discrimination
against or, persecution of, Jews and Christians in Muslim societies, as if
the chosen examples exhaust the history of relations between Muslims
and non-Muslims during some thirteen centuries of Islamicate rule.

The objective of this new genre of Zionist rewriting of Islamicate history
is clear. It seeks to fabricate an Islamic anti-Semitism as the engine driving
Arab opposition to political Zionism and Israel. Ephraim Karsh concludes,
". . . much of the Muslim and Arab anti-Zionist argument and the widespread hostility to the State of Israel is the result of a deep, and profound,
antagonism towards Jews and Judaism."[5] Once Western audiences accept
this fabrication, they can be persuaded to ignore Israel's colonial character,
its usurpation of Arab lands, its ethnic cleansing of Palestinians, its wars of
aggression, or its brutal oppression of Palestinians. The Palestinians' plea
that they are engaged in resisting a colonial occupation and ethnic cleansing can be conveniently ignored. Westerners will view every act of Palestinian resistance as violent expressions of anti-Semitic hate mongering. On
the other hand, it will become easier to defend Israel, to justify its attacks
on Palestinians as acts of self-defense against a hate-soaked adversary. The
Arabs, the West can proclaim, oppose Israel because it is Jewish.

In a second version, Arab anti-Semitism is a phenomenon of more
recent vintage that emerged in the wake of repeated Zionist military victories over Arabs. Arabs, it is argued, have discovered in anti-Semitism an
outlet, a compensation, as it were, for the shame and humiliation of their
defeat at the hands of Israel in 1948, 1967, and 1973. Bernard Lewis,
a leading exponent of this view, writes that the "Western form of anti-
Semitism—the cosmic, satanic version of Jew hatred—provided solace to
wounded [Arab] feelings."[6] Yes, the Arabs would find consolation for their
defeats in nothing less than "the cosmic, satanic version of Jew hatred."
Instantly, despite deep differences that set them apart from the Europeans—in their religion, their theology, their history of relations with
the Jews, their manner of constructing the Other—the Arabs adopted
in its entirety Europe's ancient, full-blown "cosmic" and "satanic" hatred
against Jews. It is this anti-Semitism that has driven and still drives Arab
refusal to come to terms with Israel, to accept it as a full member of the
community of Middle Eastern nations.

More recently, the Zionists have launched and nurtured a variety of
new myths to distract attention from the growing strategic costs that the
United States incurs in supporting Israel. As anger in the Islamicate has
grown over Israel's wars against Arabs, its ethnocide of Palestinians, and
repeated devastation of Lebanon, the Zionists have sought to convince
Americans that Islamicate anger against them is not provoked by their

unconditional, sustained and massive support for Israel. Instead, they blame this anti-Americanism on the Islamic doctrine of Jihad, which—some Zionists argue—preaches unremitting warfare against all infidels.[7] In other words, if the Islamists vent their anger at the United States, it is not because of its policies, but because it is Christian. It is an argument that finds many partisans among evangelical Christians in the United States, who have preached a similar doctrine.

A second explanation of growing Muslim antipathy toward the United States seeks to paint this as a "clash of civilizations." The West arouses deep "rage" among Muslims, argues Bernard Lewis, because it humiliated their once-great civilization—in the past, by colonizing their societies and giving equal rights to non-Muslim minorities, and now by subverting their youth and women with the allure of Western freedoms. It is natural, Lewis concludes, "that this rage should be directed primarily against the millennial enemy and should draw its strength from ancient beliefs and loyalties."[8] What Bernard Lewis will not explain is why the Muslims have directed their rage almost exclusively at the United States—which had no connection to Western colonialism in the Islamicate before World War II—or why the United States commanded a great deal of goodwill in the Middle East well into the 1950s. Finally, in the early 1990s, Samuel Huntington argued that Islamicate societies directed their hostility at the United States because it embodies freedom, democracy, equality, and human rights, values that are antithetical to Islam.[9] It has been the chief aim of the clash thesis, by focusing attention on a direct and eternal conflict between the West and Islam, to acquit Israel of serving as the chief source and conduit of this conflict. In large measure, this explains the tremendous vogue this thesis has attained in the West, especially since the attacks of September 11, 2001.

Zionist success in attracting the support of Americans owes much to their similar histories as colonial settler movements. "In great part," writes Portis, "the US understanding of the Israeli-Palestinian conflict involves an image of the US itself, an image first projected onto the Zionist settlements, and then onto the state of Israel."[10] In addition, these parallels recalled hallowed myths—rooted in the conquest narratives of the Torah—from which both colonial enterprises drew divine sanction and inspiration. The British and Jewish colons sought legitimacy by claiming that they were treading in the path of the "divinely chosen" Hebrews who first conquered Canaan. Since Yahweh—in the conquest narratives of the Torah—directed the campaign of the Hebrews to dispossess and exterminate the ancient Canaanites, the self-appointed Hebrews, the British colons in North America and the Jewish colons in Palestine, too, could drive out the "wild" natives with an easy conscience.

Never slow to exploit opportunities to win allies, the Zionists drew frequent attention to the history of the American colonies. Leading Zionists, during the 1920s and 1930s, wrote numerous articles for the leading American newspapers describing the Zionist "pioneers" as Jewish versions of America's "brave and religiously pious settlers."[11] In an article that appeared in New York Times in June 1922, Bernard Rosenblatt, the American representative on Zionist Executive Committee, writes that the "Jewish pilgrim fathers . . . are building the new Judea even as the Puritans built a new England three hundred years ago." "These immigrants to Palestine," continues Rosenblatt, "were indeed the Jewish Puritans: Hederah [a Jewish colony in Palestine] and her sister colonies are the symbols of the Hebraic revival—they are the Jamestown and the Plymouth of the new House of Israel." The Jewish settlers are like the "followers of Daniel Boone who opened the West for American settlers" while "facing the dangers of Indian warfare."

The parallels between the Zionist settlers and the American pioneers, however, are not complete. The Zionists did not have the benefit of pathogens to aid their colonial mission. In addition, their colonial project unfolded in a less "barbarous" age, when Western "conscience" was less eager to support the extermination of natives. At about this time, national liberation movements in Asia and Africa were also gathering steam, and, after World War II, the Soviet Union too would act as an additional check on the rapacity of Western powers. All this made it inconvenient to pursue ethnic cleansing in the broad daylight of history. Certainly, like all the white colonial settlers before them, the Jewish colons too had argued that the Palestinians they sought to displace were savages, Bedouins, barbaric impediments to the forward march of civilization. Nevertheless, there were concerns that ethnic cleansing would not go down well with the Western powers at the dawn of the new era of decolonization. Self-interest too imposed restraints on the ability of the Zionists to act too openly on their plans for ethnic cleansing. The Jews as well as the new state of Israel would have to give up their claims to Western guilt if they were to engage openly—so soon after the Holocaust—in massacres and mass expulsions of Palestinians. At the least, it would have been a little indelicate for Holocaust survivors to appear before the world as perpetrators of ethnic cleansing.

Yet, there was *no* escape for the Zionists from ethnic cleansing: their project of creating an ethnically pure Jewish state depended vitally on voiding the Palestinians from their land. In order to escape the censure and shame of such a crime, the Zionists would use their vast propaganda machinery to deny it vigorously. And so the myth was circulated—and

soon established as "fact" in Western accounts of the creation of Israel—
that the Palestinians had willingly left their homes at the urging of Arab
leaders, so that they would not stand between the advancing Arab armies
and the Jewish centers of population. Since the Palestinians or their sympathizers had little access to Western media, it was relatively easy for
the Zionists to ensure that Western publics heard only their account of
events. This account absolved Israel of any blame for the dispossession of
Palestinians; they had brought this fate upon themselves.

Israel placed itself on thin moral and legal ground again by denying
the Palestinians the right to return. On the one hand, the Israelis maintained vociferously that they had not engaged in ethnic cleansing; but
they were also determined to ensure the same result by preventing the
Palestinian refugees from returning to their homes. Israelis answered this
charge by arguing that allowing the Palestinians to return would endanger
their security, since they would resume their war for the destruction of the
Jewish state from within its borders.

All its resources and media prowess notwithstanding, Israel could not
completely insulate itself from its colonial settler origins. The Palestinians, Arabs, and Muslims—despite their muted voices—would continue
to remind the world of this. More importantly, Israel was not free to
leave its past behind and start its life as a normal state. Its present could
not be divorced from its past. Western audiences might forget, identify
with—even feel good—about Israel's colonial character; but Palestinians,
Arabs, Muslims, and, more broadly, the Third World would take the
opposite view. They would resist Israel, reject it as an egregious colonial
fact, and demand that Palestine should be restored to its rightful owners,
the Palestinians.

Israel could not just leave its past behind. The events on the ground—
the raids, the reprisals, the tensions and wars in the Middle East—would
continue to demand explanations. In addition, at world forums, the Islamicate countries would continue to confront Israel and the West with
demands to do justice to the Palestinians. Gradually, the Palestinians,
Arabs, and Muslims—joined by their sympathizers in the West—would
use scholarship to challenge the hegemony of the Zionist narrative in
Western discourse. In other words, the Zionists would continuously have
to produce and reproduce their myths about the creation of Israel to
counter the growing thrust of reality and scholarship.

The United States could bury its colonial past in mythology because
its victims were mostly dead. Israel would not be so privileged. It could
not take a break from defending its past and its present, which since 1967
has looked more and more like its past. The Zionists would continuously

have to assert their superior rights to Palestine. A single myth would not suffice. They would have to produce a deluge of myths, produce new ones when the old ones seemed to fail, and, then, resurrect old ones with new sets of fabrications or with a new twist of logic. It is the fate of the Zionists to continue, obsessively, to elaborate upon their divine rights and historical connection to Palestine. Unfailingly, they continue to muster the Torah, Talmud, archaeology, and genetics to prove these connections. They continue to draft new social Darwinist claims to Palestine by constantly reminding the world of Israel's military, economic, political, and scientific achievements. They vigorously press claims about how Israel defends the West, how it alone has stood between Arab radicalism, Islamic fundamentalism, or Islamic terrorism, and Western interests. At the same time, the Zionists mobilize Western sympathy by painting itself as a victim, by portraying Israel as uniquely vulnerable.

Above all this profusion of Zionist myths stands one that seeks to make Israel untouchable, to place it beyond reproach or criticism. The Zionists sought, and succeeded in claiming, for the Jewish colonists—the new Western pioneers in the Arab world—the crown of supreme victimhood. Not only had the Jews endured the most unimaginable suffering at the hands of the Nazis, now the Palestinians and Arabs had surrounded their tiny state, laid siege to it, and were preparing to destroy their state and drive them into the sea. The Zionist machinery ran at full speed to paint their Palestinian victims as their new tormentors: now, they and their Muslim allies were the new anti-Semites.

This would be Israel's most effective defense—the perfect cover for its colonial enterprise. The Zionists have proved themselves past masters in inverting reality, in painting themselves as the victims of Arab intransigence, Arab wars and terror. They have convinced many Europeans—and most Americans—that their lives are constantly at risk from Arab attacks; their peaceful "neighborhoods" in the West Bank under siege from predatory natives. Once this inversion was complete, they could claim continuity with their past as the eternal victims of anti-Semitism.

Israel has effectively insulated itself from criticism by identifying itself definitively with the victims of the Holocaust. It has used the call of "Never Again" to silence its critics, by telling them that criticism of Israel is anti-Semitism in disguise, that it is anti-Semitism "in effect, if not in intent." Criticism of Israel, therefore, must cease—or it will lead to another Holocaust. It is surely one of the sad ironies of history that Israel takes cover behind the screen of the Holocaust, that the "survivors" of the Holocaust use the tragedy of their ancestors to buy impunity for their own crimes.

CHAPTER 6

A SECULAR MESSIANISM

The spirit of the age is approaching ever closer to the essential Jewish emphasis on real life.

—Moses Hess, 1862[1]

Today we may be moribund, but tomorrow we shall surely awaken to life; today we may be in a strange land, but tomorrow we will dwell in the land of our fathers; today we may be speaking alien tongues, but tomorrow we shall speak Hebrew.

—Eliezer Ben-Yehudah, 1880[2]

We must seek a home with all our hearts, our spirit, our soul.

—Peretz Smolenskin, 1881[3]

Palestine is first and foremost not a refuge for East European Jews, but the incarnation of a reawakening sense of national solidarity.

—Albert Einstein, 1921[4]

ZIONISM HAD MANY FATHERS, EVEN BEFORE ITS successes could call new ones into existence. The standard Zionist narrative has always explained the creation of Israel as a response to anti-Semitism. Anachronistically, according to one version of this claim, Zionism was a response to the Holocaust, that most horrendous outbreak of the West's anti-Semitic malaise.

The plot of this Zionist narrative is simple. The return of anti-Semitism in Western Europe, in the last decades of the nineteenth century, was beginning to trouble some Jews that assimilation was not working. A few Jews were more zealous in their critique of assimilation. They claimed that assimilation would never work because the anti-Semites hated the Jew's race more than they hated his religion. In the acerbic words of Moses Hess, the German "objects less to the Jews' peculiar beliefs than to their peculiar noses."[5] These Jewish thinkers concluded that only a Jewish state could provide security to the Jews. The Jews must separate from the Gentiles; only the gathering of all Jews in a Jewish state would end anti-Semitism.

This narrative runs into a problem at the outset. It fails to explain the Zionist fixation on Palestine. If the Zionist objective was to put distance between the Jews and the Gentiles, the Zionists would have opted for a pragmatic approach to the choice of a territory for the Jewish state. Indeed, Leo Pinsker, in 1882, had emphasized that "the selection of a national and permanent land, meeting all requirements, must be made with all care, and confided to one single national institute, to a commission of experts selected from our directorate."[6] It should have been easy enough to agree on the territorial requirements of the proposed Jewish state. Three quickly come to mind. This territory should be large enough to accommodate several million Jews; it should have the best chance of winning the support of one or more great powers; and, securing this territory would evoke the least opposition from its present owners and their neighbors.

Palestine did not satisfy any of these conditions. In 1952, Hayim Greenberg, a New York Jewish intellectual, acknowledged that "the land we call the Land of Israel is not the best [for a new Genesis], not politically the most convenient, and if history were rationally planned some other country in some other continent might have been more easily the assembly point for Israel." He adds, "But that is the way it happened."[7] It happened that way for good reasons too. For the Zionist strategists, Palestine was a rational choice.

Palestine was too small to fulfill Zionist ambitions to house all or most of the world's Jews. In 1914, there were 13.4 million Jews in the world, of whom a little more than nine million lived in Europe.[8] At this time, the territory that would become the British mandate of Palestine contained 731,000 Arabs and 60,000 Jews.[9] In other words, the world population of Jews at this time was more than eighteen times the Arab population of Palestine. With the technology then available, the Zionists could not have expected Palestine to provide water for more than a fraction of the world's Jewish population. One might demur that the Zionists had more expansive ideas of what they meant by Palestine. Of course, a more expansive Palestine that could match the borders of the mythic Kingdom of David might be large enough to accommodate the world's Jews.[10] This expansive Palestine, however, would be that much harder to secure.

In the late eighteenth and early nineteenth century, Britain and France had expressed some interest in Zionism, but conditions had changed since then. In this early period, when both powers sought dominion over the Indian Ocean, a Jewish state in Palestine offered a tempting prospect for securing a land bridge connecting the Mediterranean to the Red Sea. In 1815, however, Napoleon's defeat at Waterloo settled this rivalry in Britain's favor. When a modernizing Egypt—under Muhammad Ali Pasha—began to challenge the Ottoman Empire during the 1830s, some

British leaders proposed the creation of a Jewish state in Palestine; this would prevent the Egyptians from threatening the weak Ottoman Empire. This threat too disappeared in the early 1840s when the European powers cut Egypt down to size. In 1882, when it occupied Egypt, Britain was well on its way to becoming the paramount Western power in the Middle East. It had a military base in Aden, it was offering protection to Arab tribes on the eastern shores of Arabia, and its influence over the Iranian monarchy was growing. It is hard to imagine, under these circumstances, how the creation of a Jewish state in Palestine could serve any British interests in the region. On the contrary, a Jewish state in Palestine was certain to cause grave and enduring damage to British standing in the entire Islamicate.

The creation of a Jewish state in Palestine was certain to unleash escalating resistance. It would first come from the Palestinians, the primary victims of Zionism. In time, however, the circle of resistance was certain to grow; it would be joined by the Arab world, the Middle East, and eventually the Islamicate. The Zionists could have learned a few lessons from the French, who had to wage long, arduous, and costly wars in the nineteenth century to occupy and colonize Algeria. The Zionists had chosen a more formidable country to colonize, since Palestine was more central to the sacred geography of Islam. In addition, the Zionists exceeded the French in their colonial ambitions: they wanted to establish an exclusionary colony in Palestine. The history of the Crusades too should have given the Zionists pause because of the clear parallels between their movement and the Crusades. In the end, despite repeated invasions, the Crusaders had to return to their homes in Europe.

The Zionists may never have recalled the Crusades when setting their own sights on the Levant. Nearly six centuries separated their own colonial venture from the Crusades, too remote in time to encourage or deter the Zionists. By the late nineteenth century, more importantly, the Western powers had accumulated a formidable military superiority over the Arabs. The Zionists were confident that they could press this Western military superiority into their service. In addition, they did not lag behind the Western Gentiles in their conviction of racial superiority over peoples of color. They viewed the Arabs of Palestine as savages who, for small inducements, could be persuaded to fold their camps and steal away to new desert pastures.

The Zionists saw the Ottoman rulers as weak and malfeasant, who could be persuaded with an appropriate baksheesh to part with Palestine. In 1896, Theodore Herzl traveled to Istanbul to seek audience with the Ottoman Sultan, Abdul Hamid II. Herzl was confident that he could sway the Sultan with an offer to help him with his foreign debts. The Sultan disappointed the founding father of Zionism; he refused to see Herzl, and instead sent him a message that the Zionists might have done well to heed. "My people have won this empire," he stated, "by fighting for it with their blood and have fertilized it with their blood. We will again cover it with our blood before we allow it to be wrested away from us . . . Let the Jews save their billions."[11] The Ottoman Sultan knew better than to alienate his Muslim subjects by cutting deals with the Zionists over the destiny of Palestine.

Why then did most Zionists insist on choosing Palestine? Although the Zionists, from time to time, considered proposals to establish a Jewish state in other territories, they saw these alternatives only as stopgap arrangements. They explored these alternatives as a means of stimulating Jewish interest in Zionism, as they worked on their schemes to secure Palestine. The consensus, especially among Zionists from Eastern Europe, strongly favored the creation of a Jewish state in Palestine.[12] When Herzl invited the sixth Zionist Congress in August 1903—after the horrors of Kishinev pogrom in Russia earlier that year—to investigate the Uganda offer, it encountered the strongest opposition from the Russian delegates. Although this Congress passed, over strong objections, a modest proposal to send a delegation to examine the Uganda offer, two years later when this offer was brought before the seventh Zionist Congress, it was rejected decisively. At the time, a perplexed Theodore Herzl had remarked to Chaim Weizmann, "I do not understand; the rope was (and still is) round our necks, and yet we said: 'No.'"[13]

Only a small minority of delegates to the sixth Congress took the position that Palestine was both unattainable and inferior to alternative sites for the creation of a Jewish state.[14] Led by Israel Zangwill, they broke away from the mainstream Zionists to pursue what came to be known as territorial Zionism. In 1912, they secured a commitment from Portugal to build their Jewish state in Angola; but, lacking support from mainstream Zionists, this project came to nothing.

It is clear that the Zionists had decided quite early that it would be Eretz Israel or nothing. This appeared to be an incongruous—perhaps, indefensible—position for a movement that claimed that it was dedicated to saving Europe's Jews from the rising tide of anti-Semitism. No doubt, saving Jewish lives was important to the Zionists. However, this did not exhaust their ambitions. The creation of a Jewish haven was only part of a more grand vision to establish the Jews as major historical players.

· · ·

Zionists have argued that their choice of Palestine was decided by the perennial Jewish yearning for Jerusalem. "The relationship to the land of their forefathers," writes Michael Brenner, "which was maintained through the centuries with prayers and poems, language and imagination, made Zionists across the spectrum cling to the territorial claim of the Jews to Palestine."[15] Theodore Herzl too had invoked this Jewish connection to "our ever-memorable historic home." "The very name of Palestine," he wrote, "would attract our people with a force of marvelous potency."[16]

We face two different claims here. Michael Brenner asserts that Palestine is so central to the Jewish experience that the Zionists could not choose any other territory. All rational considerations of an appropriate territory for the Jewish state were overruled by the irresistible Jewish yearning for Zion. A state of their own was the Jewish imperative, the Zionists argued, since only this would secure Jewish lives. Nevertheless, the same Zionists were determined to create their state in Palestine, even if this put the success of their movement and the viability of their state, once it had been created, at risk. This way of thinking strains credulity, to say the least.

Theodore Herzl makes a different claim. He is quite willing, for instance, to examine the merits of locating the Jewish state in Argentina. This country is one of the most fertile in the world, it is spacious, sparsely populated, and enjoys a mild climate. In addition, he thinks that the Zionists can make it profitable for the Argentines to cede a part of their territory to them.[17] Palestine offered none of these advantages, but it possessed mythic power— or so the Zionists claimed. Implicitly, Herzl is conceding that Argentina, despite all its advantages, would attract few Jewish colons. This concern appears to contradict the Zionist narrative. If anti-Semitism was a grave menace to Jews in Europe, it is odd that they would turn down the offer of a Jewish safe haven that came with so many advantages. The more pertinent question, however, is whether Herzl was right in claiming that Palestine would attract Jews with "a force of marvelous potency."

History does not support the presence of an irresistible Jewish yearning for Palestine. "Why, during these two thousand years," Abraham Leon had asked in 1946, "have not the Jews really tried to return to this country? Why was it necessary to wait until the end of the Nineteenth Century for a Herzl to succeed in convincing them of this necessity? Why were all the predecessors of Herzl, like the famous Sabbatai Zebi, treated as false Messiahs? Why were the adherents of Sabbatai Zebi fiercely persecuted by orthodox Judaism?"[18] Indeed, the Jews had developed a millenarian theology to explain why they did not seek to return to Palestine even though they yearned to hasten this in their daily prayers; this was God's work. When the time for their restoration was ripe, God would send a Messiah to restore the Jews to Zion.

Most troubling for the thesis of Jewish yearning for Zion is the presence of a large Jewish population *outside* Palestine long before the destruction

of the Second Temple in 70 CE. Louis Brandeis writes, ". . . throughout centuries when Jewish influence was greatest, during the Persian, the
Greek, and the Roman empires, only a relatively small part of the Jews
lived in Palestine; and only a small part of the Jews returned from Babylon
when the Temple was rebuilt."[19] In addition, we observe the near-absence
of Jews in Palestine during the Islamicate era, when Jewish communities
flourished in nearly every major urban center of the Middle East, North
Africa, and Spain. In the 1530s, there were only five thousand Jews living
in Palestine when it had a population of 157,000; in the late seventeenth
century, the Jewish presence had dwindled to two thousand out of a population of 232,000; and in 1800, there were seven thousand Jews out of
a population of 275,000.[20] In the seventeenth century, both Algiers and
Fez—and several other Islamicate cities besides—contained larger Jewish
populations than there was in all of Palestine.[21]

The official launching of Zionism did not spur a Jewish rush to Palestine either, when a growing stream of Jews was leaving Europe for Western destinations. Only some 75,000 Jews arrived in Palestine between
1882 and 1914, compared to 1.7 million who left for the United States
during this period. Moreover, only half of those who arrived in Palestine
chose to make it their permanent home.[22] Jewish emigration to Palestine
picked up only in the 1930s, but this was because Western countries had
closed their doors to Jewish immigrants in the preceding decades. In the
period since its founding in 1948, despite rapidly advancing prosperity,
Israel has attracted only a trickle of immigrants from the prosperous Jewish communities in Western countries.[23] Starting in the 1950s, most of
the Jewish arrivals in Israel have consisted of economic migrants who
could not gain entry into Western countries.[24] None of this means that
Eretz Israel is not a venerable place in Jewish religious imagination, or
that biblical history centered in Eretz Israel does not occupy an important
place in Jewish ethos. The historical evidence, however, shows that this
Jewish connection to Israel as a spiritual center has not translated into a
decision to migrate to Israel, when Jews have been free to choose more
prosperous and safer destinations.

. . .

The official narrative views Zionism as a nationalism of the last resort,
a project to save Jewish lives, to find a safe haven for the Jews from the
destructive and recurrent gales of anti-Semitism. Zionist writers have
paid scant attention to the part that Jewish nationalism per se played
in the launching of this movement. This is not accidental; there were

important political gains in describing Israel as a refuge for the survivors of the Holocaust.

Zionism was primarily the product of growing Jewish successes during the nineteenth century, not a heightened sense of victimhood. In large measure, during its formative early decades, Zionist thought drew on the growing successes of Jewish communities in the West, and the opportunities and temptations this created to galvanize the Jews and anchor their growing social and economic power in a Jewish state. This nationalist élan is already on display—in the writings of the Zionist precursors—during the early and middle decades of the nineteenth century. It strains credulity to imagine that the Zionist precursors were worrying about anti-Semitism at a time when legal discrimination against Jews was rapidly disappearing: and they were swiftly moving into the mainstream of many Western societies.

Jewish success during the nineteenth century helped to instill a new Jewish identity, based primarily on race. In their success, Jews began to see confirmation of biblical claims that they are a distinct people. In their rapid, almost effortless rise to the highest echelons of society—within a few decades of the lifting of the legal barriers against them—they found proof of their superiority, their chosenness. Paradoxically, as they moved out of the ghettoes, gave up the outward marks of their Jewishness, and assimilated into the cultures of the Gentiles, they also began cultivating a sense of racial distinctiveness as Jews. More and more, they began to define their Jewishness in terms of pedigree, easily supported by the emphasis in biblical narratives on lineage. As assimilation slowly pushed Jews to relinquish their local identities, they sought to replace this with a new overarching identity that emphasized racial superiority. They connected themselves to the Hebrews, to the ancient "history" that is commemorated in their scriptures. More and more, they began to view the Jews as a race, as one large family with a common lineage going back to the tribes, Moses, Isaac, and Abraham.

Max Nordau provides eloquent testimony to the thesis advanced in this chapter. He attributes the rise of Zionism to "the internal compulsions of Judaism" and "two impulses which came from without," the rise of nationalism in Europe and anti-Semitism. In part, he writes, the "new Zionism" has grown "out of the internal compulsions of Judaism itself, out of the enthusiasm of modern educated Jews for their history and martyrology, out of the awakened consciousness of their racial qualities, out of their ambition to save the ancient blood, in view of the farthest possible future, and to add to the achievements of their forefathers the achievements of their posterity." In addition, these "internal compulsions" were shaped and sharpened by the "principle of nationality, which for half a century ruled thought and feeling in Europe, and governed the politics of the world." The dominant nationalist currents in Europe induced Jews "to remember who and what they are; to feel themselves, what they had unlearned, a people apart; and to demand for themselves a normal national destiny." Anti-Semitism too, he acknowledges, "has also taught many educated Jews the way back to their people." "It is not correct to say," he adds, significantly, "that Zionism is but a 'gesture of truculence' or an act of desperation against anti-Semitism."[25]

This is the proper context of Zionism. As the Jews acquired a racial consciousness, with an ancient and distinguished pedigree, they would also create the interlocking organizations that drew upon and reinforced this distinctiveness. Zionism should be seen as an extension of this tendency. It sought to embody a "unique" Jewish people in a nation state, and articulate, enhance and safeguard their power through instruments that are available only to a nation state. At the same time, these tendencies were encouraged by the romantic nationalism that was redrawing the map of Central and Eastern Europe during the nineteenth century. This romantic nationalism too glorified the nation as an organic entity, united by blood and language, each endowed with a unique genius that could only find fulfillment, create its own history, by embodying itself in a state.

This new organic nationalism resonated with the Zionists. Proudly, they claimed that Judaism had been the first nationalism. It was the most enduring nationalism too, because of its success in creating an identity based on race, language, land, and, above all, chosenness. This "national definition of the modern Jew" began to emerge in the 1840s when nationalist movements, based on blood and language, vied with each other to change the political map of Central and Eastern Europe.[26] Since Jews did not yet possess their own land, their nationalism found expression in a secularized messianism. The Zionists would pursue Jewish distinctiveness—Jewish chosenness—within the secular framework of a Jewish "return" to Zion. Contrary to Jewish traditions, they would pursue this return *now*, through human agency; they would not wait for divine intervention. They would seek to reconstitute Jewish power, to recombine their "chosenness" and "uniqueness," in a Jewish state in Palestine. The Zionists wanted the Jews, reconstituted as a nation state in Palestine, to express their chosenness within the ambit of Western civilization, and, perhaps, embody the Western ideals of Enlightenment more completely than any Western nation.[27] Perhaps, historians should look for the deepest wellspring of Zionism in this resurgent nationalism, not in a reaction to anti-Semitism.

Confirming this thesis, one of the earliest Jewish statements of Zionism came from the United States, where Jews labored under fewer disabilities than in Europe. In a speech delivered in 1818, Mordecai Noah, the leading American Jew of his times, candidly grounded his Zionist plan in Jewish demographics and power. "There are upwards of seven million Jews," he said, "known to be in existence throughout the world . . . and possessing more wealth, activity, influence and talents, than any body of people their number on earth . . . they will march in triumphant numbers, and possess themselves once more of Syria, and take their rank among the governments of the earth." In 1844, he was confident that the time for such action had arrived. The Jews, he wrote, "are in a most favorable position to repossess themselves of the promised land, and organize a free and liberal government."[28] Abandoning his previous self-reliant plan, however, he now urged the Jews to lobby Western powers to regain possession of Palestine. Unlike the later Zionists, Mordecai Noah acknowledged that the Jews, at present, "are a sect, not a nation." Once restored to Palestine, however, "we shall, beyond doubt, be secure and protected in all our national rights."[29] Mordecai Noah was ambitious but pragmatic. He did not embellish his Zionist plan with claims of Jewish uniqueness or embed it in visions of Jewish glory.

The grand ambitions enter the Jewish nationalist discourse in the writings of the European precursors of Zionism. The Zionist precursors felt at home in an era of capitalist dominance, nation states, the growing mobility of peoples, and the centrality of knowledge in the economy. This had always been the world of Jews, asserted Moses Hess.[30] The Israelites were the world's first nation to emerge in a world of empires. They were a unique nation too, the chosen instrument of God's will, and the first to value the individual, his liberty, and conscience. In their separate enclaves, the Jews had preserved these values through the age of empires, feudalism, obscurantism, and intolerance. Now was the time for the Jews to return to Palestine, to reenter the stream of history, and claim a leading role in a world that had at last decided to live by Jewish ideals. More than any other people, the Jews had a deeper grounding in the values and structures of the modern world.

It is unlikely that anti-Semitism was the chief catalyst in the thinking of the Zionist precursors. In the mid-nineteenth century, the Jews of Western and Central Europe were moving toward legal equality with the Gentiles; they were making their mark in Europe's finance, industry, politics, science, academia, and in artistic and literary circles. At this time, Jews were keenly aware of their success; they were acquiring a sense of their growing economic and social power.[31] The Zionist precursors wanted to leverage this power, only recently acquired, to claim nation-hood for the Jews.[32] Anti-Semitism may not have been too far from the minds of these Zionist precursors, but, primarily, they were seeking Jew-ish national self-expression, a chance for the Jews to become important actors on the stage of world history.

The highest goal of the early Zionists was not to shelter Jews from the storms of anti-Semitism. They were thinking of reviving the glories of their heroic age that are celebrated in the Torah. Moses Hess, one of the precursors of Zionism, spoke of "new transcendent values" which would issue from the Jewish state; he also projected a grand civilizing role for this state among the backward nations of the Middle East. In *Rome and Jerusalem*, published in 1862, he endorsed the vision of Jewish power that Ernest Laharanne, the private secretary to Napoleon III, had offered in 1860. "A great calling is reserved for the Jews: to be a living channel of communication between three continents . . . You shall be the mediators between Europe and far Asia, opening the roads that lead to India and China."[33] In 1896, Theodore Herzl had proposed a similar mission for the Jewish state in Palestine: it "would form a portion of the rampart of Europe against Asia, an outpost of civilization as opposed to barbarism."[34]

This secular Zionist messianism was joined by another Jewish ten-dency. In the middle of the nineteenth century, some Jews began to expe-rience a growing anxiety at the prospect of losing Jewish religion and Jewish distinctiveness to modernity and assimilation. They were afraid of losing Jewish law, of losing the glue that has always bound Jews to their history, the scripture, and to each other.[35] This Jewish angst over assimila-tion was another stream that contributed to the appeal of Zionism. To Jews alarmed at the impending loss of their uniqueness, Zionism offered hope that they could preserve their heritage in a Jewish state. The ethos of Jewish uniqueness that resisted assimilation also drove Zionist messian-ism. The two are convergent manifestations of the same phenomenon.

Some early Jewish critics of Zionism had warned that the creation of a Jewish state would expose diaspora Jews to charges of dual loyalty. These worries were well founded; in its early decades, Zionism may well have helped to confirm some Gentiles in the view that Jews owe their primary loyalty to world Jewry.[36] After the creation of Israel, however, once the Christian West was redefined as Judeo-Christian, concerns about dual loyalty became an anachronism. These critics also failed to anticipate the synergy that would emerge between Zionism and the Jewish diaspora. In the United States, in particular, the Zionist movement galvanized the Jews, as they created Zionist organizations, built coalitions with civil rights groups, and became more actively involved in domestic politics;

the aim was to win the support of the American public and mobilize the U.S. government behind Zionism. Since 1948 too, a stronger Jewish diaspora has contributed vitally to Israel's success, most importantly by working to maintain Western economic, military, and diplomatic support for Israel. The major Jewish organizations in the United States and Israel work seamlessly as two manifestations of the same movement.

A few Zionists had anticipated this reciprocity. As early as 1897, Ahad Ha'am could visualize how

> the very existence of a Jewish state will also raise the prestige of those who remain in exile . . . As [the Western Jew] contemplates this fascinating vision, it suddenly dawns on his inner consciousness that even now, before the Jewish State is established, the mere idea of it gives him almost complete relief. It provides an opportunity for communal work and political excitement; his emotions find an outlet in a field of activity which is not subservient to non-Jews; and he feels that, thanks to this ideal, he stands once more spiritually erect and has regained his personal dignity, without overmuch trouble and purely by his own efforts.[37]

Indeed, the deepening synergy between Israel and the Jewish diaspora has been a vital factor in the success of Zionism.

Zionism derived its galvanizing power from its messianic nationalism. The Zionists inspired awe by the singular daring of their conception, by their plan to abrogate two thousand years of Jewish history. They challenged the Jews to make a complete break from their history since the second destruction of the Temple, leave behind the lands they had called home for centuries, gather in "ruined Palestine" and rebuild it as a home worthy of the Jews, and bring together Jews of different ethnicities and forge them into a single nation. This would be a unique project in nation building; nothing like this had been done before.

Zionism was a risky project too: even quixotic. The Zionists were proposing to launch a colonial settler project without a "mother country." This was not a project for the weak-hearted or the weak-willed. It could only be led by men who were fired by visions of greatness, of glory, of restoring Jews to history, elevating them into major political players. This was not the work of a defeated people, fleeing persecution, of refugees seeking shelter. Indeed, very few Jews fleeing persecution have chosen to go to Palestine or (later) Israel when safer destinations were available to them. Zionism is a movement of zealots. At first, these zealots were mostly secular, but, increasingly, they have been inspired by religious messianism.

The seemingly impossible goals of Zionism also explain its initial difficulties. Zionism could only appeal to an elite committed to visions of

Jewish greatness. It is impossible to read the writings of the Zionist founders and their precursors—men like Moses Hess, Theodore Herzl, Ahad
Ha'am, Vladimir Jabotinsky, and David Ben-Gurion—without coming
away with the sense that these men were moved by a sense of destiny, that
they understood the deep structures of history, and they were inspired by
visions of Jewish power. They evinced tremendous energy, resolution, and
a strong conviction of their ability to intervene in the affairs of the great
powers. The Zionists knew that the Jews lacked the two ingredients that
make a nation, a common land and a common language; but this did
not deter them. Zionists would create these missing ingredients with "the
élan" of their "nationalist will."[38]

This nationalist drive for Jewish self-expression also explains their fixation on Palestine. The focus on Palestine did not flow from any perennial
Jewish yearning to be reunited with Zion; this we have seen before. This
argument becomes weaker if we recall that few of the early Zionist leaders
had strong religious leanings; in fact, some of them were indifferent Jews.
We have to ask if the Zionists insisted on Palestine because they understood the advantages of its location. A Jewish state in Palestine would
advance their quest for power better than any alternative territory. It is
doubtful if a Jewish state in East Africa, Angola, Argentina, Australia, or
even Europe would command the strategic importance of a Jewish state
in Palestine.[39] This was true even in nineteenth century, before Middle
Eastern oil had become a vital factor in geopolitics.

A Jewish state in Palestine could expect to play a major role in world
affairs. In large part, this was because of Palestine's location: though, later,
Arab oil would also contribute to the appeal of the Jewish state. A Western colonial settler state located at the nexus of three continents could
project its power over the Middle East, East Africa, and North Africa.
As an extension of Western civilization into the Islamicate heartland,
the Zionists knew they could draw, on a sustained basis, upon a variety
of Western emotions and interests to support their expansive colonial
enterprise. Israel would seek to earn the gratitude of the Christian right
in the West by claiming to keep Islam, its perennial adversary, in check.
If ten million Jews could be attracted to Israel, they might even fulfill
the biblical prophecy of establishing a Jewish state stretching from the
Nile to the Euphrates.[40]

In Palestine, the Jewish settlers would hold the world's attention
because this was the land of the Jewish prophets and patriarchs. It was
also the Holy Land to the Christians, where Jesus had walked, where he
had been crucified. No less, Palestine belonged to a region that had layers
of ancient history; it had been ruled by empires whose names resonated

in European consciousness. By possessing Palestine, by dominating this ancient region, Israel could claim a centrality that it would never possess in any other territory. Once it was established on this elevated stage, Israel could dream of imitating the storied empires of the ancient world. Like them, it could aspire to become the source of a new civilization.

The Zionist fathers indulged in dreams of Jewish glory. It never appears that their ambitions or their plans were modest, limited to establishing a national relief agency, whose only job would be to build a shelter for persecuted Jews. Moses Hess, the most distinguished of the early Zionist visionaries—according to Arthur Hertzberg—"speaks mystically of new transcendent values which are to issue from a restored Zion . . . and of a new Jewish nation to act as the guardian of three continents and to be the teacher of the somnolent peoples of the East—i.e., he imagines a distinguished, *but not a determinant*, part for the Jew to play in the general *mission civilizatrice* of an expanding West."[41] Max Nordau, a close associate of Theodore Herzl, wrote that Zionists were "going to Palestine to extend the moral boundaries of Europe as far as the Euphrates."[42] The Zionists were not about to settle for the part of a bit player in Argentina, East Africa, Angola, or some territory on the edge of Europe when they had before them the prospect of becoming the dominant power in the Middle East. It was clear to Ahad Ha'am, wrote Arthur Hertzberg, "that a restored Zion would surely mean more to humanity than a sovereign Albania."[43]

The Jews were not a nation by the ordinary usage of the term. Even without their connection to a common land, elements of *Western* Jewry had acquired a strong sense of group identity. "The Jewish people," writes Peretz Smolenskin, "has outlived all others because it has always regarded itself as a people—a spiritual nation."[44] This Jewish consciousness of themselves as a distinct people was sustained by Judaism, which singled them out and placed them above all nations. Historically, the Jews had preserved their identity by living in intimate contact with the Torah, by adherence to Jewish religious law, and by memorializing the triumphs and tragedies of Jewish history in their holidays. The sense of Jewish distinctiveness was also reinforced by the conditions of their dispersion; by their precariously small numbers, which produced a sense of siege; and by the mobility they acquired from their professions as traders, craftsmen, goldsmiths, and doctors, unattached to the land, the military, and governments. In the nineteenth century, moreover, as assimilated Jews began to distance themselves from their religious identity, they began to define themselves in terms of a common race, as a people descended from the ancient Hebrews.

The condition of Western Jews then exemplified a paradox. Without a common land, language, or ethnicity, as Jews gained prominence, they had acquired a growing sense of being a distinctive people and privileged in the evolving capitalist world order. It was the ambition of Zionists to deepen this paradox by emphasizing Jewish distinctiveness and superiority, and by emphasizing "race" as the basis of Jewish identity. Indeed, they would claim that the Jews were already a nation, an "abnormal" nation because they did not have a land or state of their own. Although few Jews were willing to become pioneers in Palestine, eventually most of them would be persuaded to support the Zionist cause. Once growing numbers of Jews had been galvanized by their cause, the Zionists would use their considerable financial, intellectual, and political resources to secure the backing of Western governments for their movement. The Zionists were convinced that their cause was world-historical, that the paltry lives of "semicivilized" Arabs could not be allowed to stand in the way of their grand ambition to create a Jewish nation and a Jewish state. The Zionists were determined to emerge as a world-historical force: and they would muster the resources of Western Jews and the West to ensure that nothing would stop them from reaching this goal.

CHAPTER 7

A PEOPLE WITHOUT A LAND

Jews are a nation which, having once acted as the leaven of the social
world, is destined to be resurrected with the rest of the civilized nations.
—Moses Hess, 1862

Let sovereignty be granted us over a portion of the globe large enough to
satisfy the reasonable requirements of a nation; the rest we shall manage
for ourselves.
—Theodore Herzl, 1896

We are a generation of settlers, and without the steel helmet and the gun
barrel, we shall not be able to plant a tree or build a house.
—Moshe Dayan, April 1956

Zionism comprises a belief that Jews are a nation, and as such are entitled
to self-determination as all other nations are.
—Emanuele Ottolenghi, 2003[1]

ZIONISM WAS FOUNDED ON THE PREMISE THAT the Jews are a nation, and
they have always been one. What they have lacked for many centuries is
a state of their own, a Jewish state; but that deficit was now going to be
remedied by the Zionist movement.[2]

At the time the Zionist movement was launched, this premise was
indefensible. The Jews could be described as a collection of ethnicities,
having this in common, that they had various degrees of attachment to
Judaism. In the thinking of Theodore Herzl, this and "a common enemy"
sufficed to make the Jews a "nation."[3] However, as it is commonly understood, the Jews were not a nation because no sizable Jewish community
constituted a majority in any territory. In 1882, Leo Pinkser, an avid early
proponent of Zionism, acknowledged that the Jewish people lack "most
of those attributes which are the hallmark of a nation. It lacks that characteristic national life which is inconceivable without a common language,
common customs, and a common land."[4]

Arguably, Pinsker errs in denying "common customs" to the Jews. In the late nineteenth century, Jewish customs—centered on the Halacha, rituals, reverence for the Torah, and celebration of sacred holidays—carried enough weight among Jews to identify them as a religious community. In addition, although they did not possess a common spoken language, Hebrew still commanded a sufficiently central place in Jewish religious life to qualify at least as a force that brought Jews together. Jews could also revive this language—as they had done in Umayyad Spain—as the language of literary discourse. Yet, the recovery of Hebrew alone would not earn the Jews the title of a nation.

Starting in the nineteenth century, as assimilation got underway, Jewish thinkers began to redefine Jewish identity in terms of race. In part, this compensated for the gradual loss of those religious markers that had hitherto set them apart from Gentiles. It also equipped Jews with one of the two ingredients—race and fatherland—that defined nationhood in the nationalist thinking that was gaining ground in East and Central Europe. In tandem, a new myth of the Jewish diaspora too gained currency. All the scattered Jewish communities of the world—this myth asserted—are descended from the ancient Israelites forced into exile by the Romans in the second century CE. The Jews were now taking ownership of the anti-Semitic slander, that the Jews, descended from the ancient Hebrews, are an alien race.

The Jews lacked an actual and existing homeland; but they could lay claim to Palestine as their virtual homeland. Palestine had one vital advantage over alternatives destinations for the Jewish colons; using the mythic power of Eretz Israel was the Zionist's only chance of overcoming Jewish apathy toward their project. The Jewish connections to Eretz Israel would also make it easier to explain this theft of land that the Zionists were proposing. Palestine is the eternal Jewish homeland, the Zionists would repeat *ad nauseum*. It was theirs because Yahweh had granted it to their ancestors in perpetuity. It was theirs because—purportedly—their ancestors had lived there. It was theirs also because the Jews had never stopped yearning for it during their "exile."[5] Moreover, these arguments would go down well with the Protestants who, also, had been raised on the same beliefs. With ingenuity, the Zionists had furnished the second ingredient of Jewish nationhood: they had acquired a "virtual" fatherland.

A "virtual" fatherland would not make the Jews a nation. The "virtual" fatherland must be made real if the Jews were going to become a nation on the map of the world. The Jews would have to appropriate Palestine, they would have to conquer it, possess it physically, and make it exclusively a property of the world's Jews. This was the kernel of the Zionist program.

There were two ways to create the territorial basis of a Jewish state. The Zionists could first acquire that territory by force and create a Jewish majority there through colonization, natural increases of the Jewish population, ethnic cleansing, or some combination of the three. Alternatively, they could first try to create a Jewish majority in some country, or some region within a country, through immigration, natural increases in the Jewish population, or some combination of the two. Once they had created a clear majority, the Jewish colons could secede to form their own state or appropriate the existing state through the force of demography.

With near certainty, both scenarios would involve violence. In the first scenario, violence would be needed at the outset to secure and open a territory to Jewish colons; it would also persist as long as the natives did not give up the fight to regain their lands. In the second scenario, colonization *per se* might occur without the use of force if it could proceed gradually, imperceptibly, and without arousing the suspicion of the natives chosen for displacement. Concealment was extremely unlikely, however, because of Zionism's declared goal of creating a Jewish state. Concealment was nearly impossible also because the Zionists were in a hurry to create a Jewish majority. Once their suspicions had been aroused, the natives would seek to cut off the entry of Jewish colons. The Jewish colons could stay and grow only if they had developed the capacity to use violence.

In 1896, Theodore Herzl had warned that the second method of "gradual infiltration"—as it had been employed until that point in Palestine and Argentina—would eventually backfire. "It continues," he wrote, "till the inevitable moment when the native population feels itself threatened, and forces the Government to stop further influx of Jews." With singular clarity, Herzl concluded that often "immigration is consequently futile unless based on an *assured supremacy*" (emphasis added).[6] The Zionists could only pursue the first scenario; they would have to conquer a territory before they could create a Jewish majority.

Starting from the ground reality of Jewish dispersion, therefore, a Jewish state could only be created through conquest, followed by colonization. In a word, the reality about Zionism was that it was a settler colonial movement. No matter how hard they might try to disguise this—with protestations about wanting to share Palestine with the Arabs or the benefits Jewish colonization would bring to the Arabs—the Zionist founders understood this elementary logic from the outset.

Lacking a Jewish mother country, they also quickly concluded that they would have to depend on surrogates to do the conquering on their behalf. The Zionists would have to prevail on one or more Western powers to seize and hold Palestine, open it up to Jewish colonization, and allow or help the Zionists to create the infrastructure of a Jewish state. At some point, however, the Zionists would displace the mother country, and use force to drive out the natives.

. . .

It is necessary to take a closer look at the connections, the organic links, between the two tendencies in Zionism—the nationalist movement and the colonial settler enterprise.

We need to explore the pathways that lead all too quickly from the Jewish nationalist to the Jewish colon; from the Jewish patriot to the Jewish pioneer; from the "liberation" of Jews to ethnic cleansing and massacre of Palestinians; from one putative "abnormality"—the "homelessness" of Jews in Europe—to another "abnormality," the only colonial settler state of the twentieth and twenty-first centuries, a Jewish garrison state, armed to the teeth, planted in the heart of the Islamicate.

A climate of opinion favorable to political Zionism first emerged with the Reformation. In Catholic theology, God had abrogated His covenant with the Jews when they rejected Jesus as the Messiah. Indeed, with this rejection, the covenant had passed to the Catholic Church, which was now the chosen instrument of God's will on earth. In rejecting Catholicism, the Protestants also restored the Jews to their covenant and their eternal rights to Palestine. Slowly, this gave rise to demands by some Protestants for a Jewish "restoration" to Palestine and the creation of a Jewish state in Palestine.

In time, the idea was born that this restoration could—indeed, should—be effected with help from the European powers. In the nineteenth century, the idea of Jewish restoration took an ominous new turn in some evangelical circles in Britain, who would later pass it on to the United States. The evangelicals developed a new reading of the Bible, which made the Jewish restoration a necessary prelude to the Second Coming.[7] This idea gained political traction during the first half of the nineteenth century, when Britain and France sought to control the Levant as the land bridge to the Indian Ocean. It is little known that in 1799, during his siege of Acre in Palestine, Napoleon issued a proclamation inviting Jews to reclaim Palestine.[8] Over the course of the nineteenth century, a few British leaders, of evangelical persuasion, expressed sporadic interest in settling Jews in Palestine.[9] With few exceptions, however, these overtures were rebuffed by the Jews.

Ironically, an active Jewish interest in the restoration emerged in the last decade of the nineteenth century, long after the idea had lost its allure in European politics. The competition for the control of Palestine, as a land bridge to the Indian Ocean, had been settled decisively in Britain's favor.[10] The British offer in 1903, of self-rule for the Jews in East Africa—instead of Palestine—testifies to the absence of British interest in colonizing Palestine at this time. Had the Jews taken up this offer, a Jewish state in this part of the world may have followed a different trajectory. This would have been no less tragic for the East Africans; and it would be opposed by all of Africa. It would also be strongly opposed by African Americans in the United States, producing frictions there between them and the American Jews. A Jewish state in Africa would do little to excite the millenarian fantasies of America's evangelicals. In addition, East Africa does not possess any resources that could be sold as vital to the U.S. economy. One wonders how the Jewish lobby would seek to turn this Jewish state into America's strategic asset in Africa.

Several factors account for the late Jewish interest in Zionism, a question examined in Chapter 6. In short, the conditions for the emergence of Jewish nationalism were created during the nineteenth century, when legal barriers against Jews were disappearing in much of Europe. As Jews entered into the mainstream, assimilated, moved up, and gained prominence in European society, they began to create a new Jewish identity based primarily on race. At the same time, assimilation caused some Jews to feel a growing angst over the loss of Jewish distinctiveness that was rooted in observance of Halacha. Jewish success and angst, reinforced by the new racial identity, persuaded some Jews that they were a nation and deserved their own state. In the late nineteenth century, the resurgence of anti-Semitism, especially in Eastern Europe, was used by the Zionists to create support for Zionism. The Zionists would seek to enlist the support of anti-Semites as well as their Jewish victims.

The Zionists' plans flowed from their analysis of the "abnormal" condition of the Jews in Europe—the Jewish question. The Jews were a nation without a land or a state of their own; they were a homeless people. Their homelessness was the "core defect in the Jewish condition"; it was also the source of anti-Semitism.[11] Contrary to the assimilationists, the Zionists asserted that the Jews are a distinct nation, not only a religious community. Indeed, they argued, Judaism was wedded to, and inseparable from, the national existence of Jews.[12] In his Zionist manifesto, Theodore Herzl declared pointedly that the Jews are "a people—one people." Moreover, "the distinctive nationality of Jews neither can, will, nor must be destroyed." It follows that the Jewish question was a "national question," not a social or religious one.[13] The Jewish question would have to be solved collectively, based on the recognition that the Jews are, and always have been, a distinct and indestructible nation. It is this belief, this fundamental premise, on which Zionism was founded.

The Zionist demand for the creation of a Jewish state flows directly from their diagnosis of the Jewish question. If Jewish dispersion was the cause of their "abnormalcy," it could be terminated only by aggregating, concentrating, ingathering the Jews in some country they could call their own. Moreover, the Zionists insisted that this ingathering would not produce security for the Jews, unless it led eventually to the creation of a Jewish state. This is the *raison d'être* of Zionism.

In his manifesto, *The Jewish State*, Theodore Herzl wastes no time in setting out this goal. "The idea which I have developed in this pamphlet," Herzl states in the opening sentence of his book, "is a very old one: it is the restoration of the Jewish state." Later, when describing the mechanisms for the creation of the Jewish state, he explains, "Let the sovereignty be granted us over a portion of the globe large enough to satisfy the reasonable requirements of a nation; the rest we shall manage for ourselves."[14] Unknown to him, it appears, Herzl had been preceded in his analysis and conclusions by several Jewish thinkers—including Mordecai Noah, Zvi Kalischer, Moses Hess, and Leo Pinsker, among others—who had written extensively on the Jewish question and its Zionist solution.

Zionism was a utopian nationalism: it would have to *create* the ingredients of a nation. The Jewish peoples of Europe did not yet possess a national home; neither did they share a common language. Judging too from the trickle of European Jews who had chosen to make the *Aliya*—migration to Palestine—before the 1930s, it would appear that a Jewish "nation" did not even want to be called into existence. In choosing diverse Western destinations over Palestine, the Jews indicated quite clearly that becoming a nation was not their priority. The assimilated Jews in Western Europe and the Americas would eventually support Zionism with their purse, their pen, and their votes. However, these were the only roles they would play in building the Jewish state; they did not want to become colons in Palestine.[15]

The Zionists would create the Jewish nation that existed only in their imagination.[16] This they would accomplish by the force of their commitment, their Nietzschean energy, their daring and rhetoric. They would articulate visions of Jewish power, recall the mythic glory of the Davidic kingdom, resuscitate their near-dead ancient language, and set in motion a settler colony in Palestine under the aegis of Western powers. They would lay the foundations of a Jewish state in Palestine by creating Jewish communes, Jewish towns, Jewish labor organizations, Jewish banks, Jewish centers of learning, a Jewish land-holding company, and a Jewish army. In Palestine, they would forge a Jewish nation through endless wars, by demonizing the Palestinians, by creating a permanent state of war with the Arabs, by instituting compulsory military service, and offering Israeli citizenship to all Jews in the diaspora. They would press archeology and genetics into their service—to validate biblical history and fabricate the purity of Jewish lineage.

Israel emerged as a nation state not in the manner that was normal in the twentieth century. It was not as if the Jews were already in Palestine, their putative homeland, ruled by foreign elites who had to be expelled to create a Jewish state.[17] The state of Israel arose in Palestine by expropriating another people, the Palestinian Arabs. The Jewish "nation" could not reach its goal unless it first acquired land; and since the land it coveted was not "empty"—no land ever is, except in the imagination of colonists—the Jews would have to take it from those who now possessed it. In other words, Israel was the product of a colonial settler movement.

. . .

At first, the Zionists did not seek to conceal the colonial character of their movement from their Western audience. Concealment was not necessary in the age of high imperialism and triumphant racism. Once national liberation movements in the colonies got under way, however, they had to change tack.

In the latter half of the nineteenth century, Western elites were convinced that they had the right—even the duty—to colonize the still-free territories in Africa and Asia, and deal with the natives as they deemed appropriate.[18] Even the smaller nations of Western Europe—such as Portugal, the Netherlands, and Belgium—would acquire colonies in Asia and Africa. Colonies could also be acquired as personal fiefdoms. In the early 1880s, King Leopold of Belgium created a vast personal estate, the Congo Free State. During the fifteen years of its existence, from 1884 to 1908, the brutal regime of exploitation practiced in this private colony had killed between five and fifteen million Congolese and maimed many millions more.[19] In the meanwhile, European statesmen feted King Leopold as a great humanitarian who was civilizing the Congolese.

In this milieu, the Zionists had little to worry about the morality of their plan. As the twentieth century unfolded, however, blatant violations of the rights of "darker races" would be accepted less routinely. On the one hand, as liberation movements in the colonies gained momentum, the European powers did not want to be seen as openly flouting the rights of natives. In addition, colonial empires were put on the defensive when President Woodrow Wilson proclaimed the principle of self-determination. In 1918, he informed Congress that "self-determination is not a mere phrase. It is an imperative principle of action which statesmen will henceforth ignore at their peril."[20] This was convenient for the United States, which owned few colonies but could expect to gain considerably from the dismantling of colonial empires. In particular, Britain could not sustain its global dominance without its extensive colonies.

The emergence of national liberation movements in the colonies during the first half of the twentieth century made the Zionists uneasy. The Zionist movement had been advanced in the era of a confident and expansive European imperialism, whose deeply ingrained racism showed scant regard for the rights of colored peoples. Indeed, the Zionists had openly sought to become a part of this colonial movement; their plan was to hitch a ride on the bandwagon of European imperialism and create their own state in Palestine at the expense of the "backward" Arabs. Increasingly, however, the Zionists discovered that they were part of an imperialist expansion that was now on the defensive and would soon be on the retreat. The Zionists understood that they could lose the moral high ground to the Palestinians: they were on the wrong side of history.

In order to gain time and legitimacy, the Zionists would seek to obscure their kinship to European colonialists. Supported by a thousand ideologues, they would work to *re*frame their movement. Quite simply, they would seek to recast Zionism as a national liberation movement. With not-too-clever sophistry, they would make the argument that Jews are an oppressed people, victims of centuries of anti-Semitic hatred, struggling to liberate themselves *in* Palestine. A Jewish faction from Europe, colonizing Palestine under the aegis of the British Empire, would henceforth masquerade as a movement for the liberation of Jews.

The Zionists would still have to explain *why* Palestine, since this land belonged to another people. Where else, the Zionist ideologues would argue. They would now invoke, more insistently than before, the ancient myths of a chosen people, of the divine covenant Yahweh had made with their "ancestors," and the land grant he made to the Israelites in perpetuity. They would invoke their ancient connection to Palestine, they would claim that their patriarchs were buried there, and they had never given up hopes of reclaiming and returning to this land. They would claim that Jews had always maintained a presence—no matter how tiny—in Palestine. Hence, their present ownership rights in Palestine had been kept alive.

The Zionists used their differences with the British—their surrogate mother country—to support the deceit that they are a liberation movement. These differences emerged early, but they did not become serious until 1939. The Zionists complained bitterly when the British, in 1922, demarcated Transjordan—then a part of their mandate in Palestine—into an autonomous territory and closed it to Jewish settlers.[21] More disappointments followed, as the British, reacting to rising Palestinian resistance, took measures to distance themselves from Zionist aims. Finally, eager to secure

Arab support for the imminent war with Germany, the British issued a White Paper in May 1939, announcing tight new restrictions on Jewish immigration into Palestine over the next five years; after this period, immigration would depend on the consent of the Palestinians. This was a blow to the expectations of Zionists who condemned it as treachery, and resolved to oppose it by all means. The mainstream Zionists would defy the White Paper covertly, while smaller, more militant groups would inaugurate a campaign of terror against the British once the war was over.

The White Paper was not without a silver lining. It created an opportunity for Zionism to masquerade as a liberation movement. Since it would now be seeking to evict colonial Britain from Palestine, Zionism had acquired a superficial resemblance to liberation movements. The Jewish settlers would insist that they are victims of a colonial power; to give it an air of credibility, they would banish the Palestinians from their discourse. This was a clever strategy, since the Zionists were quite confident that they could force a British withdrawal. In the early 1940s, the Jewish settlers in Palestine—the *Yishuv*—had grown to 30 percent of the population of Palestine. In addition, they did not face a potent resistance from the Palestinians. After their failed uprising of the late 1930s, the ranks of the Palestinian resistance had been seriously depleted, with many of their fighters dead and their leaders in prison, in hiding or in exile.

The Zionists would read from a new script. The *Yishuv* were the rightful owners of Palestine, and they were now fighting against a colonial power to gain their freedom.[22] This has since become part of the official narrative of Zionism. Avi Shlaim, a liberal Zionist, writes, "Zionism is the national liberation movement of the Jewish people, and the state of Israel is its political expression."[23] The Zionists now claimed kinship with the Indians, Indonesians, Vietnamese, Filipinos, and Egyptians: together, these colonized nations were engaged in a common struggle against the tyranny of Western colonial powers.

The Zionists preferred not to put all their eggs in one ideological basket. They employed a broad strategy to deflect attention from their colonial character, of setting up contrasts, real and putative, between themselves and the Arabs. Several such contrasts have been emphasized over time. In the decades before the creation of Israel, as also in the early decades of Israel's history, the Zionists emphasized their progressive and socialist character in contrast to the tribal and feudal character of Arab society. The Zionists could point to the socialist thinkers in their ranks—such as Ber Borochov and Aaron David Gordon—who analyzed Zionism in the Marxist language of class struggle, and claimed that Zionism is a movement of the Jewish proletariat seeking to establish their classless society in Palestine. In support of their socialist character, they drew attention to the Jewish communes in Palestine that were based on an ethic of respect for labor, shared work and communal living. The dominance of the Labor Party in the Zionist movement and, for several decades, in Israeli politics, was another socialist feather in the Zionist cap. Not least, the Soviets too appeared to authenticate the socialist claims of the Zionists by offering them crucial diplomatic support at the UN in 1947, becoming the first country to give *de jure* recognition to Israel, and instructing Czechoslovakia to supply heavy weapons and military aircraft to the *Yishuv* during the crucial years from 1947 to 1949. As Maxine Rodinson points out, the Jewish settlers in Palestine were establishing a society "deeply permeated with the leaven of socialism."[24] How could anyone accuse the Zionists of being imperialist or colonialist?

To burnish their credentials, the Zionists never cease to draw attention to the contrast between their "democracy" and Arab autocracies. In stark contrast to Israel's democracy, they point out, the Arab world is populated with despotic regimes—monarchies, family-owned oligarchies, and personal dictatorships that are passed on to sons. Over time, the Zionists have expanded this inventory of contrasts. Only a few may be listed here. Israel has a profound respect for human life; the Arabs do not. Israel gives equal rights to women; the Arabs do not. Israel gives equal rights to homosexuals; the Arabs do not. One should note that this is almost entirely a one-sided rhetorical engagement. In the United States especially, one only hears the *pros* for Israel and the *cons* for the Arabs. Israel has succeeded almost completely in keeping the attention of Americans focused on how good Israel is and how vile the Arabs are.

Masters at creating and propagating myths about Zionism and Israel, the Zionist leaders are far too clever to start believing their own lies. Indeed, it would be fatal for a colonial enterprise if those who planned and implemented it began to take their own myths seriously.[25] If it is to succeed—and failure can be very costly—an exclusionary colonialism must do what needs to be done without sentimentalism. It must expropriate the natives; it must daily ratchet the pressures on them to leave; if they do not leave voluntarily, they must be driven out by force; and those who remain inside their borders must be dispatched to the margins of the settler society. The Zionists have shown little sympathy for their Arab victims. Indeed, the Zionists vilify the few Jews, inside Israel or outside, who cross the red line and urge consideration for the rights of Palestinians. They are seen as traitors, as self-hating Jews. Inside Israel, but especially in the United States, Jewish dissenters are not given the light of day.

Chapter 8

A Land Without a People

As soon as we have a big settlement here we'll seize the land, we'll become strong, and then we'll take care of the Left Bank [of the Jordan River]. We'll expel them from there, too. Let them go back to the Arab countries.
—Jewish settler, 1891

[We] must be prepared either to drive out by the sword the [Arab] tribes in possession as our forefathers did or grapple with the problem of a large alien population, mostly Mohammedan and accustomed for centuries to hate us.
—Israel Zangwill, 1905

Palestine shall be as Jewish as England is English, or America is American.
—Chaim Weizmann, 1919

I support compulsory transfer. I do not see in it anything immoral.
—David Ben-Gurion, 1938

Without the uprooting of the Palestinians, a Jewish state would not have arisen here.
—Benny Morris, 2004[1]

CONSIDER A FEW DATES AND NUMBERS THAT bear testimony to the demographic transformation effected by the Zionists in Palestine during the first half of the twentieth century.

At the start of the nineteenth century, there were 7,000 Jews living in Ottoman Palestine: a were 2.5 percent of its population.[2] In 1882, their numbers had increased to 24,000 and their share in the total population had grown to 8 percent. In 1918, following 36 years of organized efforts to establish Jewish colonies, the Jewish population of Palestine had grown to 60,000; their share was not much higher at 9.1 percent. Over the next three decades, following the Balfour Declaration of 1917, the rate of growth of the Jewish population accelerated dramatically. In 1946, the Jewish population had increased to 543,000, a ninefold increase since 1918. Over the same period, their share had also increased more than threefold to 30 percent. In 1949, the Jewish population of Israel—incorporating 78 percent of mandatory Palestine—had climbed to 1,014,000. On the contrary, the Arab population of this territory had plummeted to 160,000. Proportionately, the Jewish and Arab shares in the population of Israel now stood at 86.4 and 13.6 percent.[3] In no time, the Palestinians had become a minority in 78 percent of their own country.

In a single year, during 1948, the Arab population of the territory captured by Israel had plummeted from close to a million to 159,000.[4] Where had all these Arabs gone? Had they been ethnically cleansed—under the cover of the War of 1948—by the Israeli military and other armed Jewish groups? Strenuously, in their official historiography, the Zionists have maintained that they had not driven out the Arab population of Israel; there were no massacres of Arabs, no rapes, no looting of Arab property. The Arabs had left voluntarily, following the advice of their leaders, to move out of the way of the victorious Arab armies that were advancing on Palestine. This is one of the entrenched myths created by Zionism after the War of 1948.

Israel would never allow the Palestinian Arabs to return to their homes inside Israel.[5] Israel argued that the Arabs could not return because they had left "voluntarily." In leaving "voluntarily," they had demonstrated hostile intent toward Israel; if they returned, they would seek to undermine Israel from within. Israel denied that it had engaged in ethnic cleansing of its Arab population. Yet, it ensured the same outcome by preventing their return. Israel can eat its cake and have it too.

This is one of many Zionist myths that circulate as history in the West. According to official Zionist "history," the Jews in Palestine have always wanted to live in peace with the Arabs, to share the land equitably with them. Did they not accept the partition plans proposed by the Peel Commission and the United Nations? Cohabitation was rejected by the Arabs; they attacked Israel on the eve of its independence, fully determined to destroy the fledgling state and drive the Jews into the sea. Israel won the War of 1948 by a narrow margin, and has since been forced to fight many more wars imposed upon it by the Arabs. Israel has made many peace overtures since 1948, only to be rebuffed by Arabs. Every nation believes in its own myths; myths of Israeli provenance are lapped up in every Western country.

The myth of a voluntary Palestinian departure from Israel was first challenged by four Israeli historians in the late 1980s. Drawing upon official archives recently opened to the public, they presented a new narrative of the early history of Israel that is greatly at variance with the official accounts.[6] Most importantly, the revisionist historians set the record straight on the question of the Palestinian refugees of 1948. The Palestinians had *not* left voluntarily, but had been forced out violently by the Israelis according to a preconceived plan. In the process, the Israeli military and other armed Jewish groups had perpetrated dozens of massacres of Palestinian civilians and committed hundreds of rapes. Not surprisingly, this revisionist history has done little to discredit the long-entrenched myth of voluntary Palestinian departure. Indeed, a new literature has grown up to discredit and disparage the work of the revisionist historians.[7]

. . .

Mainstream Zionists had long viewed the displacement of Palestinians, by one means or another, as necessary to their mission; but they preferred to keep this under wraps.

The Zionist plan for a Jewish state in Palestine was radical by any account. It called for the creation of a state of the Jews, for the Jews, and by the Jews in Palestine. The Jewish state would be an *exclusionary* colonial settler state; it would reenact the history of the United States and Australia, whose native populations were mostly exterminated and their remnants confined to reservations. The Zionists did not want any Arabs in their state, not even as cheap labor; they only wanted their land.

In part, the Zionists were inspired by the romantic nationalism of the nineteenth century, which defined a nation as a people united by blood, lineage, history, and land. To this brew of romantic nationalism, the Zionists added another ingredient drawn from Judaism—chosenness.[8] As the political and historical instrument of the Jewish nation, the Jewish state would consist of, and represent, only Jews. If Palestinian Arabs had to be accommodated—for unavoidable reasons—inside the borders of the Jewish state, they could not enjoy equal rights with the Jews. Moreover, at some appropriate time, they would have to be driven out. The Jewish state could belong only to the Jews.

In principle, the Zionists could create a large Jewish majority in Palestine without driving out the natives. In 1919, Chaim Weizmann spoke of creating such conditions in Palestine "that as the country is developed, we can pour in a considerable number of immigrants, and finally establish such a society in Palestine that Palestine shall be as Jewish as England is English, or America is American."[9] However, this was not practical. The Zionists could not expect to attract millions of Jews to Palestine—enough to reduce the Palestinians to a small minority—in the time they had to create a Jewish state. The Zionists were in a tight race against the Arab nationalists who were rapidly gaining ground. To win this race, the Zionists could not wait for the arrival of millions of Jewish colons; this would require more than a few decades. Only by driving out the natives could the Zionists expect to create a large Jewish majority in Palestine: and such a majority was the *sine qua non* of a Jewish state.

Alternatively, the Zionists could choose to create a Jewish state *without* a Jewish majority. Armed with the power of the state now, they would have the time to attract the millions of Jewish immigrants: and create a Jewish majority without resorting to ethnic cleansing of the natives. Although superficially attractive, this would not be workable. It would force the Jewish state to become authoritarian, since they could give the vote to the Jews only if they denied it to the Arabs. An undisguised Israeli apartheid, at this stage, would have invited sanctions from the Third World. Israel would also lose face with Western audiences. Under the circumstances, the Palestinians would find it advantageous to demand equal rights in the new state. If the Palestinians, moreover, chose armed struggle to resist Israeli apartheid—with the support of neighboring Arab states— it would be difficult to continue to attract Jewish colons. Indeed, some Jewish settlers might choose to move to safer locations. Swiftly, therefore, the Zionists created a Jewish majority at the first opportunity that became available—the War of 1948.

The creation of an exclusionary colonial settler state was justified—the Zionists argued—by the threat of anti-Semitism. The founders of Zionism had argued that anti-Semitism flows inescapably from the cohabitation of Jews and Gentiles. It arises whenever Jews attain social and economic visibility, or when Gentiles have to compete with Jews for entry to or advancement in the trades, industry, professions, and academia.[10] If the Jewish state was going to offer a safe haven against anti-Semitism, if it was going to shield Jews from anti-Semites, it followed that it would have to insulate them from Gentiles. Only an overwhelming Jewish majority could ensure this. It would be "utter foolishness," wrote Israel Zangwill, to convert Palestine into "a country of two peoples. This can only cause trouble."[11]

Secular Zionists argued that a significant Arab presence in Eretz Israel would threaten their goal of creating a center of Jewish power. Not only would these Arabs, who have their own religion, culture, and history, oppose the state's Jewish orientation: they would constitute an internal threat to its security. In December 1947, when reviewing the demographic composition of the Jewish state proposed by the UN Partition Plan—Arab Palestinians made up 42 percent of its population—David Ben-Gurion told the Central Committee of the *Histadrut*, "There can be no stable and strong Jewish state so long as it has a Jewish majority of only 60 percent."[12] The creation of a Jewish majority was not an end in itself; it was a prerequisite for attaining the more ambitious goals of Zionism. Ben-Gurion argued that the "majority is but a stage along our path, albeit an important and decisive stage in the political sense. From there we can proceed with our activities in calm confidence and concentrate the masses of our people in this country, *and its environs*" (emphasis added).[13] In order to pursue their ambitions in "calm confidence," the Zionists would have to ensure a clear Jewish majority in their state.

The Labor Zionists too pushed for the creation of an ethnically homogeneous population in Palestine. The absence of a Jewish working class in the diaspora, they argued, had deformed Jewish character; excluded from agriculture, the military, and government, the Jews had been forced to become traders, shopkeepers, and moneylenders.[14] In order to restore the Jewish nation to the wholeness that comes from working on the land and in factories, the Labor Zionists were committed to creating a Jewish working class in the colonies. Most importantly, this meant that Jewish enterprises would not employ any Arab workers. In their insistence on creating a Jewish working class, the Labor Zionists would help to establish a society that had no place in it for Arabs, not even as a class of exploited workers. The objectives of Labor Zionism ensured that the Jewish society—unlike the apartheid in South Africa—would have no use for native workers. Ironically, then, more than any other political tendency in Zionism, the "socialists" made the strongest case for an exclusionary colonial settler state in Palestine.[15]

A few Zionists argued against the exclusion of Arabs, but they remained peripheral to the Zionist movement. In particular, there were two small groups—the *Brit Shalom*, which became defunct in the early 1930s, and the *Ihud*, which emerged in 1942—who advocated accommodation with Arabs in a binational state. They warned about the difficulties, even disasters, that would flow from a Zionist vision that excluded Arabs from Palestine. Although these Zionists included some eminent names—such as Judah Magnes and Martin Buber—they remained marginal to the politics of Zionism.[16]

.   .   .

Understandably, the Zionists sought to conceal their intent to create a Jewish majority in Palestine, with or without the ethnic cleansing of Arab Palestinians. They discussed these matters privately or penned their thoughts in diaries and personal letters. In public, the Zionists continued to insist, well into the 1940s, that there was room in Palestine for both people.[17] Indeed, they continued to remind the Arabs of the inestimable benefits that Jewish colonization would bring to them.

Theodore Herzl offers an early example of this duplicity in a letter he wrote in March 1899 to Youssuf Zia Al-Khalidi, Mayor of Jerusalem and member of the Ottoman parliament. With graciousness, Herzl explained to Al-Khalidi all the ways in which Jewish colonization would benefit the Ottoman state and no less, the Arabs in Palestine. Addressing the Mayor's concern that the Jews intended to displace the Arabs from Palestine, he wrote, charmingly, "But who would think of sending them away? It is their well-being, their individual wealth which we will increase by bringing in our own." Palestine, he added, "is their historic homeland."[18] Yet, in 1897, the Zionists—led by Theodore Herzl—had dedicated themselves to creating a Jewish state in Palestine. Could they do this without "sending them [the Arabs] away?"

That was not all. Theodore Herzl had ethnic cleansing on his mind several years before he wrote to the Mayor of Palestine.[19] In 1895, he confided in his diary, "We must expropriate gently the private property on the state assigned to us. We shall try to spirit the penniless population across the border by procuring employment for it in the transit countries, while denying it employment in our country."[20] In 1901, Herzl drafted a charter for the Jewish-Ottoman Colonization Association in Palestine— which the Ottomans refused to sign—demanding that the Association be granted the right to acquire territory in Palestine in exchange for territory in other provinces of the Empire. The residents of the territories thus acquired in Palestine would be resettled, with assistance from the Association, in the other Ottoman provinces.[21] Clearly, the Zionists had been working on schemes for deportation since the earliest days of their movement.

Occasionally, the mask slipped even in public. Chaim Weizmann, the consummate diplomat in the ranks of the Zionists, could not always maintain his discretion. Two years after the Balfour Declaration, he announced to a London audience that the Zionists planned to make Palestine "as Jewish as England is English, or America is American."[22] In 1921, *The Jewish Chronicle* of London, a leading Jewish weekly of its time, echoed identical sentiments. In its lead article, the *Chronicle* proposed that Jews should be given "those rights and privileges in Palestine which shall enable Jews to make it as Jewish as England is English, or as Canada is Canadian. That is the only reasonable or, indeed, feasible meaning of Jewish National Home."[23] It is indisputable that Zionists had always had ethnic cleansing on their mind. This was no secret, despite their prevarications.

Zionist rhetoric too gave away their intentions. Most famously, the Zionists summed up the essence of their movement in their trademark slogan of "The land without people—for the people without land."[24] Like other white colonists, they saw Palestine as "empty," and some took this to be literally true. More often, however, they understood this to mean that the natives of Palestine were not a people; they had no attachment to their land. In 1914, Chaim Weizmann had spoken with great charm of the creation of a Jewish state as a "marriage" between a people that "has no country" and "a country without a people." It was as simple as fitting a gem (the Jews) into the ring (Palestine). To consummate this "marriage," the Zionists only needed the consent of the Turks, the owners of the "ring."[25] In 1920, Israel Zangwill explained that the Palestinians were not a people because they were not "living in intimate fusion with the country, utilizing its resources and stamping it with a characteristic impress: there is at best an Arab encampment." The Zionists could "gently persuade them [the Palestinians] to trek." In any case, as Bedouins, it is their "proverbial habit" to "fold their tents" and "silently steal away."[26] In essence, Palestine was "empty" because it could easily be *emptied* of its population.

British politicians too had a clear grasp of the demographic implications of Zionism. In a review of Palestinian affairs in October 1919, Winston Churchill, a strong supporter of Zionism, wrote that the Jews "take it for granted that the local population will be cleared out to suit their convenience."[27] Yet, two years before the Balfour Declaration, the British had assured the world "that nothing shall be done which may prejudice the civil and religious rights of existing non-Jewish communities in Palestine." In a secret memorandum to the British cabinet, Lord Balfour wrote that Zionism, "be it right or wrong, good or bad, is rooted in age-long traditions, in present needs, in future hopes, of far profounder import than the desires and prejudices of the 700,000 Arabs who now inhabit that ancient land." Lord Balfour admits that "so far as Palestine is concerned, the Powers had made no . . . declaration of policy which at least in the letter, they have not always intended to violate."[28] British leaders were colluding with the Zionists to dupe the "natives."

Although they might be discrete in their public discourse, the Zionists could not camouflage the "facts" they were creating on the ground. Since the earliest years, the Zionist organizations in Palestine—their agricultural communes, trade unions, banks, schools, hospitals, and newspapers—rigorously excluded Arab Palestinians; they sought to enforce a boycott of the Arab economy, even attacking Jewish housewives who bought from Arab farmers; they attacked Arab farms, destroying their produce; banned the resale of lands by Jews to Arabs; and, under the pretext that they did not want to exploit Arab labor, the "socialist" *kibbutz* denied employment to Arab workers.[29] In addition, the Zionists were working to build an economy that would also exclude Arabs from using their infrastructure—their trains, postal services, ports, and even roads.[30] If the Arabs could not be expelled immediately, they should be excluded from participating in the Jewish economy and society. This exclusion carried another tactical advantage. It would ensure that the expulsion of the Arabs, whenever this became feasible, would cause no disruption to the economy of the Jewish state.

.   .   .

The Zionists had always known that the creation of a Jewish state in Palestine would entail the "transfer" of its Arab population. In the early decades of their movement, however, this was not their most pressing problem.

The first Zionist challenge was to secure the backing of one or more great powers for their colonial enterprise. Once this had been achieved in 1917, they would turn their attention to augmenting the stream of Jewish colons to Palestine and, as their numbers increased, to building the foundations of a Jewish state in Palestine. During the 1920s, the Zionists began to pay greater attention to the native problem, but Jewish advocacy of ethnic cleansing during this decade remained—in the words of Benny Morris—"uninsistent, low-key and occasional." By the early 1930s, however, "a full-throated near-consensus in support of the idea [of ethnic cleansing] began to emerge among the movement's leaders. Each major bout of Arab violence triggered renewed Zionist interest in a transfer solution."[31] Before this decade ended, most of the members of the Jewish Agency Executive (the virtual government of the *Yishuv*) were committed "to a compulsory transfer, preferring, of course, that the British rather than Yishuv carry it out."[32]

After the Arab revolt of 1936, the Zionists were convinced that the window of opportunity for creating a Jewish state was closing fast. As a result, when the Peel Commission offered them a Jewish state in 20 percent of Palestine—with a recommendation for the "transfer" of two-fifths of its population that was Arab—the Zionists voted in favor of the proposal. Indeed, Ben-Gurion considered this a godsend, since the British were offering them an exclusionary colonial settler state. It did not matter that the Zionists were receiving quite a bit less than what they wanted. Once they were established in this bridgehead, they could expand to all of Palestine.[33]

The shift in the position of the Zionist leadership toward a compulsory transfer reflected the growing capacity of the *Yishuv* to impose its will on the Palestinians. In August 1937, Ben-Gurion told the Twentieth Zionist Congress in Zurich that they will now have to carry out "transfer of a completely different scope," different from the small-scale transfers of the past. More ominously, he added, "Jewish power, which grows steadily, will also increase our possibilities to carry out the transfer on a large scale." In June 1938, Ben-Gurion announced his unreserved support for ethnic cleansing. "I support compulsory transfer," he declared. "I don't see in it anything immoral." In December 1940, Yosef Weitz, director of the Jewish National Funds' Land Department, wrote in his diary, "There is no room in the country for both peoples." Weitz was thinking of pushing out *all* the natives from Palestine. "Not one village must be left, not one [Bedouin] tribe."[34] Conscious of their growing strength, Zionist thinking was gaining in audacity.

All but a few marginal factions in the Zionist movement were agreed that the Jewish state in Palestine should contain few Arabs, preferably none. In June 1938, Menahem Ussishkin, one of the leading Zionists stated this succinctly: "We cannot start the Jewish state with . . . half the population being Arab . . . Such a state cannot survive even half an hour. It [i.e. transfer] is the most moral thing to do . . . I am ready to come and defend . . . it before the Almighty."[35] In December 1947, speaking to senior members of his Mapai party, Ben-Gurion made it clear that a Jewish share of 40 percent in the population of the Jewish state demarcated by the UN partition plan was unacceptable. "Only a state," he declared, "with at least 80% Jews is a viable and stable state."[36] The Zionist recipe of "the land without people—for the people without land" contained the seeds of the consequences that have flowed from this colonial project.

Zionist audacity was not misplaced. Within a single year, 1948, the Zionists had nearly achieved their maximalist objectives: the creation of a Jewish state in 78 percent of Palestine, with most of its Arab population dispatched beyond the borders of Israel. It should not be supposed, as some maintain, that this radical outcome flowed from unforeseen conditions—such as the attacks on the Jewish state by neighboring Arabs or the Nazi persecution of Jews in Germany. Intimidation, deadly threats and attacks against Palestinian villages—even a few villages in neighboring Lebanon and Syria—by Jewish troops had begun in December 1947, several months before the Arab armies attacked the Jewish state.[37] If the Arabs had not attacked in 1948, the Israelis would quickly have found ways to provoke them into attacking. Similarly, the Zionist consensus on the necessity of ethnic cleansing of the Arabs in Palestine was not an afterthought, precipitated by the horrors of the Holocaust; this consensus had existed well before this tragedy began to unfold. The ethnic cleansing of Palestinians flowed directly from the Zionist decision to create a Jewish state in Palestine.

CHAPTER 9

JEWISH FACTORS IN ZIONIST SUCCESS

There are upwards of seven million Jews known to be in existence
throughout the world . . . possessing more wealth, activity, influence
and talents, than any body of people their number on earth . . . they will
march in triumphant numbers, and possess themselves once more of
Syria, and take their rank among the governments of the earth.
                                                    —Mordecai Noah, 1818

In large parts of Eastern Europe [during the early decades of the
twentieth century], virtually the whole 'middle class' was Jewish.
                                                    —Yuri Slezkin, 2004[1]

WHAT ARE SOME OF THE WAYS IN which specifically *Jewish* factors have
contributed to Zionist successes in recruiting, at different times, nearly
every great Western power to their cause?

It would be easy enough to identify those characteristics of Jewish
communities in the West—their spatial distribution, wealth, intellectual
resources, organizational efficacy and political activism—that have given
them leverage over the politics of Western societies. Such an inventory,
however, identifies only the proximate sources of Jewish influence over
public opinion and politics in Western societies. A deeper look at this
question is necessary. Stepping back, we need to examine the historical
origins of Jewish influence so that we can view the history of Zionism,
and its successes, as part of a continuum that antedates its formal appearance on the stage of history.

The Zionists too invoke history to explain their origins and justify
their drive to create a Jewish state; they speak of the history of Jewish
encounters with European anti-Semites.[2] This "lachrymose" historiography has been quite serviceable to Zionists. It helped to prod and sustain Jewish insecurity at a time when vast numbers of Western Jews had

moved out of the ghetto to attain a level of prosperity and security most of them had not experienced in previous centuries. It underlined the natural interest that anti-Semites had in working for the success of the Zionists; it would have been hard for anyone to miss the complementarity between the two groups. In addition, the Zionists had an equal interest in grounding Western support for Zionism in their guilt over anti-Semitism. The lachrymose historiography pricked the Westerners' conscience, prodding them to make amends for centuries of anti-Semitism by supporting Zionism. Finally, once their guilt had been aroused, this would restrain the Westerners' criticism of Zionist actions, lest this be seen as proceeding from anti-Semitism. The Zionists have reinforced this self-restraint by making sure that every critic of Zionism is accused of anti-Semitism.

The Zionist claim that their movement has been driven by the imperative of escaping anti-Semitism is misleading. It falsifies the history of Jews and, equally, of Europe, by ignoring the vital contributions that Jews have made to the culture and history of European societies, especially since the early nineteenth century. It elides the singular fact that this was a unique period in Jewish history, when they moved rapidly into the mainstream of European societies, and soon took up leading positions in important sectors of European life. Within a few generations, Jews had left behind a largely marginal existence in the ghettoes to enter upon a period of economic prosperity and cultural creativity that they had never before experienced in Christian Europe. The Zionist motivation in exorcising this dazzling period of Jewish history is quite transparent. They wanted to emphasize Jewish victimhood the better to suppress the vital role that Jewish prosperity, power, and ambitions played in the genesis and success of their movement. Correctly, they were convinced that Zionism would be better served by presenting it as a movement of emaciated Jewish victims, seeking to escape the continent that had tormented them for nearly two millennia. This historical distortion deserves to be corrected.

. . .

During the long medieval era, the small Jewish population of Europe survived on the margins of dominant Christian societies. Despised by Christians, segregated, periodically subjected to persecutions and deportations, most European Jews were forced to make a living as moneylenders, international traders, tax collectors, craftsmen, peddlers, and pawnbrokers.

This would change dramatically during the nineteenth century. The Jews would move quickly from the margins of European society to its center. By the end of this period, they would occupy a visible, and, often, dominating position in Europe's new urban classes that were leading its capitalist transformation. The steep Jewish ascent to positions of leadership reinforced an already strong sense of Jewish uniqueness, previously rooted in religious claims, but now constructed increasingly on racial foundations. Not least, this period witnessed a rapid increase in the Jewish population in the West. In combination with a large westward migration of Jews, this established significant Jewish populations in nearly every major Western country including the United States.

Consider first the demographic changes. So dramatic was the expansion in the size of the world Jewry during the eighteenth and nineteenth centuries, some scholars have dubbed it the Jewish "demographic miracle."[3] The world population of Jews held steady at about one million between 500 and 1700 CE. In 1800, a century later, this population had more than doubled to 2.5 million. The growth in population accelerated over the next century, so that in 1900 the world Jewish population was 10.6 million.[4] Over the two centuries from 1700 to 1900, world population increased by a factor of 2.7, the population of Europe grew by a factor of 3.3, and the Jewish population experienced a more than tenfold increase.[5] Remarkably, the world Jewish population had grown to 16.7 million in 1939, an increase of nearly 58 percent since 1900.[6] Clearly, the demographic prospects for a Jewish nationalist movement in 1939 or 1900 were considerably more promising than in 1800 or 1700. This favorable demography has received scant attention in the voluminous literature on Zionism.

The changes in the spatial distribution of the world's Jewish population between 1800 and 1930 were equally important in preparing the grounds for Zionist success. In 1700, only about 16 percent of the world's Jews lived in Western and Central Europe and its overseas extensions, regions that would become centers of global capitalism over the next two centuries. At this time, 49 percent of the world's Jewish population lived in Eastern Europe and 35.5 percent in the Islamicate.[7] This demographic weakness was remedied substantially by the middle decades of the twentieth century, due primarily to the growing migration of Jews to destinations westward. In 1939, Europe's share of the world Jewish population had declined to 57 percent, while the shares of the United States, Canada, Australia, and South Africa had increased substantially.[8] Most importantly, Britain's Jewish population had increased from an estimated 12,000 to 15,000 in the early 1800s to 300,000 by 1914, due mostly to the immigration of Jews from Eastern Europe since the early 1800s.[9] The growth of Jewish population in the United States was more dramatic, having increased from 2,500 in 1800 to one million in 1900 and 3.6 million in 1920.[10]

During the nineteenth century, the Jewish population became increasingly concentrated in big cities. In 1800, only three or four cities contained more than 10,000 Jews. By the 1880s, there were several cities—including Warsaw, Vienna, Odessa, Budapest, New York, and Berlin—whose Jewish population exceeded 50,000. In 1900, Warsaw had a Jewish population of 220,000 and Odessa contained 140,000 Jews.[11] The urban concentration of Jews became even more dramatic in 1914, with 1.35 million Jews living in New York City, 350,000 in Warsaw and Chicago, 200,000 in Budapest, 175,000 in Philadelphia, 160,000 in Vienna, Lodz, and Odessa, and 150,000 in London.[12] The emergence of these large concentrations of Jewish population created opportunities for the Jews to develop educational, cultural, and religious institutions that sustained vibrant communal activities. The location of these large Jewish populations in important Western cities also gave them the opportunity to observe, participate in, and influence Gentile society. At the same time, the presence of large and flourishing Jewish communities at the center of Gentile society gave an impetus to a new form of anti-Semitism, fueled by competition and envy.

The long centuries during which the Jews were relegated to the margins of Europe's feudal society prepared them to play a dominant role in the capitalist age, once the legal constraints inhibiting their energies were withdrawn. Christian Europe generally treated its Jews as outsiders, even outcasts, because the Jewish rejection of Jesus troubled Christian theology and Christian pride. Excluded from feudal Europe's established orders, the Jews made a living as moneylenders, money changers, international traders, physicians, peddlers, pawnbrokers, and, when laws permitted, craftsmen. The most successful Jews established close relations with the rulers as moneylenders and physicians; in turn, they used these royal connections to become tax collectors, manage the ruler's military supplies, and secured permits to operate mines, distilleries, the mint, and, occasionally, to manage agricultural estates.[13] In other words, European Jews became urban, skilled, and capitalist and developed close ties with the ruling classes; they were also highly mobile, since their chief assets were portable. Ironically, then, Europe's discriminatory policies had endowed the Jews disproportionately with those assets that would give them vital advantages in Europe's emerging capitalist societies.

The nineteenth century presided over a dramatic transformation in the status of European Jews, especially those in Western and Central Europe. The slow erosion of the feudal order during the preceding centuries—followed by the French Revolution and the removal or easing of restraints against Jews in much of Europe—set the stage for the nearly explosive rise of Jewish capital, a Jewish middle class and Jewish intelligentsia in several European countries. The long centuries of Jewish exposure to finance, commerce, estate management, and the crafts had equipped them better than most Gentiles to succeed as international traders, bankers, speculators, industrialists, and stockbrokers in Europe's emerging capitalist economies. "They [the Jews] were a race of merchants and money-lenders," wrote Bernard Lazare in 1894, "perhaps degraded by the mercantile practice, but, thanks to this very practice, equipped with qualities which were becoming preponderant in the new economic system."[14] At the same time, when the intellectual skills honed in the study of the Talmud were transferred to secular pursuits, the Jews soon attained leading positions in academia, media, and the professions. In time, the economic ascent of Jews would incite the jealousy of the Gentiles, especially of migrants to the cities who had to compete with Jews for entry into the crafts, retail trades, colleges, and the professions. Thus was laid the basis of a new anti-Semitism; it may still use some of the old myths inherited from medieval times but it would be driven by the growing economic competition between Jews and Gentiles.

Drawing upon a variety of sources, Yuri Slezkin has documented Jewish success in several European countries.[15] Already, in the early nineteenth century, Jewish families owned thirty of the fifty-two private banks in Berlin; in Vienna, by the end of the nineteenth century, "40 percent of the directors of public banks were Jews or of Jewish descent, and all banks but one were administered by Jews." Jewish bankers at this time, according to Ettinger, had "established branches all over Europe and wielded considerable influence in all important capitals." In the early twentieth century, the stock exchange in Vienna and Budapest consisted mostly of Jews, 70 and 88 percent respectively.[16] Jewish preponderance in finance carried over to industry as well, since banks during this period financed and controlled investments in heavy industries in several European countries. Not surprisingly, these developments translated into a strong Jewish presence among Europe's wealthy elite.[17] The Jews had also established a visible presence in the newly emerging professional classes, including lawyers, accountants, doctors, academics, scientists, and artists. In Vienna, for instance, around 1900, "62 percent of the lawyers, half the doctors and dentists, 45 percent of the medical faculty, and one-fourth of the total faculty were Jews, as were between 51.5 and 63.2 percent of professional journalists."[18] Finally, according to Steven Beller, "in an age when the press was the only mass medium, cultural or otherwise, the liberal press [in Europe] was largely a Jewish press."[19]

Jewish bankers and contractors played a dominating role in financing the development of railways in all the countries of Europe except Britain. The Rothschilds financed the main railway networks in France, Belgium, Austria, and Italy. Similarly, the railway networks in Spain and Tunis were

built by the Pèreire brothers; and Baron de Hirsch built the railways in
the Balkans and the Ottoman Empire. In Russia, the railway networks
were built by Jewish contractors, who also operated them until they were
bought over by the Russian government. In the United States too, Jewish
banks played an important role in financing railway construction.[20]

In Britain, Jews experienced dramatic gains in all areas of life. In the
early 1800s, most British Jews were immigrants, "impoverished, poorly
educated, dependent on low-status street trades and other forms of petty
commerce, popularly identified with crime, violence and chicanery,
widely viewed as disreputable and alien." By 1880, more than four-fifths
of the Jews in London belonged to the middle class (with annual family
income between £200 and £1000), and another 15 percent were part of
the upper middle class and financial elites (with annual family income
of £1000 or more). In the general population of England and Wales, less
than 3 percent of families earned £700 or more; and less than 9 percent
earned between £160 and £700.[21] Clearly, starting with an initial handi-
cap, the Jews of London had done quite well.

In the period since the sixteenth century, Europe went through several
profound transformations that altered relations between Jews and Gentiles. On the one hand, the Reformation, the rise and consolidation of
nation states, and the nationalization of Christianity splintered Europe's
Christian unity under the Catholic Church. On the other hand, the
growing cosmopolitanism of Jewish capital during the age of commercial
capitalism brought the members of the Jewish elites into frequent contacts with each other, and this stimulated, among its members, a growing sense of a community that transcended local affiliations. During the
nineteenth century, these tendencies gathered momentum, as growing
numbers of Jews entered the middle classes and began to reflect on the
Jewish condition in their writings. In turn, as their prosperity evoked the
envy of Gentiles and, worse, a new wave of anti-Semitism, this reinforced
the bonds of Jewish unity. As a result, while Christian Europe splintered
during the centuries since the Reformation, a segment of Jews gradually emerged as the only people with a transcontinental presence who, in
addition, also began to acquire a racial identity that transcended Europe's
national frontiers.[22]

The economic integration of Jews into Gentile societies during the
nineteenth century produced important cultural ramifications. Inevitably, the entry of Jews into the mainstream of Gentile society stimulated
cultural assimilation. In order to take advantage of the new opportunities
opening up before them, the Jews moved out of the ghettos and shtetels,
and begin to acquire the languages, dress, and manners of the Gentiles.

Some Jews carried this process forward by seeking to harmonize Jewish beliefs with the ideas of the Enlightenment, giving rise to Reform Judaism as the religion of the assimilated Jews. Other Jews sought to complete the process of assimilation by converting to Christianity.

Jewish assimilation into the Gentile mainstream had its limits. Struck by the loss of their identity, their distinctive culture and history, some Jews recoiled from assimilation, began to reclaim Judaism, emphasize their Jewish identity, and began to make the case for the preservation of Jewishness and Jewish values. Indeed, this would create an urge to reconstitute the Jews into a nation, in imitation of the romantic nationalism that was sweeping the landscape of Eastern Europe. This romantic nationalism encouraged Jewish nationalism in unexpected ways too. It raised the barriers to Jewish assimilation. A Jew might acquire the language, manners, and even the spirit of a German, but he could not give himself a German lineage. In an age that glorified ethnic nationalism, an assimilated Jew could not become a German, Hungarian, or Pole by "race." The new nationalism also gave fresh impetus to anti-Semitism; since this nationalism was founded on claims of lineage, it did not wish to accommodate the Jews who were seen as aliens. In turn, pushed back by this new anti-Semitism, some assimilated Jews were forced to return to their Jewish identity, more willing than before to accept the racial basis of their identity.[23]

Already in the middle decades of the nineteenth century, some Jewish thinkers were proposing political Zionism as the solution to anti-Semitism and the perils of Jewish assimilation; this would save Jewish lives and Jewish identity. It was in the 1890s, however, that these ideas were given a practical formulation under the leadership of Theodore Herzl. Jewish nationalism was a great deal more ambitious than Polish or Hungarian nationalism—since it would have to create the territorial basis of the state it sought to create. It is unlikely that the Zionists could find the daring to promote their unique national project, based on land grab and ethnic cleansing, without the hubris that their success had bred in some Jews. This hubris radiates from the writings of Zionist founding fathers as well as their precursors. The Zionist project was predicated on the ability of Jews to influence the policies of great powers, to nudge them in directions that may not coincide with their strategic interests.

Many Jews sought the solution to anti-Semitism in revolutionary movements that sought to eradicate both class and nation at the behest of the proletariat. The Jewish attraction to radical movements was strongest in Eastern Europe, where pogroms against Jews had been on the rise, and whose Jewish populations were flocking to the cities to escape persecution and to take advantage of the new opportunities they offered in commerce, industry, and the professions. There was another reason why Jews were attracted to Marxism: the ideal society it sought to create may have struck some as the secular fulfillment of Judaism's messianic kingdom. In nearly every European country, Jews were heavily represented especially in the vanguard of the revolutionary movements; they made up most of the theorists, leaders, and activists of the Marxist parties in Europe.[24]

In addition to the internal migration of Jews in Europe—from small towns and rural centers to the cities, and from Eastern Europe to destinations in Central and Western Europe—there occurred a migration of similar magnitude from all of Europe, but especially from locations in Eastern Europe, to the new world and especially the United States. The cross-Atlantic migration of Jews was pregnant with consequences for the Zionist movement. Because of these migrations, by the third decade of the twentieth century, the United States became home to the world's largest concentration of Jews.[25] Shortly, as these new immigrants began to catch up economically with the older established Jews, together they would create a network of Jewish organizations and a tradition of political activism that would place them at the center of American political system.

In conclusion, Zionism emerged in a milieu in which Jews were established as major actors in nearly every Western country, stretching from Russia to the United States. In the early decades of its career, Zionism competed with two other tendencies—both older than Zionism—for the attention of Jews as the appropriate response to anti-Semitism: these two tendencies were assimilation and left radicalism. This triad of Jewish forces, together with their relationship to Gentile societies—containing both anti-Semites and evangelical Christians—offered several intriguing options for promoting the Zionist cause.

.   .   .

In its early years, political Zionism was regarded with deep suspicion by nearly all segments of Jewish opinion. Yet, within a few decades, the Zionists had moved from the fringes to the center of Jewish discourse; and, soon, they were drawing support from nearly all segments of Jewish opinion, from assimilated, orthodox, and radical Jews alike.

The opposition of assimilated Jews to Zionism was easy to understand, since it challenged their premise and achievements. Pointing to the return of anti-Semitism in Western Europe during the 1880s, the Zionists argued that assimilation had not worked. In addition, they argued that it could not work because the Jews were a nation, and they could not, and should not, merge their identity into different European ethnicities.[26]

Assimilated Jews worried also that Zionism gave the Gentiles cause to accuse the Jews of divided loyalties. On the other hand, the Zionists were eager to harness the power of anti-Semitism to their movement.[27] If Zionism fuelled anti-Semitism, this reassured its protagonists; it meant that the movement could expect to strengthen one of its chief allies. In the presence of this strong antipathy between the two tendencies, it might appear that the Zionists had little prospect of harnessing the wealth, intellectual resources, and political influence of the Jewish establishment to their cause.

This appearance of irreconcilable differences is misleading; other factors operated to temper the opposition between the two camps. The assimilated Jews were worried about the slow return of the new anti-Semitism, even in places where it had long been in retreat. They also knew that the new anti-Semitism was being fueled by the rapid migration of poorer Jews from the shtetels of Eastern Europe to the cities in both Eastern and Western Europe, where they competed for jobs, markets and housing with the poorer Gentiles. In Britain, the Anglo-Jewish community assisted and encouraged Jewish immigrants to go back to Eastern Europe.[28] Anxious to stem this influx of Jewish immigrants, some establishment Jews concluded that only Zionism could stem the rising tide of crude anti-Semitism. The diversion of Jews from Eastern Europe to Palestine, away from destinations in Western Europe, could help to attenuate the chief source of the new anti-Semitism in Europe.

Zionism was also available in a softer variant—the cultural Zionism of Ahad Ha'am—that appealed to liberal assimilated Jews. Since this emphasized the development of Palestine as a center of Jewish culture and learning, it was likely to raise fewer concerns about divided loyalties. In addition, cultural Zionism allowed liberal Jews to support projects—establishing Jewish communities in Palestine, the revival of Hebrew as a living language, the establishment of universities and *yeshivas* in Palestine—that did not immediately threaten indigenous Palestinians with marginalization. Although the cultural Zionists did not strive to create a Jewish state in Palestine, their activities contributed vitally to building the demographic, economic, and educational infrastructure of such a state.

Over time, political Zionism would also overcome Orthodox objections over its political interpretation of the Jewish "restoration." On the one hand, some Reform Jews had been developing a new reading of Jewish messianism; the Jewish mission was not to return to Zion but to bring Zion—the ideals of Zion—to the world. The Jews had been dispersed among Gentile nations, they argued, so that they could bring the light of Zion to the world. The Orthodox Jews objected to political Zionism because it sought Jewish restoration through human agency; traditional Judaism held that a

Jewish Messiah would accomplish this, as part of the divine plan for the end times. As the political Zionists propagated their vision of Jewish restoration, as they organized, as they gained access to the leading Western statesmen—in short, as the Zionist movement gained momentum—it would become harder for Reform and Orthodox Jews to continue to oppose Zionism.

The opposition to Zionism became harder to sustain as political Zionists mobilized the iconic power of Zion, kindled hopes of restoring Jews to the "promised land," raised expectations of establishing the Jews as a nation with their own state, and as the dominant civilizing force in the Middle East. Zionism's nationalist goals were so attractive, most Jews would find it hard to withhold their support for Zionism, even if they would not consider voting for it with their feet. Only small but shrinking pockets of Orthodox Jews would continue to oppose Zionism as an apostasy.

Europe's radicals—Jews and Gentiles alike—thought Zionism was a reactionary movement, a wasteful distraction from the primary goal of creating a classless society. They did not think that the Jews were a nation, and, although they had been important players in Europe's capitalist transition, it was their destiny to be assimilated into Gentile societies.[29] In Eastern Europe, Chaim Weizmann wrote to Theodore Herzl in 1903, "the larger part of the contemporary younger generation is anti-Zionist, not from a desire to assimilate as in Western Europe, but through revolutionary conviction." Indeed, their attitude "towards Jewish nationalism is one of antipathy, swelling at times to fanatical hatred."[30] The Zionists would have to remedy this strong antipathy to their movement in the Jewish left, since its success might well depend on attracting a growing stream of Jewish immigrants from Eastern Europe. They would have to build bridges between their own movement and socialism, make Zionism attractive to Jewish youth stirred by socialist ideals of justice and equality.

The Zionists on the left—Nahman Syrkin, Ber Borochov, Aaron David Gordon, Berl Katznelson, David Ben-Gurion and others—developed two sets of arguments to integrate socialism with Zionist goals.[31] Some argued that Jews could contribute most effectively to socialism only within a Zionist framework, with Jewish workers taking the lead in the creation of a socialist state in Palestine. Others preached a new glorification of manual work to reverse the erosion of Jewish virtues due to centuries of specialization in service occupations—as peddlers, traders, tailors, moneylenders, and bankers. Jews, they argued, could recover their ancient virtues by working the land with their own hands; this required the exclusion of Arab labor from the Jewish colonies. Under the impact of these ideas, a new generation of Jewish immigrants from Eastern Europe—the Second *Aliya*—established Jewish communes, known as *kibbutzim*, based on the principles of collective ownership and the sharing of work and responsibilities. In 1920, they founded the *Histadrut*, a Jewish worker's federation that provided benefits to Jewish workers, established banks, factories, and schools, and soon became the largest employer in Palestine. In short, this Labor Zionism soon established itself as the dominant force in the *Yishuv*. The socialist movements in the West—especially their Jewish membership—now had a new reason for supporting Zionism; the Zionists were laying the foundations of a socialist society in Palestine.

The growing support for Zionism among Western Jews opened up several possibilities for leveraging Jewish power to promote the Zionist cause. As the great powers recognized the growing Jewish commitment to Zionism, they sought to align themselves with the Zionists in order to win the Jews to their side. Increasingly threatened by radical movements, the great powers also sought to drain Jewish support for these movements by giving encouragement to Zionism. In turn, the Zionists themselves lobbied the great powers by promising to mobilize Jewish support for them, or using Jewish power to align policies in one country to suit the interests of another. Indeed, not only did the Zionists seek to use the levers of Jewish power, they promoted an exaggerated opinion of the powers possessed by Jews. These questions are taken up in the next two chapters. As evangelical Christians took up the Zionist cause, their influence too would be added to the Zionist arsenal, a subject we examine in Chapter 13.

· · ·

In their public pronouncements, the Zionists strongly disavow that they have the power—or having it, they use it—to bring the policies of Western powers into closer alignment with Israeli interests in the Middle East.

This disavowal lacks credibility. We have already examined the logic by which the Zionists succeeded in advancing their project from the margins to the center of Jewish discourse in the early decades of their movement. Once Zionism began to draw substantial support from Jewish communities in the West, and from important centers of Jewish power—in finance, industry, politics, media, and academia—we can expect that these Jewish communities would increasingly use their influence to mobilize the support of Western governments for the Zionist cause. Over time, indeed, as their commitment to Zionism deepened, we can expect that these Jewish communities would develop new community structures to promote Zionist goals with greater efficacy. Disavowals of the efficacy of Jewish lobbying are hard to reconcile with the growing resources that have been channeled into this activity.

In their early deliberations, the Zionists never concealed their conviction that Western powers alone could launch their project. In consequence, Zionist leaders concentrated their efforts on using Jewish influence to push the Western powers ever closer to the Zionist point of view. Zionist lobbying of great powers began early; this is best exemplified in the careers of some of the most successful early advocates of Zionism, including Theodore Herzl, Chaim Weizmann, Louis Brandeis, Nahum Sokolow, and Abba Silver. The lobbying power of the Zionists has grown over time, especially in the United States. It is scarcely an exaggeration to claim that after the founding of Israel, the Zionists have continued to nurture their lobbying prowess with the greatest care.

A quick examination of the short career of Theodore Herzl, the founder of the Zionist movement, illustrates convincingly the central importance of lobbying in the pursuit of Zionist goals. Very impressive indeed is the list of public figures who gave audience to Theodore Herzl during the eight years between his launching of the Zionist movement at Basel in 1897 and his death in 1904. Not counting dukes, ambassadors, and ministers of lesser standing, during this short period Herzl gained access to the Ottoman Sultan, Kaiser Wilhelm II, the Grand Duke of Baden, King Victor Emanuel III of Italy, Pope Pius X, the English colonial secretary, Joseph Chamberlain, Lord Cromer, the Russian minister of interior, Vyacheslav Plehve, and the Russian minister of finance, Count Sergei Witte.[32] In 1902, he also gave testimony in London before the Royal Commission on Alien Immigration, a rare privilege for a foreigner.

Walter Lacqueur thinks that Theodore Herzl's ability to gain audience with European leaders was "miraculous," since, at first, he "represented no one but himself, and later on a dedicated but uninfluential minority among the Jewish communities."[33] Theodore Herzl's "miracle," though, would not have been possible outside the context of Jewish wealth, influence, and political activism that was created during the nineteenth century. It is true that the Zionists had not yet succeeded in recruiting wealthy Jews to their cause, but few people knew about this outside the inner circle of Zionist leaders. With a deft combination of confidence and bluster, Theodore Herzl managed to persuade his interlocutors that he could indeed mobilize Jewish wealth and influence to deliver on his promises. Thus, he promised to relieve the debt of the Ottomans, convinced that if he could extract important concessions from the Sultan, this would help him to sway wealthy Jewish financiers to his side.[34] As the occasion demanded, he could also play on the fears of European statesmen concerning socialist revolutionaries, which drew many of its leaders from the ranks of Jews.[35] He piqued the interest of European statesmen in the proposed Jewish state by offering to place it under their protection, or claiming that the creation of Jewish state would stem the influx of Jews from Russia. Once he had gained audience with one European leader, he played on interstate rivalries to gain access to his competitors. Finally, it should not be forgotten that the Zionists even at this early stage in their movement often found help from well-placed Jews in high places.[36]

The Zionists insist that they have had strategic luck on their side. Western support for Zionists is not the product of lobbying, but flows from a convergence of Western and Zionist interests in the Middle East. The West and Zionists have overlapping strategic interests in suppressing Arab independence and unity. The West supports Israel because a strong Israel obviates the need for the United States to station its own troops in the Middle East or wage wars against the Arab world and the Islamicate. In other words, Israel is a strategic asset, not a liability.

This thesis is weakly founded. If British or American support for Israel has flowed from their strategic interests, it would be difficult to explain the existence of the vast, layered and well-oiled lobbying apparatus that the Zionists keep on the ready, especially in the United States. It does not stand to reason that Israel and the Jewish diaspora would make such an enormous investment of their resources—of time, intellect, organization, money—if this did not serve some vital function useful to the Zionist project. The financial support that Zionist organizations mobilize from Jewish communities is relatively small compared to the material support that the United States has provided to Israel. Certainly, the complex, interlocking network of Zionist organizations in the United States—and their complex and dense interactions with different sectors of the American political system—do not exist merely to channel the financial support of American Jewry to Israel.

Finally, consider for a moment the fate of a hypothetical colonial project, similar to Zionism, but without its resources of persuasion. If Europe's Gypsies had wanted to colonize a province of India—on the claim of historical links to that country—they too might have relied on two forces. On the one hand, European countries with a Gypsy presence would have been eager to support a colonial scheme that promised to rid their countries of a population they had always regarded as unwanted aliens. In addition, during the early twentieth century when Indian demands for independence were growing louder, the British might well have been persuaded that a colonial Gypsy state—in, say, Sind or Baluchistan—could serve important strategic interests. A Gypsy state on India's western borders could serve as a buffer—a more effective buffer than Afghanistan—between their Indian possessions and Russian ambitions; such a state could also be used to project British power over Iran. A Gypsy colonial project, however, had little chance of being adopted by the British or any other Western power. The Gypsies lacked the cultural, intellectual, and financial resources to advance their project in Western political discourse. A Gypsy "restoration" could never have gotten off the ground.

CHAPTER 10

A SURFEIT OF
MOTHER COUNTRIES

The beginning of the Redemption will come through natural causes by human effort and by the will of the governments to gather the scattered of Israel into the Holy Land.

—Rabbi Kalischer, 1836

I considered it a duty to call upon the free people of this country [the United States] to aid us in any efforts [at restoration] which, in our present position, it may be prudent to adopt.

—Mordecai Noah, 1845

France, beloved friend, is the savior who will restore our people to its place in universal history.

—Moses Hess, 1862

From the first moment I entered the Movement, my eyes were directed towards England, because I saw that by reason of the general situation of things, there it was the Archimedean point where the lever could be applied.

—Theodore Herzl, February 1898

Maybe England will chance upon an empty piece of land in need of a white population, and perhaps the Jews will happen to be these whites . . .

—Chaim Weizmann, 1914[1]

ZIONISM ABOUNDS IN IRONIES. NOT LEAST, IT has derived its greatest strength from a deficit that would have killed another colonial project before it got off the ground. Zionism proposed to create a Jewish settler state without a Jewish mother country to bring it to fruition. The ease with which the Zionists have found surrogates for the missing mother country is the result of a curious marriage—in modern times—between two rival tendencies within Western civilization, the Christian and Jewish. The peculiarity of the Zionist colonial project, its durability and capacity to engender widening circles of conflict, derives in no small measure from the manner in which it has produced and continues to reproduce this improbable union between two historical adversaries.

The Zionists could not have executed their colonial project without the support of one or more major Western powers. In order to create their exclusionary colonial settler state, they would first have to take Palestine from the Ottomans and follow this up with a second, more brazen act of expropriation by taking Palestine from its Arab owners who had lived there for centuries. Only a great power could deliver this radical plan. It would be nearly impossible to create the Jewish state surreptitiously, through the slow infiltration of Jewish colons into Palestine. "An infiltration is bound to end badly," warned Theodore Herzl in 1896. "It continues till the inevitable moment when the native population feels itself threatened, and forces the Government to stop the further influx of Jews. Immigration is consequently futile unless based on an *assured supremacy*" (emphasis added).[2] The Zionists could make their plan work only if they first seized control over Palestine.

The creation of nearly every one of the white settler colonies in the Americas had been backed by European powers. Could the Jews in the Western diaspora now seize Palestine without the backing of a state? In 1818, Mordecai Noah, an early American Zionist, thought that they could. There were seven million Jews in the world—he argued—with more wealth and talent than any other people of comparable size; if they made up their minds, they could create a Jewish state in Syria. "This is not fancy," Noah assured his audience. Jews "hold the purse strings, and can wield the sword; they can bring 100,000 men into the field."[3] This self-reliant plan was born of a flight of fantasy; it would not be proposed again by serious Zionists. Indeed, when Noah returned to this subject in 1844, he proposed that Jewish advocates of the "restoration" would have to mobilize the support of Western societies. He expected Christian nations to provide this help, and he pinned his hopes on two in particular: the United States and Britain.[4]

Zionist leaders were of one mind on the need to recruit one or more Western powers to play mother country to their colonial settler project. In 1862, Moses Hess called for the founding of a public corporation to finance the Jewish "restoration," but as a practical man he knew that this could not be accomplished without the intervention of a great power. "France, beloved friend," he exclaimed, "is the savior who will restore our people to its place in universal history."[5] Leo Pinsker, a younger contemporary of Hess, was of the same opinion. In 1882, he wrote that "it is obvious that the creation of a Jewish home could never happen without the support of governments."[6]

Theodore Herzl had a more ambitious plan; he sought to place the might *and* moral authority of the Western world per se behind the Zionist project. In 1896, he argued that the Zionist solution to the Jewish question could only succeed by turning it into "a political world-question, to be discussed and controlled by the *civilized nations of the world in council*" (emphasis added). The Zionist project would have to be "inaugurated in absolute conformity to law." In other words, the proposed theft of land from the Palestinians would have to be given legitimacy in international law by the consent of the great powers. It would require "the friendly intervention of interested Governments, who would derive considerable benefits from it."[7]

The Zionists were no idle visionaries. In two decades after its official launching, they would succeed in converting their "orphan" colonial plan into a *collective* Western enterprise backed by the moral and diplomatic authority of much of the Western world.[8] In another three decades, they would also have their Jewish colonial settler state. No colonial settler state in recent centuries comes close to matching this record.

. . .

The task of recruiting a surrogate mother country was daunting by any calculation. Why would any country undertake a colonial project whose chief beneficiaries were *not* its own citizens? Yet the Zionists rarely evinced serious doubts about their ability to recruit such a surrogate. On the contrary, they exuded an eerie confidence in their ability, eventually, to mobilize the support they would need. So large was the field of potential surrogates that the Zionist thinkers were not always in agreement about the best candidate they should pursue. In practice, they pursued several candidates simultaneously, hoping, thereby, to win the support of all or to maximize their chances of winning the support of at least one. At various times, the Zionists fixed their sights on the Ottoman Empire, Russia, Italy, France, Britain, Germany, and the United States.[9] Why were the Zionists so confident that they could persuade one or more Western powers to sponsor their project?

Zionist confidence was inspired by the strength and variety of the pro-Zionist forces that were already in place toward the end of the nineteenth century. Jewish assimilation and westward migration of Jews during the nineteenth century had established important communities of assimilated Jews, who were often concentrated in the chief commercial cities of the major Western powers. In Eastern Europe, the Jews made up much of the vanguard of its revolutionary movements. Anti-Semitism was on the rise, more noticeably in Eastern than in Central and Western Europe. The evangelical movement too, which evinced a growing fervor for Jewish restoration, had crossed from Britain to the United States. Finally, the dramatic growth of Jewish population, their concentration in the big cities, and their entry into the highest echelons of Western society had generated frequent contacts among the leading Jews across national boundaries. These contacts stimulated growing coordination over Jewish concerns and a stronger Jewish unity, grounded increasingly in the myth of racial purity. In short, the last decades of the nineteenth century, more than any previous period, offered manifold opportunities for the growth and success of the Zionist movement.

The geographic dispersion of Jews—by the end of the nineteenth century—offered the Zionists multiple points of entry into the politics of nearly every major Western country. The westward migration of Jews—and their tendency to locate in the leading commercial and financial centers—had created influential Jewish communities in each of the pivotal countries of the West, including Britain, Germany, the United States, and France. The Zionists could also draw upon the support of sizable Jewish communities in the Netherlands, Italy, Canada, Australia, South Africa, Argentina, and Mexico. In addition, the October Revolution would place Jews in important leadership positions in the Soviet Union. After World War II, as communist parties gained power in the wake of the Soviet invasion, the Jews also extended their influence over several countries of Eastern Europe.[10]

Western civilization, as a whole, could make common cause with Zionism for at least three reasons. A Jewish state in Palestine promised to fulfill the anti-Semite's dream of a Europe free of Jewish presence and competition. Protestant sentiment too favored Jewish to Muslim control over Palestine; although hated, the Jews were a biblical people, easily preferred over the "infidel" Muslims.[11] In its perennial contest against the Islamicate, the Christian West would construe each Zionist victory as a blow against its most hated adversary. In addition, Western publics could be persuaded into believing that a Jewish state in the Middle East would be a Western bastion, projecting Western values and influence throughout the Middle East.

The presence of complementarities between Zionism and different Western constituencies, however, did not automatically translate into pro-Zionist policies. Zionist writers would work to convert pro-Zionist sentiments into political ideas, and Zionist organizations would work to incorporate these ideas into the programs of political parties. In some cases, the complementarity—such as that between the strategic interests of Western powers and Zionism—may only be transitory or illusory, with adverse consequences for the powers that might support Zionism. These imagined or temporary complementarities must be made to look real and enduring. In this task of manufacturing perceptions, Zionist lobbies—organized, led, and supported primarily by the Jewish diaspora—have played a pivotal role.

Zionist ability to shape Western perceptions and beliefs constitutes one of their chief strengths. Once again, this strength derives, in large part, from the pattern of Jewish dispersion across the Western world. Jewish leverage over the economy, film, media, and academia—in key Western countries—has been the strongest asset of the Zionist movement. Clearly, Jewish lobbying in support of Zionist aims has been more effective in some countries than in others. In no Western country of any importance, however, can the power of the Jewish lobby be ignored by its media, politicians, academics, and writers. The ability of the Jewish diaspora to work in tandem with the Zionist leadership, inside and outside Israel, has grown steadily over time.

The Zionists—including the *Yishuv*—and the Jewish diaspora have been linked to each other in a virtuous cycle. On the one hand, the growth of the *Yishuv* depended on immigrants and financial support from the diaspora; in turn, every expansion of the *Yishuv* brought more financial support from the diaspora. Once Zionism gained Gentile support in 1917, more diaspora Jews were drawn to Zionism; and as Zionist demands on the Jewish diaspora increased, they organized more effectively to lobby their governments to support Zionist demands. At some point in this cumulative process, as the *Yishuv* gained in numbers and organizational strength, its leaders would seek a growing role in the decisions of Zionist organizations in the Jewish diaspora. Over time, there emerged a sustained synergy between the *Yishuv* and the diaspora Zionists, with the latter continuing to play a dominating part in mobilizing the Jewish diaspora and Gentile support for the *Yishuv*. With the creation of Israel, however, the Jewish state would assume the leading role in directing the Zionist activities of the Jewish diaspora.

The diaspora Zionists have worked very hard to secure the strongest Gentile commitment to their goals. They encouraged all those tendencies in the West that were supportive of Zionist aims, including Christian Zionism, anti-Islamic bigotry, and anti-Arab racism. When appropriate, they made political alliances with groups that drew strength from these tendencies. At times, they were even willing to cooperate with anti-Semitic regimes.[12] At another level, the apex Zionist organizations orchestrated the activities of pro-Zionist Gentile groups to prod Western governments to support their goals. Increasingly, as Zionist influence has grown, the Jews and Gentiles have worked together to secure primacy for Zionist goals in the policies of key Western governments. Since the creation of Israel, Zionist success in appropriating the economic, military, and diplomatic support of the United States is nearly complete. In the absence of compelling strategic interests, a mother country's support for its colons is quickly exhausted. Support for settlers cannot long persist in the face of rising costs—in blood and treasure—incurred to support them against indigenous resistance; as domestic pressures in the mother country build up, this will lead to abandonment of the settlers. These pressures were at work during the period before 1948 when Britain operated as the surrogate mother country on the ground, using its troops and personnel to hold Palestine on behalf of the *Yishuv*. Once the *Yishuv* had acquired its own state, the new surrogate mother country—the United States—did not have to make any direct military commitments in defense of the Jewish colons. The economic and diplomatic support of the United States for Israel, although quite costly, could be disguised; it was, therefore, less vulnerable to democratic pressures. A second factor too has helped to maintain the support of the United States for the Jewish settler state. Israel derives its primary support in the United States from the Jewish diaspora, whose identity, pride, messianic expectations, power, and hopes of finding refuge during another eruption of anti-Semitism are closely tied to the success of the Jewish colonial state. While enjoying all these advantages, the Jewish diaspora in the United States bears only a very small part of the costs of supporting their colonial cousins. Overwhelmingly, Gentile taxpayers incur the financial costs of supporting Israel. As a result, the escalating costs of the Zionist enterprise—incurred by Americans—are unlikely to produce any weakening of the primary base of their support in the United States.

·   ·   ·

The Zionists have made up for the absence of a natural sponsor with something considerably better. Given the presence of Jewish communities in key Western societies, the influence they wielded over their "host" societies, and the presence of Gentile groups and tendencies aligned with Zionism, the Zionists had the luxury of enlisting one or more mother countries.

This was Zionism's trump card as a colonial settler movement. Instead of being stuck with one mother country—the fate, for instance, of the French colons in Algeria and Morocco, or British colons in Kenya and Rhodesia—the Jewish colons could shop around for one that best served their interests. If one mother country should begin to lose interest in the

Zionist enterprise, the Zionists could shop for its replacement or replacements from the pool of potential surrogates. In addition, at all times, the Zionists could count on the political support of influential segments of the population in nearly *all* Western countries. In consequence, the Zionist enterprise has enjoyed a wide range of options for meeting its financial, technological, military, and diplomatic needs. If one country turns them down, they can make the same demands on several other countries. Only the Zionist colonial settler project has enjoyed this kind of flexibility.

In a career that spans more than a century, the Zionist project has sought and received support from a variety of Western countries. Indeed, it would be a long list that identified all the Western countries that have provided moral, political, diplomatic, financial, military, technological, or intelligence support to the Zionist project since its launching in 1897. It is generally agreed, however, that Britain and the United States—the first before 1948 and the second since—have supported the Zionist project over extended periods and in ways that were indispensable to its success. These great powers, more than any other, deserve the title of mother country to the Jewish colonial settlers in Palestine.

The Zionists drew vital support from an unexpected source during the critical period before and after the creation of Israel. In stark defiance of its anti-imperialist and anticolonial stance, the Soviet Union joined the United States in supporting the creation of a colonial settler state in Palestine. Together with its allies in Eastern Europe, the Soviets helped the United States to secure the two-thirds majority at the United Nations General Assembly in November 1947 necessary to approve the plan to partition Palestine. It is important to note also that without the massive infusion of heavy armaments, including aircrafts, from Czechoslovakia during the first Arab-Israeli war, the Israeli army may have faced defeat in 1948, bringing the Zionist colonial enterprise to an early end.[13]

In the first two decades of its existence, Israel received vital support from two major Western countries besides the United States. At a time when the United States did not wish to be seen by the Arabs as supporting Israel, France stepped in to take on the role of the leading supplier of heavy arms to Israel. France also provided Israel with nuclear technology, which it would use to develop nuclear weapons. Starting in 1953, under a treaty commitment, Germany provided Israel with commodities and services worth three billion marks over a period of twelve years. Under this treaty, the Israelis acquired power stations, railways, improved port facilities, ships, copper mines, machinery for 1,300 plants including a steel plant, and more.[14] No developing country has received financial assistance and technology on this scale from any developed country. Under a secret program that ran from 1958 until its discovery in 1965, Germany also supplied heavy arms to Israel; this was in addition to a soft loan of $500 million given in 1960 to develop the Negev.[15] It is doubtful if Israel could have scored the stunning victory in the June War of 1967 without the financial assistance, technology, and military hardware provided by France and Germany since the early 1950s. Over the past century, each of the five greatest Western powers, at one time or another, have offered support that has been vital to the success of the Zionist project. This is a unique record for *any* colonial settler project.

Collectively too, the West demonstrated its nearly unanimous support for Zionism in November 1947 when the proposal to partition Palestine was put up for a vote before the UN General Assembly. In reality, the vote for partition was a vote to carve a Jewish state out of territories that belonged to the Palestinians. The terms of the partition too were unjust. Although the Jewish settlers in 1948 owned less than 7 percent of the land, the UN proposal gave them 55 percent of Palestine.[16] In addition, it gave the Jewish state access to the Jordan River, Lake Tiberias, the Red Sea, the Mediterranean Sea, and, incredibly, the Gulf of Aqaba. In order to give the Jewish state access to the Gulf of Aqaba, the UN plan severed the only continuous land link between the eastern and western segments of the Arab world. The geography of the new states—Israel and Arab Palestine—proposed by the UN partition plan was also preposterous. Each of the proposed states consisted of three parcels of land, connected only by narrow land corridors. Yet nearly all the Western countries voted for the UN partition plan; only Greece voted against the plan, and Britain and Yugoslavia abstained. Several Latin American countries also abstained.[17] Clearly, the vote at the UN in 1949 showed that Zionism was a core Western project. Of the thirteen countries that voted against the plan, ten were members of the Islamicate world. Even at this early date, the Zionist movement had drawn the battle lines between the West and the Islamicate world. Was this a precursor of things to come?

CHAPTER 11

BRITISH INTERESTS AND ZIONISM

Dr. Weizmann, it's a boy.

—Sir Mark Sykes, October 31, 1917[1]

IN NOVEMBER 1917, THE BRITISH MADE A commitment to use their "best endeavors" to create a "national home for the Jewish people" in Palestine. Famously known as the Balfour Declaration, this historic commitment was conveyed in a letter from Lord Balfour, British Foreign Secretary, to Lord Rothschild, a leading pillar of Jewish society in Britain, an active Zionist and a close friend of Chaim Weizmann.

The Balfour Declaration gave the Zionists nearly everything they could have asked for. The world's greatest power had declared that that it would be the mother country to their colonial project. Shortly, in pursuance of their commitment, the British would grant Jewish colons nearly unlimited access to Palestine. The Declaration signaled to Western Jews and Christian evangelicals alike that the Zionist project was no fantasy. The Zionists were now assured that their movement was on a fast, nearly irreversible, track to success.

The Zionists operated within a historical matrix thickly populated with forces and tendencies that could be hitched to the wagon of their colonial ambitions. The pro-Zionist forces identified in previous chapters included the Jewish diaspora, anti-Semitism, Christian Zionism, racism, anti-Islamic bigotry, Crusading ambitions, real and putative Western interests in the Middle East, and the rivalries of Western powers. It was the Western Jews, however, who would soon become the strongest advocates of Zionism. These Jews were often located at strategic nodes of Western societies, positions from which they could rally pro-Zionist forces in key Western societies, and leverage their strength to shape Western policies toward Zionism.

In their public rhetoric, however, the Zionists have nearly always chosen to emphasize their project's strategic value to Western powers: both when they have sought Western support, and no less when they are explaining the support that Western powers have so readily extended to Zionism nearly since its inception. Western leaders too employ the same rhetoric. This is scarcely surprising. The Zionists as well as Western leaders—the lobbying party and the targets of their lobbying—have an equal interest in covering up that lobbying. The Zionists do not wish to be seen as the real architects of policies toward the Middle East, which have imposed sizable strategic and economic costs on the Western powers. Western leaders too do not want the people to learn how their decision-making powers are constrained by Zionist lobbying.

Other factors too have sustained the myth that Israel is America's strategic asset in the Middle East. Ironically, many of the writers on the left in the United States have chosen to blame American imperialism for the wars and repressive policies of Israel. The United States supports Israel, giving it a carte blanche to repress the Palestinians, because it keeps the Middle East in a straitjacket. In addition, the Zionist movement in the United States—in all its components—has accumulated enough deterrent power to banish criticism of Israel from the public discourse. Careers can end quickly if one insists on pointing to the elephant in the room—the Israel lobby.

The Zionists began to harp on the strategic value of their project quite early on. Writing in 1862, Moses Hess could foresee the dismantling of the Ottoman Empire as nationalist movements in its territories gained strength; when this happened, he hoped that a Jewish state could be inserted in Palestine by Western powers expecting to benefit from its presence in the Middle East.[2] Moses Hess pinned his colonial hopes on a partnership with the imperial ambitions of the French. Once France had conquered the "modern Nebuchadnezzar," it will be persuaded by its interests and politics to "extend its work of redemption also to the Jewish nation. It is to the interest of France to see that the road leading to India and China should be settled by a people which will be loyal to the cause of France to the end."[3]

Theodore Herzl too played up the putative strategic value of Zionism in his manifesto of 1896. Israel, he wrote, would "form a portion of the rampart of Europe against Asia, an outpost of civilization as opposed to barbarism. We should, as a Neutral State, remain in contact with all Europe, which would have to guarantee our existence."[4] In a few words, Herzl had defined the nature of Israel. Lacking a Jewish mother country, the Jewish settler state would have to be created by European powers, who would also find it necessary to "guarantee" its existence against the resistance of the natives.

. . .

Britain and France had shown some interest in the insertion of a Jewish state in the Levant from the late eighteenth to mid-nineteenth centuries.

Toward the end of the nineteenth century, however, they had lost interest in this project.

In the eighteenth century, when the European powers competed with each other to secure—or expand—their presence in the Indian Ocean and China, they saw the Levant as a vital land bridge, offering quick and direct access to the Indian Ocean. As Ottoman and Safavid power continued to decline, Britain, France, and Russia, the leading European powers, sought to gain footholds in the Middle East by extracting privileges for their traders and entering into alliances with the non-Muslim minorities in the region. Catholic France took the Maronites under its wing, while the Russians promoted themselves as the protectors of the Orthodox Christians. Only Protestant England had no natural clients in the region, and they tried to make up for this deficiency by championing the cause of the Jews and, at times, the Druze in Syria.[5]

During this period, some elements in Britain and France argued that the interests of these powers in the Indian Ocean might be advanced by inserting a Jewish state in the Levant. In April 1799, during his siege of Acre, Napoleon invited the Jews of Europe to establish a Jewish state in Palestine with Jerusalem as its capital. Napoleon's move was not inspired by biblical prophecies; neither did he expect that European Jews would be rushing to Palestine to take up his offer. Instead, his appeal was intended to sway Europe's Jews to his side. In any case, not much came of this appeal since Napoleon had to lift his siege of Acre and return to France in a hurry. Nevertheless, this episode reveals quite starkly the importance that a major European leader accorded—even at this early date—to the support of Europe's Jews in securing his imperial ambitions.

Britain too was moving in the same direction. Having taken the Oriental Jews under its protection, Britain proceeded in 1839 to open the first European consulate in Jerusalem.[6] A year later, Lord Palmerston, the British Foreign Secretary, wrote to the ambassador in Istanbul that the return of the Jews to Palestine "under the sanction and protection of the Sultan, would be a check upon any future evil designs of Mehmet Ali or his successor." From this point onward, we encounter repeated formulations by leading British officials regarding the strategic importance of the Middle East to British ambitions. Some of these officials also argued that British interests would be well served by creating a Jewish presence in the Levant. Strikingly, in 1876 Lord Shaftesbury argued that it would serve British interests to "foster the nationality of the Jews and aid them . . . to return as a leavening power to their old country."[7]

Toward the last decades of the nineteenth century, however, the great powers had lost interest in schemes to establish a Jewish presence in the Levant. Three developments account for this change. First, the rivalry between Britain and France had been settled decisively in favor of the former after Napoleon's final defeat at Waterloo in 1815. Second, the challenge mounted by Mohammad Ali, the ambitious new sovereign of Egypt, to the Ottoman Empire—and, therefore, to Western interests in the Ottoman Empire—was rolled back firmly in 1840. Finally, when the British occupied Egypt in 1882, including the Suez Canal, this made Britain quite capable of protecting and advancing its interests in the Middle East without invoking help from the Jews. By this time, Britain had already established a bridgehead in Aden, and would soon draw Oman and the Arab tribal chiefs along the eastern shores of Arabia into the net of its protection.

.   .   .

Questions concerning the motives, forces, personalities, and events that played a leading part in the formulation of the Balfour Declaration continue to generate a variety of answers.

No single sentence, containing an official statement of a government's foreign policy, was the product of more strenuous maneuvers, jockeying, and word parsing among a greater number of parties than the statement that would gain notoriety as the Balfour Declaration. Yet, the Declaration was presented to the world—in the words of J. M. N. Jeffries—"as an *entirely* British communication embodying an *entirely* British conception" (emphasis added). It was little known to most British, Western, Jewish, or Arab audiences that "Zionists of all nationalities had collaborated" on the text of the declaration or that they had "written most of it."[8] In hindsight, this comes as no surprise. Since 1897, the leading Zionists had engaged in intense lobbying in every major European capital—not to forget, Ottoman and Arab capitals as well—to promote their colonial project. This also explains why the Declaration was presented to the world as an "entirely British conception." In the middle of a war, any indications to the contrary would be read as signs of British weakness in the prosecution of the war.

Several theories have been advanced to account for the origins of the Balfour Declaration. At various times, the Declaration has been explained as the product of Zionist diplomacy, Jewish power, Britain's strategic interests in the Middle East, a bargain struck between an imperiled Britain and powerful Jews, the influence of Christian Zionists in Britain and the United States, a restitution for the historical wrongs done to Jews by Europeans, or the result of anti-Semitic delusions about the extent of Jewish power. Implausibly, David Lloyd George—whose government had issued the Declaration—claimed in his memoirs that it was a thank you note to Chaim Weizmann for his discovery of a new process for synthesizing acetone, a vital ingredient in explosives.[9] Primarily, this chapter will make the case for a negative. The British did not adopt Zionist goals because it would promote their vital and enduring interests in the Middle East. It is plausible, however, that during a vulnerable phase of the war in 1917, the Zionists offered to help the British by mobilizing Jewish support for their cause especially in the United States—and received the Balfour Declaration as *quid pro quo*.

Once it became clear that the Ottomans could not be bribed or pressured to part with Palestine, the Zionists concentrated on taking it by force. Even as they worked to create a Western consensus on their project, most leading Zionists were convinced that Britain was their best choice for securing control over Palestine. The advantages of this choice were quite compelling. Britain was better equipped than any other great power to seize control of Palestine. It was not only the world's paramount power. It had already established a dominating presence in the Middle East, with military bases in Cyprus, Egypt, and Aden surrounding the southern flanks of the Ottoman Empire; it had acquired sole policing rights over the Persian Gulf; it had also brought southern Iran within its sphere of influence. In some sections of Britain's upper classes, there also existed a strong sentiment that it was Britain's destiny to restore the Jews to Palestine. Increasingly, the Zionists also recognized that they could use their leverage over the United States—itself incapable of sponsoring their project—to bring pressure on Britain if it hesitated or wavered in its support of Zionism.

Over a period of seventeen years since its launching in 1897, the Zionists had made great strides in gaining the support of Jewish communities all over the world. Although the Zionists had not quite won over a majority of Western Jews in 1914, they had succeeded in establishing a network of organizations with representatives in nearly every Jewish community. They had won over a growing pool of Jewish activists to their cause, recruited some very talented Jews from major Western countries to their leadership, placed or identified allies in high places in many Western capitals, and carried the Zionist plea to Gentile leaders in every Western capital. "And yet," in the words of Walter Laqueur, "despite the collections, the cultural and propagandist work, the enthusiasm of the rank and file, and the perseverance of the leaders, the realization of its aims seemed in 1914 as remote as ever."[10]

Zionism first attracted the interest of British statesmen—during this period—when domestic concerns increased over the growing immigration of Jews from Eastern Europe. Theodore Herzl helped to focus this interest when he argued, before the Royal Commission on Alien Immigration in July 1902, that the creation of a Jewish state would stem the flow of Jewish immigrants to Britain. A few months later, in October

1902, this testimony led to a meeting between Herzl and the British colonial secretary, Joseph Chamberlain. At this meeting, Herzl identified three British territories as potential locations for his Jewish state: Cyprus, el-Arish, and the Sinai. Palestine was not on his list because it was not a British territory. Chamberlain could only discuss Cyprus; as colonial secretary, he had no jurisdiction over the two territories in Egypt. Cyprus was not on offer, however, because its Christian Greek majority could not be displaced in favor of Jews. Nevertheless, Chamberlain helped Herzl in arranging a meeting with the Foreign Secretary, Lord Lansdowne, who did have jurisdiction over el-Arish and the Sinai.

Herzl failed to persuade the British to part with either of these territories in Egypt. Lansdowne took little interest in Herzl's proposal for establishing a Jewish colony in el-Arish, but agreed to introduce him to Lord Cromer, British consul-general of Egypt. Lord Cromer refused to accommodate Herzl either; he was concerned that Jewish colonization of el-Arish would inflame Egyptian sentiments. At this point, Herzl went back to Chamberlain, who offered him a tract of land in Kenya, although this has come to be known as the Uganda Plan. The Zionists rejected this plan at the sixth congress of the World Zionist Organization in August 1903.[11] At Zionist urging, Lloyd George again submitted a proposal to the British government to permit Jewish colonization in Sinai, but without any success.[12]

The peregrinations of Theodore Herzl through British officialdom show conclusively that the British, at this time, had no interest in locating a Jewish state anywhere in the Middle East. The British had been in control of Egypt since 1882, of Cyprus since 1878, and besides they were masters of the Persian Gulf. Moreover, the British, who had long protected the Ottoman Empire against disintegration, did not anticipate any Ottoman threat to their interests in the Middle East. By no stretch of imagination could the insertion of a Jewish state in the Levant serve any of Britain's strategic interests; but it was certain to arouse the strongest sentiments against the Jewish state and their British sponsors in the entire region. It is therefore scarcely surprising that the British offered to shunt the Jewish state to an obscure location in East Africa, at a safe distance from Palestine. If the Zionists had taken up this offer, it might still help to attenuate the flow of Jewish immigrants into Britain.

It has been argued that the new realities created by World War I—and, in particular, the Ottoman decision in October 1914 to join the Central Powers—endowed the Zionist project with a new significance in Britain's strategic plans. In an essay written before the Balfour Declaration, Herbert Sidebotham—an Anglo-Zionist and one of the architects of the

Balfour Declaration—wrote, with some exaggeration, that the alliance between Germany and the Ottoman Empire "is so close that, for military purposes, Turkey is Germany." In light of this new reality, too hastily, Sidebotham concludes that the defense of Egypt now requires the creation of a buffer state between Egypt and Ottoman Syria. He argued that the least burdensome way to create such a buffer state would be to establish it as a settler colony. In another breathtaking leap, he concludes that this buffer state should be founded as a Jewish colony: the "only possible colonists of Palestine are Jews." Only the Jews can establish a state that will be allied with Britain, "at once a protection against the alien East and a mediator between it and us, a civilization distinct from ours yet imbued with our political ideas, at the same stage of political development, and beginning its second life as a nation with a debt of gratitude to this country as its second father."[13]

Herbert Sidebotham's case for the creation of a Jewish state in Palestine had little merit. The British in Egypt certainly had an interest now in extending their present frontiers to include Palestine; this would increase the distance between an Ottoman land attack and the Suez Canal.[14] But there was little plausibility to the argument that the Jews could take control of Palestine, bring in a few millions of Jews, colonize it, develop it, build an army, in short, establish a full-fledged Jewish state that would serve as a buffer against an Ottoman attack on Egypt. What makes this argument utterly fantastic is that this work of establishing a strong Jewish state would have to be telescoped within a few months—certainly within a very short time—if it was going to hold back an imminent Ottoman invasion. Needless to add, Sidebotham gives no indication of the strategic costs of his proposal. He passes over in silence the deep antagonism against Britain that the creation of a Jewish state in Palestine was certain to arouse in all of the Middle East and beyond.

The fate of an initiative by Herbert Samuel to persuade his cabinet colleagues to adopt the Zionist project also demonstrates that the war had not altered British attitudes toward Zionism. In January 1915, Herbert Samuel, the first person of Jewish faith to serve as a member of a British cabinet, submitted a memorandum to Prime Minister Herbert Asquith, urging him to establish a British protectorate in Palestine and open it up to Jewish immigration, a policy that he argued would contribute to the strength of the British Empire. In personal correspondence, Lord Asquith observed, "I confess I am not attracted by this proposed addition to our responsibilities." A revised version of Herbert Samuel's memorandum was circulated two months later, but it too was voted down by every member of the cabinet except Lloyd George, an ardent Zionist who had been hired as an attorney by Theodore Herzl in 1903 to persuade Lord Cromer to hand over el-Arish to the Zionists.[15]

We get no indication from the arduous negotiations that went into determining the terms of the secret Sykes-Picot Accord that Britain or France intended to accommodate Zionist plans for Palestine. Indeed, Britain and France both wanted to control Palestine. As a compromise, the Accord gave Britain control over Acre and Haifa and a stretch of territory that would allow it to construct a railway to Iraq. The rest of Palestine was to be placed under international control whose conditions were left undetermined. All Arab territories of the Ottoman Empire outside Palestine were promised to the Arabs, who would be allowed to form one or more states under the control of Britain and France. The Sykes-Picot Accord made no promises to the Zionists: it contained no plans for creating a Jewish state in Palestine. In the words of Lloyd George, British Prime Minister from December 1916 to January 1919, Palestine, under Sykes-Picot Accord, was "to be mutilated and torn into sections. There would be no more Palestine. Canaan was to be drawn and quartered." "But 1917 saw a complete change in the attitude of nations towards this historic land," added Lloyd George.[16] On November 2, 1917, after resisting Zionist demands for close to twenty years—and more than three years after the start of the war—the British cabinet declared its support for the creation of a "national home for the Jewish people" in Palestine. This was a dramatic shift in British policy. It would initiate a new alignment of forces between the Jews and the West whose ramifications are still being worked out by growing circles of conflict in the Middle East.

. . .

How then are we to explain this shift in British policy that was announced in November 1917?

It was inconceivable before 1914 that Britain—or any great power—could have espoused Zionist aims in the Levant. Inevitably, such a commitment would have involved Britain in a war against the Ottomans, which, in turn might have drawn in the other great European powers—the French, Germans, and Russians. Quite possibly, this could have escalated to a major conflict involving all these powers, allied with or against the Ottomans. In other words, supporting Zionism carried risks of war, and it had few countervailing advantages.

This calculus changed when the Ottomans decided to join the Allied Powers in November 1914. In a reversal of its earlier policy, the British now examined various proposals for carving up the Ottoman Empire.

The British had an interest in keeping Palestine under their control or in friendly hands, as a barrier against an Ottoman attempt to occupy the Suez Canal. A Jewish buffer state in Palestine, however, was not practical because of its small Jewish population. In addition, the creation of a Jewish buffer state would make it difficult for the British to rally the Arabs to its cause in the war, an important British objective at this time; the British were also keen to avoid alienating the Muslims in India. If the British were keen to safeguard the Suez Canal, they would have much preferred to annex Palestine to Egypt rather than set it up as a Jewish buffer state.[17]

As the war entered its fourth year, without a resolution in sight, British calculations began to change. The British now sought to end the stalemate by recruiting the United States to its side. At the other end, Germany had an opposite interest in keeping the United States out of the war. This set up a contest between Britain and Germany for the support of the Jewish diaspora in the United States, who—both believed—could expedite or delay American entry into the war. More to the point, since American Jewry leaned increasingly toward Zionism, both Britain and Germany were anxious to court the Zionists as the most effective way to win the support of Jewish America.[18] The Zionists gained influence over Britain and Germany because of their courtship of American Jews. Walter Laqueur writes, "The news about the talks between the German representatives and the Zionists was noted in London and Paris; so were the pro-Zionist articles in the German press."[19] There existed a similar contest between the two Entente powers—Britain and France—and Germany in relation to Russia. Britain sought to keep Russia in the war, while Germany sought its exit. The Zionists gained also from the rivalry between Britain and France, allies in the war, for securing control over Palestine; both powers were now willing to use Zionism as a cloak for their ambitions in Palestine. Cumulatively, these contests helped to augment the lobbying power of the Zionists in London and Berlin.

Western interest in Zionism was piqued by another development: the growing threat of revolutionary movements in Eastern and Central Europe. It was common knowledge that the radical movements drew their leaders and activists disproportionately from Jewish populations. The Zionists too underlined this connection when they pressured Western governments to support their cause; this would divert Jews away from their support for revolutionary causes. Admittedly, Britain and Germany did not host strong communist parties. Nevertheless, all Western powers had a strong interest in preventing the accession to power of communists in Eastern Europe.

Great power competition for the support of Zionists intensified in 1917. In June of that year, Jules Cambon, the Director General of the French Foreign Ministry, issued a declaration stating that the French government "cannot but feel sympathy for your [Zionist] cause, the triumph of which is bound up with that of the Allies."[20] On their part, the Germans used their influence with the Ottomans to ease pressures on the Jewish colons in Palestine. However, they could not offer direct support to the Zionists because of the determined opposition of their Ottoman allies to Zionism. Nevertheless, the Zionists continued to lobby the German government if only to ratchet the pressure on Britain.[21] Who can claim that these pressures, as they built up, did not play an important part in pushing Britain toward embracing the Zionist plan?

Two additional developments in 1917 gave a boost to the Zionist case in Britain. The Allied prospects in the war continued to worsen during 1917.[22] The opposing armies were still bogged down on the Western front, increasing the pressure on Britain for a breakthrough in the Middle East. According to Lloyd George, the French army "was exhausted," the Italians had suffered a "shattering defeat" at Caporetto, and "the unlimited submarine campaign had sunk millions of tons of our shipping." On the eastern front, the Russians were demoralized after suffering numerous defeats, raising British fears that they would pull out of the war. Although the United States had entered the war in April 1917, it had yet to make a major contribution to the Allied war effort. Under these conditions, the British leadership was convinced that the Zionists were more useful than ever before. In the words of Lloyd George, "we had every reason at that time to believe that in both countries [the United States and Russia] the friendliness or hostility of the Jewish race might make a considerable difference."[23]

The British cabinet that took office in December 1916 was also decidedly more sympathetic to Zionist claims. At least five of its members—the Prime Minister; Lord Balfour, Foreign Secretary; Lord Milner, member of the war cabinet; Lord Cecil, Minister of Blockade; and Winston Churchill, Secretary of State for Munitions—were committed Zionists. Despite the detailed and eloquent memoranda submitted by Herbert Samuels, Zionist advocacy made little progress during the tenure of Herbert Asquith, the previous Prime Minister. With Lloyd George leading Britain, the Zionists had a much more sympathetic audience. Perhaps by coincidence, during 1916, three powerful assistant secretaries in the all-important war cabinet "rapidly became converts to Zionism." During the last two years of the war, Zionists or recent converts to Zionism also rose to high office in the Foreign Ministry and the Whitehall. In Washington, "the ascendant Zionist spin on British Middle East policy" during 1917 was monitored with growing concern. Col. Edward Mandel House, the aide to President Wilson, wrote, "It is all bad and I told Balfour so. They are making the [the Middle East] a breeding place for future war."[24]

The British decision to announce its support for Zionism in November 1917 was the product, then, of the convergence of several conditions connected to the war. There was the three-way rivalry—among Britain, France, and Germany—for Jewish support to influence the disposition of the United States and Russia toward the war. Zionists gained influence also because of the impetus the war gave to revolutionary movements. In turn, this led the great powers to promote Zionism as a means of diverting Jews from supporting socialist revolutions in Europe. Jewish centrality came into play in 1917, when, Britain, offered to sponsor Zionism in exchange for the support of the Jewish diaspora. Perhaps, the assumption of power by Lloyd George in December 1916, an ardent Zionist, was a coincidence. In any case, it completed the quartet of conditions that dropped Palestine in the lap of the Zionists.

Behind these forces, at a deeper level, other forces had been ripening for decades, if not centuries. Most importantly, they included the rise of Jewish power in key nodes of Western civilization, the rise of Christian Zionism, and the emergence of revolutionary movements—again, not unconnected to each other—which also contributed less directly but no less importantly to the success of Zionism. If Zionism has succeeded, thus far, it is because—by luck and design—its proponents have cleverly positioned themselves to take advantage of history, even the history of their own tragedies.

.   .   .

If the British had promulgated the Balfour Declaration because they expected a Jewish state in Palestine to serve its strategic interests in the new Middle East, this is not borne out by subsequent events. "By 1921," Walter Laqueur attests, "the pattern had been set for many years to come. The process of whittling down the mandate begins early and proceeds slowly."[25]

The British retreat from the Balfour Declaration began soon after the end of the war. In March 1921, overriding Zionist objections, the British detached eastern Palestine—renamed Transjordan—and awarded this protectorate to Prince Abdullah, a scion of the Sharif family.[26] In addition, after an episode of violent Palestinian resistance in May 1921, the British administration in Palestine "went out of its way to promote Arab political frameworks parallel to Zionist institutions."[27] Soon the British took additional steps to knock down Zionist ambitions in Palestine. In June 1922, the Churchill White Paper clarified that Britain did "not contemplate that Palestine as a whole should be converted into a Jewish National Home, but that such a home should be founded in Palestine" (emphasis added). The White Paper clarified that the "Jewish National Home" would only be "a centre in which the Jewish people as a whole may take, on grounds of religion and race, an interest and a pride." More importantly, the White Paper set out economic criteria to restrict Jewish immigration; proposed the creation of legislative bodies in Palestine based on proportional representation, not on parity as demanded by the Zionists; and excluded Jewish settlements from the Transjordan.[28]

The Zionists successfully challenged several British moves to derail their colonial project during the 1930s. In March 1930, following Arab violence a year ago in Jerusalem, the Shaw Report blamed this violence on Arab fears of coming "under the economic domination of Jews," and to allay these fears recommended tighter regulation of Jewish immigration and land acquisition. When they could not implement these recommendations, in part because of Zionist opposition, the British government shifted the responsibility to another investigative committee headed by Sir John Hope-Simpson. This committee endorsed the conclusions of the Shaw Report and, in addition, maintained that discriminatory Zionist policies on labor and land—denying employment to Arabs and making the lands they acquired inalienable—violated the terms of the Mandate. Incorporated into the Passfield White Paper in October 1930, these analyses and recommendations ran into determined opposition from the Zionists. When they threatened to lobby the United States to impose economic sanctions on Britain, Prime Minister MacDonald capitulated. In a letter whose terms were dictated by Chaim Weizmann, the Prime Minister abrogated the Passfield White Paper.[29] This was an important Zionist victory. It would keep Palestine open to Jewish immigration during the crucial 1930s when the flow of immigrants accelerated.

The conflict between Britain's strategic interests and the Zionist project grew during the 1930s, leading eventually to a British decision to disengage from Zionist goals. Two developments were driving this change. First, and more importantly, the 1930s were marked by growing tensions between Britain and the Axis Powers, leading to near certainty that another great war was imminent. In addition, Palestinian anger erupted in two successive revolts, in 1936 and 1937, creating worries that this might persuade the Arabs to throw their lot with the Axis Powers. In July 1937, the Peel Commission, set up after the first revolt died down, proposed partition as a solution to the Palestinian problem, with 20 percent of Palestine going to the Zionists. This led to a more violent second Arab revolt starting in September 1937.

Although this revolt too was suppressed, the British became more concerned about the costs of supporting the Zionist project. In January 1939, British strategists declared that failure to "bring about a complete appeasement of Arab opinion in Palestine and in neighboring countries" at the outbreak of the war would drive the Arab states into the camp of the Axis Powers.[30] On the other hand, the British knew that the costs of alienating the Zionists would be minimal. As matters stood in the late 1930s, with the aggressive anti-Semitic policies of the Nazis, there was practically no risk that world Jewry would abandon the British for the anti-Semitic Germans.

The stage was now set for Britain to repudiate the Balfour Declaration. In January 1938, the British Foreign Office prevailed upon the Woodhead Commission to review the feasibility of partition. When the Zionists rejected the partition plans proposed by this Commission, the government issued the White Paper of November 1938 declaring that partition was "impracticable," and invited Jewish and Arab leaders to a conference in London to settle their differences. When this conference failed, the British concluded that they could not alienate the Arabs at a time when another great war was imminent.

In a dramatic shift, the White Paper of May 1939 declared that "His Majesty's Government believe that the framers of the Mandate in which the Balfour Declaration was embodied could not have intended that Palestine should be converted into a Jewish state against the will of the Arab population of the country." Over the next five years, Britain restricted Jewish immigration to a maximum of 75,000, after which it would require the consent of the Palestinian Arabs. Jewish land purchases too would be restricted to designated areas along the coast. In addition, sometime over the next ten years, Palestine, with an Arab majority, would be granted independence.[31] The exigencies of World War I had persuaded the British to sacrifice Palestinian rights in favor of the Zionist colonial project; now, some twenty-two years later, in anticipation of another great war, the British appeared to be reversing course.

The backtracking in British policy toward the Zionist project, effected in the face of Zionist opposition, confirms that Jewish lobbying—in and of itself—was not the overriding factor behind the Balfour Declaration of November 1917. If Zionist lobbying had prevailed in 1917, this was the result of a peculiar set of circumstances—described earlier—that would not be repeated. After World War I, with complete Allied victory and the extension of British control over much of the Middle East, the Zionists were much less effective in preventing overt British backtracking on Zionism. This weakness of the Zionist lobby in Britain contrasts substantially—as we will show in Part III—with the trajectory of Zionist influence in the United States. Jewish influence over the political system in the United States has been substantially stronger, as this has been exerted at multiple levels—through trade unions, the media, the Congress, the President's office, and a growing partnership with the Christian Zionists. We will return to this subject in Part III of this book.

CHAPTER 12

ANTI-SEMITISM AND ZIONISM

The struggle of Jews for unity and independence . . . is calculated to attract the sympathy of people to whom we are rightly or wrongly obnoxious.

—Leo Pinsker

The anti-Semites will become our most dependable friends, the anti-Semitic countries our allies.

—Theodore Herzl

If we allow a separation between the refugee problem and the Palestine problem, we are risking the existence of Zionism.

—David Ben-Gurion, 1938

If I am asked could you give money from UJA [United Jewish Appeal] moneys to rescue Jews? I say "No; and I say again, No."

—Itzhak Greenbaum, 1943

Anti-Semitism is no longer a problem [in the United States], fortunately. It's raised . . . because privileged people want to make sure they have total control, not just 98% control . . . they want to make sure there's no critical look at the policies the US (and they themselves) support in the Middle East.

—Noam Chomsky, 2002[1]

ZIONISTS HAVE LONG CLAIMED THAT THEIR MOVEMENT was a reaction and a solution to anti-Semitism. They favor this explanation because it provides a convenient moral cover to their colonial project; as perennial victims of Gentile persecution, the Jews have an unqualified right to their own state. This explanation is scarcely plausible. Broadly, three responses to anti-Semitism had emerged during the nineteenth century: assimilation, revolution, and political Zionism. Political Zionism was the last to appear on the scene; and until the start of World War I, it was also by far the weakest of the three.

It is quite a bit more helpful to think of Zionism—our approach in this book—primarily, as a movement inspired by and founded on Jewish success and ambitions.[2] At first, most prosperous Jews would scarcely consider giving up their gains for what they considered to be the utopian dream of the Zionists; and the poorer Jews from Eastern Europe preferred to move westward in the footsteps of their assimilated cousins, or they were drawn to revolutionary movements. Under the circumstances, the small band of early Zionists looked upon anti-Semitism to propel their movement from the margins of Jewish political discourse to its center stage. They took early notice of the complementarities between anti-Semitism and their own movement, and decided to harness these complementarities to propel their movement. If assimilation or revolution could abolish or attenuate anti-Semitism, few Jews would be attracted to Zionism. The success of Zionism was closely tied to the proposition that assimilation cannot work: anti-Semitism is ineradicable. Jews could not escape anti-Semitism in a Gentile society, but, in a Jewish state, they could turn their backs on anti-Semites.

What were the complementarities between Zionism and anti-Semitism? Most importantly, the Zionists shared a common goal with anti-Semites: they wanted the Jews out of Europe. The anti-Semites had pursued this ambition over many centuries by expelling, killing, or segregating the Jews. Now—with Zionism—it appeared that the Jews themselves were proposing to remove themselves from Europe, voluntarily, if only one or more Western powers would help them to secure a Jewish state in Palestine. The Zionists offered the anti-Semites a historic opportunity to accomplish their long-standing goal with little trouble. The offer was unexpected because Jews, in the past, had never cooperated in their own deportation. It was an attractive opportunity too because the anti-Semites would attain their goal without any of the unpleasantness associated with deportations and pogroms. In the measure that anti-Semitism—in its diffuse and concentrated forms—was still prevalent in Europe, the Zionists could rely on the cooperation of European leaders, themselves driven by anti-Semitism or acting to appease strong anti-Semitic sentiment in their societies. Thus, Zionism promised to create an extraordinary convergence in the primary goals of two historical antagonists—Jews and anti-Semites.

Anti-Semitism also provided the rationale for Zionism, both when its protagonists were appealing to Western guilt, and when they were seeking to overcome Jewish diffidence toward their movement. Perhaps for the first time in Christian Europe, the Enlightenment had created in some segments of Europe's intellectual class a growing remorse over the persecution of the Jewish minorities. In turn, during the nineteenth century,

Jewish writers sought to cultivate and enhance this remorse by exaggerating the persecution they had endured at the hands of Christians.[3] Now, the Zionists could count on a measure of support for their movement from Europe's intellectual classes, who wished to expiate for their past sins. In the past, Europe's Jews had cultivated this guilt when demanding equal rights. The Zionists would use the same tactic to gain support for the creation of a Jewish state in Palestine.

Anti-Semitism was useful to Zionism in other unexpected ways. It would help to reverse the strong opposition of assimilated Jews to Zionism. Faced with rising anti-Semitism in the last decades of the nineteenth century—caused by a growing tide of Jewish immigrants from Eastern Europe—the assimilated Jews, selfishly, would see in Zionism a solution to this new wave of anti-Semitism. In a meeting in June 1919 with Lord Balfour, Louis Brandeis explained that his conversion to Zionism occurred in the backdrop of concerns about the influx of Jews, especially Russian Jews with revolutionary tendencies, into the United States. With these sentiments, Lord Balfour, himself a lifelong anti-Semite, expressed his complete agreement, adding, "Of course, these are the reasons that make you and me such ardent Zionists."[4]

Since the creation of Israel, anti-Semitism has performed a third vital function in the history of Zionism. In the postwar period, when Western nations occupied the moral high ground with their rhetoric of human rights, the Zionists had to ensure that Israeli violations of Palestinian rights did not enter the public discourse in Western societies. Similarly, they would seek to prevent Americans from questioning their country's partisanship toward Israel and the role that the Israel lobby plays in creating this special relationship. In order to stifle any debate on Israel, American relations with Israel, or the influence of the Israel lobby on U.S. policies toward the Middle East, the Zionist organizations have worked with great effectiveness to equate any criticism of Israel with anti-Semitism. They have routinely employed charges of anti-Semitism to discredit, ostracize, intimidate, and deny employment to Americans—especially politicians and academics—who criticize Israel, the Israel lobby, or the deeply partisan relations that the United States maintains with Israel.[5]

.   .   .

The early Zionists understood quite well that the Jewish nation they wanted to establish in Palestine did not yet exist. Instead, they would have to create this nation out of the disparate communities of Jews spread across Europe, many of whom had assimilated and gained acceptance, prosperity, and influence in Gentile societies. The Jews in Eastern Europe still faced anti-Semitic persecution, but they too were seeking deliverance in emigration, assimilation, or revolutionary movements that would banish anti-Semitism by creating a classless society.

In order to gain converts, in competition with assimilation and revolutionary movements, the Zionists would of course appeal to Jewish pride in their "chosenness" and their messianic ambitions. Nationalist Jews were the natural constituency of Zionism, those who believed that the Jews are a distinct nation—set apart from and above other nations—that should take its place among the great nations of the world. Many Jews in the nineteenth century might have felt the pull of these nationalist sentiments, but few were convinced that it was practical to bring the Jews together in a Jewish state.[6] The creation of a Jewish state from scratch looked like a remote, even quixotic, prospect; in comparison, assimilation and revolution appeared to offer far better prospects for fulfilling Jewish ambitions. Nevertheless, a few Jews of strong mettle and overweening ambition found their métier in the call of Zionism; they turned to this enterprise because it promised so much. With excitement barely concealed, they took up this challenge because it offered an opportunity to take advantage of the power that Jews had accumulated. These Jews made up the core of the Zionist movement—its leaders and its most eager colons.

The Zionists' best hope of creating a mass following lay in cultivating *Judennot*—Jewish misery. They would seek to arouse Jewish anxiety by arguing that there could be no salvation for Jews in concealing their Jewishness. The Jews were a distinct people who could give up the outward signs of their religion but could not escape their Jewish ethnicity. The English and Germans would never accept the assimilated Jews as one of their own; even those who converted would be seen as baptized Jews. No matter how troubling the irony, the Zionists' most dependable allies were the Jews' most dreaded enemy. Although this was a marriage of convenience, it was enduring.

Theodore Herzl clearly saw these connections. In his Zionist manifesto, he had asked the question vital to Zionism, "What is our propelling force?" His answer was unequivocal, "The misery of the Jews." In the ensuing discussion, Herzl scarcely distinguishes between "the misery of the Jews" and anti-Semitism, the source of this misery. He compares the force of anti-Semitism to "steam-power, generated by boiling water, lifting the kettle-lid." Attempts by Zionists and "kindred associations" to check anti-Semitism are like trying to put a lid on the boiling kettle. Fighting anti-Semitism is futile; worse, it is misguided. Instead, he argues that "this *power*, if rightly employed, is powerful enough to propel a large engine and to despatch passengers and goods: the engine having whatever form men may choose to give it" (emphasis added). Far from becoming extinct, as the assimilated Jews believed, anti-Semitism could be expected to grow. Herzl confided in his diaries, "Anti-Semitism has grown and continues to grow, and so do I."[7] Clearly, he expected rising anti-Semitism to be immeasurably more effective in recruiting Jewish colons than the wasted appeals hitherto made in the name of Jewish nationalism.

If anti-Semitism was so closely tied to Zionism, would the Zionists shrink from exploiting this connection? In launching the Zionist movement, had not the Zionists also declared their opposition to all those hopes of a better future that Europe's Jews pursued in assimilation, migration, and various radical movements? Ironically, since Zionist hopes rested on rising Jewish misery, a check on anti-Semitism might doom their movement from the start. "Am I before my time?" Theodore Herzl had worried in 1896. "Are the sufferings of the Jews not yet grave enough?"[8] Barring the period of Nazi persecution, this has been a recurrent problem for the Zionists. At first, most Jews were opposed to, or skeptical of, Zionism; even when they had been won over to Zionist goals, their support was mostly limited to "pocketbook Zionism." This is a problem that Zionists face to this day. As long as developed Western countries are open to Jewish immigrants, few Jews emigrate to Israel.

What actions might the Zionist leaders contemplate or execute in order to generate stronger Jewish support for their movement? "If Zionism," writes David Hirst, "as a historical phenomenon, was a reaction to anti-Semitism, it follows that, in certain circumstances, the Zionists had an interest in provoking the very disease which, ultimately, they hoped to cure."[9] Although the Zionists might not give overt encouragement to anti-Semitism, they were more willing to produce the same results covertly. According to Alfred Lilienthal, there were zealous Zionists who wanted the Jewish leadership to keep anti-Semitism alive.[10] We do not know if Zionist agents engaged in covert actions to provoke anti-Semitism *before* the creation of Israel. However, we do have evidence, presented later in this chapter, of such covert actions in Iraq during the early 1950s.

If the Zionists did not directly provoke anti-Semitism, there was little to restrain them from capitalizing upon actual and existing manifestations of anti-Semitism. They would identify, record, rehearse, publicize, project, analyze, and, thus, exaggerate every incident of anti-Semitism so that its shadow would loom larger in the Jewish imagination. Indeed, the efforts to document, publicize, and magnify anti-Semitism remain an important part of the activities of most Zionist organizations; and there are quite a few who make this their exclusive duty.

Since anti-Semitism fed directly into the Zionist movement, it is unlikely that the Zionists would take actions to check its growth, much less roll it back. Stoking anti-Semitism carried unacceptably high political risks, but it was quite safe to withhold actions to combat anti-Semitism. Sins of omission are far less visible than sins of commission. One of the most serious sins of omission on the part of Jewish organizations and leaders during the first three decades of the twentieth century was their near silence on the moves to restrict immigration into Western Europe and the Americas.[11] These restrictions were indispensable to the success of Zionism in attracting Jewish colons to Palestine. Open borders threatened to sever the connection between anti-Semitism and Zionism; the dramatic increase in the flow of Jews to Palestine since the 1920s would not have occurred if they could gain entry into Western Europe or the Americas. In the words of the eminent Palestinian historian, Walid Khalidi, "This is the unmentioned and, presumably, unmentionable rock upon which the Anglo-Zionist and American-Zionist entente was established in the twenties and thirties of this century, long *before* the rise of Hitler."[12] It should also be noted that the old assimilated Jews in Western Europe and the United States could not have been too displeased either with the new restrictions on immigration. They did not want to see their gains threatened by the growing anti-Semitism that was being aroused by new Jewish immigrants.

The Zionists were opposed to any schemes to rescue the Jews of Europe if it would end in their repatriation to destinations other than Palestine. In 1938, they refused to attend a conference at Evian, a town on the shores of Lake Geneva, convened by Western governments to consider ways of rescuing and resettling Jews whose lives were seen to be at risk in Germany and Austria. Should such schemes succeed, the Zionists were afraid, they would greatly diminish the stream of Jews heading for Palestine.[13] Similarly, an American plan to admit close to half a million Jewish refugees—in the middle of World War II—into Western countries was shelved because of lack of support from Jewish organizations.[14] The plan was initiated by President Franklin D. Roosevelt, who was convinced he could persuade the Congress to admit 150,000 Jewish refugees if Britain also agreed to accept a similar number. In addition, President Roosevelt believed he could count on Brazil, Chile, Canada, and Australia, among others, to admit an additional 150,000 or more. The President instructed Morris Ernst, one of his close friends and advisers, to explore, unofficially, on one of his trips to England, the willingness of British leaders to support this plan. Although the British gave their consent to President Roosevelt's plan, it was never implemented. Ernst writes that "the failure of leading Jewish groups to support with zeal this immigration program may have caused the President not to push forward with it at that time."

This is an understatement. Because of his support for President Roosevelt's plan, Ernst writes, "active Jewish leaders decried, sneered and then attacked me as if I were a traitor."[15] When news of the systematic killings of Jews reached the United States in 1942, the American Jewish establishment did not respond with alacrity to the unfolding horror.[16]

The complementarities between Zionists and anti-Semites were a constant invitation to both parties to work together to achieve their common goals. "It was in this spirit," writes Maxine Rodinson, "that in 1903 Herzl reached a general agreement on fundamentals with the sinister Plehve, Czarist minister of the interior and organizer of pogroms, inaugurating a political tradition of converging the Zionist program with that of the anti-Semites (something Herzl proudly admitted), and which was to be almost fatal."[17] In the 1930s, the Nazis banned all Jewish organizations except those with Zionist aims; they even allowed the Zionists to fly their blue-and-white flag with the Star of David at its center. In violation of the *Jewish* boycott of the Nazi economy, the Zionists promised cash and trade concessions to Nazi Germany if they directed Jewish emigrants to Palestine. This collaboration with fascist forces was not limited to Zionist revisionists, who are often painted as extremists for espousing in public views privately held by the Zionist mainstream. Brenner has documented several episodes of collaboration between the mainstream Jewish organizations and fascist governments in Germany, Italy, and Japan.[18]

The evidence of Zionist collaboration with the Nazis forces us to a speculation. Would the history of Jews in the first half of the twentieth century be different, even very different, if the Western Jewish diaspora, instead of channeling its energy into the Zionist movement, had pooled its resources to curb and defeat all those political tendencies that sharpened anti-Semitism in the West? This question can scarcely be regarded as idle, since the Jews, both during this period and later, have demonstrated, on numerous occasions, their capacity to influence the domestic politics of key Western countries.

Nothing better illustrates the critical dependence of Zionist success on anti-Semitism than the annual record of Jewish arrivals in Palestine since it became a British colony. Contrary to Zionist expectations, the Balfour Declaration did not produce a stampede of Jews eager to enter Palestine. After reaching an annual peak of 33,801 in 1925, Jewish arrivals in Palestine declined steeply to 2,713 in 1927; over the next four years, the annual Jewish arrivals barely exceeded 5,000. At this rate of colonization, the Zionist project would almost certainly have to be abandoned. What saved the day for Zionism was the exodus of German Jews precipitated by the anti-Semitic measures imposed by Nazi Germany during the 1930s. Since nearly all Western countries had closed their doors to immigrants by the early 1920s, many of these Jewish émigrés had nowhere to go but Palestine. As a result, the Jewish population of Palestine increased dramatically during the 1930s: from 172,300 in 1931 to 445,457 in 1939. In 1946, the Jewish population had grown to 608,225, and their share in the total population of Palestine had risen to 33 percent.[19] With their incomparably higher education and skills, their superior organization, their access to the resources of the Jewish diaspora, and the support they received from British administrators, the balance of social and economic power in Palestine had swung heavily toward the Zionists.

. . .

As a self-defined movement for "liberating" Europe's Jews *from* Europe's Gentiles, Zionism had an anomalous relationship with the Gentile nations of Europe.

The Zionists did not regard Europe's Gentile nations as their adversary, since they depended on the anti-Semitism of these Gentile nations to rescue their movement from obscurity and failure. Unlike nationalists who seek to secede from a state or empire by creating new borders, the Zionists did not ask to redraw the map of Europe; they planned to establish their Jewish state *outside* the borders of Europe. In other words, the Zionists were offering to execute what any state battling secessionists would have embraced avidly. The Zionists were "secessionists" who wanted to sail away from Europe, and hence, they could count on Europeans to help them with their plans to sail away.

This was a novel approach to national liberation. As a first step, the Zionists proposed to "liberate" Jews from European persecution by arranging for their exodus from Europe. This had always been the dream of Europe's anti-Semites: to cleanse Europe of all its Jews. Over the past centuries, different states in Europe had periodically attempted this voiding of Jews through forced conversions, pogroms, expulsions, and segregation of Jews from Gentiles. The Zionists were now proposing to purge Europe of its Jews on a scale never attempted before, and without the inconvenience of deportations and pogroms. Kerekes writes, "Some Britons actually supported the creation of a Zionist state . . . because it expressed their ultimate wish fulfillment: a modern day expulsion, but one which, while resolving the Jewish Question, would have been achieved with the Jews' cooperation."[20] The Zionists had made an offer to Europe's Judeophobes that they would have difficulty turning down.

This was a clever stratagem. The Zionists were pursuing a plan to convert an impossible nationalism—with little prospect of ever achieving its goal *inside* Europe—into a settler colonial project. In addition, they would convert the Jews' perennial adversaries into strategic partners. The Zionists expected to persuade at least one European power to play the part of mother country to the Jewish colons in Palestine. It appeared that the Zionists would outshine the exploits of Moses. In biblical narration, Moses too had chosen to liberate the Hebrews of Egypt by marching them out of Egypt and into Canaan, where they would create their own state. Moses was not as lucky as the Zionists; he could not persuade the Egyptians to help the Hebrews to colonize Canaan. There was no basis for such cooperation in the biblical narrative; the Egyptians had no desire to be rid of the Hebrews who were their slaves. Most Westerners, on the other hand, were all too happy to be rid of the Jews.

.   .   .

The partnership between Zionism and anti-Semitism did not end with the creation of Israel. The Zionists now became more daring, and more innovative, in their uses of anti-Semitism, since the needs of Zionism were changing as Israel sought to consolidate its power over the Middle East. There were few anti-Semites in Europe now: and those in the United States, now converted to dispensationalism, adulated Israel. Nevertheless, Israel still needed anti-Semitism as a tool to discipline the West.

In 1948, the ingathering of the world's Jews in Palestine had only begun; at the time, Israel contained less than 6 percent of the world's Jews. In terms of its borders too, the Israel of 1948 was not a finished work. The Zionists had been dreaming of recreating the mythic Davidic kingdom whose borders extended beyond the outlines of mandatory Palestine. The logic of Israel's creation too—its conflicts with the Arab world—would constantly tempt and force the Israelis to expand. The Zionists were not yet ready to bid farewell to the anti-Semites.

The pressures on Israel to expand its demographic base were nearly as great in the decade following its creation as in the preceding two decades. The events of 1948—the creation of Israel, the defeat of Arab armies, and the massive ethnic cleansing of Palestinians—had ignited an Arab nationalism that was dedicated to rolling back the Zionist state. Israel would have to expand its demographic base if it was to deter and defeat this surging Arab nationalism. Once again, the Zionists ramped up their efforts to produce a fresh influx of Jews into Israel. Their goal was ambitious; they planned to bring an additional four million Jews into Israel during the 1950s.[21]

The Zionists did not hesitate to use violence and deception in their drive to recruit Jewish colons for Israel. When the displaced Jews in German refugee camps insisted—despite intense pressures from the Jewish Agency—on settling in the United States, they were subjected to a variety of coercive measures. The Zionists stopped their food rations, fired them from their jobs, smashed the machines they had received from Americans, and denied them legal protections and visa rights. In several Jewish communities—in Mexico, Uruguay, Brazil, Argentina, and Peru—Jews were ostracized and denied access to community services when they refused to contribute funds to the Zionists.[22] Most histories of Israel do not mention these unsavory Zionist tactics.

The Zionists now spoke openly of using anti-Semitism to shock Jews into leaving their host societies. In 1952, a columnist for *Davar*, the official organ of *Mapai* (Israel's ruling party), explained how *he* would incite anti-Semitism in order to bring Jews to Israel. The columnist wrote,

> I shall not be ashamed to confess that if I had the power, as I have the will, I would select a score of efficient young men . . . and I would send them to the countries where Jews are absorbed in sinful self-satisfaction. The task of these young men would be to disguise themselves as non-Jews, and plague Jews with anti-Semitic slogans such as "Bloody Jew," "Jews to Palestine" and similar intimacies. I can vouch that the results in terms of a considerable immigration to Israel from these countries would be ten thousand times larger than the results brought by thousands of emissaries who have been preaching for decades to deaf ears.[23]

This was no mere Zionist fantasy. Methods more daring than those outlined by the *Davar* columnist had been employed to produce the exodus of Iraqi Jews in 1951.[24] The campaign worked on three fronts. Secret Zionist agents egged young Iraqi Jews to leave their ancient homeland, luring them with promises of prosperity in Israel. At the same time, the Western Zionist media began publishing reports of pogroms against Iraqi Jews in order to embarrass the Iraqi government into allowing the Jews to leave. Finally, to clinch their efforts, secret Israeli agents launched bomb attacks against three Jewish targets in Iraq—including Jews celebrating Passover along the banks of Tigris, the U.S. Information Center and a synagogue—when the rate of departure of Iraqi Jews did not meet Zionist expectations. According to Shiblak, there were at least five bomb attacks against Jewish targets in Iraq during this period. In combination, these methods produced a dramatic flight of Jews from Iraq; by March 1951, only 5,000 of Iraq's 140,000 Jews remained in the country.[25]

Israel's dependence on anti-Semitism has not weakened in recent decades. The leading Zionist organizations in the West constantly hold their ears to the ground, ready to pick up the faintest signals of anti-Semitism, amplify them, and offer them to the world as proofs of ever-present Jewish victimization. This serves important Zionist needs. Diaspora Jews continue to play a vital role in securing Western support for Israel. In part at least,

Israel's ability to mobilize the support of diaspora Jews still depends on keeping alive fears that their citizenship in Western countries rests on precarious foundations. Israel continues to remind them that a new wave of anti-Semitism could at any time force them to seek refuge in Israel. At the same time, Western societies could not be allowed to forget their complicity in the history of anti-Semitic crimes; they too must be told *ad nauseum* that anti-Semitism still stirs in the Gentile breast, barely concealed under the surface of a genteel tolerance. As long as Western guilt over centuries of anti-Semitism can be maintained, the Zionists can muzzle criticism of Israel by equating it with anti-Semitism. In the United States, the fear of being charged with anti-Semitism succeeds almost completely in suppressing any voices critical of Israel in the public discourse.

The two-way relationship between Zionism and anti-Semitism has become more explicit over time. Israeli violations of human rights, its repeated wars against Lebanon, its advocacy of wars against Iraq, its repeated threats of war against Iran, its alliance with Armageddon-seeking Christians in the United States, and its deepening alliance with extremist Hindus in India are now increasingly seen as major sources of global instability. Recently, two apologists of Zionism, Prager and Telushkin, wrote, "The establishment of the Jewish state has produced the most hated state in the world."[26] Moreover, since major Jewish organizations in the Western world—the visible face of diaspora Jews—are inflexibly committed to the official policies of Israel, and vigorously attack anyone disagreeing with these policies, the anger at Israel is occasionally, although unfairly, directed at diaspora Jews. In some measure, as long as this anger can be painted as anti-Semitism, this too would be grist to Israel's propaganda mill.

Zionism's cleverest use of anti-Semitism comes in a slightly disguised form now. Over the past century, Zionism has not only energized the religious right in the United States; its successes have also encouraged them to embrace a dispensationalist theology of end times. In their early years, Protestants were drawn to support Jewish "restoration" because they hoped that, once in Palestine, Jews would convert to Christianity *before* the Second Coming. More recently, as their enthusiasm for dispensationalism has grown, the Christian Zionists adjusted their theology to allow the Jews to convert *after* the Second Coming. In as much as Zionism has energized dispensationalism, then, it has effectively catalyzed anti-Semitism in the United States into its opposite—a fanatical devotion to the state of Israel. As a result, the Republican Party, with its strong base among dispensationalists, has now emerged as a stronger champion of Israel than the Democratic Party that is still supported overwhelmingly by American Jews. It is a transmutation that might well put the medieval alchemists to shame.

CHAPTER 13

CHRISTIAN ZIONISM

We welcome the friendship of Christian Zionists.
—Theodore Herzl, 1897

The entire Christian church, in its variety of branches . . . will be
compelled . . . to teach the history and development of the nascent Jewish
state. No commonwealth on earth will start with such propaganda for its
exploitation in world thought, or with such eager and minute scrutiny, by
millions of people, of its slightest detail.
—A. A. Berle, 1918

Christian Zionists favor Jewish Zionism as a step leading not to the
perpetuation but to the disappearance of the Jews.
—Morris Jastrow, 1919

Zionism has but brought to light and given practical form and a
recognized position to a principle which had long consciously or
unconsciously guided English opinion.
—Nahum Sokolow, 1919

Christian Zionism and Jewish Zionism have combined to create an
international alliance superseding anything that NATO or UN has to
offer.
—Daniel Lazare, 2003

Put positively: Other than Israel's Defense Forces, American Christian
Zionists may be the Jewish state's ultimate strategic asset.
—Daniel Pipes, 2003[1]

THE ZIONISTS DESCRIBE THEIR MOVEMENT ALMOST EXCLUSIVELY in terms
of Jewish history, Jewish aspirations, and Jewish nationalist thought. They
claim that political Zionism and the creation of Israel were the inevitable fulfillment of Jewish messianism, a biblically inspired, centuries-old

Jewish yearning to return to and reclaim Palestine. Political Zionism is traced back exclusively to Theodore Herzl and his Jewish predecessors in the nineteenth century, who worked out the secularist vision of a Jewish "restoration" that would be achieved by human agency.[2] This historiography is misleading since it leaves out the Christian antecedents of, and connections to, Zionism.

In the early decades of the nineteenth century, British and French politicians and writers proposed several schemes for restoring the Jews to Palestine. Their intent was to gain control of a land bridge to the Indian Ocean; if they chose to couple their imperialist goal with Jewish restoration, this was because "belief in the Restoration and its speedy fulfillment was already widespread in Britain."[3] Some three centuries before, the Reformation had set in motion changes in Christian theology that spoke again of Jews as a "chosen people" and hence of Palestine as a land promised to the Jews.

In several ways, the Reformation prepared an important segment of the Christian world—especially Britain and its overseas extensions that would dominate the world, starting in the nineteenth century—to champion the return of Jews to Palestine. This idea had long been heretical with Catholics, who believed that God had cancelled his covenant with the Jews when they rejected Jesus Christ. The Catholic Church did not see Palestine as a Jewish inheritance; they revered and coveted it because of its associations with Jesus and the apostles. The medieval Catholics waged their Holy War to regain control of Palestine for the Christians, not to restore it to the Jews. On the contrary, upon capturing Jerusalem, the first Crusaders massacred its Jewish population.

The Reformation marks a watershed in the history of the Latin West. By overthrowing the authority of the Catholic Church, it introduced a deep religious schism in Western Europe that led to centuries of religious wars between Catholics and Protestants. Quickly, the Protestants too splintered into sects, and these sectarian theologies were soon appropriated to serve the needs of the newly emerging nation states. The Reformation also laid the foundation for a new relationship—a rapprochement—between the Jews and several of the new Protestant sectarians. In their contest against the power of the Catholic Church, the Protestants sought the Jews as their political allies; in some circles, a philo-Semitism went hand in hand with anti-Catholicism.[4] More importantly, since the Protestants rejected the Catholic Church as God's vehicle in history, this opened up the theological space for regarding the Jews as a covenanted people. With appropriate qualifications, the Protestants were willing to recognize the Jews as God's chosen people with eternal rights to Palestine.[5]

This shift in theology did not always bring marked relief to the Jews. It may well have increased the friction between Protestants and Jews as the former hoped, prayed, and worked more zealously than the Catholics to bring "salvation" to God's chosen people. Nevertheless, after having reached its lowest point in the middle of the sixteenth century, the Jews reestablished a significant presence in much of Western Europe by the end of the eighteenth century.[6] In addition, this new theology, and later extrapolations thereof, would lay the foundations for Christian Zionism and, therefore, of an alliance between Protestants and Jews against the Islamicate world.

In order to distance themselves from the Catholics, the Protestants sought, in a variety of ways, to Judaize Christianity. This new movement, wrote Bernard Lazare in 1894, took "its roots in Hebrew sources . . . The Jewish spirit triumphed with Protestantism. In certain respects the Reformation was a return to the ancient Ebionism of the evangelical ages."[7] In their theology and affections, the Protestants replaced Rome with Jerusalem, the Pope and the Catholic saints with Hebrew prophets and warrior heroes, and some of their ministers read the Old Testament in Hebrew.[8] As a result, the Gospels lost some of their former primacy in order to accommodate the Protestant fascination with the prophets and prophecies of the Old Testament and the Apocalypse.[9] The violence and ethnocentrism of the conquest narratives in the Old Testament also were in better accord with the frequent wars waged by Protestant nations as well as their colonizing ambitions in the Americas, Africa, and Asia.

The English Puritans went farther in their Judaizing tendencies. They baptized their children under Old Testament names, made a bid to observe their Sabbath on Saturday, some rejected the divinity of Christ, and a few converted to Judaism.[10] Indeed, according to a leading Zionist, the Puritans viewed their history "as the continuation, their own lives the reflection, their own achievements the fulfillment, of the experience of a Palestine of so many centuries before; for they were, in very deed, the Jews."[11]

Contrary to the Catholics who eschewed the apocalyptic expectations of the early church, the Protestants began to develop an eschatology inspired by a literalist reading of the prophecies of the Old Testament and the Apocalypse. Already in the seventeenth century, the belief was common in England that the Second Coming of Christ would be preceded by the ingathering of all Jews in Palestine. Nahum Sokolow, a leading Zionist, has documented the interest a variety of eminent Protestant figures—including John Sadler, a close friend of Cromwell, John Milton, Isaac de la Peyrère, a distinguished French-Huguenot scholar, and others—took in Jewish restoration during the seventeenth century. "As early as the seventeenth century," writes Nahum Sokolow, "Interest [in England] in the restoration of *Israel* had become deep and general, England providing the earliest stimulus to Zionism."[12] In 1648, two English Puritans in Amsterdam petitioned the English government to repeal the Act that had banished the Jews from England. The petition expressed the hope that "this Nation of England, with the inhabitants of the Netherlands, shall be *the first and the readiest* to transport Israel's sons and daughters in their ships to the land promised to their forefathers, Abraham, Isaac and Jacob for an everlasting inheritance" (emphasis added).[13]

Not even the philosophers and scientists of the Enlightenment were immune to the new Protestant eschatology. John Locke wrote, "God is able to collect the Jews into one body . . . and set them in flourishing condition in their own land."[14] Isaac Newton too maintained a deep interest in biblical prophecies pertaining to Jewish restoration. Following a literalist reading of the Old Testament, he believed that the Jews were a chosen people, that God's covenant with them was everlasting, and he made lists of passages in the Bible that predict the return of Jews to Palestine; although, unlike his contemporaries, he thought this event was still centuries away.[15] In short, the return of Jews to Palestine was central to Newton's understanding of the final dispensation.

The fervor of the English Puritans went through a period of decline in the eighteenth century, when the rationalism of the Enlightenment was ascendant. During the nineteenth century, however, England came under the sway of evangelical ideas that recalled the fundamentalist energy of the Puritans.[16] The English evangelicals accepted the Bible as the actual words of God, and, in addition, followed the literal sense of these words. They also adopted dispensationalist eschatology—developed, among others, by an Anglo-Irish preacher, John Nelson Darby—that divided human history into seven epochs or "dispensations." Their eschatology predicted a time of growing troubles—together with the ingathering of the world's Jews in Palestine—culminating in the Second Coming, the defeat of anti-Christ, and a millennium of peace. These waves of Judaizing tendencies in Protestant Christianity—in their Puritan, evangelical, and dispensationalist versions—eventually found their way across the ocean to become even more firmly established in the United States, many of whose early settlers were convinced that *they* were the new Hebrews and the American continent was their Canaan to conquer and convert into a new Israel.

John Nelson Darby introduced his dispensationalist theology during several trips in the mid-nineteenth century to the United States, where he gained a wide following particularly among Presbyterians and Baptists. His ideas were taken up and propagated, among others, by Dwight Moody, C. I. Scofield, and William Eugene Blackstone. In 1910, Scofield published the *Scofield Reference Bible,* an annotated translation of the Bible, which developed John Darby's dispensationalist eschatology, and soon became the most influential single source of dispensationalist teachings. It has sold more than two million copies to date. William Blackstone combined his proselytizing—through books such as *Jesus Is Coming,* which has sold millions of copies—with an active campaign to persuade the U.S. government to effect the "return" of Jews to Palestine. In 1891, he sent a petition to President Benjamin Harrison and Secretary of State, James G. Blaine, together with 413 signatures—henceforth known as the Blackstone Memorial—that urged them to use "their good offices and influence with the governments of the European world to secure the holding at an early date of an international conference to consider the condition of the Israelis and their claims to Palestine as their ancient home."[17] The wide acceptance of the Memorial's restorationist message among America's elites can be gauged by its signatories, which included a former president, chief justice of the Supreme Court, the speaker of the House of Representatives, John D. Rockefeller, J. P. Morgan, members of the Congress, and editors of all the major newspapers in the five cities where the petition was circulated.[18] In 1903, Blackstone resubmitted the memorial to President Roosevelt, and submitted a new memorial to President Wilson in June 1917, a few months before the launching of the Balfour Declaration.[19]

In 1916, when Justice Brandeis discovered the Blackstone Memorial, he worked avidly to compile forty-seven pages of handwritten notes on the document. At the same time, Brandeis and Blackman also started a correspondence that lasted until the death of Blackstone in 1934. In 1916, Nathan Straus, a philanthropist and friend of Justice Brandeis, wrote to inform Blackstone that Justice Brandeis "is perfectly infatuated with the work you have done along the lines of Zionism . . . In fact, he agrees with me that you are the Father of Zionism, as your work antedates Herzl."[20]

At least one leading Zionist has acknowledged the debt that the Zionists owe to the English Puritans and Evangelicals. It was the English Christians, wrote Nahum Sokolow in 1919, who "taught the underlying principles of Jewish nationality."[21] Long before Hess, Pinsker, and Herzl, these Christians were insisting on Jewish nationhood, Jewish chosenness, and their divine right to "return" to Palestine. More importantly, they continued to make the vital connection between Jewish return and the power of Western nations.[22] It was the religious duty of Protestant nations, they insisted, to use their resources to advance this Jewish restoration. In the nineteenth century, when the strategic and economic interests of Western nations increasingly directed their attention to the weakened Ottoman Empire, the Christian Zionists became increasingly vocal. On several occasions during and after World War I, Christian Zionists in Britain used their official positions to push their country to take a favorable view of Zionist claims. It is not easy to brush aside the suspicion that the strong Zionist leanings of the British cabinet that took office in December 1916 were a relevant factor in their decision to support Zionist ambitions.

The Christian and Jewish Zionists energized each other not only at a distance; increasingly, they strengthened each other through direct contacts too. These collaborative efforts began quite early. In 1848, when Mordecai Manuel Noah sought Jewish restoration in a "new Judea," under the protection of Western powers, he presented his plan to audiences consisting mostly of Christian Zionists. In 1879 and 1882, Sir Thomas Oliphant, a former journalist and British diplomat, engaged in abortive negotiations in Istanbul to facilitate Jewish immigration to Palestine, anticipating the diplomatic exertions that would be undertaken later by Theodore Herzl. Herzl gained access to German statesmen through the efforts of William H. Hechler, a Christian Zionist.[23] In this regard, however, the most fruitful and sustained collaboration occurred between Chaim Weizmann and Christian Zionists in Britain, both before and after the launching of the Balfour Declaration.

In the United States, the collaboration between Jewish and mainstream Christian Zionists occurred informally, as in the long-drawn correspondence between William Blackstone and Justice Brandeis; but they also supported each other through the work of at least two influential organizations, the American Palestine Committee (APC) and the Christian Council on Palestine. The APC was launched in 1932 by leading American Jewish Zionists, after the British announced a partial retreat from the Balfour Declaration in the Passfield White Paper of 1930, to organize Christian support for Zionism. After a period of inactivity, the APC was revived in 1941, and its membership quickly included 70 U.S. senators, 120 congressmen, the Attorney General, the Secretary of Interior, 21 state governors, and many eminent civic, religious, and labor leaders. Very quickly, to this list were added the governors, mayors, members of state legislatures, and other prominent public figures. Most importantly, the APC and other organized groups of Christian supporters of Zionism, orchestrated support for Zionism in the ranks of the elites. In addition, the members of the APC—eventually numbering some 15,000—mobilized popular support for Zionism by taking up frequent speaking engagements.[24] Also working closely with the Jewish leadership of American Zionism, the leading Protestant thinkers—including such luminaries as Paul Tillich and Reinhold Niebuhr—created the Christian Council on Palestine in 1942 to promote Zionist goals among the

Protestant clergy.[25] The Council spread its message through conferences, seminars, and publications.

In order to grasp the significance of the Reformation for the career of political Zionism, it is important to consider briefly the attitude of the Catholic Church to this movement. Theodore Herzl gained audience with Pope Leo XIII in January 1904, some three years after he first sought this meeting. The Pope, however, refused to endorse Zionism. "We cannot prevent the Jews from going to Jerusalem," he told Herzl, "but we could never sanction it." Strikingly, according to Herzl's testimony of this meeting, the Pope added, "If you come to Palestine and settle with your people there, we shall have churches and priests ready to baptize all of you." Pietro Cardinal Gasparri, the Secretary of State to the Pope, opposed the Balfour Declaration and the British mandate over Palestine. In March 1922, the Cardinal argued that the Zionist plan would establish "an absolute economic, administrative and political preponderance of Jews," and "would act as the instrument for subordinating native populations." However, the pope preferred to see "a third power, neither Jew nor Arab," in control of Palestine. [26] That "third power," presumably, would be Christian and Western.

The Protestant Reformation created much more than a climate of opinion, which favored the launching and success of Zionism. For nearly three centuries before Theodore Herzl launched the Jewish nationalist movement, Protestants of various denominations had popularized the idea of Jewish restoration, made it a part of Protestant eschatology, brought this scheme to the attention of Western governments, and, later, made peremptory efforts to incorporate it into the political agenda of Britain and the United States. Without this preparatory work, without the wide support that Christian Zionists had created for Jewish restoration, without the interest that Western governments had shown during the early nineteenth century in Jewish restoration, the Jewish Zionists may have had to struggle harder to launch their project and carry it to completion. The evangelical support for Zionist causes, especially in recent decades, has greatly enhanced the ability of the Jewish lobby to shape U.S. policies toward the Middle East.

CHAPTER 14

A SUMMING UP

> The ultimate goal . . . is, in time, to take over the Land of Israel and to
> restore to the Jews the political independence they have been deprived of
> for these two thousand years . . . The Jews will yet arise and, arms in hand
> (if need be), declare that they are the masters of their ancient homeland.
> —Vladimir Dubnow, 1882[1]

ZIONISM IS BEST DESCRIBED AS AN ABNORMAL nationalism. This singular
fact has engendered a history of deepening conflicts between Israel—in
alliance with Western societies—and the Islamicate more generally.

Jewish "nationalism" was abnormal for two reasons. It was homeless: it
did not possess a homeland. The Jews of Europe were not a majority in, or
even exercised control over, any territory that could become the basis of a
Jewish state. We do not know of another nationalist movement in recent
memory that started with such a land deficit—that is, without a homeland.

Arguably, Jewish nationalism was without a nation too. The Jews were
a *religious* aggregate, consisting of communities, scattered across many
regions and countries, some only tenuously connected to others, but who
shared the religious traditions derived from, or an identity connected
to, Judaism. Over the centuries, Jews had been taught that a divinely
appointed Messiah would restore them to Zion; but such a Messiah never
appeared; or when he did, his failure to deliver "proved" that he was false.
Indeed, while the Jews prayed for the appearance of the Messiah, they
had no notion about when this might happen. In addition, since the
nineteenth century, Reform Jews have interpreted their chosenness meta-
phorically. Max Nordau complained bitterly that for the Reform Jew, "the
word Zion had just as little meaning as the word dispersion . . . He denies
that there is a Jewish people and that he is a member of it."[2]

Since Zionism was a nationalism without a homeland or a nation, its
protagonists would have to create both. To compensate for the first deficit, the Zionists would have to *acquire* a homeland: they would have to
expropriate territory that belonged to another people. In other words, a

homeless nationalism, of necessity, is a charter for conquest and—if it is exclusionary—for ethnic cleansing. At the same time, the Zionists would have to start *creating* a Jewish nation out of the heterogeneous Jewish colons they would assemble in their newly minted homeland. At the least, they would have to create a nucleus of Jews who were willing to settle in Palestine and committed to creating the infrastructure of a Jewish society and state in Palestine. For many years, this nucleus would be small, since, Jews, overwhelmingly, preferred assimilation and revolution in Europe to colonizing Palestine.

A Jewish nation would begin to grow around this small nucleus only if the Zionists could demonstrate that their scheme was not a chimera. The passage of the Zionist plan—from chimera to reality—would be delivered by three events: imposition of tight immigration restrictions in most Western countries starting in the 1900s, the Balfour Declaration of 1917, and the rise to power of the Nazis in 1933. As a result, when European Jews began fleeing Nazi persecution, most of them had nowhere to go to but Palestine.

In their bid to create a Jewish state in Palestine, the Zionists could not stop at half-measures. They could not—and did not wish to—introduce Jews as only *one* element in the demography of the conquered territory. The Zionists sought to establish a Jewish state in Palestine; this had always been their goal. Officially, they never acknowledge that the creation of a Jewish state would have to be preceded, accompanied, or followed by ethnic cleansing. Nevertheless, it is clear from the record now available that Zionists wanted nothing less than to make Palestine "as Jewish as England is English."[3] If the Palestinians could not be bribed to leave, they would have to be forced out.

The Zionists were determined to reenact in the middle of the twentieth century the exclusive settler colonialism of an earlier epoch. They were determined to repeat the supremacist history of the white colons in the Americas and Oceania. By the measure of *any* historical epoch, much less that of an age of decolonization, the Zionist project was radical in the fate it had planned for the Palestinians: their complete or near-complete displacement from Palestine. A project so daring, so radical, so anachronistic could only emerge from unlimited hubris, deep racial contempt for the Palestinians, and a conviction that the "primitive" Palestinians would prove to be utterly lacking in the capacity to resist their own dispossession.

The Zionists faced another challenge. They had to convince Jews that they are a *nation*, a Jewish nation, who deserved more than any nation in the world—because of the much greater antiquity of Jews—to have their own state, a Jewish state in Palestine. It was the duty of Jews, therefore, to work for the creation of this Jewish state by supporting the Zionists, and, most importantly, by emigrating to Palestine. Most Jews in the developed Western countries had little interest in becoming Jewish pioneers in Palestine; their lives had improved greatly in the previous two or three generations and they did not anticipate any serious threats from anti-Semitism. The Jews in Eastern Europe did face serious threats to their lives and property from anti-Semites, but they too greatly preferred moving to safer and more prosperous countries in Western Europe, the Americas, South Africa, and Australia. Persuading Jews to move to Palestine was proving to be a far more difficult task than opening up Palestine to unlimited Jewish colonization. Zionism needed a stronger boost from anti-Semites than they had provided until the early 1930s.

The Zionists always understood that their movement would have to be driven by Jewish fears of anti-Semitism. They were also quite sanguine that there would be no paucity of such assistance, especially from anti-Semites in Eastern Europe. Indeed, now that the Zionists had announced a political program to rid Europe of its Jews, would the anti-Semites retreat just when some Jews were *implicitly* asking for their assistance in their own evacuation from Europe? This was a match made in heaven for the anti-Semites. Once the Zionists had also brought the anti-Semites in messianic camouflage—the Christian Zionists—on board, this alliance became more broad-based and more enduring.[4] Together, by creating and continuing to support Israel, these allies would lay the foundations of a deepening conflict against the Islamicate.

Zionism was a grave assault on the history of the global resistance to imperialism that unfolded even as Jewish colons in Palestine laid the foundations of their colonial settler state. The Zionists sought to abolish the ground realities in the Middle East established by Islam over the previous thirteen hundred years. They sought to overturn the demography of Palestine, to insert a European presence in the heart of the Islamicate, and to serve as the forward base for Western powers intent on dominating the Middle East. The Zionists could succeed only by combining the forces of the Christian and Jewish West in an assault that would almost certainly be seen as a new, latter-day Crusade to marginalize the Islamicate peoples in the Middle East.

It was delusional to assume that the Zionist challenge to the Islamicate would go unanswered. The Zionists had succeeded in imposing their Jewish state on the Islamicate because of the luck of timing—in addition to all the other factors that had favored them. The Islamicate was at its weakest in the decades following the destruction of the Ottoman Empire; even a greatly weakened Ottoman Empire had resisted for more than two decades Zionist pressures to grant them a charter to create a Jewish state in Palestine. The first wave of Arab resistance against Israel—led by secular nationalists from the nascent bourgeoisie classes—lacked the structures to wage a people's war. Taking advantage of this Arab weakness, Israel quickly dismantled the Arab nationalist movement, whose ruling classes began making compromises with Israel and its Western allies. This setback to the resistance was temporary.

The Arab nationalist resistance would slowly be replaced by another that would draw upon Islamic roots; this return to indigenous ideas and structures would lay the foundations of a resistance that would be broader, deeper, many-layered, and more resilient than the one it would replace. The overarching ambitions of Israel—to establish its hegemony over the central lands of the Islamicate—would guarantee the emergence of this new response. The quick collapse of the Arab nationalist resistance in the face of Israeli victories ensured that the deeper Islamicate response would emerge sooner rather than later. As a result, Israel today confronts—now in alliance with Arab rulers—the entire Islamicate, a great mass of humanity, which is determined to overthrow this alliance. If one recalls that the Islamicate is now a global community, enjoying demographic dominance in a region that stretches from Mauritania to Mindanao—and now counts more than a billion and a half people, whose growth rate exceeds that of any other collectivity—one can easily begin to comprehend the eventual scale of this Islamicate resistance against the Zionist imposition.

In the era preceding the rise of the Nazis, the Zionist idea—even from a Jewish standpoint—was an affront to more than two millennia of their own history. Jews had started migrating to the farthest points in the Mediterranean long before the second destruction of the Temple, where they settled down and converted many local peoples to the Jewish faith. Over time, conversions to Judaism established Jewish communities farther afield—beyond the Mediterranean world. In the 1890s, however, a small but determined cabal of European Jews proposed a plan to abrogate the history of global Jewish communities extending over millennia. They were determined to accomplish what the worst anti-Semites had failed to do: to empty Europe and the Middle East of their Jewish population and transport them to Palestine, a land to which they had a spiritual connection—just as Muslims in Bangladesh, Bosnia, and Burkina Faso are connected to Mecca and Medina—but to which their racial or historical connections were nonexistent or tenuous at best. Was the persecution of Jews in Europe before the 1890s sufficient cause to justify such a radical reordering of the human geography of the world's Jewish populations?

A more ominous implication flowed from another peculiarity of Zionism. Unlike other white settlers, the Jewish colons lacked a natural mother country, a Jewish state that could support their colonization of Palestine. In the face of this deficiency, the career of any settler colonialism would have ended prematurely. Instead, because of the manner in which this deficit was overcome, the Zionists acquired the financial, political, and military support of much of the Western world. This was not the result of a conspiracy, but flowed from the peculiar position that Jews—at the end of the nineteenth century—had come to occupy in the imagination, geography, economy, and the polities of the Western world.

The Zionists drew their primary support from the Western Jews, many of whom by the middle of the nineteenth century were members of the most influential segments of Western societies. Over time, as Western Jews gravitated to Zionism, their awesome financial and intellectual assets would become available to the Jewish colons in Palestine. The Jewish colons drew their leadership—in the areas of politics, the economy, industry, civilian and military technology, organization, propaganda, and science—from the pool of Europe's best. It can scarcely be doubted that the Jewish colons brought overwhelming advantages to their contest against the Palestinians and the neighboring Arabs. No other colonists, contemporaneous with the Zionists or in the nineteenth century, brought the same advantages to their enterprise vis-à-vis the natives.

Pro-Zionist Western Jews would make a more critical contribution to the long-term success of Zionism. They would mobilize their resources—as well-placed members of the financial, intellectual, and cultural elites of Western societies—to make the case for Zionism, to silence criticism of Israel, and generate domestic political pressures to secure the support of Western powers for Israel. In other words, the Zionist ability to recruit Western allies depended critically upon the peculiar position that Jews held in the imagination, prejudices, history, geography, economy, and politics of Western societies.

The Jews have always had a "special" relationship with the Christian West; they were special even as objects of Christian hatred. Judaism has always occupied the unenviable position of being a parent religion that was overtaken by a heresy. For many centuries, the Christians regarded the Jews, hitherto God's "chosen people," with disdain for rejecting Jesus. Nevertheless, they incorporated the Jewish scriptures into their own religious canon. This tension lies at the heart of Western ambivalence toward Jews; it is also one of the chief sources of the enduring hatred that Christians have directed toward the Jews.

In addition, starting in the fifteenth century, the Protestants entered into a new relationship with Judaism and Jews. In many ways, the Protestants drew inspiration from the Hebrew Bible, began to read its words literally, and paid greater attention to its prophesies about end times. The theology of the English Puritans, in particular, assigned a special role to the Jews in their eschatology. The Jews would have to gather in Jerusalem before the Second Coming of Jesus; later, this theology was taken up by the English Evangelicals who carried it to the United States. Over time, with the growing successes of (Jewish) Zionism, the Evangelicals slowly became its most ardent supporters in the United States. The obverse of the Evangelical's Zionism is a virulent hatred of Islam and Muslims.

Most importantly, however, it was the entry of Jews into mainstream European society—mostly during the nineteenth century—that paved the way for Zionist influence over the politics of several key Western states. The Zionists very deftly used the Jewish presence in the ranks of European elites to set up a competition among the great Western powers—especially Britain, Germany, and France—to gain Jewish support in their wars with each other, and to undermine the radical movements in Europe that were also dominated by Jews. Starting with World War II, the pro-Zionist Jews would slowly build a network of organizations, develop their rhetoric, and take leadership positions in important sectors of American civil society until they had gained the ability to define the parameters within which the United States could operate in the Middle East.

Serendipitously, it appears, pro-Zionist Jews also found, ready at hand, a rich assortment of negative energies in the West that they could harness to their own project. The convergence of their interests with that of the anti-Semites was perhaps the most propitious. The anti-Semites wanted the Jews out of Europe, and so did the Zionists. Anti-Semitism would also become the chief facilitator of the Jewish nationalism that the Zionists sought to create. In addition, the Zionists could muster support for their project by appealing to Western religious bigotry against Muslims as well as their racist bias against the Arabs as "inferior" nonwhites.

The Zionists would also argue that their project was closely aligned with the strategic interests of Western powers in the Middle East. This claim had lost its validity by the end of the nineteenth century, when Britain was firmly established in Egypt and it was the dominant power in the Indian Ocean. Indeed, the insertion of an *exclusionary* Jewish colonial settler state into the Islamicate geographical matrix was certain to provoke waves of resistance from the Muslim peoples. Western interests in the Islamicate were not positively aligned with the Zionist project. Yet, once Israel had been created, it would provoke anti-Western feelings in the Middle East, which, conveniently, the Zionists would deepen and offer as the rationale for supporting and arming Israel to protect Western interests against Arab and, later, Islamicate threats.

Israel was the product of a partnership that seems unlikely at first blush, between Western Jews and the Christian West. It is the powerful alchemy of the Zionist idea that produced and sustained this partnership. The Zionist project to create a Jewish state in Palestine possessed the power to convert two historical antagonists, Jews and Gentiles, into allies united in a common imperialist enterprise against the Islamicate. At different times, the Zionists have harnessed all the negative energies of the West—its imperialism, anti-Semitism, Crusading zeal, anti-Islamic bigotry, and racism—and focused them on a new project, the creation of a surrogate Western state in the Islamicate heartland. At the same time, the West could derive considerable satisfaction from the success of the Zionist project. Western societies could take ownership of, and revel in, the triumphs of this colonial state as their own; they could congratulate themselves for helping "save" the Jewish people; they could feel they had made adequate amends for their history of anti-Semitism; they could feel they had finally paid back the Arabs and Turks for their conquests of Christian lands. Israel possessed a marvelous capacity to feed several of the West's egotistical needs.

As a vehicle for facilitating Jewish entry into the stage of world history, the Zionist project was a stroke of brilliance. Since the Jews were influential, but without a state of their own, the Zionists were going to leverage Western power in their cause. As the Zionist plan would unfold, inflicting pain on the Islamicate, evoking Islamicate anger against the West and Jews, the complementarities between the two ancient adversaries would deepen, and, over time, new commonalities would be discovered or created between these two antagonist strains of Western history. In the United States, the Zionist movement would encourage Evangelical Christians—who looked upon the birth of Israel as the fulfillment of end-time prophecies—to become fanatic partisans of Israel. The West had hitherto traced its central ideas and institutions to Rome and Athens; in the wake of Zionist successes, it would be repackaged as a Judeo-Christian civilization, drawing its core principles, its inspiration from the Old Testament. This reframing would not only underscore the Jewish roots of the Western world: it would also make a point of emphasizing that Islam is the outsider, the eternal adversary opposed to both.

Zionism owes its success solely to this unlikely partnership. The Zionists could not have created a Jewish state in Palestine by bribing the Ottomans into granting them a charter to colonize Palestine. Despite his offers of loans, investments, technology, and diplomatic expertise, Theodore Herzl was repeatedly rebuffed by the Ottoman Sultan.[5] It is even less likely that the Zionists, at any time, could have mobilized a Jewish army to invade and occupy Palestine, against Ottoman and Arab opposition.[6] The Zionist partnership with the West was indispensable for the creation of a Jewish state.

This partnership was also fateful. It produced a powerful new dialectic, which has encouraged Israel—as the political center of the Jewish diaspora and the chief outpost of the West in the heart of the Islamic world—to become ever more aggressive in its designs against the Islamicate. In turn, a fragmented, weak and humiliated Islamicate, more resentful and determined after every defeat at the hands of Israel, has been driven to embrace increasingly radical ideas and methods to recover its dignity, wholeness, and power, and to seek to attain this recovery on the strength of Islamic ideas. This destabilizing dialectic has now brought the West itself into a direct confrontation against the Islamicate. This is the tragedy of Israel. It is a tragedy whose ominous consequences, including those that have yet to unfold, were contained in the very idea of an exclusive Jewish state in Palestine.

PART III

GROWING A SPECIAL RELATIONSHIP

The expansion and consolidation of United States Jewry in the late nineteenth and twentieth centuries was as important in Jewish history as the creation of Israel itself; in some ways more important. For, if the fulfillment of Zionism gave the harassed diaspora an ever-open refuge with sovereign rights to determine and defend its destiny, the growth of US Jewry was an accession of power of an altogether different order, which gave Jews an important, legitimate and permanent part in shaping the policies of the greatest state on earth.

—Paul Johnson[1]

CHAPTER 15

BEFORE THE SPECIAL
RELATIONSHIP

The Jews from every tribe have descended in force, and they are
determined to break in with a jimmy if they are not let in.
                                    —Edward House, October 1917[2]

Don't worry, Dr. Wise, Palestine is yours.
                                    —Woodrow Wilson, March 1919[3]

IF THE BRITISH DID NOT QUITE VIEW Zionism as serving their strategic
interests in the Middle East—except, temporarily, in the middle of World
War I—did the successive U.S. administrations view this colonial project
any differently? This question gains urgency during the years 1939 to
1948, when the United States took over from Britain the mantle of surrogate mother country to the Zionist colonial settler movement.

Why did the United States step into the breach, starting in 1939,
just when the British were convinced that carrying the Zionist project to
completion would seriously damage their strategic interests in the Middle
East? Considering that the United States, soon after the war, would succeed Britain as the paramount power in the Middle East, it would appear
that the calculations that Britain had made concerning the strategic costs
of supporting Zionism would apply with equal force to the United States.
Indeed, in the years after World War II when global communism and
Arab nationalism were looming on the horizon, the U.S. government
should have viewed the strategic costs of Zionism with even greater concern than Britain. If these strategic costs did not dampen President Truman's espousal of the Zionist project, was that because his hands were tied
by the imperatives of domestic politics flowing from Zionism?

In order to analyze the sources of U.S. commitment to Zionism, it
may be helpful to begin by identifying the successive stages of this relationship. The first stage spans the years from 1897 to the start of World

War I, when the United States played no significant role in Zionist efforts to secure Palestine for Jewish colonization. This changed during the second stage, from 1914 to 1939, when the United States assumed a supportive role in securing British and international support for the Zionist project and, later, exerting pressure on Britain to prevent it from backtracking on its commitment to Zionism. Starting in 1939, when Britain put its Zionist commitment on the backburner, the United States began to ratchet its pressures on Britain, and, after the war, assumed the leading role in shepherding the Zionist project through the United Nations. However, once the demands of the Cold War began to take center stage in America's strategic thinking, the United States sought to camouflage its support for Israel. During this fourth phase, Israel enjoyed the patronage of three mother countries, including the United States, France and Germany, with the United States leading from behind the scenes. Israeli relations with the United States entered a new phase, starting in the late 1950s, when the latter began to assume a more direct and visible role in building Israel's military superiority over the Arabs. The level of U.S. support for Israel—military, economic, and diplomatic—grew rapidly starting in the early 1970s, and, by the early 1980s, Israel, with the support of a powerful Israel lobby, had acquired the power to determine within wide limits the terms of its "special relationship" with the United States. Instead of declining after the end of the Cold War—as one might have expected—the commitment of American politicians to Israel has become nearly as important as their loyalty to the United States itself.

A comparison of the American and British relationship with the Zionist project points to important differences in their trajectories. After helping to launch the Zionist project in the middle of World War I, Britain took measures at the beginning of World War II that might well have aborted the creation of a Jewish state. In contrast, the United States made episodic interventions on the behalf of Zionists in the period before World War II, but since then its commitment to Israel has continued to grow, and since the late 1950s has become an enduring and vital part of its policies toward the Middle East. Why did the United States and Britain follow such different trajectories in their relations with the Zionist project especially during the period when they—Britain, between the two World Wars, and the United States since World War II—were the paramount powers in the Middle East? Was the Zionist project always perceived as a strategic asset by U.S. policy makers?

In subsequent chapters, we will argue that the United States continued to regard Israel as a strategic liability well into the 1950s. Israel took on the characteristics of a "strategic asset" only slowly in the period following its creation. It is our fundamental thesis that this transformation was driven by forces released by the creation of Israel itself, the power of the Jewish diaspora to mobilize Western support, and the ability of the Jewish state to leverage this support to alter the strategic map of the Middle East. A comprehensive examination of the forces that have driven this transformation—of Israel from strategic liability to a strategic asset—must be grounded, historically and dialectically, in the cumulative exchanges among four sets of actors—the Yishuv/Israel, the Israel lobby in the United States, Western governments, and the Arab and Islamicate world—that have been directly involved in or affected by the Zionist project. Nevertheless, despite the involvement of multiple actors in Zionism, as advocates or adversaries, it is important to remember that the Zionists have always occupied the driver's seat. They proposed this project, forced it upon the attention of Western publics and Western politicians, harnessed various negative Western energies to their advantage, and used the political resources of Western Jewry—their votes, their presence in Western intellectual discourse, their money, and their access to the highest levels of decision making—to constantly ratchet the pressure on Western powers to deepen and maintain their commitment to the Zionist project.

. . .

Although the U.S. president and Congress played only a supporting role in the process that produced the Balfour Declaration of November 1917—and, later, its incorporation into the colonial mandate awarded to Britain over Palestine—they brought no reservations to their advocacy of Zionism. However, this enthusiasm was not shared by the career officials in the U.S. State Department. U.S. support for Zionism was also contrary to the economic and cultural interests of Americans with a stake in the Middle East.

In opposition to his own Secretary of State, who was excluded from these deliberations, President Wilson, in October 1917, officially extended U.S. support to the Balfour Declaration. In 1920, the president went beyond the wording of the Balfour Declaration, which had offered support only for the creation of a "national home for the Jewish people," and began to pledge his support for the creation of a Jewish commonwealth in Palestine.[4] In June 1922, the Congress unanimously passed a joint resolution, stating that the United States "favors the establishment in Palestine of a national home for the Jewish people."[5] Finally, by signing the Anglo-American Convention in 1924, the United States formalized its "endorsement of Britain's control over Palestine and, by reiterating provisions of the Balfour Declaration and of the British Mandate instrument, formally accepted Zionism in Palestine."[6] Short of taking on the role of a mother country, the United States had officially extended the strongest moral support to the Zionist project in Palestine.

There is little indication, however, that the strongly pro-Zionist stance of the United States was motivated by aims—to use Noam Chomsky's phrase—that were "close to those of elite elements with real power."[7] On the one hand, this position marked a departure from the long-standing American policy of avoiding entanglements in the political rivalries of European powers. Moreover, the president did not explain, at any time, what changes in economic, political or cultural interests of the United States had made this departure from a venerable policy necessary. President Wilson's support for the Balfour Declaration also contradicted his own principle of self-determination that he believed should guide the peace settlement after the war. The U.S. administration could scarcely plead ignorance of the strong opposition to the Zionist project that existed in Palestine and every part of the Arab and Islamicate world.[8] In Palestine, however, in the words of Lord Balfour, the commitment to Zionism "would inevitably exclude *numerical* self-determination" (emphasis added).[9]

Indeed, there is no indication that the establishment of a Jewish state in Palestine would be regarded with favor by American capital with a commercial interest in the region. As Jewish capital would gain ascendancy in Palestine—and the region—it could it be expected to offer competition to American commercial interests in the entire Middle East. In addition, the establishment of the Jewish National Fund in 1901, with the aim of acquiring and retaining *exclusive* ownership of all lands in Palestine, could not have augured well for American developers who had their own plans for investments in real estate in Palestine.

It is also far from obvious that the parceling of Arab territories of the Ottoman Empire between the British, French, and a future Jewish state, was in the best interests of American oil corporations.[10] Given that oil had emerged as a key military asset during World War I, the United States could have pushed for granting early independence to the former Ottoman territories, since this would have leveled the playing field for U.S. oil corporations in the entire region.[11] Is it possible that the United States was not in a position to consider such an alternative—explaining why President Wilson shelved the report of the King-Crane Commission that proposed a U.S. mandate over the Arab territories of the Ottoman Empire—since this would have jeopardized the Zionist project? In analyzing the causation behind historical developments, it may be useful to look at some plausible alternatives that did not emerge: and ask, why?

Although the commercial interests of the United States in the Middle East were quite modest, the American Protestant establishment had very substantial interests in the Arab provinces of the Ottoman Empire. Over the past century, they had established churches, schools, and hospitals, especially in the Levant. The U.S. government had shown solicitude for these interests only a few years before, when President Woodrow Wilson excluded the Ottoman Empire from his declaration of war against the Axis Powers.[12] Toward the end of the war, the American missionary establishment in the Middle East began to lobby the United States for the Arab right to self-determination.[13] Their pressures at the Paris Peace Conference in 1919 persuaded President Wilson to dispatch a commission to the Middle East to ascertain the readiness of the people of the region for self-determination. This Commission—known as the King-Crane Commission—concluded that the Zionist program was tantamount to a "gross violation" of the principle of self-determination. It also recommended that the mandate over the former Arab Ottoman territories (minus Iraq), in accordance with the wishes of the people of the region, should be awarded to the United States. In the event, the Commission's report was published in 1922, only after President Wilson was out of office. There is no evidence that the president had read the report.[14]

In the assessments made by the U.S. State Department during these years, the Zionist project did not advance the strategic interests of the United States. President Wilson's Secretary of State, Robert Lansing, was opposed to Zionism because he believed this would alienate the Ottomans.[15] Contrary to the strongly pro-Zionist positions of the politicians, the career officials at the State Department were much less enthusiastic about Zionism; they urged a neutralist position upon the administration, with warnings that unrestricted Jewish immigration into Palestine would cause bloodshed between Jews and Arabs.[16] Zionist partisans are eager to accuse the officials at the State Department of anti-Semitism because they did not show the appropriate measure of enthusiasm for Zionism. More plausibly, the distancing of the career officials in the State Department can be explained by their insulation from electoral pressures to preserve their jobs. In any case, those who see a preponderance of anti-Semites in the State Department must explain why individuals with this proclivity would be drawn to the bureaucracy but shun politics.

It is easy to identify several domestic tendencies in the United States that were aligned with Zionism at this time. Leaving aside Jewish opinion—for now—these tendencies included anti-Semitism, Christian Zionism, Christian antipathy toward Muslims, and anti-Arab racism. In order to influence U.S. foreign policy, these tendencies would have to be articulated, mobilized, and directed by *organized* groups toward a particular project. There is no evidence that there existed, during this period, movements led by anti-Semites, anti-Arab racists, or anti-Islamic bigots, working with the Jewish Zionists, to use the power of the U.S.

government to punish the Palestinians, evict the Jews from the United States, or capture the Christian Holy Lands. We need to investigate if the Christian Zionists in the United States, at this stage, were engaged in any organized efforts to translate their eschatology into political actions.

Christian Zionism has taken two forms in American Protestant theology. At first, Jewish restoration flowed primarily from Jehovah's grant of Palestine to the Jews; it was not yet linked to any narrative of the end times. This version of Christian Zionism arrived in the United States with the English Puritans, and has since enjoyed a strong following among various Protestant denominations in the United States. Starting in the late nineteenth century, however, a new fundamentalist Christianity gained ground, which linked Jewish "restoration" to their narrative of the end times. They began to believe that the Jews would have to be gathered in Palestine *before* the Second Coming. This new eschatology was propagated by John Nelson Darby, an English evangelist, during six trips he made to the United States between 1859 and 1874. It was later enshrined in a new annotated edition of the Bible prepared by Cyrus Scofield, known as the *Scofield Reference Bible*, first published by Oxford University Press in 1909. More than any other text, this edition of the Bible helped to popularize Christian Zionism in the United States; it had sold two million copies by the end of World War II.[17]

In the early decades of the twentieth century, Christian Zionism primarily offered moral support to Jewish Zionists. There are few indications that they were exerting any organized political pressures for the restoration of Jews to Palestine. The best-known attempt by Christian Zionists in the United States to translate their beliefs into foreign policy was the petition of 1891, accompanied by a campaign of newspaper ads, urging President Benjamin Harrison to convene an international conference "to consider the condition of Israelites and their claims to Palestine as their ancient home, and to promote in all other just and proper ways the alleviation of their suffering condition."[18] However, this petition—known as the Blackstone Memorial—was almost entirely the work of one tireless campaigner, William Eugene Blackstone, a lay preacher and author of a millenarian tract. Although the petition carried 413 signatures—including those of the chief justice of the Supreme Court, the House Speaker, and two big financiers—it did not lead to any action by the U.S. government.[19] In 1916, Blackstone submitted a second petition with support from the leading American Jewish Zionists.[20]

As the Zionists ramped up their efforts during World War I, this evoked two responses from the Christian Zionists. In 1916, the American Presbyterian General Assembly passed a resolution supporting Zionist aims.[21] In addition, the British conquest of Jerusalem, the passage of the Balfour

Declaration in 1917, and the opening of Palestine to Jewish immigration—most potent signs that the ingathering of Jews in Palestine was on its way—produced two "prophetic conferences" in 1918, but failed to impart any enduring political momentum to the Christian Zionists in the United States. Indeed, in the years preceding the end of World War II, the Christian Zionists "withdrew, to a large extent, from the public arena." During the interwar years, the Christian Zionists "did not see themselves as influential national figures whose voices would be heard by the policy makers in Washington or as people who could advance a political agenda on the national or international level."[22] On the whole, there was little organized lobbying by Christian Zionists before 1948—or sometime afterward—to generate pressures on the U.S. government in support of Zionism.

In the United States, the Zionist cause found its most influential, best organized, and fully committed advocates in the American Jewish community. In 1914, the Jewish population in the United States stood at three million, having grown fifteenfold since 1870. Since this population was concentrated in key cities—including New York, New Jersey, Boston, Philadelphia, Chicago, and San Francisco—their electoral weight far exceeded their share in the population.[23] Once they overcame the early diffidence of affluent Jews of German extraction to their cause, the Jewish Zionists established a strong network of national and local organizations dedicated to the Zionist cause. Local Jewish organizations with Zionist aims and sympathies emerged as soon as the First Zionist Congress was convened in Basel in 1897. At about the same time, national organizations were also formed, most notably, the Knights of Zion, the Federation of American Zionists, and the United Zionists.[24] Several Zionist youth organizations were also set up in the years before the war; they are important because they helped to recruit several leaders of the Zionist movement in the United States, including Abba Hillel Silver and Emanuel Neumann. In 1912, the *Hadassa* was established, which soon became the largest Zionist organization for women in the United States.[25]

The Zionist movement in the United States gained prestige and political influence when Louis Brandeis took over its leadership in 1914, bringing with him several leading Jewish progressives into the movement.[26] The primary factor behind the surge in Zionist fortunes at this time, however, was the onset of the war. The central leadership of the Zionist movement, based in Europe, had been concentrating on the major European powers—mainly Britain and Germany—to obtain the international backing for their colonization project. With the onset of the war, the United States became a factor in the strategic deliberations of Britain and Germany, the first eager to expedite U.S. entry into the war as its ally, and the second anxious to keep it neutral. As a result, both Britain and Germany began their courtship of the Zionists to get American Jews on its side. Further, the Zionists had long believed that the dismemberment of the Ottoman Empire in a major war would create the window of opportunity for inserting their colonial project in Palestine. When this moment arrived, with the Ottoman entry into the war on the side of Germany in October 1914, this gave tremendous impetus to the hopes of the Zionists. They were convinced their historical moment had arrived: Palestine would soon be theirs.

The energized Zionist movement is reflected in the dramatic growth in the membership of the Zionist Organization of America (ZOA), the central organ of the Zionist movement in the United States since 1897. In 1914, the ZOA had a cadre of 12,000 activists, but this rose to 149,235 four years later. Once the Zionists had achieved their main objective—the commitment of Britain and the United States by November 1917 to the Balfour Declaration—the ZOA membership quickly fell back to 21,000 in 1920.[27] The World Zionist Organization would have different priorities for several years. It would direct its energy to attracting Jewish settlers to Palestine, acquiring land in Palestine, and building the infrastructure for a Jewish state there.

The growth in the membership of the ZOA offers only a partial picture of the support that the Zionists enjoyed in the United States at this time. Of greater significance was the success of the revitalized ZOA in mobilizing the entire Jewish community in support of Zionist demands. Once the Jewish masses had been mobilized behind the Zionist cause, the leaders of the American Jewish establishment—who had until now maintained a safe distance from the Zionist movement—were also persuaded to take a stronger interest in Zionist activities. At a preparatory conference in 1916, "it became the declared policy of *all* American Jewish organizations not only to press for equal rights for east European Jewry *but also to secure Jewish rights in Palestine*" (emphasis added).[28] In other words, virtually the entire American Jewry had thrown its full weight behind the Zionist movement when Zionist leaders began serious negotiations for the creation of a Jewish state in Palestine.

When all the advances of the Zionist movement are brought together—the dramatic growth in the cadre of activists, the mass mobilization of Jews, and the support of the American Jewish establishment—we begin to acquire a better estimate of the political influence that the Zionist movement could now exercise over the U.S. political system. The Zionists had now become a force in the elections to the Congress and the president, and they had built up a network for lobbying congressmen, senators, and the White House. This power was magnified by the visibility of the new leadership that Louis Brandeis brought into the ZOA. The early Zionist leaders, who were active before 1914, enjoyed little visibility in the wider American society. This changed after 1914. "An examination of the group of new Zionists as a whole in both American society and the Jewish community indicates that they had achieved a degree of prominence in the dominant society and were now turning to lead their minority group."[29] From their vantage points in the wider American society—as civic leaders, philanthropists, leaders of labor movements, and prominent lawyers—the new Zionist leadership was also in a position to enlist the support of the liberal and progressive segments of American society. Finally, at least two of the most prominent leaders of the Zionist movement, Rabbi Stephen Wise and Louis Brandeis, were important backers of Woodrow Wilson in the presidential elections and joined the inner circle of his advisers when he was elected to office.[30]

We can identify at least three successful cases of political interventions by the Zionists in support of their cause between 1917 and 1922. In September 1917, when the British cabinet sought President Wilson's advice on the question of issuing a declaration of support for the Zionist cause, he replied that only an expression of sympathy for Zionism was desirable, without making any commitment. This was a serious setback to the Zionist movement. Instantly, Chaim Weizmann was in touch with the Zionist leadership in the United States, who, led by Louis Brandeis, succeeded in reversing President Wilson's decision. "The Zionists had surmounted yet another major hurdle owing to the help from American Jewry."[31] The Zionist pressure on the White House was so intense, it led Colonel Edward House, close friend and advisor to President Wilson, to complain that "the Jews from every tribe have descended in force, and they are determined to break in with a jimmy if they are not let in."[32]

The passage of a joint Congress resolution endorsing the Balfour Declaration in September 1922 was almost wholly due to the efforts of American Zionists. In March 1922, two groups of Zionists, from Massachusetts and New York, approached Henry Cabot Lodge and Congressman Hamilton Fish—respectively—to bring a resolution supporting Zionism for a joint vote by the Congress. In September 1922, the Congress passed the resolution unanimously. Ten days later, it was signed by President Harding who said that returning the Hebrew people to their "historic national home" would allow them to "enter on a new and yet greater phase of their contribution to the advance of humanity."[33]

A more dramatic example of Zionist intervention in the execution of U.S. foreign policy occurred in 1917. Partly in response to the lobbying of the Protestant missionary establishment, President Wilson had dispatched Henry Morgenthau, a former ambassador to the Porte, to look into the possibilities of arriving at a separate peace with the Ottomans. The Zionists were alarmed at this move. Its success could scuttle their plan to detach Palestine from the Ottoman territory and place it under the control of the British, who could then be persuaded to open it up to Jewish colonization. With the cooperation of the British authorities, Chaim Weizmann intercepted Henry Morgenthau in Gibraltar, before he could reach Istanbul, and persuaded him to terminate his mission and return to Washington.[34] One has to wonder at the charm Chaim Weizmann must have exercised in overruling an important diplomatic initiative of the president of a great power. Alternatively, does this offer us an insight into the power that the Zionists had gained, at this early date, over the foreign policy of the United States?

Once they had demonstrated their support for the passage of the Balfour Declaration and, later, its incorporation into the British mandate in 1922, the president and Congress parted company until the beginning of World War II. Whenever the British wavered in their commitment to the Zionist plan, the Zionists lobbied different branches of the U.S. government to lean against the British. The Congress proved vulnerable to Zionist lobbying, and periodically used its powers—issuing statements, writing letters to the president, lobbying the White House, and passing resolutions—to get the President to mimic Zionist positions.[35] However, the four presidents, who served during the interwar years, generally resisted these pressures; and they had the complete support of the Departments of War and State.[36]

.   .   .

In May 1939, in anticipation of the onset of World War I, the British issued a White Paper disavowing their commitment to the creation of a Jewish state in Palestine.[37] The White Paper limited Jewish immigration to 75,000 over the next five years; after that, it would require the consent of the Palestinians. It also made land sales subject to approval by the British. This was a serious setback to Zionist aspirations.

The Zionists decided to defy the White Paper while supporting British war effort.[38] They would encourage illegal immigration to evade the limits on Jewish immigration; the aim was to quickly raise the fighting strength of the Jewish settlers in preparation for an eventual showdown with the Palestinians and their Arab allies. At the same time, taking advantage of the vacuum created by the White Paper, David Ben-Gurion advocated (in the words of Walter Laqueur) that the Jewish settlers should "behave as though they were the state of Palestine and should so act until there was a Jewish state."[39] This was not rhetoric; it was a plan of action. Since the late nineteenth century, the Zionists had been working to develop the infrastructure of a Jewish state in Palestine, and, by the late 1930s, nearly all the ingredients of a parallel Jewish state were in operation within the framework of the British mandate.

Simultaneously, the Zionists launched concerted efforts to recruit the United States as the new mother country to replace Britain. In all likelihood, this substitution would have occurred even without the White Paper. On the one hand, as Nazi armies marched across Europe, the Zionists had anticipated that this would destroy their power in continental Europe. They could also anticipate that Britain, even in the event of a German defeat, would yield its position of global hegemony to the United States. Finally, the United States, with the largest and most influential segment of the Jewish diaspora, offered a more reliable base of Zionist operations than Britain.[40] As a result, the Zionists wasted little time in organizing efforts to recruit the United States to play the role of the new mother country.[41]

Zionist activity in the United States increased dramatically after 1939. Although traveling was hazardous during the war, both Ben-Gurion and Chaim Weizmann traveled to the United States in 1940 and 1942 and stayed there for extended periods. Weizmann met President Roosevelt on both his visits.[42] In May 1942, the Zionists convened the Biltmore Conference in New York, attended by all the American Zionist parties, where they launched the openly militant phase of Zionism. Rejecting the White Paper and the partition of Palestine, the Zionists at Biltmore made a categorical demand for the creation of a Jewish state in *all* of Palestine. The Biltmore Conference placed in high gear Zionist efforts to fully engage and mobilize the resources of American Jews, and eventually the United States, behind their objectives. The Zionists accelerated their efforts to propagate their cause, published pro-Zionist books, and mailed out millions of leaflets to members of Congress and their constituents.[43] In October 1943, Rabbi Silver organized mass rallies in several large cities including New York; these were followed a month later by 118 rallies held all over the United States.[44]

The Zionist campaign produced some quick results. Most significantly, the membership of the ZOA rose from 43,000 in 1939 to 200,000 in 1945 and just under one million in 1947. Moreover, this growth was quickly translated into political activism since most members of the ZOA were actively engaged in campaigning, lobbying, writing letters, sending telegrams, and contributing money in support of Zionist causes. Zionist success may also be seen in the record of the United Jewish Appeal in raising funds: their collections increased more than fourteenfold over a similar period, rising from $14 million in 1940 to $150 million in 1947.[45]

"Sympathies for Zionism and Palestine," according to Walter Laqueur, "increased even more quickly and more extensively than is reflected in the growth of ZOA membership. American Jewry had become overwhelmingly pro-Zionist, whereas in the past the majority had been indifferent or even actively hostile."[46] In addition, the Zionists created one Christian Zionist organization and reinvigorated another—the American Palestine Committee and the Christian Council on Palestine—to lobby the Congress and to mobilize popular support to give pro-Zionist candidates an edge in elections to the Congress.[47]

The intense Zionist activity during the war years produced important gains in the public arena and in the Congress. Most importantly, the Zionists "managed to create a climate of opinion favorable to Zionism among legislators, church dignitaries, journalists and the public in general."[48] In November 1942, 68 senators, 194 congressmen, and hundreds of other prominent public figures signed a statement supporting the creation of a Jewish state in Palestine.[49] In January 1944, the Zionists lobbied the Senate to pass a resolution opposing the White Paper of 1939 and supporting the creation of a Jewish state in Palestine. Later the same year, Rabbi Abba Silver and Emmanuel Neumann persuaded the Democratic and Republican Party conventions to endorse the Taft-Wagner resolution—supporting unlimited Jewish immigration and the creation of a Jewish state in Palestine—in their party platforms. In October 1945, the Congress passed a joint resolution—after being obstructed on two previous occasions by the President and the State Department—that called for the creation of a Jewish state in Palestine.[50] In 1945, Zionist lobbying persuaded thirty-three state legislatures to pass resolutions favoring the establishment of a Jewish state in Palestine. Again, in July of the same year, before President Truman left for a summit with Churchill and Stalin at Potsdam, the Zionists prevailed upon thirty-seven governors to send cables, and over half the members of the Congress signed a statement, calling for lifting of immigration restrictions in Palestine.[51]

Zionist influence, however, had its limits under the Presidency of Roosevelt. Walter Laqueur is mostly on target when he claims that "once the Zionists came up against the State Department, the Pentagon, and the White House, they faced interests and forces superior to their own, and references to the tragedy of the Jewish people did not cut much ice."[52] While the State Department and Pentagon were steadfastly opposed to Zionist positions during the war, President Roosevelt played both sides of the aisle. He made promises to the Zionists when their pressures mounted, and, at the same time, reassured the Arabs that no decision on Palestine would be taken without their consent. Under Zionist pressure in

1939, the president sought to dissuade Prime Minister Chamberlain from issuing the White Paper, but backed away when Chamberlain warned that continuing British commitment to Zionism was certain to provoke an Arab conflagration, and that he would need 500,000 U.S. troops to suppress this Arab uprising.[53]

In one important instance, however, President Roosevelt went beyond making promises. In 1939, he began discussing with Justice Brandeis a plan to transport 200,000 to 300,000 Palestinians to Iraq; a year later, he broached this plan again with Chaim Weizmann.[54] Although the president was aware of the strong Arab opposition to Zionism, he thought the Arabs could be bought with "a little back-sheesh." In 1943, upon the urging of Chaim Weizmann but against the advice of his own State Department, the president sent Colonel Harold B. Hoskins to Saudi Arabia to offer the Saudi monarch £20 million and the leadership of an "Arab federation" in return for his cooperation with the president's plan of ethnic cleansing. The Saudi monarch refused to meet with Zionist leaders to discuss this offer; he was incensed by the suggestion that he would betray his own people for a bribe.[55] When his diplomatic mission to the Saudi King failed, the president proposed a plan to place Palestine under UN Trusteeship, and he was still pursuing this plan at the time of his death.[56]

President Truman's tenure marks a sea change in the official policy of the United States toward Zionist aspirations. In August 1945, within months of entering office, the president wrote to Clement Attlee, the British Prime Minister, suggesting that he authorize the entry into Palestine of Jewish displaced persons—"as many as possible"—then living in refugee camps in Europe. In April 1946, he came out strongly in support of the proposal of the Anglo-American Committee to permit the entry of 100,000 Jewish displaced persons to Palestine and remove restrictions on the purchase of land by Jews. At the same time, he brushed aside the primary recommendation of the Committee to place Palestine under UN Trusteeship. In July 1946, with midterm elections looming, President Truman again rejected the report of the Morrison-Grady Commission, which proposed placing Palestine under UN Trusteeship—after its division into "semi-autonomous zones"—and called upon other countries to admit Jewish refugees and not place the entire burden on Palestine. The U.S. pressure on Britain to partition Palestine and open it to Jewish immigration continued to mount, and by July 1946 the president was threatening to cut off postwar loans to Britain. In August 1946, after the Zionists retreated from the Biltmore Declaration—demanding the creation of a Jewish state in all of Palestine—without any loss of time,

President Truman endorsed the plan for partitioning Palestine.[57] In addition, during 1946 the British came under increasing pressure from the United States—including a freeze on loans negotiated earlier—to retreat from their plan to use military force to disband the *Haganah*, the military force built up by the Yishuv.[58]

Capitulating to these pressures, in February 1947, Britain took the step—unprecedented in its long colonial history—of leaving Palestine unilaterally, without putting in place a successor state or states. Simultaneously, the British dumped on the United Nations the responsibility for resolving the mess they had created in Palestine. At the United Nations, the United States held most of the cards, and President Truman used all the powers of his office to ensure that Zionist aims would be translated into American policy. The United States promoted a plan for the partition for Palestine that met nearly all the demands of the Zionists. According to Avi Shlaim, "On all salient questions—partition, trusteeship, recognition of the state of Israel, arms embargo, and disposition of the Negev—Truman, laboring under strong Zionist pressures in a presidential election year, took a consistently pro-Zionist line."[59]

President Truman's unwavering support for the creation of a Jewish state in Palestine was in sharp contrast to the clear and persistent advice he received from all the leading officials he appointed to the State and Defense Departments as well as the different branches of the military. "Here was a president," commented Abba Eban, Israel's first ambassador to the United States, "who runs against the current of specialized people with whom he surrounded himself."[60]

The opposition of these "specialized people" to the creation of a Jewish state was based on two considerations: the strategic location of the Middle East and its rich reserves of oil.[61] Although the United States had supplied 84 percent of the oil needed to fuel the war effort of the Allies, geologists in the 1940s were predicting that America's domestic reserves would be exhausted by the end of the 1950s. Among other things, this meant that the recovery of Europe would be impossible without Middle Eastern oil. In addition, the Department of Defense and the Joint Chiefs of Staff were worried that the new Jewish state would lean toward communism. Under these circumstances, the president's key foreign policy advisers warned him that support for the creation of a Jewish state would be disastrous for the United States.[62] As early as August 1945, Loy Henderson, the head of Office of Near East and African Affairs of the State Department, in a memo to the Secretary of State wrote, "At the present time the United States has a moral prestige in the Near and Middle East unequaled by that of any other great power." However, by supporting the creation of a Jewish state in Palestine, the United States "would lose that prestige and would likely for many years be considered a betrayer of the high principles which we ourselves have enunciated during the period of the war."[63] Another official in the State Department wrote that this would be "a major blunder in statesmanship."[64] In January 1948, George F. Kennan, director of policy planning wrote that as a result of its support for partition "U.S. prestige in the Moslem world has suffered a severe blow and U.S. strategic interests in the Mediterranean and Near East have been severely prejudiced. Our vital interests in those areas will continue to be adversely affected to the extent that we continue to support partition."[65]

There are commentators who would like to believe that President Truman's support for Zionist aims was principled; he did "*what* he felt was right *when* he felt it was right."[66] This is naïve: it suggests that the U.S. president is not the chief executive of the world's greatest power but the head of the Salvation Army. Moreover, there is a great deal of evidence to suggest that President Truman was a savvy politician whose policies on Palestine were influenced by Jewish lobbying, Jewish campaign contributions, and Jewish votes.

Jewish lobbying operated at three levels. On the one hand, the leading Zionists had direct access to the president and used this channel at every turn to influence his decisions on Palestine. In addition, the Zionist organizations had thoroughly impregnated the political system at federal and state levels with Zionist ideas.[67] The members of the Congress too, responding to demands orchestrated by the Zionists, were constantly bringing pressure on the president to accommodate Zionist demands. Finally, the Zionist organizations flexed their political muscle by instructing their members to deluge the White House with letters, telegrams and phone calls.[68] Altogether, these lobbying pressures on the president were quite intense. In a letter to a Jewish Congressman Arthur Klein, in May 1948, President Truman wrote that he had never seen more "lobbying and pulling and hauling" by the Jews.[69]

More importantly, President Truman, who had neither inherited nor created a personal fortune, was more dependent than any president before or after him on private donors, many of whom were Jews. His campaign as vice-presidential candidate in 1944 was financed by Dewey Stone, a wealthy and avid American Zionist.[70] During his first term in office, there grew up "a small, almost clandestine circle of wealthy Jews . . . who had entrée into Truman's inner sanctum." A few of these wealthy Jews also worked closely, as "informal, substitute ambassadors," with the leading Zionists. Further, in September 1948, when his chances of reelection were in serious jeopardy—having run out of money and facing unfavorable ranking in the polls—the president and his advisers had one last desperate plan to rescue the campaign with a whistle-stop train tour. The money for this tour, $100,000, was raised in two days by Abraham Feinberg. "If not for my friend Abe," stated Truman, giving credit where it was due, "I couldn't have made the [whistle-stop] trip and I wouldn't have been elected."[71]

In 1948, an election year, the Jewish vote could not have been far from the calculations of President Truman and his political advisers. In 1945, when four chiefs of missions from the Near East met President Truman to present their concerns about the impact of U.S. policies relating to Palestine on the Middle East, he responded with candor. "I am sorry, gentlemen," he said, "but I have to answer to hundreds of thousands who are anxious for the success of Zionism: I do not have hundreds of thousands of Arabs among my constituents."[72] On May 12 1948, in a confrontation over the timing of the recognition of Israel, Robert Lovett, Undersecretary of State, warned that premature recognition would be seen as a "very transparent attempt to win the Jewish vote." Secretary of State Marshall, also present at the meeting, recalled telling the President that the advice—given to him by Clark Clifford—to declare U.S. support for the creation of Israel the next day after its creation was "based on domestic political considerations" and a "transparent dodge to win a few votes."[73]

Finally, consider an exchange between Secretary of Defense James Forrestal and President Truman in early 1948. James Forrestal writes,

> I said, that I was merely directing my efforts to lifting the question out of politics . . . He [Truman] said this was impossible, that the nation was too far committed and that, furthermore, the Democratic Party would be bound to lose and the Republicans gain by such an agreement. I said I was forced to repeat to him what I had said to Senator McGrath in response to the latter's observation that our failure to go along with the Zionists might lose the states of New York, Pennsylvania and California—that I thought it was about time that somebody should pay some consideration to whether we might lose the United States. [74]

Since President Eisenhower, no American president, faced with the need to choose between the interests of his country and those of the Israel lobby, has had the luxury of asking whether the lobby was pushing him to make decisions that might cause irreparable damage to the United States.

CHAPTER 16

FROM LIABILITY TO ASSET

> It seems to me and all members of my office acquainted with the Middle East that the policy which we are following [support for partition] . . . is contrary to the interests of the United States and will eventually involve us in international difficulties . . . we are forfeiting the friendship of the Arab world . . . [and] incurring long-term Arab hostility towards us.
>
> —Loy Henderson, November 1947

> US prestige in the Muslim world has suffered a severe blow, and US strategic interests in the Mediterranean and Near East have been seriously prejudiced.
>
> —George F. Kennan, January 1948

> The United States has a special relationship with Israel in the Middle East comparable only to that which it has with Britain over a wide range of world affairs . . . I think it is quite clear that in case of an invasion the United States would come to the support of Israel.
>
> —John F. Kennedy, December 1962[1]

THE ZIONISTS DID NOT GAIN AMERICAN SPONSORSHIP for their colonial project because of a prior convergence of their strategic interests. Instead, a temporary and limited convergence was created by the sponsorship itself. Israel, then, deftly exploited this self-created convergence to deepen America's pro-Israel policies and make it irreversible.

It was clear to American policy makers, before and after the creation of Israel, that their support for Zionist goals would cause grievous harm to the enduring strategic interests of the United States in the Middle East. Before the creation of Israel, Zionism was a liability, not an asset, to the United States. Ironically, however, since the creation of Israel radicalized the Arab world, Zionist claims that a Jewish state in Palestine would serve the interests of the West may be seen as a self-fulfilling prophecy. The creation of Israel imparted a radical edge to Arab nationalism, pushing the leadership of liberation movements in several Arab countries toward leftist programs of nationalization, state planning, and a truculent opposition to the presence of Western capital in the region. It also lent urgency to Arab aspirations for unity and military power, since these were seen as necessary conditions for rolling back the insertion of a colonial settler state in the region. Once these radical tendencies, which threatened Western interests in the Middle East, began to take shape, Israel could, with some plausibility, claim that it alone was best placed to defend against Arab threats to Western interests. Give us massive amounts of arms, money, and immunity from international laws, the Israelis told the West, and we will disembowel the Arab nationalist movement before it can achieve any of its aims.

Arab hostility to the United States—generated by the creation of Israel—contained the logic of a vicious circle. Once the United States and other Western powers began to place themselves firmly behind Israel, Arabs began to view Israel with greater alarm than before. This alarm added impetus to radical tendencies across the Arab world and forced them to turn to the Soviets for economic assistance and arms, increasing the threat to Western allies and interests in the region. In addition, Israel, too, quickly expanded and began to use its capacity to reinforce this vicious circle. Armed with U.S. and U.S.-sanctioned weaponry, bolstered by vast amounts of economic aid and insulated from the sanction of international laws, Israel pursued policies that deepened Arab and Islamicate hostility toward the United States. In time, by defeating Egypt and Syria, Israel earned the gratitude of the United States for setting back the Arab nationalist threat to its strategic interest in the Middle East. Inspired and activated by Zionist successes, the two major factions of the Israel lobby in the United States—Jewish and Christian—expanded and became better organized to take advantage of these gains. At some point, as the strength of the Israel lobby continued to grow, it became the dominant force determining U.S. policies toward the Middle East.

. . .

Chapter 11 debunked claims that British support for the Zionist project in late 1917 flowed from its enduring strategic interests in the Middle East. Instead, this support, in part, was a *quid pro quo*—during a difficult phase in World War I—for Zionist promises to effect an early and more complete U.S. entry into the war on the side of the Entente Powers. The Zionist inclinations of the British cabinet, headed by Lloyd George, which took office in December 1916, may also have contributed to this decision. In the years before 1917, despite intense Zionist lobbying, the best offer the British had made to the Zionists was to open up eastern Kenya to Jewish settlers. In addition, soon after the end of World War I, the British began to show unease about their commitment to Zionism. They excluded Jordan from the Palestine mandate, and, in 1939, dissociated themselves from Zionist goals in Palestine. In short, British support for Zionism in 1917 was rooted in two transitory events: the accession to power of Christian Zionists and wartime exigencies.

During these early years, the United States did not support Zionism for strategic reasons either. While the Zionists lobbied the major European powers before World War I, they did not think the United States had the capacity to deliver their project. The reasons for this are plain. At this time, the United States was only a regional power, with interests in Latin America, the Caribbean, and the Philippines. It had yet to acquire any significant interests in the Middle East, a region that was almost exclusively an arena of rivalry for major European powers. If the United States, nevertheless, offered symbolic support to the Balfour Declaration—and it did so with enthusiasm—this was the result of domestic pressures. It was the work of Zionist organizations, still directed from Europe, who were mobilizing American Jews and Christian Zionists to generate support for Zionism in the state legislatures, the Congress, and the White House. The Zionists were taking advantage of a Jewish presence in the United States that was the largest, the most prosperous, and the most influential in the world.

In the early twentieth century, the Protestant missionaries were the oldest and best-organized group of Americans with interests in the Ottoman Empire; and they were opposed to Zionism. They owned churches, hospitals, schools, colleges, and printing presses—mostly in greater Syria—in support of their efforts to evangelize Christians belonging to various Eastern churches. In deference to these missionaries, President Wilson had excluded the Ottoman Empire from his declaration of war against the Axis Powers. Toward the end of World War I, the missionary establishment supported the Arab right to self-determination. They persuaded President Wilson to dispatch a commission—with delegates from the United States, France and Britain—to determine if the Arabs in the former Ottoman Empire were ready to take on the burden of self-governance.[2] Headed by two Americans, but without the participation of Britain and France, this commission opposed the creation of a Jewish state in Palestine because this violated the principle of self-determination. At the time, this principle formed the centerpiece of President Wilson's challenge to the global dominance of the European colonial powers.

Why, then, did the United States step into Britain's shoes when it reversed its position on Zionism in 1939? It would appear that the logic behind the British disengagement from Zionism would apply with equal force to the United States. It was clear to most observers that the United

States, at the conclusion of World War II, would succeed Britain as the paramount power in the Middle East. In addition, American policy makers knew that a Jewish state in Palestine would radicalize Arab nationalists and force them to seek support from the Soviets.[3] If these adverse prospects did not dampen President Truman's decisive support for Zionism in 1948—an election year—that is because the exigencies of electoral politics weighed more heavily than concerns about the long-term strategic costs of creating a Jewish state in Palestine. Domestic politics had trumped the vital interests of the United States.

Once the elections were behind, President Truman began to distance his administration from Israel. In the period leading up to the UN resolution on the partition of Palestine, he had resolutely backed all Zionist positions.[4] After 1948, however, seeking to placate the Arabs, the United States began to distance itself from Israel. Most importantly, it refused to resume the supply of arms to Israel, suspended earlier in December 1947. With a few exceptions, it also resisted Israeli demands for large-scale economic assistance. Most significantly, the United States kept Israel out of the defense arrangements it sought to make with Middle Eastern nations against the Soviets. Clearly, without an election looming ahead, President Truman felt he had more latitude in resisting the domestic pressures of Zionists.

.   .   .

The United States could not long sustain this policy of distancing itself from Israel. Israel was no ordinary liability that could be sacrificed once the costs of supporting it started coming home.

The United States could not cut Israel loose even as growing Cold War tensions raised the strategic costs of alienating the Arabs. The reason for this is obvious. The domestic forces that Zionism had mobilized in the United States had not gone into abeyance after the creation of Israel. Jewish Zionism, Christian Zionism, anti-Semitism (in its messianic incarnation, as dispensationalism), and anti-Islamic bigotry would remain enduring features of the political landscape in the United States. To these pro-Zionist forces, World War II had added a new one: the burden of guilt for the Holocaust, continually reinforced by the Zionist organizations and Zionist partisans in the United States. Indeed, these forces would continue to draw strength from the creation of Israel. In particular, the Christian Zionists would view the creation of Israel as confirming their reading of biblical prophecies. In addition, with support and leadership from Israel, the Zionist organizations in the United States too would gain strength.

Zionism encouraged Jews and Christians to look at their religions as symbiotic. Westerners would see their support for Israel—especially after the Holocaust—as the beginning of a healing process, atonement for centuries of Christian persecution of Jews. Increasingly, Israel and the United States would view themselves as the leading protagonists in a civilization with ancient roots, now redefined as Judeo-Christian. There was great promise in this symbiosis, since it would harness the energy and creativity of Jews and Gentiles to augment the power of the United States and Israel. Once this new Judeo-Christian framework was in place, the fate of the West and of United States in particular would become tied to the survival of Israel. The two were now inseparable.

There was another factor at play, cementing the Judeo-Christian framework. Should the Zionist project come to an early end, should this revival of Jewish power in Palestine in nearly two millennia be overturned, the Jews would blame the United States for this disaster. They would see this as a terrible betrayal, an unforgivable treachery. It would forever turn the Jews against the United States. It was not a prospect that American leaders could contemplate without alarm. They could not wish to become targets of Jewish hostility.

Anti-Semitism too, even in retreat, would continue to play a passive role in sustaining Western support for the Jewish state. In all likelihood, the dissolution of the Jewish state of Israel would place the burden of transporting and rehabilitating its Jewish population on the United States and Western Europe. Neither would welcome this. If Western societies—at least in part—had supported Zionism as a way of getting rid of the Jews, they would have an equal, if not stronger, interest in ensuring that Israeli Jews did not return to "trouble" these societies. Indeed, as the Jewish population of Israel has grown over time—now exceeding six million—the strength of the anti-Semitic interest in keeping these Jews *in* Israel, and *out* of the Western countries, should not be underestimated.

Israel was a source of pride for Westerners too. Many in the West felt an instinctive affinity for the new state, founded by Western Jews, projecting Western values, claiming to protect Western interests in the Islamic Middle East. At a time when Western power was in retreat across Asia and Africa, many Westerners saw the creation of Israel as going against this trend; it had reestablished Western power in the Islamic heartlands. Israel appealed to some Christians as a new Crusade, led by Western Jews, to reclaim the Holy Land from the Islamic infidels. With so many ties binding it to the Western world, Israel was no ordinary liability. The West had created this liability, and it now could not shrink from defending it.

Israel would capitalize upon the knowledge that it was a strategic liability. If Israel was a strategic liability, Israeli leaders would seek to *enhance* the *perceived* threats to Israel; the greater the threats to a "strategic" liability the stronger would be American willingness to commit resources to enhance its security. Israel was also quite willing, within limits, to ratchet up the real threats it faced from the Arabs, as long as it was convinced it was fully capably of neutralizing these threats. Far from making concessions to Palestinians and Arabs to advance peace, Israel had an opposite interest in escalating its conflicts with the Arabs. American support for Israel could only increase as Israel succeeded in escalating its conflicts with its adversaries. Israel was free to deny the Palestinians the right of return, attack the Palestinians in the refugee camps in Gaza and Jordan, accelerate the influx of Jewish colonists into Israel, augment its military superiority over the Arabs, and engage in frequent attacks against Arab targets. Anything that provoked Arab belligerence would bring rich payoffs in higher levels of American support. Israel faced powerful incentives to expand its colonial project. At the same time, the Zionist organizations in the United States would be at work, magnifying American perceptions of these threats to Israel, and bringing pressure on the political establishment to expand American commitment to Israel.

Being a liability brought another advantage. Although keen to ensure Israel's survival, the United States could not offer Israel security guarantees backed by American military presence or the threat of military intervention; this would deepen the anti-American stance of the Arabs. Instead, the United States decided to support Israel indirectly, even covertly, by building up Israel's economy and military. Israel too preferred this, since this allowed it to retain the greatest autonomy over how to use its growing military strength. Indeed, as Israel increased its lead over the frontline Arab states, it would use this military superiority to provoke Arab hostility. In due time, Arab hostility would increasingly be directed against the United States, as the leading patron of Israel. At this point, the Zionist lobby in the United States could begin arguing—with greater conviction than before—that Israel alone could defend American interests in the Middle East. As this Zionist logic played out, Israel would increasingly acquire the appearance of an asset.

In the absence of Israel, Arab nationalism would still seek to unify the Arabs, and it would seek to roll back British influence over Saudi Arabia and the Sheikhdoms in the Persian Gulf. In pursuing these far from radical goals, the Arab nationalists were more likely to turn to the United States rather than the Soviet Union, since Arab nationalism was overwhelmingly a bourgeois movement. At the same time, the United States had a natural interest in supporting the Arab nationalists since it wanted to displace the British and French from the region, and, even more importantly, keep the Soviets out of the region. U.S. support for Israel, however, made this alliance impossible. The nationalist Arab states—Egypt, Syria, Iraq, Algeria, and Libya—could not oppose Israel and be allied to the United States. They had no option but to make alliances with the Soviet Union.

Once the Arab nationalists were allied to the Soviet Union, the Middle East became a major arena of Cold War conflict. This was Israel's moment to demonstrate its strategic value to the West by defeating and downsizing the leading Arab nationalist states. In 1956, Israel waged its first war to overthrow the Arab nationalists who had seized power in Egypt. However, this was a misconceived war because it was made in alliance with Britain and France, two declining colonial powers, who sought to restore their former prestige in their still extensive colonies. As a result, the United States intervened to stop the war before it could achieve its aims, and even forced Israel to vacate its conquest of the Sinai.

Its withdrawal notwithstanding, Israel had demonstrated that it possessed the military capability to serve the West as a bulwark against Arab nationalist ambitions. According to an Israeli political columnist, writing in 1958, General Moshe Dayan believed that "the Jewish people has a mission, especially its Israeli branch. In this part of the world Israel has a mission; it has to be a rock, an extension of the West, against which waves of Nasser's Arab nationalism will be broken."[5] In 1956, Israel had made the error of choosing to ally with Western powers whose time had passed. When Israel again waged war against the Arab nationalists, in 1967, the United States had replaced Britain as the dominant Western power in the Middle East. In addition, Arab nationalist regimes in Syria, Iraq, Libya, and Algeria—in alliance with Soviet Union—posed a growing threat to both Israel and American interests in the Middle East. Israel's preemptive strike against the Arabs in June 1967 was well timed and well conceived; this time, it knew that the outcome of its war would greatly please the United States.

The domestic forces in the United States that had supported the creation of Israel had not gone into recess after its creation. On the contrary, the creation of Israel and its growing military successes would continue to galvanize these forces. Most importantly, the major Jewish organizations would continue to increase their influence over the electoral process; they would establish think tanks and use the Jewish presence in the media and academia to present Israel as a strategic asset; they would censor the public discourse to exclude critical assessments of the impact of Israel on U.S. interests in the Middle East. While Israel worked on the ground to antagonize the Arabs, the pro-Israel pressure groups lobbied the Congress and the White House to take positions uncritically supportive of Israel. They lobbied to expand U.S. military and economic assistance to Israel, to expand strategic cooperation with Israel, to give Israel immunity against violations of international laws, to grant Israel privileged access to U.S. technology and markets, and to outsource to Israel covert activities in the Third World. In other words, the Israel lobby worked on a dual agenda. They sought to enhance Israel's capacity to pursue its aggressive agenda against its neighbors, and shield Israel from the negative consequences of its actions in the Middle East.

· · ·

Once Israel was in place, its presence *per se* would invite the interest of European powers with political and economic stakes the Middle East. They would be tempted to use Israel as the spearhead of Western efforts to preempt the rise of a robust Arab nationalism. Instead of coming to terms with the nascent Arab nationalist movements, meeting them halfway to prevent their radicalization, the Western powers were tempted to use Israel to weaken or neutralize the region's nationalist aspirations. This strategy was not without risks: it could accelerate the radicalization it sought to preempt, force the Arab nationalists to seek help from the Soviets, and provoke direct Soviet intervention. Despite these risks, Britain and France would be tempted to use Israel to try to shore up their shrinking influence in the region. Once Israel was established in the Middle East, an interloper, a determined antagonist of the Arabs, it would constantly beckon Western powers whose interests clashed with the nationalist aspirations of the Arabs.

In consequence, several great powers, one after another, entered the Middle East conflict on the side of Israel, aiding and arming it in the expectation that they could use it to secure their interests in the region. In the 1950s, France discovered that its strategic interests were aligned with Israel now. It sought to strengthen Israel to neutralize the growing threat that Egypt, with her bid for leadership of Arab liberation movements, posed to her prized possessions in North and West Africa and no less her oil supplies passing through the Suez Canal.[6] French anxiety over Egypt rose when the British evacuated their forces from the Canal Zone in 1954 and, the same year, the Algerian struggle for independence took a violent turn. When the Egyptian leader, Gamal Abdel Nasser, nationalized the Suez Canal in July 1956, the British and French secretly entered into a military deal with Israel to invade Egypt. This tripartite invasion sought to defeat the Egyptian army, occupy the Suez Canal, overthrow the new nationalist government and replace it with one that would be friendly to their interests. This desperate attempt by two fading colonial powers to revive their sinking fortunes in the Middle East did not go down well with the United States: it was opposed by the Soviets too. This colonial adventure had to be called off.

After distancing itself from the Zionist project for more than a decade, starting in 1939, Britain too was back in the arena seeking an alliance with the Jewish state soon after its creation. In 1950, the British military was "carefully appraising Israel's logistical value" with an eye on the roads, bridges, and ports the British had built in Palestine during their colonial occupation. In January 1951, the British were sounding out Israel "on the chances of establishing bases in Israel, particularly in the Gaza area, as well as a strategic corridor for British troops through the Negev to Hashemite Jordan." These early attempts to create a military partnership between Britain and Israel did not reach fruition. In January 1954, the British Prime Minister concluded that they did not wish to base their military policy in the Middle East "either wholly or mainly on cooperation with Israel."[7] Two years later, however, Britain abandoned this caution when it entered into a partnership with France and Israel in a bid to reassert colonial control over Egypt following the nationalization of the Suez Canal.

The support that Soviet Union extended to the Zionists, on three occasions, is harder to explain. In 1947, it mobilized the vote of the socialist bloc in favor of the UN partition of Palestine. In 1948, it instructed Czechoslovakia to transport large supplies of heavy arms to the *Yishuv*, tilting the military balance in Israel's favor. It also became the second country to extend recognition to Israel. Why did the Soviets choose to alienate the Arabs and undermine the Arab communist parties with its vote for the establishment of a Jewish colonial settler state in Palestine? Their motivation remains murky. One hears of two arguments: they expected the creation of Israel to expedite British withdrawal from the region; they saw Israel as a natural ally because of its apparent socialist character. Neither argument is convincing. The British were on their way out, in any case; the socialist character of Israel was more apparent than real. Perhaps the Soviets were acting more strategically. Without Israel, there was little chance that any of the Arab regimes would turn away from their dependence on the West. Only Arab anger over Israel would open the Middle East to Soviet influence. Indirectly, the creation of Israel served the interests of the Soviets too.

The early Soviet support for Israel aroused concerns in the United States, which Israel was quick to exploit. In the period after 1948, Israel

carefully sought to deepen this anxiety by cultivating an ambiguous posture on the Cold War. In hindsight, it appears unlikely that Israel would
have established a socialist economy or joined the Soviet camp in the
Cold War; but this was much less obvious to Western policy makers at
the time. In order to keep it out of the Soviet camp, the United States was
keen to strengthen its ties with Israel—covert ties, to be sure—as a means
of anchoring it in the Western alliance. An Israel allied with the Soviet
Union could have altered the existing arrangements in the Middle East in
ways that might have been quite unsettling for Western powers. A Soviet
alliance that included Israel, Egypt, and Syria could have posed a serious
challenge to Western control over oil in the Persian Gulf.

Israel was the result of a lucky conjuncture. In the early twentieth
century, a variety of powerful forces supported the colonial enterprise
of Western Jews in Palestine. Israel appears "miraculous" only if we fail
to account for the forces that were working to make it succeed. Western
Jews were a leading segment of Western societies, hated by their "hosts,"
yet commanding considerable influence over major Western powers. On
the other hand, the Palestinian territory they targeted for colonization
was backward and its people without a strong national consciousness.
The larger Arab society—of which Palestine was a part—was also backward, weak, divided, still effectively under foreign occupation, and this
society, its religion and civilization, commanded little or no sympathy in
the Western discourse. At the same time, every one of the great Western
powers eyed the region for its chief strategic assets: oil and the Suez Canal.
The "miracle" of Israel was produced by the confluence of a variety of
powerful forces that favored Zionism. The Zionists would have needed
a real miracle if they had wanted to create a Jewish state in some part
of Europe, the region to which they belonged. The Zionist decision to
choose Palestine rather than Bremen or Brittany was a stroke of brilliance.
At once, this choice mobilized the support of all those Western forces,
overt and hidden, that have stood historically and culturally in opposition
to the Islamicate.

CHAPTER 17

PROVOKING ARAB HOSTILITY

[The Zionists] will seek to involve [the U.S.] in a continuously widening
and deepening series of operations intended to secure maximum Jewish
objectives.

—U.S. Joint Chiefs of Staff, 1948

During the years 1955–56 (and perhaps as early as 1954), retaliatory
strikes were also launched by the IDF in order to draw the Arab states
into a premature war.

—Benny Morris, 2001[1]

WHAT WERE THE POLICIES THAT ISRAEL CHOSE to pursue, during the first
two decades after its creation, to accelerate its transformation from a strategic liability to a strategic asset?

In April 1948, a month before Israel's creation, the U.S. Joint Chiefs
of Staff were predicting how the Jewish state would proceed to mobilize the Americans behind their ambitions in the Middle East. Anticipating Israeli strategy, they wrote that the Zionists "will seek to involve
[the United States] in a continuously widening and deepening series of
operations intended to secure maximum Jewish objectives." The Zionists
are ambitious. They would seek initial Jewish sovereignty over a portion
of Palestine, endorsement by the great powers of Jewish right to unlimited immigration, extension of Jewish sovereignty over all of Palestine,
expansion of "Eretz Israel" into Jordan and parts of Lebanon and Syria,
and establishment of Jewish hegemony over the entire Middle East. Ominously, the report added, "All stages of this program are equally sacred to
the fanatical concepts of Jewish leaders."[2]

Instead of seeking a settlement, the Israelis would pursue a policy
of provocations against the Palestinians and its Arab neighbors.[3] They
blocked the return of Palestinian refugees, attacked them when they tried
to return to their lands, and continued to create new Palestinian refugees.[4]
They bulldozed more than 400 Palestinian villages in Israel that had been

cleansed of their inhabitants in the War of 1948. They escalated the war of attrition, rejected peace overtures from Arabs, and unilaterally diverted the waters from the Jordan River. Clearly, the Israelis were not seeking accommodation with the Arabs.

These provocations served a variety of Israeli objectives. They deepened Arab anger, radicalized Arab politics, and turned Arab nationalists against the United States. The Zionists have given currency to a spurious history of the War of 1948, claiming that Jewish settlers had narrowly averted destruction at the hands of invading Arab armies.[5] After the war, Israel presented itself as a small country, beleaguered, at risk of being swamped by hostile Arab neighbors. Israel also provided intelligence to the United States that exaggerated the military strength of the Arab nationalist states.[6] In order to sustain this image, Israel continued to provoke the neighboring Arab states, who, the Israelis knew, lacked the capacity to retaliate. Nevertheless, forced to save face, the Arabs offered Israel satisfaction by spouting belligerent rhetoric. Israel used these hollow Arab threats to demand expanded military and economic assistance from the West. The Israeli policy of provocations was also designed to force the Arabs to turn to the Soviet Union for military assistance. Once this happened, the Western powers were nearly certain to turn to Israel as their first line of defense against Arab threats to their interests in the Middle East.

Complementing Israeli actions on the ground, the Zionists tirelessly lobbied the United States to recognize Israel as a strategic asset. During the 1950s, Israel repeatedly offered to become the military arm of the United States in the Middle East. In 1950 and 1951, it offered the United States military bases in the Negev, sought membership in a regional defense pact against the Soviets, and offered to raise an army of 250,000 to fight the Soviet Union.[7] In December 1950, the Israeli Foreign Minister secretly invited the United States to stockpile weapons, foodstuffs, and raw materials in Israel; supply arms to Israel; and establish Israel as a major arms producer. Known as Operation Stockpile, this proposal was part of Ben-Gurion's bid to persuade Washington to make Israel "the base, the workshop and the granary" of the Middle East. Washington turned down the proposal. It had no wish to build a Middle Eastern policy centered on Israel; its interests were better served by mobilizing the entire region against the Soviets.[8] This did not discourage the Israelis. After the nationalization of the Suez Canal, Abba Eban told a special U.S. emissary that Israel was the only reliable partner the West had in the Middle East. Hence, the United States "should take immediate steps to put [Israel] in a position to be a bastion of strength."[9] The United States was not persuaded—at least not yet.

In the years leading to Israel's creation, the leading officials in President Truman's State and Defense Departments had warned—in the words of Peter Hahn—that American support for Zionism "would trigger war in the Middle East, undermine U.S. interests in the Arab world, and drive Arab states into partnership with the Soviet Union."[10] Israel spared no efforts to ensure that these dire predictions would be fulfilled in their entirety. Israel's growing military superiority, and its close military partnership with France, caused growing concern in Egypt. When Israel conducted a large-scale military raid against Gaza in February 1955, this flagrant breach of its sovereignty alarmed Egypt. It moved swiftly, and in September of the same year acquired a large shipment of arms from Czechoslovakia. Similar Israeli pressure had before forced Syria to acquire arms from the Soviet Union. In July 1956, when Secretary of State Dulles withdrew the offer to finance the Aswan Dam, Egypt nationalized the Suez Canal. In October of the same year, France, Britain, and Israel began an invasion of Egypt, known as the Suez War, to repossess the Suez Canal and overthrow the Arab nationalist government in Cairo. Simultaneously, Israel occupied the Sinai.[11] This tripartite invasion pushed Egypt even more firmly into the Soviet camp.

The die was now cast. After Egypt and Syria initiated a military relationship with the Soviet Union, the United States—already impressed by Israel's demonstration of its military prowess in the Suez War—became more willing to look upon Israel as a useful counterweight against the rise of radical nationalism in the Arab world. Slowly, the belief that Israel was a dangerous liability was beginning to shift. In a memorandum of January 1958, the National Security Council took the position that support for Israel, "the only strong pro-West power left in the Near East," flowed as a "natural corollary" from U.S. opposition to radical Arab nationalism. Secretary of State Allen Dulles was now convinced that a strong Israel could block Egypt from intervening militarily in support of nationalist forces in Arab countries friendly to Western powers. In August 1958, he communicated to Abba Eban that the United States was ready to equip Israel to "deter an attempt at aggression by indigenous forces." This was an important turning point. For the first time, between 1958 and 1960, the United States agreed to deliver major arms systems to Israel, including antitank rifles, twenty S-58 Sikorsky helicopters, and an early warning system against air raids.[12] Henceforth, the trajectory of U.S. arms deliveries to Israel generally moved upward.

Israel's policy of provocation against the Arabs was beginning to pay off. Increasingly, the United States would take the view that Israel, with generous supplies of the latest American weapon systems, could be relied upon to neutralize the threats to its interests posed by radical Arab states allied with the Soviet Union. It did not matter that the creation of Israel, its ethnic cleansing of Palestinians, and its policy of provocations against the Arabs had produced and augmented these threats. Now, the facts were on the ground. Since the creation of Israel was irreversible in Western political calculus, the United States could best address the Arab and Soviet threat by giving Israel an overwhelming military advantage over the Arabs, and setting it free to sink the ship of Arab nationalism.

In producing this shift in American policy, the Israeli lobby played only a minor role. On two previous occasions—the passage of the Balfour Declaration in 1917 and the UN vote in November 1947 to partition Palestine—this lobby had mobilized its network in the United States to produce the results it wanted. In the years following the creation of Israel, however, the Israeli lobby's influence had weakened—for two reasons. First, in these critical early years of the Cold War, the United States was anxious to limit the fallout from the creation of Israel. Capitulating to the Israel lobby now risked losing the Middle East to the Soviet Union. The Israelis too understood this; with reservations, they too went along with the U.S. decision to deliver its support indirectly. Second, General Eisenhower was better insulated than any past or future president against the pressures of the Israel lobby. "The national hero in the White House," according to Edward Tivnan, "owed nothing to any domestic or foreign-policy interest group. A career army man, he had never been in a position to benefit from Jewish support or bear the community's enmity in Congress." In addition, the president did not stay awake worrying about losing the Jewish vote, since he had won only 36 percent of their votes in 1952.[13] In 1953, when Israel, in defiance of the United States, continued to divert water from the Jordan River, President Eisenhower secretly put a loan to Israel on hold and threatened to cancel the tax-exempt status of the United Jewish Appeal. A year later, he suspended aid to Israel over the massacre of civilians in Qibya, a village in the West Bank.[14] Finally, when Israelis leaders dragged their feet over evacuating from the Sinai, the United States threatened to cut off all aid, expel Israel from the United Nations, and invoke sanctions on the country.[15] None of these actions would have been imaginable in the 1970s, much less in more recent decades.

That is not to say that the Israeli lobby was dormant during these years. In his book on the Eisenhower administration, Sherman Adams, the White House Chief of Staff from January 1953 to September 1958, wrote, "The great body of private opinion in the United States favoring Israel was a large factor in every government decision on the Middle East issues."[16] In 1954, the Zionists founded a pro-Israeli lobbying organization, the American Zionist Council of Public Affairs, the precursor to American Israeli

Public Affairs Committee. In March of the same year, the Conference of Presidents of Major Jewish Organizations held its first meeting "to discuss how American Jewry could best help Israel in the face of the Eisenhower Administration's hostility."[17] In January 1957, when Israel was under American pressure to vacate the Sinai, the Israeli embassy launched a "massive information drive" during which they contacted key editors, Congressmen, and labor leaders. A month later, forty-one Republican congressmen met the president to convey their opposition to the Sinai withdrawal until Egypt agreed to recognize Israel. Simultaneously, seventy-five Democrats demanded that the United States guarantee Israel the right of free passage through the Straits of Tiran. When Congressional opposition to his policy grew heated, the president appealed directly to the American people to browbeat the Congress. In addition, Alan Dulles called upon non-Jewish leaders "to make themselves more felt or else there will be a major disaster." In an address to the Presbyterian Church, Dulles warned, "If the Jews have the veto on foreign policy, the consequences will be disastrous."[18]

The resurgence of the Israeli lobby began during the Presidency of John Kennedy; from then onward the sky would be the limit. President Kennedy understood the importance of winning Jewish support, and, like every good politician, he tailored his views to ingratiate the Israeli lobby. In 1958, when Philip Klutznick, President of the Council of Major Jewish Organizations, met Senator Kennedy to scout his views on Israel, the senator voiced his concerns about the Arab refugee problem and the risks of war in the region. "Look, Senator," Klutznick said, "if you plan to run for the presidency and that is what you're going to say, count me out and count a lot of other people out, too." After he won the Democratic nomination for the Presidential election, Kennedy met a group of Jewish leaders in New York, who pledged $500,000 toward his campaign. President Kennedy was not one to forget his debt. In spring 1961, after he became president, Kennedy told David Ben-Gurion, the Israeli Prime Minister, "I know I was elected because of the votes of American Jews. Tell me, is there something I can do for the Jewish people?"[19]

Toward the end of the 1950s, the elements for the recognition of Israel as a strategic asset were in place. With Western support, Israel had extended its military lead over the leading Arab nationalist states. During the Suez War, it had also given a convincing demonstration of its ability to quickly defeat the military of the leading Arab nationalist state. Israeli policy of provocations had brought Arab nationalists to power in three key Arab countries, and pushed them ever closer to the Soviet Union. For the United States, these new threats contained their own solution: turn Israel loose to clean up the threats it had created.

Two factors still restrained the United States from a whole-hearted embrace of Israel. The Americans were concerned that this would persuade the Arab nationalist states to host Soviet military bases in their territories. By the same logic, the Soviets too would exploit a closer identification between the United States and Israel to push for closer ties with the Arab nationalists. Finally, there was the fear that Arab nationalist forces, with support from Egypt, Syria, and Iraq, might incite a nationalist takeover in the oil-rich Gulf states. Alternatively, in order to preempt such a takeover, the Arab royalists may decide to distance themselves from the Americans.

Clearly, this was not a stable equilibrium. An observer, unfamiliar with the relative strengths of the Arab nationalists and Israel, might imagine that the Middle East, with equal chance, could evolve in one of two opposite directions. The Arab nationalists, with Soviet help, could continue to gain strength until they could deal a knockout blow to Israel. Alternatively, Israel could defeat the Arab nationalists, and, thereby, create conditions for their incorporation into the Western sphere of influence. As it turned out, Israel would be the winner in the next throw of the historical die. In every historical situation, there are imponderables—the difference that the human spirit, chance, and luck of leadership can make to historical outcomes—but if we discount these, Israel, in this slice of time, had won because it was the favorite of history.

.   .   .

At this point, it may be useful to settle a question of timing. When did American policy makers begin to treat Israel as a strategic asset rather than a strategic liability?

Zionist writers prefer to examine the timing of this switch exclusively in terms of the volume of U.S. aid flows to Israel.[20] Since these flows rose dramatically only after the June War, this becomes the hinge on which the U.S. relationship with Israel turns. The trends in U.S. aid flows to Israel are very clear. Annual U.S. aid to Israel averaged $65 million from 1952 to 1970. It jumped from $71 million in 1970 to $601 million in 1971, and the trend since was upward until the early 1980s. The annual average aid flow for the period 1971–1980 was $1081 million, marking a nearly seventeenfold increase over the average annual aid flows for the previous period.[21] However, this focus on aid flows to Israel is misleading. It ignores the shift in U.S. policies toward Israel that had been underway since the late 1950s.

Once President Truman had secured UN sanction for the partition of Palestine *and* won the election to boot, he began efforts to limit the damage done by his pro-Zionist policy. Under the new approach, he would minimize the risks to Israel's security by offering help indirectly and covertly. The stage for this was set in December 1947, when the United States imposed an arms embargo on *all* the countries in the Middle East, to show that it was evenhanded between Israel and the Arabs. At the same time, in violation of the arms embargo, the United States allowed Israel to import World War II surplus personnel carriers and to recruit American Jewish veterans of World War II to fight in Israel, the latter in violation of U.S. citizenship laws.[22] While refusing to ship any major arms systems to Israel until the late 1950s, the United States worked out deals with NATO allies to step into the breach.[23] It provided training to Israeli military personnel in the United States; allowed large numbers of American Jews to serve in the Israeli military; facilitated the transfer of technology to Israeli arms industry; and covertly provided Israel with funds to buy arms. The United States extended its covert support also to Israel's nuclear program. In 1955, the United States gave Israel a small nuclear reactor, together with a library of research reports on nuclear topics, and trained some fifty-six Israeli nuclear scientists. In addition, according to CIA, the two hundred pounds of enriched uranium (enough to make thirteen to twenty bombs) that went missing in 1966 from a company in Apollo, Pennsylvania, were smuggled by Mossad to fuel Israel's nuclear weapons program.[24]

The United States turned down repeated Israeli demands, during the 1950s, to give formal guarantees to protect its security. These formal rebuffs, however, were mostly for Arab consumption. Official documents of this era "are full of remarks suggesting that protecting Israel was a matter of official concern. The Israeli archives reveal the following message from [Secretary of State] Dulles to the Israeli Foreign Ministry, 'Even without a formal link, which we will reach when the time comes, Israel should trust that the USA will not abandon her.'"[25]

Starting in the late 1950s, the United States began to reverse its policy of appearing to distance itself from Israel. Two developments during this decade, both inevitable, brought about this change in policy. With a steady inflow of Western arms and military technology, Israel had widened its military lead over the neighboring Arab states. Moreover, in the Suez War of 1956, it also provided convincing demonstration of its superiority in battle against the leading Arab state. Official American assessments of Israel's military during this period state that Egypt "would be decisively defeated" in the event of war with Israel.[26] In the meanwhile, by the late 1950s, Arab nationalists had gained control of three key Arab states—Egypt, Syria, and Iraq—that were now allied with the Soviet Union. Under these circumstances, it is scarcely surprising that the United States began to tilt more visibly toward the view that Israel could play a useful, perhaps indispensable, role in countervailing the growing threat that Arab nationalism posed to American interests in the region.[27] The time had arrived for a shift in American policy toward Israel.

Starting in the last years of President Eisenhower's second term, the United States began supplying—openly and without any intermediaries— large weapon systems to Israel. This trend accelerated under President Kennedy, who told Golda Meier in December 1962, "The United States has a special relationship with Israel in the Middle East really comparable to that which it has with Britain over a wide range of world affairs . . . We are in a position, then, to make clear to the Arabs that we will maintain our friendship with Israel and our security guarantees." In 1962, President Kennedy acceded to Israeli demands to supply Hawk antiaircraft missiles. The direct military relationship between the United States and Israel received a further boost during the Johnson administration. In February 1965, when West Germany canceled an arms deal after its discovery, leading to protests by Arab states, the United States decided to "compensate" for the loss by supplying Israel with 200 Patton tanks even though Germany had completed delivery of 70 percent of the arms promised. In February 1966, the United States decided to supply Israel with forty-eight lightweight and high-speed Skyhawk bombers.[28] It should be clear that well before the War of June 1967, the United States had begun to replace France as the major supplier of arms to Israel.

The United States also helped Israel pay for the weapon systems whose deliveries it ensured one way or another. Over 1948 to 1965, with no domestic savings on average, Israel financed its imports of armaments and capital and consumer goods entirely from foreign financial inflows. Much of these financial flows consisted of unilateral transfers from three sources: West German reparation payments, official government aid, and donations from the Jewish diaspora.[29]

Overwhelmingly, the private contributions from the Jewish diaspora came from the United States, helped in considerable measure by the tax-free status of these contributions even though they did not satisfy the legal criteria for charitable contributions. In the United States, the United Jewish Appeal (UJA) orchestrates the drive to mobilize private contributions to Israel. Instead of spending these funds through its own distribution channels, the UJA hands them over to the Jewish Agency of Israel, a quasi-governmental organization, which then allocates it mostly to new settlements, religious institutions, and the absorption of new colonists.[30]

American support was also vital in persuading West Germany to accede to Israeli demands for reparations and making these payments generous. First, West Germany was not obliged to make these payments, since it had not waged war against Israel; it agreed to these payments under pressure from Western powers and in particular the United States.[31] In addition, the Western powers sacrificed their own claims to allow West Germany to increase its reparations to Israel. In order to allow the West Germans to accommodate Israeli demands, Western creditor nations delayed the settlement of their own debts, and, in some cases, agreed to reduce them. In addition, the U.S. High Commissioner in Germany pressed the West Germans to accede as nearly as possible to all of the Zionist demands for reparations. The influence that Jewish banking circles could exert on the course of the London Debt Conference—that convened in October 1950—also persuaded the West Germans to be generous in its reparations to Israel.[32]

Because of these pressures, Israel succeeded in extracting the most generous reparations from West Germany. In September 1952, under the first of these agreements, West Germany agreed to transfer $845 million in reparations to Israel to be paid out over fourteen years.[33] Over time, these payments increased dramatically. According to one source, by 1998 "the totality of German expenditures for reparations, indemnifications, and restitutions exceeded DM 100 billion, and the single largest beneficiary of these distributions was the nation of Israel. Altogether, the infusion of *Wiedergutmachung* had saved the little country during its most precarious early years of economic vulnerability."[34] In the first decades after its creation, Israel could not have built a first-world economy, industry, and military without these transfers from West Germany.

The transformation of Israel from a strategic liability to a "strategic" asset had begun long before Israel's stunning victory in the June War of 1967. Indeed, this transformation had started soon after Israel's creation, driven by the recognition that Israel was a "strategic liability": it could not be abandoned. Israel reinforced this logic on two fronts. First, on the ground, it continued to provoke the weak Arab states to respond with belligerent rhetoric, become more radical in their nationalist goals, and move into the Soviet camp. Once this had persuaded Western nations to arm Israel, and give it a decisive lead over the combined forces of Arabs, Israel began to claim that it was a strategic asset. It had the ability to defend Western interests in the Middle East. Inside the United States, simultaneously, the Israeli lobby worked very hard to create support for Israeli positions at the highest levels of civil society and the government. Finally, in June 1967, Israel delivered the *coup de grace*—by defeating the two leading Arab nationalist states. It had now gained the gratitude of the Western world by greatly diminishing the Arab nationalist threat to their interests in the region. Israel would now capitalize upon this gratitude to deepen Western support for its policies and, more importantly, ensure that the United States—unlike Britain—would never be free to backtrack from its support for Israel.

CHAPTER 18

THE JUNE WAR

AFTERMATH

The glory of past ages no longer is to be seen at a distance but is, from now on, part of the new state.
> —*Haaretz* editorial, June 8, 1967

We have returned to our holiest places, we have returned in order not to part from them ever again.
> —Moshe Dayan, June 9, 1967

A messianic, expansionist wind swept over the country. Religious folk spoke of a "miracle" and of "salvation"; the ancient lands of Israel had been restored to God's people.
> —Benny Morris, 2001

You can trace the resurgence of what we call Islamic extremism to the Six Day War.
> —Michael Oren, 2007[1]

BY THE MID-1960S, ISRAEL WAS POISED TO alter decisively the balance of historical forces in the Middle East. It showed growing eagerness to engage the Arabs in a major war, and dramatically alter the geopolitical realities in the region.

The confrontation between Israel and the Arabs was coming to a head. Since its launching in 1897, Zionism challenged the Palestinians to respond with their own nationalism. It also raised the tempo of the nascent Arab nationalist movement, especially after the British declared their support for the creation of a Jewish state in Palestine. In 1948, the creation of Israel, followed by its defeat of five Arab armies, gave the Arab nationalists a new urgent task: they would have to roll back this Jewish colonial settler state. Once this goal began to radicalize Arab nationalism,

Israel would offer itself to the West and especially the United States as the chief bulwark against this rising threat to Western interests. Indeed, the belligerent rhetoric of the Arab nationalists was so useful to the Zionists that they would do everything in their power to keep this pot boiling. Israel would continue to provoke the Arabs in order to give a radical direction to their national aspirations, direct Arab anger against the United States, and provoke them into a premature war against Israel. The West was quite pleased with these developments. By tying down Egyptian and Syrian forces on the Israeli front, Israel set clear limits to the spread of Arab nationalism to the oil-rich Arab kingdoms around the Persian Gulf.

Arab nationalism lacked the grit and stamina that could mobilize the Arabs for their confrontation with Israel. This fledgling nationalism contained two flaws from the outset. It was not deeply rooted in the history or traditions of the Arabic-speaking peoples of the Middle East and North Africa. In the late nineteenth century, the Christian Arabs of Syria—the first Arabs to reap the benefits of a Western education and embrace Western ideas—began to cultivate this new *ethnic* identity; this would form the basis of a new Syrian state or, more ambitiously, unite all the Arabic-speaking peoples in a larger Arab state. During World War I, the British also briefly invoked this identity when inciting the Arabs to revolt against the Ottoman state. Not only did Arab nationalism lack historical precedents, but it also sought to turn its back on the religious identity of the Arabic speaking Muslims with its strong emphasis on secularism. Arab nationalism sought to build a new ethnic identity by drawing inspiration from a distant Arab past—of the glorious caliphate of the Umayyads and Abbasids—but without its beating heart, Islam. By emphasizing the secularist character of their resistance, the Arab nationalists would also fail to connect to and mobilize the deep sympathies of the larger non-Arab Islamic world for the iconic importance of Palestine in Islamic sacred geography.

Arab nationalism had a second serious flaw. It espoused goals that were radical—uniting the Arab world, terminating Western control over Arab resources, and dismantling the Jewish state in Palestine—but, in nearly all its components, this was a movement led by members of the petty bourgeoisie, who were also divided by tribal loyalties. This led to a troubling contradiction, between the class character of the Arab nationalist movement and its radical aspirations. In fact, their anti-imperialism and rhetoric of Arab unity were superficial, adopted, in considerable part, to accommodate populist—Islamist—anger over the creation of Israel. Among other things, this meant that the Arab nationalist leadership did not have the stomach for mounting a sustained resistance.

This contradiction was visible in the strategy that the Arab nationalists adopted to defeat Israel. Instead of creating a mass base among their people and preparing for a long drawn peoples' war against a technologically superior adversary—as the Vietnamese or Algerians were doing—the Arab nationalists sought to match Israel on its own ground, by acquiring modern weapon systems from the Soviets. Their hollow radicalism became a trap for the Arab nationalists. Without Israel's sophisticated industrial, educational, and scientific assets, the Arab nationalists should have known that they could not win conventional wars against so advanced an adversary. Yet, the Arab nationalist leadership never departed from their commitment to fighting conventional wars against Israel. Not even repeated defeats in their wars with Israel—in 1948, 1956, 1967, and many smaller encounters besides—could persuade them to rethink their strategy. The petty bourgeois Arab regimes were not willing to make the sacrifices demanded by a guerilla war. They also knew that their people could not be inspired to fight a peoples' war in the name of a newfangled, secular Arab nationalism.

Unavoidably, as a result, the Arab nationalists were heading toward a final confrontation with Israel that they could not win because they had chosen to fight on the enemy's terms. The Israelis knew this. By the early 1960s, it was clear to Israelis that they possessed the military capability to knock out the opposing Arab armies in a matter of days. The Americans too knew this. According to official American assessments before the 1967 war, the Israeli army would need only "five to seven days" to win a war against Arabs, regardless of who initiated the hostilities. When President Johnson criticized this estimate as too "optimistic," the intelligence services went back to the drawing board. Only trivially less positive, their revised estimates predicted that Israel would need no more than ten days to defeat the Arab armies.[2] President Gamal Abdel Nasser of Egypt too knew that he could not go to war and win.[3] Yet, the Arabs lost no opportunity to threaten Israel and blundered headlong into a war they should have done everything to avoid until they were better prepared.

They paid dearly for this bravado. On the first day of the war, within a few short hours, Egypt and Jordan lost their entire air force. Syria too lost half its air force; they saved the other half by flying their aircrafts out of the reach of Israeli jets. Two hours after Israeli attacks began, General Ezer Weizman, deputy chief of general staff, called his wife to say, "We have won the war."[4] This was no exaggeration. Without air cover, the Arab armies fell apart within days. By the time hostilities ended on June 10, Israel had captured all of the Sinai, Gaza, the West Bank, and the Golan Heights. The Zionists had exceeded the official Zionist aim of creating a Jewish state in *all* of Palestine.

The United States had bestowed its blessings on Israel's preemptive strike against the Arabs. At first, the U.S. president warned Israel against taking unilateral action to lift the Egyptian blockade of the Straits of Tiran; he preferred international action. In the days before June 5, however, he changed his mind. Convinced that Israel—in the words of President Johnson—"could whip the hell out of them," Secretary of State McNamara effectively "gave Israel a green light to take military actions against Egypt."[5] The United States also assisted Israel's war efforts by supplying timely intelligence on the damage caused by Israeli bombing of Egyptian airfields, and, later, on Egyptian troop locations and movements.[6] This intelligence may have helped Israel to achieve its military aims before the imposition of a ceasefire.

Israel and the United States would now work, singly and together, to extract the greatest political capital from the new situation in the Middle East. Their goals were not identical, however. It might appear that the United States and Israel had a shared interest in gaining Arab recognition of Israel, establishing peace with the Arabs, and bringing the Arab nationalist states out of the Soviet camp. This is deceptive. The United States *did* have a strong interest in pursuing these goals. A comprehensive peace with the Arabs, however, could not be in Israel's interest. Should the Arab nationalist states make peace with Israel and abandon the Soviets, this would greatly diminish Israel's value to the United States. Israel could not claim the privileges of a strategic asset if key Arab nationalist states—like Egypt and Syria—too joined the American camp.

Israeli objectives after the June War were quite different from what the Americans would want to pursue. The stunning victory of 1967 had created new opportunities for Israel to pursue the maximalist goals of Zionism. Israel had triumphed over the Arabs; they now possessed all of Palestine, all of the Sinai, and they looked down upon Damascus from the Golan Heights. Why should they retreat now? Certainly, they were not going to retreat from the West Bank and Gaza. This was the new frontier of their colonial project. They would bring a million Jewish colons into these new lands, and, when the time was ripe, they would drive out the Palestinians. The Israelis knew that their plan to extend their colonial frontier clashed with American interest in moving toward an Arab-Israeli peace settlement. It would be the task of the Israel lobby to finesse this conflict. The several components of this lobby would flex their muscle to "persuade" the United States to continue to support Israel—indeed, deepen its partnership with Israel—despite this fundamental clash in their interests.[7]

Israel would have its way, since it held the trump card of Arab territories conquered in June 1967. Both Israel and the United States understood—each in its own way—that they would use the conquered territories as bargaining chips to force the Arabs to recognize Israel. On

June 19, within days after the war ended, at a secret meeting, the Israeli cabinet offered Egypt and Syria the terms of a "peace agreement based on the international border and the security needs of Israel."[8] This decision was communicated to Secretary of State, Dean Rusk, but there is no mention in the American records that the Israelis asked Dean Rusk to transmit this decision to Egypt or Syria. The Arabs too deny receiving this message. Avi Shlaim concludes, "One is left with the impression that Eban was more interested in using the cabinet decision of June 19 to impress the Americans than to engage the governments of Egypt and Syria in substantive negotiations." In addition, the Israeli leaders, in public and private, quickly began to backtrack from this "decision," and less than a month later, they were approving plans for Jewish settlements on the Golan Heights. "The decision of 19 June," writes Avi Shlaim, "became a dead letter even before its formal cancellation in October."[9]

Moreover, the terms of the "peace agreement" offered by Israel were designed for Arab rejection. A single defeat, no matter how quick and decisive, could not have persuaded the Arab nationalist regimes to swallow their humiliation, recognize Israel, and accept Israel's dominance over the Middle East. Even if some of these Arab regimes may have been inclined to sign a humiliating peace, their population demanded continuation of the struggle to roll back the Israeli state. On September 1, 1967, in a great show of defiance and unity at the Khartoum Summit, the Arab states proclaimed the three no's: no negotiation, no recognition, and no peace with Israel. The summit could only accept unconditional withdrawal of Israeli troops from all Arab territories conquered in June 1967.

Taking advantage of this rejection—that they must have anticipated all along—the Israeli cabinet, on October 30, secretly revoked its earlier offer of peace with Egypt and Syria based on international borders; they would now seek to adjust these borders to enhance Israeli security. In principle, the United States endorsed the new Israeli position. In the words of Walt Rostow, special assistant to the president, the United States was "opposed to any UN resolution that would require Israel to concede war gains except in return for an Arab-Israeli final settlement."[10] The ostensible congruence of Israeli and US positions produced the UN Security Council Resolution 242 of November 22, which called for "peace" with the Arabs in exchange for the return of their territories. Israel now had the legal cover of the UN Security Council to hold on to the territories it had conquered in June 1967 until the Arabs agreed to its terms for "peace."

On the surface, there were few changes in the Arab world in the aftermath of their stunning defeat of June 1967. There would be no change in the strategy they had pursued in their confrontation with Israel and the United States. They would prepare once again to wage conventional wars against Israel. Very quickly, the Egyptians and Syrians replenished the military hardware they had lost during the war. Their stunning defeat brought no change in leadership in the Arab world. Falsely, some Arab commentators took all this as a sign that the Arabs remained politically undefeated despite their military losses. One leading Arab scholar, Hisham Sharabi, wrote that Israel's "crushing victory" had not produced an Arab "surrender." "On the contrary," he concluded, "new forces emerged which pushed political capitulation still further away."[11]

This was hubris—in the face of defeat. The absence of significant changes—much less fundamental ones—in the Arab world was a portent of paralysis. This could scarcely be construed as evidence of the "astonishing Arab capacity to cope with . . . defeat."[12] In the years following June 1967, there would be no accountability for defeated Arab leaders, no soul-searching among nationalist elites, no rejection of defeated military strategies, no urge to uncover structural causes of the Arab defeat, no renewed efforts to forge a united Arab front to reverse the Zionist gains since 1917. Instead, the Arab elites responded to their defeat by reinforcing the *status quo ante*.

Arab peoples were not happy over the absence of an appropriate response to the defeat of 1967. There was discontent in the ranks of the army and protests among workers and students: but the Arab regimes quickly suppressed all opposition with purges from the army, arrests, and torture.[13] Alienated from their own population, these regimes would hold on to power by becoming police states. In addition, there emerged a growing gap between the ideology of the Arab nationalist states—still seeking legitimacy in the language of secular Arab nationalism—and the Islamist rhetoric of the populist opposition to the Arab regimes. Over time, as the Islamist opposition gained strength across much of the Arab world, the discredited "nationalist" regimes sought to ensure their survival through repression and accommodation—openly and secretly—with Israel and the United States.

In the contest of nerves that followed the June War, Israel held all the cards. It had won a stunning victory, it had nearly quadrupled its territory, it now had the United States visibly and firmly on its side, and it had the legal cover of UN Security Council Resolution 242 to hold on to the conquests as long as it took to engineer the "peace" that it wanted. Israel had time on its side. It would use this advantage to create new facts on the ground to make its territorial acquisitions irreversible. On the other hand, time worked against the defeated Arab regimes. Their defeat had eroded their legitimacy, and they were under growing pressure to reverse this erosion by making individual deals with Israel to recover their territory. The nationalist Arab states could expect little help now from the oil-rich, royalist Arab regimes either. Now that the Arab nationalist threat to their regimes had diminished, they were under no pressure to continue to support the Arab nationalist policy of confronting Israel indefinitely. Their interest too lay in dismantling Arab nationalism.

The conditions were now ripe for an Arab capitulation. Ironically, Egypt, the leader of the Arab nationalist movement, would be the first to break rank. Clearly, Israel wanted to retain all the territories it had gained in the war; but this was risky. This could extend the life of a tottering Arab nationalism and encourage renewed Soviet intervention in the Arab-Israeli conflict. Its next best option, therefore, was to give up the Sinai and make a separate deal with the Egyptians. The Egyptian defection would break the back of Arab nationalism, giving Israel a free hand in dealing with the Palestinians and the other Arabs. Israel also knew that, among the defeated Arab states, Egypt had the strongest incentive for making a separate peace. It had suffered the largest territorial losses. Its economic losses too were the heaviest because of the closure of the Suez Canal and the loss of the Abu-Rudeis oil fields in Sinai. Once it had recovered the territories it had lost, Egypt could claim that it had redeemed its honor.

In January 1971, within months of entering office, President Anwar Sadat began making peace overtures to Israel. He was eager to sign a separate peace with Israel. The Israelis showed little interest; they wanted a peace agreement to precede any talk about territorial concessions. Rebuffed by Israel, and impatient to force it to the negotiating table, President Sadat planned a limited preemptive war to cross the Suez Canal and dislodge Israelis from its eastern bank. He had calculated that this would force the Israelis to negotiate. In October 1973, the Egyptian army successfully executed a surprise crossing of the Suez Canal. In a swift counteroffensive, however, Israel regained the upper hand, crossed the Suez, cut off supplies to the Egyptians in Sinai and surrounded the Egyptian Third Army. Although Egypt lost this war too, President Sadat would get his separate peace with Israel. The October War persuaded Israel and the United States to negotiate the terms of a separate peace treaty with Egypt. In September 1978, at Camp David, President Sadat broke away from the Arab world to recognize the legitimacy of the colonial settler state and its expropriation of 78 percent of Palestine. In return for recognizing Israel, breaking ranks with the Arabs, and abandoning the Palestinians to their own devices, Egypt got back the Sinai (on condition that it would be demilitarized) and a perpetual commitment of $2 billion in U.S. aid. It was a tremendous bargain for Israel and the United States.

At Camp David, Egypt formally declared the end of the era of Arab nationalism. Four limited wars, waged intermittently over a period of twenty-five years, had exhausted Egypt. It had had enough of leadership; it would now mind its own house. The Palestinians, Syria, Jordan, and Lebanon would now be on their own. They too would seek to make their separate "peace" with Israel. In reality, they would acquiesce to whatever fate Israel would choose to deal out to each of them separately. Abandoned, under Israeli occupation or scattered in refugee camps in the Arab world, the Palestinians—it appeared—had lost everything. In hindsight, the Arab nationalist movement—in its utter failure—appeared to be a huge distraction and, perhaps worse, a monumental waste of opportunities. Instead of delivering sovereignty, unity, and dignity to the Arabs, it had reinforced the combined power of Western imperialism working in tandem with the Jewish colonial settler state. Almost certainly, no other region of the world, in the postcolonial era, had failed so completely in pushing back the legacy of Western imperialism.

CHAPTER 19

THE LOBBY GAINS CLOUT

Without this lobby, Israel would have gone down the drain.

—Isaiah (Si) Kenen

During every congressional campaign, each candidate for every seat
is asked to describe his or her views on the Middle East. Most office-
seekers happily comply in writing. AIPAC then shares the results with its
members, helping them to decide who is the most pro-Israel.

—J. J. Goldberg, 1996

AIPAC has one enormous advantage. It really doesn't have any
opposition.

—Douglas Bloomfield, 2003

In the last two decades between 1980 and 2000, American Jews gained
power and influence beyond anything that they had ever experienced.

—Stephen Schwartz, 2006

A lobby is like a night flower: it thrives in the dark and dies in the sun.

—Steven Rosen, 2005

If Israel nuked Chicago, Congress would approve.

—Steve Reed, 2009[1]

IT IS IMPOSSIBLE TO FORM A PROPER estimate of Israel—its creation, wars,
and expansionist policies—unless we examine it as part of a triangular
relationship; the Jewish diaspora and the Western powers are the other
actors in this relationship.

It was no ordinary feat to create in the middle of the twentieth century an exclusionary colonial settler state—based on ethnic cleansing—
in the heart of another civilization. The early Zionists knew this; they
were visionaries with a firm grasp of reality, not naïfs and dreamers. They
knew that they would be contending with the people whom they would

displace from Palestine, as well as the near and far Islamicate. If the Zionists could somehow displace the Palestinians without directly impacting their neighbors—say, by transporting *all* the Palestinians to Argentina—the Islamicate would still resist this intrusion.[2] Colonial settlers are not tourists who enter a region, take in its sights, spend a few nights in the hotels—and leave with a few mementos of their visit. When these settlers create their own exclusionary state, they declare war not only against the people they displace. They declare a more general war, entailing violence against the demography, cartography, geopolitics, and the historical memory of the region on which they impose themselves.

We cannot explain the creation of Israel—and its economic and military successes—as the manifestation of Jewish power alone. The Zionists had succeeded because they were capable of amplifying Jewish power by recruiting allies. The Western Jews would have been foolhardy had they, on their own, undertaken so daring a project, one that was certain to produce collision with the great mass of Islamicate peoples. The Zionists had proposed this project because they were convinced they could use Western Jews—embedded in Western societies—to harness the resources, arms and drives of Western societies in support of their project. In order to oppose, contain and subdue the Islamicate world, the Zionists would have to oppose against it the much greater mass of the Western world.

Israel's dependence on Western power—and hence on Western Jews—did not, and could not, end with its creation. On the contrary, this dependence would grow. It was easy enough to plant a Jewish settler state in the Middle East at a time when Western control over this region was at its height, and when the disparity between the West and the Islamicate was greater than it had ever been. However, this disparity would decline in the postwar period. As the Islamicate countries gained a measure of independence, they would build their economic, industrial, and military capabilities. In addition, the Israeli intrusion was certain to evoke a countervailing response, perhaps a delayed one, from the Islamicate. At first, this response took the form of Arab nationalism, but, later, when this first wave of resistance was defeated or co-opted, it was followed by a second wave of resistance that drew upon Islamic ideas and ideals. Driven by its maximalist ambitions as well as reacting to the deepening Islamicate response to its insertion in Palestine, Israel too has drawn increasingly upon the financial, military, and diplomatic support of its new mother country, the United States.

Israel's growing reliance upon the United States could become a liability. The Zionists could not afford a repeat of Britain, their first mother country, which had dramatically scaled down its commitment to Zionism in 1939, when the strategic costs of this policy became too high. In choosing to found its colonial project now on the power of the United States, Israel faced a similar risk. Indeed, the cost of abandonment would rise as Israel's Jewish population grew. In 1948, at the time of its creation, Israel contained less than 6 percent of the world's Jews. That share would rise dramatically after 1948, and as Israel's share of world Jewry increased, so would the cost of abandonment by the United States. The Zionists would have to avoid or, at least, minimize the risk that the United States might abandon Israel.

This was the great challenge before the Zionists. How could they get the United States firmly in Israel's corner, and, more importantly, keep it there? This called for a two-pronged approach. On the ground, Israel would have to sustain and deepen Arab and Islamicate anger against the West and the United States in particular. Israel's expansionist policies could only succeed by creating the anti-American backlash against which it could "defend" the United States. Simultaneously, the Zionist Jews would expand and use their influence over domestic politics in the United States to shape its Middle Eastern policy. In short, the Zionists would have to craft a "special relationship" between Israel and the United States, whose reigns they would firmly keep in their own hands. The Jewish lobby would maximize American support for Israel, promote strategic cooperation between the two countries, magnify and misrepresent Arab and Islamist threats to the United States, and obtain for Israel the license to police the Middle East. This chapter will examine how the Jewish lobby, since the creation of Israel, acquired the power to pursue and achieve these goals.

.   .   .

Consider first some of the chief characteristics of the special relationship that has developed between the United States and Israel in the decades since the creation of Israel.

One frequently used index of the special relationship tracks the volume of aid that Israel has received from the United States. The value of annual economic and military assistance to Israel increased dramatically in 1970 and 1974, never dipped below $3 billion between 1985 and 2000, and has declined only trivially since then.[3] Moreover, Israel has received this aid on terms that are not available to other aid recipients. For many years now, the Congress has approved aid commitments to Israel automatically, without any discussion or dissent. Israel has received all its aid in the form of grants since 1985, spends most of it on weapon systems, receives all of its assistance at the beginning of each year, bypasses the Department of

Defense in making military purchases, spends its aid without any oversight, and it is free to refinance the debt owed to the U.S. government.[4] The loans to Israel have been eventually forgiven; according to one estimate, between 1974 and 1989, $16.4 billion in military loans received by Israel were forgiven.[5] In addition, the United States has provided $19 billion in loan guarantees to Israel since the 1990s.[6] This has allowed Israel to lower the cost at which it can borrow from the U.S. capital market.

Nearly always, the economic costs of the special relationship to United States are equated with the value of direct financial assistance given to Israel. In terms of 2001 dollars, between 1973 and 2001 Israel has received $240 billion in economic and military assistance from the United States. This figure seriously underestimates the total economic cost of America's special relationship with Israel. A comprehensive accounting of these costs would also include the higher energy costs because of the oil embargo imposed by the Arabs, the aid to Egypt and Jordan in return for signing peace treaties with Israel, the costs of the Arab boycott of U.S. corporations that traded with Israel, the costs of prepositioning supplies in Israel, and so on. According to Thomas Stauffer, the total economic cost to the United States of its special relationship with Israel—between 1973 and 2001—comes to $1.6 trillion.[7]

The aid program is only one aspect of the special relationship between the United States and Israel. Starting in the 1980s, the United States began cooperating with Israel in a variety of military areas: including military planning, joint military exercises, logistics, intelligence gathering, and the development of new weapon systems. In November 1983, the United States and Israel agreed to form a Joint Political-Military Group (JPMG), which meets every six months to deliberate on issues relating to military planning, joint military exercises, and the prepositioning of military supplies in Israel. In May 1986, Israel became the third U.S. ally to join the Strategic Defense Initiative (SDI), which gave it the right to bid for SDI contracts. A year later, Israel became the third country—after Japan and Australia—to become a "major non-NATO" ally; this gave Israel access to advanced weapon systems as well as the right to bid on equal terms for NATO defense contracts.[8] In addition, caving in to Israeli pressure, the United States conducted less than rigorous inspections of Israel's nuclear facilities in the 1960s, and, later, gave Israel a blank check when it became known that it possessed a stockpile of nuclear weapons.[9] Indeed, Cockburn and Cockburn maintain that the United States, in return for Israeli withdrawal from the Sinai in 1957, had allowed Israel to divert 200 pounds of enriched uranium from the Apollo plant in Pennsylvania.[10] According to another source, Israel is reported to have stolen nuclear material on at least three other occasions, without facing any consequences.[11]

Incredibly, the United States has bought little influence over Israeli governments with its annual and ongoing largesse to Israel. On the one hand, as American financial support for Israel has grown, it has been offered increasingly on the most generous terms. Yet, this has almost never stopped Israel from pursuing policies—such as creating illegal Jewish settlements in the West Bank and Gaza, the annexation of Jerusalem and the Golan Heights, engaging in targeted assassinations, and the wars against Lebanon—that are contrary to the wishes of the United States and damage its strategic interests. Rarely, when the U.S. president has dared to disagree with Israel, the Congress has intervened to neuter the president. In September 1991, when President George H. W. Bush sought to delay approval of $10 billion in loan guarantees, the Congress opposed the delay, with enough votes to override a veto.[12] Despite the massive aid it extends, the United States can "elicit cooperation" from Israel only by offering "additional carrots." It cannot employ "sticks (threats to withhold aid)."[13]

On the diplomatic front, the United States gets its directives from Israel. At the United Nations Security Council, in recent decades, it has logged a nearly uninterrupted record of vetoing every resolution that is opposed by Israel. Starting in September 1972, the United States exercised its veto power on thirty-nine occasions to shield Israel against the force of international law. It has vetoed resolutions that affirmed the right of Palestinians to self-determination, the right of Palestinian refugees to return to their homes, or the inadmissibility of acquiring territory by the use of force. On other occasions, it has disallowed resolutions condemning Israeli violations of Palestinian rights in the West Bank and Gaza or repeated Israeli attacks against neighboring countries.[14] If an Arab or African country had Israel's record of violating international laws, it would have invited the full force of international sanctions many years ago.

The United States and Israel have established a special relationship also in the area of trade. Israel became the first country to sign a free-trade agreement with the United States in 1985, nearly a decade before the latter established free trade with Canada and Mexico, its two closest neighbors. The benefits of this free trade agreement have been quite asymmetrical. The share of Israel's exports absorbed by the United States nearly doubled between 1980 and 1997; whereas the U.S. share in Israel's imports remained virtually unchanged over the same period.[15] In December 2004, the United States signed a limited a free trade accord to admit exports from designated areas in Egypt provided they contained 11.7 percent of Israeli components.[16] Perhaps, this is the only free trade accord between two countries that ties the exports from one of these countries to imports from a third country.

. . .

In the evolution of U.S. relations with Israel since 1948, as the latter mutated from a strategic liability to a strategic asset, Israel and its Zionist allies in the United States have always occupied the driver's seat. President Truman had shepherded the creation of Israel in 1947 not because the American establishment saw it as a strategic asset. "No one," writes Cheryl Rubenberg, "not even the Israelis themselves, argues that the United States supported the creation of the Jewish state for reasons of security or national interest."[17] Domestic politics, in an election year, was the primary force behind President Truman's Zionism. In addition, the damage to U.S. interests from the creation of Israel—although massive—was not immediate. The first blows from Israel's creation would be borne by the British who were still the paramount power in the region.[18] Nevertheless, soon after he had helped create Israel, President Truman enacted measures that *appeared* to distance the United States from the Jewish state. Instead of committing American troops to protect Israel, when it fought against five Arab armies, he imposed an even-handed arms embargo on both sides in the conflict.[19] Had Israel been dismantled, the United States would have urged international action to protect the Jewish colonists in Palestine, but it would have accepted Israel's premature demise as *fait accompli*. Zionist pressures failed to persuade President Truman to lift the arms embargo. Ironically, military deliveries from Czechoslovakia, at Soviet urging, may have saved the day for Israel.

Once Israel had defeated the armies of the Arab proto-states and expelled the Palestinians to emerge as an exclusively Jewish state in 1949, these brute facts would work in its favor. Led by the United States, the Western powers would recognize Israel, aware that they had helped create a liability that they would have to defend. At the same time, the humiliation of defeat gave an impetus to Arab nationalists across the region, who directed their anger against Israel and its Western sponsors. Ironically, this placed Israel in a strong position to accelerate its transformation into a strategic asset. In tandem with the Jewish lobby in the United States, Israel sought to maximize Western assistance through policies that stoked Arab nationalism; as its military superiority grew, Israel ratcheted its aggressive posture toward the Arabs. Israel had the power to set in motion a cumulative process that would soon create the Arab threat against which it would "defend" the West. As a result, at various points during the 1950s, France, the United States, and Britain came to regard Israel as a strategic asset.

America's embrace of Israel did not begin in 1967. Israel's victory in the June War only accelerated a process that had been underway since before its creation. Indeed, the Zionists had decided in 1939 to pursue the United States as their new mother country; the large and influential population of American Jews was a resource waiting to be exploited by the Zionists.[20] This decision paid off handsomely in 1947, when American support carried the day for Zionism as the United Nations voted on a partition plan for Palestine.

For several years after 1947, the United States sought to contain the damage to its strategic interests caused by the creation of Israel. However, these efforts were self-defeating; the die had been cast. Israel—not the United States—was now in the driver's seat, and it would do everything in its power to increase and exploit the negative fallout from its insertion in the Middle East. As Israel succeeded in enhancing—within limits—the Arab threat to itself and the United States, the Jewish lobby too would regain confidence; it would reorganize to promote Israel as a strategic asset. We have here another vicious circle—virtuous, for Israel. The Jewish lobby would gain strength as the combined Arab and Soviet threat to the United States grew.

When Israel scaled back the Arab threat in 1967, the Jewish lobby would have a field day. Quickly, it moved in to start cashing the enormous political capital that victory in the June War had garnered for Israel in the United States. The Israeli capture of Jerusalem in 1967 also greatly energized the Christian Zionists, who, with encouragement from Jewish Zionists, would organize, enter into Republican politics, and soon become a major ally of the Jewish lobby. The sky was now the limit for Israel and the Zionists in the United States. The special relationship would become more special under every new presidency.

Several writers on the American left have pooh-poohed the charge that the Jewish lobby has been a leading force shaping America's Middle East policy. They argue that the United States has supported Israel because of a convergence of their interests in the region.[21] Middle Eastern oil, these convergence theorists point out, correctly, is "a stupendous source of strategic power, and one of the greatest material prizes in world history."[22] Incorrectly, however, they conclude that this is what has driven U.S. policy toward the Middle East. *A priori*, this is an odd position to maintain, since Britain—up until the early 1950s—had managed to maintain complete control over Middle Eastern oil without Israel, an accomplishment that the United States could not sustain despite (or, is it because of) the "strategic support" of Israel. Successively, the convergence theorists argue, Western control over oil came under threat, starting in the 1950s, from

Arab nationalism and, later, from militant Islamism. Israel has demonstrated its strategic value by holding in check and, later, defeating, the Arab nationalist challenge. Since then, Israel has contained the Islamist challenge to U.S. hegemony over the region.

It may be useful to examine Noam Chomsky's analysis of the special relationship between the United States and Israel, since he enjoys iconic status among liberals and leftists alike in the United States. Chomsky frames his analysis of the "causal factors" behind the special relationship as essentially a choice between "domestic pressure groups" and "U.S. strategic interests." He finds two limitations in the argument that the "American Jewish community" is the chief protagonist of the special relationship between Israel and the United States. First, "it underestimates the scope of the 'support for Israel,' and second, it overestimates the role of political pressure groups in decision-making." Chomsky points out that the Israel lobby is "far broader" than the American Jewish community; it embraces liberals, labor leaders, Christian fundamentalists, conservative hawks, and "fervent cold warriors of all stripes."[23] While this broader definition of the Israel lobby is appropriate, Chomsky thinks that the presence of this "far broader" support for Israel diminishes the role that American Jews play in the Israel lobby.

Two hidden assumptions underpin Chomsky's claim that a broader Israel lobby shifts the locus of lobbying to non-Jewish groups. First, he fails to account for the strong overlap—barring the Christian fundamentalists—between the American Jewish community and the other domestic pressure groups he enumerates. In the United States, this overlap has existed since the early decades of the twentieth century, and increased considerably in the postwar period. It is scarcely to be doubted that Jews, deservedly, hold a disproportionate share of the leadership positions in corporations, the labor movement, and those professions that shape public discourse. Starting in the 1980s, the ascendancy of Jewish neoconservatives—together with their think tanks and media presence—gave American Jews an equally influential voice in conservative circles. Certainly, the weight of Jewish neoconservative opinion during the early years of President Bush—both inside and outside his administration—has been second to that of none. The substantial Jewish presence in the leadership circles of the "other" pressure groups undermines Chomsky's contention that the Israel lobby is "far broader" than the American Jewish community.

There is a second problem with Chomsky's argument. Implicitly, he assumes that the different pro-Israel groups have existed, acted, and evolved independently of each other; alternatively, the combined impact of the lobbying efforts of these groups is merely additive. This ignores the galvanizing role that Jewish organizations have played in mobilizing Gentile opinion behind the Zionist project. The activism of the American

Jews—as individuals, groups, and networks—has operated at several levels. Certainly, the leaders of the Zionist movement have directed a large part of their energies to lobbying at the highest levels of official decision making. At the same time, they have created, and they orchestrate, a network of Zionist organizations that are dedicated to creating support for their aims in the broader American civil society.

American Jews have worked through several channels to deepen Zionist influence over civil society. As growing numbers of American Jews embraced Zionist goals during the 1940s, as their commitment to Zionism deepened, this forced the largest Jewish organizations to embrace Zionist goals. In addition, since their earliest days, the Zionists have created the organizations, allies, networks, and ideas that would translate into media, congressional, and presidential support for the Zionist project. In addition, since Jewish Americans made up a growing fraction of the activists and leaders in various branches of civil society—the labor, civil rights, and feminist movements—it was natural that major branches of civil society came to embrace Zionist aims. It makes little sense, then, to maintain that the pro-Israeli positions of mainstream American organizations had emerged independently of the activism of the American Jewish community.

Does our contention fail in the case of the Christian Evangelicals because of the absence of Jews in their ranks? In this case, the movement has received the strongest impetus from the "ingathering" of Jews in Israel since the late nineteenth century. The dispensationalist stream within Protestant Christians in the United States—who believe that Jews must return to Israel as a prelude to the Second Coming—has been energized by every Zionist success on the ground. They have viewed these successes—the launching of Zionism, the Balfour Declaration, the creation of Israel, and the capture of Jerusalem, "Judea" and "Samaria" in 1967—as so many confirmations of their dispensationalist eschatology.[24] The movement expands with every Zionist victory. At the same time, it would be utterly naïve to rule out direct relations between the Zionists and the leaders of the evangelical movement. The Zionists have rarely shrunk from accepting support even when it has come from groups with unedifying beliefs. It did not matter that the dispensationalists believed that the Jews who rejected Jesus at his Second Coming would face a fate worse than the Holocaust—their total obliteration.

Noam Chomsky raises a second objection against the ability of the pro-Israeli lobby to influence policy on its own steam. "No *pressure group*," he maintains, "will dominate access to public opinion or maintain consistent influence over policy-making unless its aims are close to those of *elite elements with real power*" (emphasis added).[25] One problem with this argument is easily stated. It pits the Jewish lobby as *one* "pressure group" arrayed against all the others that hold real power. This equation of the Jewish lobby with a narrowly defined "pressure group" is misleading. We have argued—a position that is well supported by the evidence—that Jewish protagonists of Zionism have worked through many different channels to influence public opinion, the composition of political classes, and political decisions. They work through the institutions and media that shape public opinion to determine *what* Americans know about Israel, *how* they think about Israel, and *what* they can say about Israel. Once we recognize the scale of financial resources the Israel lobby commands, the array of political forces it can mobilize, and the tools it commands to direct public opinion on the Middle East, we would shrink from calling it a lobby.[26]

Chomsky quickly proceeds to undermine his own argument about "elite elements with real power." He explains that the "[elite] elements are not *uniform* in interests or (in the case of shared interests) in tactical judgments; and on some issues, *such as this one* [U.S. policy toward Israel], they have often been divided" (emphasis added).[27] Yet, despite the differences in their interests and tactics, and their divisions, Chomsky maintains that these "elite elements" have "real power." Oddly, these "divided" elites—whoever they are—exercise the power of veto over the multifaceted Jewish lobby with its deep pockets, hierarchy of organizations, and influence exercised through key organs of civil society, campaign contributions, and popular votes.

Chomsky's argument shifts again—a second time in the same paragraph—away from "elite elements" to "America's changing conceptions of its political-strategic interests" in the Middle East.[28] This suggests a new approach to defining the chief determinant of U.S. policy toward Israel. At the heart of these "political-strategic interests" is the oil wealth of the Middle East, threatened by Arab nationalists and the Soviets. Presumably, Israel protected these "political-strategic interests" by holding the Arab nationalists *and* the Soviets at bay. Conveniently, Chomsky forgets that the Arab threat to U.S. interests in the Middle East was—in large part—the product of Israel's creation, its policy of ethnic cleansing, diverting the waters of the Jordan River, and constantly offering provocations to the Arabs. It is unnecessary to account for the Soviet threat, since they entered the region on the back of Arab nationalist discontent. Indeed, had Israel never been created, it is more than likely that *all* the states in the Middle East—just like Turkey and Pakistan—would have remained firmly within the Western sphere of influence.

In another attempt to convince his readers that oil has driven U.S. policy toward the Middle East, Chomsky claims that the United States was "committed to win and keep this prize [Saudi oil]."[29] Presumably, it could not do so without help from Israel. This argument fails because it ignores history. Starting in 1933, American oil corporations—who later merged to form *Aramco*—gained exclusive rights to explore, extract and market Saudi oil. Saudi Arabia first acquired a 25 percent ownership stake in *Aramco* in 1973. Had there emerged an Arab nationalist threat to U.S. control over Saudi Arabian oil in the 1950s and 1960s—in the absence of Israel—the United States and Britain could have confronted these threats on their own.[30] Far from helping to reinforce American control over Saudi oil, Israel, by radicalizing Arab nationalism, gave Saudi Arabia the excuse to first gain a 25 percent stake in *Aramco* and then nationalize it in 1988.

Was the United States actually committed to winning and keeping the "stupendous" prize? If the United States were indeed committed to this goal, it would have pursued a Middle East policy that could be expected to maximize—with low risks of failure—the access of U.S. oil corporations to exploration, extraction, and distribution rights over oil in this region. However, this is not what United States did. In creating, arming, and shielding Israel, the United States has followed a policy that could have been foreseen—and, indeed, was foreseen by the officials at the State and Defense Departments—to produce exactly the opposite effects. U.S. policies toward the Middle East, together with the reinforcing actions of Israel, stirred up Arab nationalism, radicalized it, and led within a few years to the Arab nationalist takeover of three of the four key states in the Arab world. In turn, this contributed to the nationalization of oil wealth even in those Arab countries that remained clients of the United States, not to speak of countries taken over by Arab nationalists, who excluded the U.S. oil corporations from this industry altogether. In addition, since U.S. partisanship of Israel forced Arab nationalists to seek Soviet support, the Middle East became a leading cockpit of Cold War conflicts as well. In the October War of 1973, the United States provoked the Arab nations—by massively resupplying the Israeli army during this war—to impose a costly oil embargo against the United States. In opposition to the pleadings of its oil corporations, the United States prohibited them from doing business with three oil-producing nations in the Middle East—Iran, Iraq, and Libya.[31]

If oil had been driving America's Middle East policy, we should be able to see the fingerprints of the oil lobby all over this policy. In recent decades, according to Mearsheimer and Walt, the oil corporations have aimed their lobbying efforts almost entirely at "their commercial interests rather than on broader aspects of foreign policy." They have worked to get the best deals on tax policies, government regulations, and drilling rights. Even the AIPAC bears witness to this. In the early 1980s, Morris J. Amitay, former executive director of AIPAC, noted, "We rarely see them [oil corporations] lobbying on foreign policy issues . . . In a sense, we have the field to ourselves."[32]

. . .

In order to study the efficacy of the Israel lobby, we must examine its movement in time, in a dialectical framework. The Jewish lobby is part of the forces—including Israel, Palestinians, Arab nationalists, Islamists, the United States, and Soviet Union—that affect and are affected by the destabilizing logic of Zionism. It has gained strength from Israeli actions on the ground to transform itself into a strategic asset. It has grown as Israeli victories have galvanized American Jewry, Christian Zionists, and the wider American public.

Over the course of the twentieth century, American Jews elevated themselves to leadership positions in nearly all areas of American life, barring professional sports. During the 1920s and 1930s, there were quotas restricting the entry of Jews into the most prestigious colleges, the best legal and accounting firms refused to employ Jews, and major corporations excluded them from their managerial cadres. Nevertheless, despite these barriers, the Jews steadily moved forward; and, as their standing in society improved, they worked actively to bring down these barriers. A half century later, "virtually every field of endeavor was open to Jews in America."[33] Although their share in the population was about two percent in the late 1960s, Jews constituted 20 percent of the faculty of elite universities and 40 percent of professors of elite schools.[34] In addition, they "make up one fourth or more of the writers, editors, and producers in America's 'elite media,' including network news divisions, the top newsweeklies and the four leading daily newspapers."[35] Further, in the early 1990s, the three largest television networks, the four largest film studios, and the most prestigious newspaper were headed by Jews.[36]

Other indicators too corroborate a strong Jewish presence in the highest echelons of American society. In the last three decades of the twentieth century, according to two leading American sociologists, Jews "made up 50 percent of the top two hundred intellectuals, 40 percent of the Nobel prize winners in science and economics, 20 percent of the professors at leading universities, 21 percent of high-level civil servants, 40 percent of partners in the leading law firms in New York and Washington, 26 percent of the reporters, editors, and executives of the major print and broadcast media, 59 percent of the directors, writers, and producers of the 50 top-grossing motion pictures from 1965 to 1982, and 58 percent of directors, writers, and producers in two or more primetime television series."[37] Similarly, Jews had come to play a "central role" in American finance during the 1980s. They accounted for nearly half the billionaires in the country, "more than 25 percent of the elite journalists and publishers, more than 17 percent of the leaders of important voluntary and public interest organizations, and more than 15 percent of the top ranking civil servants."[38]

It would be naïve to suppose that American Jews have not mobilized—some of them methodically—their very considerable social, economic, and intellectual power in the service of Zionist objectives. No doubt, there are other "ethnicities" in the United States who are also successful—such as Americans of Norwegian, Swedish, or Japanese origins—although they do not come close to matching the success of Jews relative to their numbers. However, these groups—after their assimilation into American mainstream culture—do not identify themselves by their origins, nor ordinarily do they espouse beliefs, practice rituals, or engage in political activities that define them by their ethnic origins. That is not the case with most American Jews.

The American Jewish community has worked hard to preserve its distinctive religious culture and cohesiveness. Several aspects of Judaism and Jewish traditions have historically served to reinforce a strong Jewish identity. As the putative early history of the Hebrews, the Torah powerfully reinforces Jewish distinctiveness. The Jews follow a calendar of holidays that recapitulates—through rituals, prayers, and recitals—the ancient myths and history of the Jews; it preserves, no less, the memory of the persecutions they endured in Europe.[39] Since the mid-nineteenth century, Western Jews have given currency to the myth that Jews are descended from the ancient Hebrews; they have preserved their racial purity despite thousands of years of dispersion. Together, Jewish spirituality and culture reinforce the Jewish sense that they occupy a special place in God's plans for humanity; they are a "light unto the nations."

In turn, the strong sense of Jewish identity, combined with a sense of mission, has encouraged among Jews high levels of political activism, charitable work, and philanthropy. This activism has been motivated too by the Jewish need, as they entered into the mainstream of Western societies in the nineteenth century, to overcome the remaining formal and informal barriers to entry into various professions. As a result, Jewish political activism has been directed overwhelmingly toward progressive issues—relating to civil rights, human rights, the rights of workers and women, and religious freedom. One important result of this focus is a strong Jewish presence in labor unions, civil rights organizations, women's organizations, and various liberal causes.

Over the first six decades of the twentieth century, American Jewry directed their political energies primarily toward defending and expanding the opportunities available to them in the American economy and society.[40] This placed the Jews in the vanguard of nearly all the progressive and liberal movements that emerged during this period. Since the Jews made up a very small part of the population of the United States, they could most effectively safeguard and expand their own rights by adopting the broadest conception of rights, one that embraced the rights of all groups that were socially and economically handicapped, including racial minorities, religious minorities, women, workers, immigrants, and, eventually, homosexuals. "In civil rights, immigration policy, abortion rights, labor organizing, and Democratic campaign financing," writes J. J. Goldberg, "the Jewish community plays a crucial role in American liberalism, as it has through much of the twentieth century."[41]

During the first half of the twentieth century, American Jews normally directed their activism toward domestic issues. On at least two occasions, however, they redirected their activism toward Zionist goals; the two occasions were the launching of the Balfour declaration of 1917 and the period leading up to the UN resolution of 1947 calling for the partition of Palestine. Indeed, the ease and swiftness with which Zionist emissaries from Europe achieved this reorientation of Jewish activism toward Zionist goals, especially in 1947, speaks to the organizational sophistication of American Jewry and their readiness to subscribe to Zionist ambitions. Notwithstanding their activism for Zionist causes, few American Jews have been willing, before or after the creation of Israel, to emigrate to Israel. Yet, their organizations—and the activism of their members—have shown the capacity to quickly generate massive financial and political support whenever Israel has needed it.

Zionism had won over most American Jews to its cause by the end of the Second World War. In part, the dramatic growth in the membership of the Zionist Organization of America (ZOA) shows this: from 8,400 in 1932 to 43,000 in 1939 and more than 200,000 by 1945. In 1947, the United Jewish Appeal succeeded in raising $50 million, compared to $3.5 million in 1940. In the words of a leading historian of Zionism, Walter Laqueur, "American Jewry became overwhelmingly Zionist [during the 1940s], whereas in the past the majority had been indifferent or even actively hostile."[42] This is not surprising. Once Britain decided to distance itself from the Zionist project in 1939, and Germany rapidly extended its control over continental Europe, the United States—with its large and influential Jewish population—became the central theater of Zionist activities. Overwhelmingly, now, Zionist efforts were directed to recruiting the United States as the new mother country to the Jewish colonial project in Palestine. It is a testament to the efficacy of their lobbying that American Jews met with nearly complete success in placing the power of the United States behind the Zionist enterprise in 1947. This was no mean victory. The Zionists had won this support in the face of a near-consensus in the highest policy-making circles that President

Truman's support for Zionism would inflict enduring damage on the strategic interests of the United States in the Middle East.

Once it had delivered the Jewish state, the United States sought to limit its damage. In the years following 1948, it sought to avoid any show of overt support for the new state of Israel. The American Jewish leadership went along with this policy for two reasons. Opposing a vital U.S. interest at the height of the Cold War would be politically untenable, when the Soviet Union was eager to use Arab anger to gain entry into the Persian Gulf. In addition, this U.S. distancing from Israel was mostly a diplomatic ploy, and, more importantly, it contained the mechanism for its own reversal. Covertly, the United States prodded other members of the NATO to accommodate Israel's military needs. At the same time, it leaned on Germany to make generous reparations payments to Israel. While the Israelis did not too strongly protest U.S. refusal to provide direct support to Israel, they were determined to reverse this. Over the next two decades, Israel worked through several different channels to compound Arab threats to American interests in the Middle East, on the calculation that they could use these threats to turn Israel into a strategic asset. In the United States, the American Jewish community would ramp its efforts to convince—and build pressure on—the American public, media, the Congress and the president to strengthen Israel, economically and militarily, to serve as a strategic asset.

. . .

According to an American commentator, "Eisenhower and Kennedy often considered the Israel lobby more nuisance than titan."[43] Perhaps this is a fair assessment of the relationship between President Eisenhower and the Jewish lobby; but, already, during the term of President John F. Kennedy, the Jewish lobby was on its way to becoming more of a titan than nuisance.

We have examined above why the Jewish lobby was not quite as effective under President Eisenhower as it would later become. This is less because this lobby was weak in itself—in its personnel, organization, and finances; only a few years back it had corralled President Truman to support the creation of a Jewish state. The Jewish lobby in the 1950s had greater electoral strength than it would later have, because of a declining share of Jews in the general population; it had created a strong pro-Israeli bloc in the Congress through its ability to define the issues, raise and direct campaign contributions, and mobilize public opinion. The lobby remained actively engaged with issues dear to Israel during this period, but it now faced a president who was less beholden to special interests, less dependent on Jewish votes, and still trying to neutralize the negative fallout from the creation of Israel.[44] President Eisenhower believed that there was still an opportunity to stop the slide of Arab nationalists toward the Soviets. It is clear to us that the game was actually over, that the historical forces released by the creation of Israel would force the major actors to take the course that they *did* take over the subsequent decades. This inexorable logic flowed from the simple brute fact that the West, led by the United States, could not abandon Israel.

The failure of the Jewish lobby during this period is only relative. It could not convince the United States to embrace Israel as a strategic asset, but, taking advantage of Israel's status as a strategic liability, it did succeed in pushing policies that strengthened Israel's economy and military, shielded Israel from pressures to take back Palestinian refugees, and, most importantly, pushed even harder to drive a wedge between the United States and Egypt. Israel faced huge trade deficits during the 1950s, as it absorbed new immigrants and developed its industry and infrastructure. In part, the United Jewish Appeal financed these deficits through tax-exempt funds raised in the United States. Generous German reparations payments, however, paid for the greater part of these deficits; this was the result of Jewish pressure applied through the United States.

Israel's muscular approach to the Arabs was beginning to produce the desired effects by late 1950s.[45] Washington now began to think of building up Israel to check the growing anti-U.S. forces in the Arab world, itself a reaction to the creation of Israel. In 1958, President Eisenhower began to supply large weapon systems to Israel, still covertly. In 1962, when President Kennedy made an overt commitment to deliver antiaircraft missiles to Israel, U.S. military support for Israel had finally stepped out of the closet. In 1966, President Johnson expanded the delivery of heavy weapons to include tanks and bombers.[46] Contrary to a common claim, the foundations of a special relationship between Israel and the United States were not laid by Israel's stunning victory in the War of June 1967. This victory only imparted fresh momentum to forces, ascendant since the late 1950s, that were pushing for a stronger U.S. commitment to Israel as a strategic asset. The forces that established the special relationship—as well as the basic contours of this relationship—long preceded Israel's victory in the Six-Day War.

Israel's defeat of Egypt, Syria, and Jordan in June 1967 gave a new boost to the Zionist cause. For self-serving reasons, the Zionists had exaggerated Arab nationalism as a menace to Western interests and a threat to Israel's existence. This was mischievous but clever. This exaggeration had twofold objectives: to push the United States to look to Israel as its savior, and, equally, to alarm pro-Israel forces to exert growing pressure on the U.S. government to support Zionist aims. This strategy worked. In the weeks before the June War, there was growing anxiety about Israel's fate among audiences in both Israel and the United States. As a result, when the Israelis defeated the Arabs, they saw this victory as stunning and even miraculous; some saw this as confirmation of their messianic expectations. Most of all, by defeating what had come to be seen as the greatest threat to America's interests in the Middle East, Israel had created a huge reserve of political capital with Americans.

The Jewish lobby would waste no time in drawing upon this political capital. The lobby would not foolishly expend this capital on a few big trophies, and go home. Instead, it would use this capital to gain American support for policies—American and Israeli—that reinforced Israel's image as a strategic asset, thus allowing it to replenish its fund of political capital with Americans. The Jewish lobby would channel the energy, support, and expectations—in the American Jewish community, the Christian Zionists, and others—raised by the June victory into organizations, alliances, commitments, and policies that would continue to provide support for Israel for many years to come.

The Israeli victory was a clear signal for American Jews to place their weight more confidently behind their advocacy for Israel. There would be no taint of dual loyalty in their partisanship for Israel, since Israel had "proved" that its interests are the same as those of the United States. At the same time, Israel's stunning victory in the Six-Day War inspired a new era of Jewish pride in Israel. American Jews now identified more closely than ever with Israel; they increasingly viewed Israel as the center and pivot of the global Jewish community. The Jewish triumphalism inspired by the June War also helped many Jews to erase feelings of guilt over their failure to rescue more Jews from the Holocaust. In the post-1967 period, as a result, the Jewish lobby could draw upon growing political and financial support from the American Jewish community, even as it prepared to ratchet the demands it would make on the United States.

Israel's military victory in the Six-Day War tilted the balance of forces within the Zionist movement toward its more conservative and hawkish segments. This shift toward the right had a long history. Underneath their liberal and socialist veneer—never troubled by the colonial aims of Zionism—nearly all segments of the Zionist movement had been moving toward the right. This shift was inevitable, as the Zionists confronted the central demand of their movement: they could not establish a Jewish state in Palestine without the ethnic cleansing of Palestinians. Instead of stepping back from their goal of creating a Jewish state, the Zionists increasingly shifted to the right in their rhetoric and their policies—and prepared for the inevitable war against the Palestinians and the neighboring Arabs.

The liberal and socialist orientation of many of the early Zionists—a legacy of their struggle against anti-Semitism in Eastern Europe—would become discordant in Palestine. As the settlers confronted the resistance of the natives, as they realized that they could not "spirit the penniless population across the border," the Zionists began to make plans to remove the Palestinians by force. Quite early, the Labor Zionists—the dominant segment of the Zionist movement—had adopted an exclusionary program. Nearly from the outset, their *kibbutz*, their labor unions, and the services they offered strenuously excluded Palestinians. At the same time, in order to attract Jewish colons, create a nation out of these colons of diverse ethnic backgrounds, militarize Israel's settler society, and prepare to cleanse the Palestinians, the early secular Zionism began to yield ground to religious Zionism. All these tendencies came to a head during the 1940s, as the Zionists ratcheted their plans to take possession of Palestine. The *Irgun* began its campaign of terror against British targets in February 1944; soon they were joined by the *Stern Gang*. In the War of 1948, following the UN-sanctioned partition of Palestine, the *Haganah, Irgun, Stern Gang* and other armed Jewish colons expelled more than 80 percent of the Palestinians from the territories they conquered. The shift toward the right would not let up in the period after 1948, as Israel marginalized the Arab population still inside Israel, repeatedly used overwhelming force to prevent the return of Palestinians, and pursued a policy of provoking the neighboring Arabs into fighting wars they could not win.

Israel's victory in the War of June 1967 provided a major new impetus for Israeli politics to move to the right; there were two reasons for this. In order to gain greater latitude in pursuing its goals in the Middle East, Israel would aggressively support America's imperialist goals in other regions of the world. Israel would increasingly transform itself into an overt and covert tool of American imperialism; often, gaining leverage over American administrations by doing their dirty work when this was illegal under American laws. The colonization of the territories acquired in 1967 too gave a boost to fundamentalist right-wing factions in Israel. Overwhelmingly, Israelis supported this second round of colonization, but its leadership consisted of religious zealots. They became the new pioneers, taking the place of the labor Zionists in the previous round of colonization. Since most Israelis viewed the new settlements as engaged in the task of extending Israel's borders—making them less vulnerable to attacks from the Arabs—the right-wing forces that led and organized this colonization grew in strength and prestige. As a result, the extreme right wing parties began to gain in the polls at the cost of the Labor Party. With the rise of the Likud to power in 1977, the Israeli right became the dominant force in Israeli politics. This was the first time that the Labor Party had lost power in Israel.

Similar shifts toward the right occurred in the Jewish core of the Zionist movement in United States. Most visibly, a new cadre assumed the leadership of the mainstream Jewish organizations. The new leadership reshaped these organizations to articulate the more radical demands made by an overtly expansionist Israel committed to colonizing the territories it had conquered in June 1967. The major mainstream Jewish organizations now functioned more and more as mere extensions of the Israeli government, openly pursuing the Israeli agenda through their growing influence over the domestic politics of the United States, and using their clout to suppress dissent in the Jewish community. The major Jewish organizations had become "an engine of geopolitics," working to uphold Israeli interests through their influence over the domestic politics of the United States.[47]

A leading Jewish commentator explains this shift in the character of Jewish politics a bit differently. J. J. Goldberg argues that a small minority of Jews—"a minority with an edge"—propelled this shift. These Jews were alarmed by "Israel's isolation at the United Nations, outraged by black anti-Semitism in New York, and haunted throughout by the specter of the Holocaust." So moved were these Jews by this experience, by their conviction that no one can feel the pain of the Jews but the Jews, they "took over the machinery of Jewish politics."[48] This is a theory of geopolitical shifts by epiphany. The Zionists were too much of realists to tie their fortunes to popularity contests at the United Nations. It is equally implausible to suppose that black anti-Semitism—always a marginal phenomenon—was ever a serious factor in Jewish politics. Finally, it is even less credible that America's Jewish leadership, with knowledge of Israel's overwhelming military superiority over Arab nationalist states, could have seriously contemplated the prospect of a second Holocaust in the weeks leading to, or during, the June War of 1967. The Zionist leaders invoked the specter of a second Holocaust to arouse a new, more intense American Jewish commitment to Israel.

It makes a great deal more sense to regard this shift in Jewish politics as an adjustment to the new demands that Israel made on American Jewry in the aftermath of the June War of 1967. The *domestic* interests of American Jewry were still largely aligned with the liberal tendencies in American society. It would have been difficult and unwise to try to push the entire Jewish community to the right. This would have lost them the support of all those Gentile groups that had worked with Jews, and often with Jewish leadership, in a variety of liberal and progressive causes over the past half-century and more. The right-wing Zionists chose a smarter course. They took over the leadership of major Jewish organizations and deployed them more aggressively in support of Israel without alienating the Jewish base. Interestingly, the Jewish community—as if complicit in this coup—offered no resistance to this change in the leadership of the "mainstream" Jewish organizations. "Hardly anyone tried to stop them," writes J. J. Goldberg. The majority of American Jews had not abandoned their liberalism, but they "left the community structures to the New Jews."[49]

The June War enhanced the power of the Jewish lobby by offering it an opportunity to intervene directly in U.S. policies toward the Soviet Union. Stirred by the Israeli victory in the Six-Day War, the Soviet Jews began to demand the right to emigrate freely from the Soviet Union. When the Soviets refused this demand, the Jewish lobby in the United States decided to flex its muscle. Backed by the American Jewish establishment, and, working with the hawkish elements in the Congress, the Jewish lobby introduced an amendment to the East-West Trade Reform Act, which tied the recognition of Most Favored Nation status for the Soviet Union to the right of Soviet Jews to emigrate. Although opposed by the White House, the lobby mobilized the House of Representatives to pass the amendment on December 13, 1973, with 388 votes in favor and 44 against the amendment. This was a milestone in the career of the Jewish lobby. "Jewish activists," wrote J. J. Goldberg, "had taken on the Nixon administration and the Kremlin and won. Jews had proven to the world and to themselves that they could stand up and fight for themselves."[50] This legislative victory gave a tremendous boost to the reality and mystique of the power of the Jewish lobby. It had acquired the reputation of being invincible on the floor of the Congress.

In the aftermath of the June War, a new closer relationship developed between Israel and the Jewish lobby, on the one hand, and the evangelical Christians in the United States. Since the theology and passions of evangelicals is tied up intimately with Israel and the "restoration" of Jews to Israel, they perceived in the emergence of Israel and its victories the fulfillment of biblical prophecies. It was Israel's victory in June 1967, however, that gave the strongest impetus to the millennial hopes of the evangelicals; it encouraged expectations that the Second Coming might occur in their lifetime. Galvanized by these messianic expectations, the evangelicals—together with the broader Christian Right—began to create the organizations that would influence domestic politics and steer the United States toward a more staunchly pro-Israel policy.[51] They received encouragement from the Jewish lobby in these efforts. Since the support of mainstream Christian churches for the Israeli occupation of the West Bank and Gaza had been declining—and some were becoming openly critical of Israeli repression of Palestinians—the Zionists, starting in the mid-1970s, sought to compensate for this loss by allying themselves with the evangelicals. This alliance has deepened over time, giving the Jewish Zionists an army of zealots in the American body politic. Since the evangelicals began flexing their electoral muscle, sending growing numbers of their delegates to the Congress and Senate, their fanatical support for Israel has become the mainstay of the

Republican Party. Indeed, Daniel Pipes, a leading American Jewish advocate of Israel, claims that apart from the Israeli military, "America's Christian Zionists may be the Jewish state's ultimate strategic asset."[52]

The ascendancy of the Christian Zionists in the Republican Party coincided with the growing prominence of the neoconservatives, a mostly Jewish elite group who sought to place American power in the service of Israel. Some of the "New Jews"—who took over the leadership of mainstream Jewish organizations after the 1967 War—were former liberals who were convinced that they could best serve Israel's core interests in alliance with the American right. As a result, they left the Democrats, joined the Republican Party, where, in alliance with a few leading hawkish Gentiles, they began advocating a more expansionist, a more militarist U.S. foreign policy.[53] In addition, the neoconservatives—so described, to set them apart from the traditional conservatives—advocated a deeper partnership with Israel and using its military to gain direct control over Middle Eastern oil.[54] This was also the goal of the maximalists inside Israel, the Likudniks, among others, who wanted to redraw the map of the region to facilitate Israel's total and irreversible dominance over the region.[55] Over time, the Jewish neoconservatives cultivated close ties with right-wing Israeli politicians and ideologues; they often worked together in American and Israeli right-wing think tanks. Together, they advocated placing the U.S. military behind Israel's hegemonic ambitions in the Middle East.

The American neoconservatives are an elite group, small but dynamic, combining a prolific intellectual output with political activism, who had been positioning themselves since the 1970s to shape U.S. foreign policy. With support from the largest mainstream Jewish organizations, they established several influential magazines and think tanks, which have relentlessly made the case for extending and using U.S. military superiority to reshape the map of the Middle East and prevent the rise of any rival power—even regional powers—with threats or actual use of military force. The neoconservatives first gained important policy-making positions in the Reagan administration.[56] Put out to pasture during the Clinton years, they moved to right-wing and pro-Israel think tanks, magazines, and newspapers, where they worked out their plans for an imperial United States, deepened their alliances with Israeli Likudniks, and made deeper inroads into the hierarchy of the Republican Party. With the election of George W. Bush in 2000, they had gained control over many key positions in the offices of the Vice President, the Pentagon and the State Department. In September 2000, the neoconservatives had wished for a "catastrophic and catalyzing event—like a new Pearl Harbor" to accelerate their plans for transforming the U.S. military to ensure American military eminence for decades.[57] On September 11, 2001, they got their wish. Playing upon American fears, the neoconservatives instantly seized the opportunity to implement their plans for world domination through military means. They called it the Global War on Terrorism: the invasions of Afghanistan in October 2001 and Iraq in March 2003 were the opening volleys in this war.

In the aftermath of September 11, the Zionists appeared to be close to realizing their maximalist vision of establishing their dominance over the Middle East on an enduring basis. The two projects launched by Zionism—in Palestine and the United States—had grown dramatically in the decades after the June War. After defeating its Arab nationalist rivals and co-opting Egypt, Israel had gained a strong upper hand over the remaining Arab states, who were now eager to cooperate with the Jewish state. In the United States, too, propelled by forces emanating from Israel's victory in the June War, the power of the Jewish lobby grew cumulatively, until it was calling the shots on nearly all matters relating to the Middle East—and, occasionally, on some matters beyond this region as well. "In the last two decades between 1980 and 2000," writes Stephen Schwartz, "American Jews gained power and influence beyond anything they had ever experienced."[58] J. J. Goldberg too acknowledges that American Jewry emerged, during the post-1967 period, as "a force on the international stage."[59]

Is it the American Jewish community or Israel that has positioned Jews so prominently on the stage of history? J. J. Goldberg takes the view that the American Jewish community constitutes the real center of world Jewry—the real locus of its power.[60] It would be unhistorical to see the rise of American Jewish power as a force in isolation from Israel. The fortunes of the two have been deeply interconnected, especially since 1939 when Britain decided to distance itself from the Zionist project. In this mutually reinforcing relationship between the two largest concentrations of Jewish population since World War II, however, it is the *Yishuv* in Palestine—and later the Jewish state of Israel—that has directed the global Zionist enterprise. American Jewry has been galvanized by the escalating demands, no less than the successes, of the Zionist center; it created new organizations, reoriented others, made powerful new allies, and magnified the impact of these organizations and alliances on domestic politics to firmly place the power of the United States behind Israel. In the web of interactions between Israel and the American Jewish community, the latter shaped its institutions, values, and even alliances more and more to serve the needs of Israel. Surely, without Zionism and Israel, the American Jewish community would still occupy a distinguished place in many areas of the economy, society, and culture. It is unlikely, however, that it would be a pivotal force in the politics of the United States.

CHAPTER 20

A SUMMING UP

My God! Is this the end? Is *this* the goal for which our fathers have striven
and for whose sake all generations have suffered? Is *this* the dream of a
return to Zion which our people have dreamt for centuries: that we now
come to Zion to stain its soil with innocent blood?

—Ahad Ha'am, 1921[1]

THIS STUDY HAS EMPLOYED A DIALECTICAL FRAMEWORK for analyzing
the destabilizing logic of Zionism. We have examined this logic as it has
unfolded through time, driven by the vision of an exclusionary colonialism,
drawing into its circuit—aligned with it and against it—nations, peoples,
forces, and civilizations whose actions and interactions impinge on the trajectory of Zionism, and, in turn, who are changed by this trajectory.

It would be a bit simplistic to examine the field of interactions among
the different actors in this historic drama on the essentialist assumption
that these actors and their interests are unchanging. Instead, we need
to explore the complex ways in which the Zionists have worked—and,
often have succeeded—to alter the behavior of the other political actors
in this drama: and, how, in turn, the Zionists respond to these changes.
Most importantly, we need to explore all the ways in which the Zionists
have succeeded in mobilizing the resources of the United States and other
Western powers to serve their specific objectives.

Consider a list of the political actors who have had more than a passing
connection to the Zionist project and, who, at one time or another, have
affected or have been affected by this project. First, there are the different
Zionist factions, the Jewish diaspora, and, later, the state of Israel. These
entities are overlapping, with the degrees of overlap between any two of
them changing over time. The second set of actors consists of Western
powers—especially, the United States, Britain, and France—the Christian
Zionists especially in the United States, and the Soviet Union and its allies
in Eastern Europe. Finally, there are actors who are the direct and indirect
victims of the Zionist project, those who have paid the costs of Zionist

success. They form four concentric circles around Israel, including the Palestinians, the Arabs, the Middle East, and the Islamicate. These three sets of actors make up the *dramatis personae* in the unfolding tragedy of the Zionist project.

Clearly, the number of actors involved, their variety, and, not least, the multilayered power commanded by the Zionists and their allies would indicate that Zionism is no sideshow. Directly, it has involved much of the Western world, on one side, and the global Islamicate on the other side, who will soon make up one-fourth of the world's population.

Many white settlers established colonies in Africa during the nineteenth century. In Palestine, the Jews established the only white settler colony to be established in the Middle East—or for that matter, anywhere in Asia. Of all these colonial settler projects, only the Jewish settlers in Palestine have endured. In 1948, only three decades after they gained British backing for their project, the Jewish colons created their own state, Israel, which, almost overnight, became the dominant power in the region, capable of defeating any combination of the military forces of the neighboring states. Within two decades of its founding, the "tiny" Jewish state had also acquired an arsenal of nuclear weapons, the only country in the region with such weapons of mass extermination. In recent decades, militarily, Israel has ranked behind only three other countries, the United States, Russia, and China. In addition, Israel has forged a special relationship with the United States, which finances its military, arms it, and shields the country from the sanction of international laws, leaving it free to expand its colonial project, and threaten and attack its neighbors at will. After September 11, Israel and its allies were a major—if not decisive—factor in pushing the United States to invade and occupy Iraq. For several years now, they have been itching to instigate the United States into a war against Iran.

How did the Zionists manage to do all this?

In part, the answer to this question lies in taking a measure of the forces that underpin Israel's capacity to endure. Had the French colons survived in Algeria, had they partitioned the country to create a white colonial settler state along the Mediterranean coast, like Israel, this settler state too would be armed to the teeth, backed by a special relationship with France, and perpetually at war with Algerian refugees and with its Arab/African neighbors. In 1960, David Ben-Gurion had urged Charles De Gaulle, the French president, to create a colonial settler state in Algeria in the rich agricultural areas along the Mediterranean coast. In the Algerian civil war, Israel had supported the faction within the *Organisation Armée Secrète* (OAS), the underground militant organization of the colons in Algeria, which wanted to partition Algeria.[2] Had it gone through, the partition would have prolonged the conflict in Algeria, created an Israeli twin in North Africa, and deepened the bond between France and Israel. Unluckily for Israel, de Gaulle firmly rejected partition. He was convinced that French rule could not be maintained in Algeria and conceded independence to the Algerians.

How did the Jewish colons in Palestine succeed in creating an exclusionary colonial settler state in the middle of the twentieth century and continue to grow with support from a surrogate mother country, while the French colons in Algeria, the Italians in Libya, or the British colons in Kenya had to give up their colonial projects?

The answer to this question is simple. The white colons in Algeria, Libya, or Kenya simply did not have enough influence over the mother country—over France, Italy, and Britain—to overrule what the elites in the mother country had decided was in their interest: to pull out of their colonies. The Jewish colons in Palestine had more power than the white colons in Algeria, Libya, and Kenya. Where did their power come from?

The success of Jewish colons in Palestine and the failure of the colons in Algeria, Libya, or Kenya is a paradox. The French, Italian, and British settlers had a *natural* mother country, a country of origin, with whose people they shared an ethnic bond. The Jewish colons in Palestine did not have a natural mother country, a powerful Jewish state to support their colonial project. Yet, their colonizing project succeeded, and they drove out the Palestinians to create a nearly pure Jewish state in Palestine. The Jewish colons did not pull off this feat on their own; they succeeded because of their ability to recruit the greatest Western powers, and many others besides, to support their colonial project. Somehow, the Zionists turned what could well have been a fatal deficiency in their colonial project— the absence of a natural mother country—into their greatest asset. They gained the freedom to pick and choose their mother country.

How did the Zionists bring this about? The Jews were not a majority in any one country, but there existed a Jewish minority in nearly every Western country. In itself, the presence of Jewish minorities could not have been a source of strength; a weak Jewish minority in any country could do little to help their coreligionists in another country. What made the Jewish minorities different was that they carried a weight that far outweighed their numbers. Over the course of the nineteenth century, they had become an important, often vital, part of the financial, industrial, commercial, and intellectual elites in several of the most important Western countries, including Britain, France, Germany, Russia, and the United States. Moreover, the most prominent members of these elites had cultivated ties with each other across national boundaries.

Once these Jewish elites, spread across the key Western countries, had decided to support the Zionist project, they would become a force in global politics. On the one hand, this would tempt the great powers to support Zionism, if this could buy them the help of the Jewish communities based in a rival or friendly country, to push their host country in a desirable direction. Conversely, once the Zionists recognized this tendency, they too would seek to win support for their cause by offering the support of Jewish communities in key Western countries. It would be in their interest to exaggerate the *results* that Jewish communities in this or that country might be able to deliver. During periods of intense conflicts—such as World War I—when the fate of nations hung in the balance, the competition for Zionist support became more intense than ever. This placed the Zionists in a strong position to trade their favors for the commitment of the great powers to their goals. In September 1917, this competition persuaded Britain, at a difficult moment in the execution of its war, to throw its support behind the Zionist project.

The Zionists continue to market their colonial project as a haven for Jews, fleeing anti-Semitic persecution. This is misleading. Overwhelmingly, Jews fleeing persecution in Europe have stayed away from this "haven" when alternatives were available. On the contrary, the Zionists were counting on support from the anti-Semites to propel their nationalist-cum-colonial project. They were counting on anti-Semitic persecution to *send* Jewish colons to Palestine; and they were counting on the European anti-Semite's desire to be rid of Jews to recruit Western powers to support their colonial project in Palestine. Zionism was primarily a nationalist movement, whose origins predated the resurgence of anti-Semitism in the late nineteenth century. Even then, most Jews sought to combat anti-Semitism through assimilation, Jewish autonomism, and socialist revolutions. When forced to emigrate, they overwhelmingly preferred destinations outside Palestine. The fortunes of Zionism improved only when most Western countries closed their doors to Jewish immigrants. When these doors were closing in the early 1900s, it was little opposed by the Jewish diaspora, whose leadership now identified increasingly with Zionist goals. Little pressure too was applied to reopen these doors before the 1960s.

The Zionists have received support, since the launching of their movement, from the dominant Protestant segment of Christianity, whose theology reinstated the Jews to their covenant with God. As a result, a few Protestants began calling for the "restoration" of Jews to Palestine in the seventeenth century; at the time, Jews looked on these proposals with deep suspicion. Since the nineteenth century, a new group of evangelical

Christians began to support the restoration of Jews, because they believed this was a necessary prelude to the Second Coming. From its home in Britain, this movement spread to the United States, where, in recent decades, cheered by Israeli victories, it has become an important source of support for Zionism in the United States.

In no small measure, the success of the Zionist colonial project was magnified by the weakness of the Arabs in the Middle East. Unlike Algerians in the nineteenth century or Libyans between the two World Wars, the Palestinians were slow in resisting Jewish colonization—the first serious resistance was mounted in 1936—and, once beaten, in 1939, they could not reorganize for more than two decades. More fatefully, the Jewish colonization of Palestine did not evoke a response in the larger Arab/Islamicate world that was commensurate with the scale of the Zionist threat to the Islamicate. This period is marked by the absence of any concerted efforts in Syria, Egypt, Iraq, or the Arabian Peninsula to resist Jewish colonization before it would become undefeatable. The Arab nationalists began to stir when it was too late, *after* Israel had established itself and soon would be in a position to smash them before they could build their strength.

Anxious to conceal the power of the Jewish lobby, Zionists often argue that the Western powers supported Zionism only because the Jewish state served their strategic interests in the Middle East. We have shown that Zionism was in conflict with the long-term interests of Britain and the United States. Exigencies of war and the presence of a strong contingency of Christian Zionists in the cabinet of Lloyd George explain British support for the Balfour Declaration in 1917. On the other hand, the strong U.S. support in 1948 for the partition of Palestine—and later—was the product of a domestic Jewish lobby.

In the 1940s—and even later—the United States commanded considerable goodwill in the Arab world. The populist movements in the Arab world directed their anticolonial animus against the British and the French, not the Americans. In addition, the Arab dynasties and petit bourgeoisie, who expected to gain power after the departure of the colonial rulers, would have been quite happy to work with their former rulers and the United States. Arab and local nationalisms—weakly founded, in any case—had no radical thrust. It takes little prescience to see that the insertion of Israel in the Middle East—far from serving Western strategic interests—was certain to create threats to these interests, where none existed before. Nor was this prescience lacking in Washington. The officials at the State and Defense Departments saw this clearly, but they were overruled by the exigencies of presidential politics.

Once created, however, Israel had the resources to create and entrench the perception that it is a strategic asset, that it defends the vital interests of Western powers in the Middle East. The creation of a Jewish colonial settler state in the Arab world—one that would have to engage in massive ethnic cleansing—was the perfect incitement for starting a rising spiral of anger against Israel's Western backers, chiefly, the United States. Arab anger over Israel, exacerbated by Israel's truculent policies, would continue to fuel Arab nationalism and push it in a radical, anti-Western direction. Even so, the United States persisted in its doomed efforts, during the 1950s, to bring about peace between the Arabs and Israel. Israel would ensure that these efforts would not succeed, forcing the Arab nationalist states to turn to the Soviet Union. Inevitably, at this stage, Washington would see radicalized Arab nationalism as a threat to its interests in the Middle East. The first circle was complete. Israel had *manufactured* the threats that would make it look like a strategic asset. In a preemptive strike in June 1967, Israel confirmed this by defeating Egypt and Syria, the two leading Arab nationalist states.

Once this paradigm was in place, Israel and its Jewish allies in the United States worked hard to ensure that it stayed in place. Jewish Zionists in the United States, working both inside and outside the Jewish community, worked to whittle down the ability of the American political system to take any positions contrary to the interests of Israel. In the aftermath of the victory in the June War, and Israel's new policy of expanding its frontiers to incorporate the West Bank, Gaza and the Golan Heights, a new, more aggressively pro-Israel cadre of Jews took over the leadership of the mainstream Jewish organizations in the United States. They worked to suppress dissent within the Jewish community, used campaign contributions to elect the strongest pro-Israeli candidates to the Congress, and maintained discipline inside the Congress by punishing dissenters at the next election. They cultivated the Christian Zionists, who were being energized by Israeli successes. At the same time, pro-Israeli think tanks produced hundreds of position papers, journal articles, magazines, reports, and books, resurrecting atavistic fears of a dangerous, resurgent, anti-Western Islam that was the greatest threat to the power of the United States.

The secret of Zionist success, then, lies in the manner in which it overcame the chief flaw in its design: it did not have a natural mother country to support its colonial project. By winning over the Jews in the Western diaspora, and galvanizing them to use their wealth, intellect, and activism to promote Zionist causes, the Zionists succeeded in substituting the West for the missing natural mother country. Over time, nearly every major Western country (including the Soviet Union) has offered critical help in the creation, survival and success of Israel. Most importantly, the two greatest Western powers, Britain and the United States, successively, have placed their military might squarely behind the Zionist project despite the damage that this inflicted on their vital interests in the Middle East.

The United States has already paid dearly for its pro-Zionist policies since 1948. Over time, these costs would include the hundreds of billions of dollars in subsidies to Israel and its Arab allies, the alienation of the Arab world, an oil embargo, higher oil prices, the rise of Islamic radicalism, and several close confrontations with the Soviet Union in the Middle East. After September 11, 2001, under strong pressure from Israel—working in league with their neoconservatives allies—the United States launched a costly but unnecessary war against Iraq. In turn, this war galvanized the Islamist radicals, giving them a new theater where they could engage the United States. The United States has financed this war—and the war in Afghanistan—by borrowing from China and the oil-rich Arabs. We must also add two other consequences of the Iraq War to the debit in America's Israeli account: the rise of Iran and the growing challenge to U.S. hegemony in Latin America.

The costs that the United States—and the rest of the Western world—might incur in the future are likely to be much greater. We can only speculate about these costs, or when they will come due. The repressive, pro-American regimes in the Arab world are not sustainable. When these unpopular regimes begin to fall, and are replaced by Islamist governments, it may become difficult for the United States to maintain its presence in the region. Indeed, it is likely that the United States itself or Israel might trigger this outcome with an attack on Iran. In the opinion of some, this is an accident waiting to happen.

Should Israel wither away, the United States will bear much of the collateral damage of this collapse. The withering of the Jewish state could occur due to international pressures against its apartheid regime, a slow loss of nerve as Jewish settlers lose their "demographic war" with the Palestinians, or loss of deterrence as Israel continues to engage in failed attempts to destroy the Hizbullah and Hamas. Israel and the United States have been joined at the hip for many years. In America's public discourse, the two have become more and more like each other: they are two exceptional societies, marked by destiny, chosen by God, created by brave pioneers, who have shaped and continue to shape their common destiny through territorial expansion and ethnic cleansing. Should the Jewish state wither away, its much larger twin may begin to wobble.

Some consequences of the withering away of Israel might be easy to predict. Over the past century, the successes of the Zionist movement have galvanized many American Jews and Zionist Christians; they will now be disillusioned, in despair, confused, and angry. Probably, most Israeli Jews will want to migrate to the United States, which most Americans will be loath to refuse. Yet, this will give rise to frictions between some sections of Gentiles and Jews and may give rise to pockets of anti-Semitism. Tensions will also rise between Jews and Muslims in the United States. The disillusioned Christian Zionists too may seek to scapegoat all peoples of color, but especially Arab-Americans and Muslims. In all likelihood, the United States will experience growing conflicts among different sections of its population; there will be more racism, hate crimes, and, perhaps, worse. None of this will be good for America's image as a great country.

Although the domestic fallout of the withering of the Israeli state will be serious, the more serious losses for the United States will flow from the erosion of its control over the oil-rich states in the Persian Gulf. It would be foolhardy to predict the contours of the new map that will eventually emerge in the Middle East and the Islamicate. Whatever new structures emerge, these transformations are likely to be violent. On the one hand, the fragmentation imposed on the Islamicate has created local interests that will seek to maintain the status quo. These local interests now will confront Islamist movements that seek to create more integrated structures across the Islamicate. These conflicts will be deeply destabilizing, as India, China, Europe and Russia may choose sides, each eager to replace the United States. Once the U.S.-Israeli straitjacket over the region has been loosened, it will not be easy to fashion a new one made in Moscow, Beijing, Brussels or New Delhi. The Islamicate world today is not what it was during World War I. It is noticeably less inclined to let foreigners draw their maps for them.

NOTES

CHAPTER 1

1. Said, "Foreword," ix.
2. Davis, *Zionism in Transition*, 76; Neusner, *Comparative Hermeneutics of Rabbinic Judaism*, 341; Morris, *Righteous Victims*, 343.
3. At its conclusion, the first World Zionist Congress issued a declaration of its intentions, known as the Basel Program. It stated, "Zionism strives for the establishment of a publicly and legally secured home in Palestine for the Jewish people." Khalidi, *From Haven to Conquest*, 89. In public declarations of their aims, the Zionists did not restrict their program to European Jews; but there is little doubt that this was a movement of, for, and by Western Jews. The Zionists brought non-Western Jews into their movement only later to compensate for the paucity of Western Jews willing to vote for Zionism with their feet.
4. See Sokolow, *History of Zionism: 1600–1918*; Hertzberg, *The Zionist Idea*; Laqueur, *History of Zionism*; Vital, *Origins of Zionism*; Davis, *Zionism in Transition*; Shimoni, *Zionist Ideology*; Shlaim, *Iron Wall*; Hertzberg, *Fate of Zionism*; Falk, *Fratricide in the Holy Land*; Rose, *Myth of Zionism*; Rose, *Question of Zion*; M. Brenner, *Zionism*; Kovel, *Overcoming Zionism*.
5. In an exclusionary settler colony, the settlers work to *exclude* the natives from their territory. The settlers may seek the exclusion of natives from two motives: the presence of cheaper native labor will bring down the wages of settlers below European levels; alternatively, the natives resist their dispossession and are a threat to the settlers.
6. Following Marshall Hodgson, "Islamicate," as a noun, will refer to a society consisting mostly of Muslims; as an adjective, it will refer to some characteristic of an Islamicate, which may or may not derive from Islam as a faith. Hodgson, *The Venture of Islam 1*, 57–60.
7. In a recent book published in Hebrew in Israel, Sand (*The Invention of the Jewish People*) questions the validity of a central claim of Zionism: that the Jewish "diaspora" emerged when the Romans expelled the Jews from Palestine after the destruction of the Second Temple. Starting in the nineteenth century, Zionist thinkers began to propagate the myth of a common descent to provide a racial foundation to their claim that the Jews are a nation. Historical evidence indicates that mass conversions, mostly during the first millennium of the Common Era—not migrations from Palestine—created the Jewish communities of North Africa, Yemen, and Europe, among other places. The Jews of Palestine converted, first, to Christianity, and, after the Arab conquest, most of them converted to Islam. In a similar vein, Paul Wexler writes, "The Sephardic Jews are largely descended from a mixed population consisting of a majority of proselytes of Near Eastern, Arabian and North African origin and a small community of ethnic Palestinian Jews (and their mixed descendants)." Wexler, *Non-Jewish Origins of the Sephardic Jews*, 229. Patai and Wing (*Myth of the Jewish Race*) showed—in the words of a reviewer—"that Jews are genetically closer to their

non-Jewish neighbors than they are to Jews in other lands. Most particularly was this true when Oriental Jews were compared to those of Central and Eastern Europe." Schnall, "Review," 182. Claims that the Jews are a race were carefully debunked in 1894 by Lazare, *Anti-Semitism*, 119–28. In a recent book, Corcos (*Myth of the Jewish Race*), a biologist, has debunked the notion of a Jewish race.

8. The Orthodox Jews opposed Zionism because it wrote the Jewish Messiah out of the narrative of Jewish restoration. See Rabkin, *Threat from Within*. At the same time, the Reform movement in Germany dropped the doctrine of restoration from its creed in 1845; the reform movement in the United States followed suit in 1885. See Jewish-encyclopedia.com, "Zionism"; and Neusner and Avery-Peck, *Routledge Dictionary of Judaism*, 116. In 1897, the German Rabbinical Council and the leaders of the Jewish community of Munich opposed Zionist plans to hold their first Congress in Munich. Theodore Herzl failed to garner financial support from two of the leading Jewish philanthropists of his time—Barons Rothschild and Hirsch—for his Zionist scheme. M. Brenner, *Zionism*, 26.

9. Dror, "On the Uniqueness of Israel," 247.

10. See Said, "An Ideology of Difference," 38.

11. Studies that seek to establish a genetic link among Jews or seek to trace them back to common ancestors have engaged the interest of many geneticists in Israel and the United States. See Goldstein, *Jacob's Legacy*.

12. According to Hertzberg and Hirt-Manheimer, "Affirming Jews cleave to their Jewish-ness in the conviction that they are a chosen people. This may be a delusion, or at the very least an exaggeration, but this is at the very core of their self-image." They also write, "it is the central affirmation of the Jewish faith that God had singled out their ancestors and entered into an eternal covenant with them." Hertzberg and Hirt-Manheimer, *Jews*, 15–16.

13. Herzl, *Jewish State*, 12.

14. The doctrine of Jewish election incorporates three interlocking choices made by the God of the Jewish scriptures. First, God chose Abraham's lineage through Isaac to be His "treasured people" (Deuteronomy 7:6), a people "consecrated" to the Lord and "a kingdom of priests and a holy nation" (Exodus 19:5). He also chose a land for His people; although its borders vary, this land always included the land between the Jordan River and the Mediterranean Sea. Like the chosen people, this land too was unique: it was a pure land, "flowing with milk and honey" (Exodus 33:3), devoid of impurities, the best of all lands on the earth; it was also a holy land, set apart from other lands, because it was His earthly dwelling place. Finally, God made a covenant with His chosen people. He promised to make them owners and rulers over this land, and to guide, bless and favor them as long as they observed His laws. Conversely, He threatened them with dire punishments, including exile from the promised land, if they break their covenant (Exodus 19:5). It appears that the cumulative moral deficit in Jewish conduct finally led to their expulsion from the promised land in the first century CE. In their centuries of exile, the overwhelming majority of the Jews have lived in Europe and the Middle East, outside of Palestine. All quotes from the Jewish Bible in this book are from Berlin and Brettler, *Jewish Study Bible*.

15. According to Arthur Hertzberg, "The Jewish people had been warned [in the Tal-mud] that they should not try to predict the time of their redemption, because that was a mystery known only to God; nor should they engage in any active endeavors, and certainly not in the use of arms, to force "the end of day." Hertzberg, *Fate of Zion-ism*, 6.

16. Rose, *Question of Zion*, 16–17.

17. See Vital, *Origins of Zionism*, 369, and Herzl, *Old-New Land*, ii, for the two quotes from Theodore Herzl.
18. Rose, *Question of Zion*, 16.
19. Goldman, *Jewish Paradox*, 72.
20. Apparently, the profound irony of this position escaped the Zionists. They denied peoplehood to the Palestinians because the land they occupied was not a sovereign state: and yet, the Jews were a people, although they possessed neither a land nor a state.
21. Peters (*From Time Immemorial*) revived this argument. Falsely, she attributes the natural increase in the population of Palestine since the 1850s—a result largely of improvements in health care and sanitation—to immigration. A similar natural increase occurred in Israel's Palestinian population, whose numbers had plummeted to 150,000 after the ethnic cleansing of 1948–49. In 2004, this population had grown to some 1.3 million. Although it was widely acclaimed by the leading Zionists in United States—including such luminaries as Saul Bellow and Barbara Tuchman—Peter's book, according to Finkelstein (*Image and Reality*, xxxii) is a "colossal hoax."
22. This was the starting point, the chief inspiration for nearly all the early Zionists. Shapira writes, "One of the covert assumptions present among all the poets and the majority of Zionist thinkers and leaders was that Jews had a special right to the Land of Israel, that is, Palestine." Ahad Ha-Am, quoted in Shapira, commented that this was "a land to which our historical right is beyond doubt and has no need for far-fetched proofs." Shapira, *Land and Power*, 40–41.
23. In 1919, in an address to British Zionist Federation, Chaim Weizmann declared, "I repeat it again. By a Jewish national home I mean the creation of such conditions that as the country is developed we can . . . finally establish such a society in Palestine that *Palestine shall be as Jewish as England is English, or America American*" (emphasis added). Rose, *Question of Zion*, 121–22.
24. In an essay he wrote in 1891, after a short trip to Palestine, Ahad Ha'am wrote that Jews in Europe believe that "all Arabs are savages of the desert, a people similar to a donkey." Shapira, *Land and Power*, 42.
25. The Lord's instruction to the Israelites, as they prepared to take possession of the promised land, was unequivocal: "When the Lord your God brings you to the land that you are about to enter and possess, and He dislodges many nations before you . . . and the Lord your God delivers them to you and you defeat them, you must doom them to destruction: grant them no terms and give them no quarter." Deuteronomy 7:1–3.
26. These more expansive promises are made in Genesis 15:18, Deuteronomy 11:24, and Joshua 1:4.
27. Shahak, *Jewish History*, 8–9.
28. In 1904, Rabbi Kook, the chief Ashkenazi rabbi of Palestine, wrote, "So on the collective level of Israel, God ordained these two faculties: a faculty corresponding to the physical entity, that aspires to material improvement of the nation . . . and a second facet devoted to the cultivation of spirituality. By virtue of the first aspect, Israel is comparable to all the nations of the world. It is by dint of the second aspect that Israel is unique, as it says, 'The Lord leads it [Israel] alone'; 'Among the nations it [Israel] shall not be reckoned.' It is the Torah and unique sanctity of Israel that distinguish it from the nations." Kook, *When God Becomes History*.
29. Dror "On the Uniqueness of Israel," 247.
30. In the fifteenth century, Isaac Abravanel, a Jewish statesman and Bible commentator, offered a clear statement of the doctrine that Jewish election—in the words of his

modern biographer—offered them "exemption from the laws of nature and society that govern gentiles." Feldman, *Philosophy in a Time of Crisis*, 137–38.

31. Stannard writes of other ways in which chosenness may escalate to racism "with its special emphasis on the maintenance of blood purity (e.g., Deuteronomy 7:3; Joshua 23:12–13), and on the either tacit or expressed pollution fear of corrupting that purity with the defiling blood of others, the ideology of the Covenant intrinsically is but a step away from full blown racism and, if the means are available, often violent oppression of the purportedly threatening non-Chosen." Stannard, "Politics of Genocide Scholarship," 275.

32. Thus, Johnson, a Catholic and a fierce partisan of Israel, writes, "In the last half-century, over 100 completely new independent states have come into existence. Israel is the only one whose creation can fairly be called a miracle." Johnson, "The Miracle," 21.

33. Israel, Ministry of Foreign Affairs, "Address by Prime Minister Netanyahu."

34. Pipes, "[Michael Oren's] Six Days of War."

35. Kook, "Rebirth of Israel," 425.

36. Rose, *Question of Zion*, 73.

37. Israel, Ministry of Foreign Affairs, "PM Rabin Response."

38. "[Israel] has provided its citizens with the highest standard of living of any nation in the Middle East." Brownfeld, "Judaism and the Jewish State," 194.

39. Israel, Ministry of Foreign Affairs, "Address by Prime Minister Netanyahu."

40. Esther Benbassa develops this thesis in her book, *La Souffrance Comme Identité*. The thesis of a "lachrymose" conception of Jewish historiography was first offered in 1928 by Salo Wittmayer Baron, a leading historian of Jewish history in the twentieth century. He maintained that Jewish historians distort the history of Jews in Europe when they make anti-Semitism—that is, the discrimination, deportations and pogroms endured by Jews—the centerpiece of this history. Liberles and Lyman, *Salo Wittmayer Baron*, 340. This lachrymose tradition is far from dead, as it is an imperative of Zionism. For a recent example of this lachrymose history, see Vital, *A People Apart*. According to his reviewer, Vital "does not seem to find much to value in that existence [in exile] outside the Jews' eventual reach for self-determination in their own land." Young, "Bad for the Jews."

41. See Ye'or, *Dhimmi* and *Decline of Eastern Christianity*; Karsh, *Islamic Imperialism*. See M. Cohen, "Jews under Islam," for an extensive review of the literature on Jews under Islam.

42. Prager and Telushkin, *Why the Jews?* 3.

43. Jewish sacred history speaks of two attempts in antiquity to destroy the Jews in their entirety: by the Egyptians in Exodus, and by Haman, the chief minister to Persian king Ahasuerus, in the *Book of Esther*. There is no evidence, however, that these events actually occurred.

44. Merom, "Israel's National Security," 413.

45. Ibid., 414.

46. Ibid., 413–14.

47. Jabbour (*Settler Colonialism*) and Rodinson (*Israel: A Colonial-Settler State?*) offered the earliest and most exhaustive analyses of whether Israel is a colonial settler state.

48. On premeditation in the ethnic cleansing of Palestinians, the two best sources are Masalha, *Expulsion of the Palestinians*, and Pappe, *Ethnic Cleansing*.

49. Close to 800,000 Palestinians were expelled from the territories that Israel seized in 1948, and another 320,000 were expelled from the West Bank in 1967. Farsoun and Aruri, *Palestine and the Palestinians*, 303.

50. Qumsiyeh, *Sharing the Land of Canaan*, 87.
51. See Carter, *Palestine*.
52. Findley, *They Dare to Speak Out*.
53. Cook, *Blood and Religion*, 7.
54. Ibid., 8.

CHAPTER 2

1. Merom, "Israel's National Security," 411.
2. Ben-Gurion, *Ben-Gurion Looks at the Bible*, 35.
3. Telegraph, "Angola Is Offered for Zionist Colony," 8.
4. Brenner, *Zionism*, 19–22.
5. Hertzberg, *The Zionist Idea*, 15–16.
6. Hertzberg, *The Zionist Idea*, 19.
7. Dror, "On the Uniqueness of Israel," 257.
8. Consider the testimony of Ahad Ha'am ("A Truth from Eretz Israel," 14–15), who was writing after a trip to Palestine in 1891. "We who live abroad," he wrote, "are accustomed to believing that the Arabs are wild desert people who, like donkeys, neither see nor understand what is happening around them." The Jewish colons, he continued, "deal with the Arabs with hostility and cruelty, trespass unjustly, beat them shamefully for no sufficient reason, and even boast about their actions."
9. Most recently, Benny Morris, a leading Israeli historian, told an interviewer, "There was no reason in the world why it [the Jewish people] should not have one state. Therefore, from my point of view, the need to establish this state in this place overcame the injustice that was done to the Palestinians by uprooting them." He continued, "Even the great American democracy could not have been created without the annihilation of the Indians. There are cases in which the overall, final good justifies harsh and cruel acts that are committed in the course of history." See Shavit, "Survival of the Fittest,"
10. Neusner, "A 'Holocaust' Primer," 978, quoted in Finkelstein, *The Holocaust Industry*, 47.
11. Glazer, *American Judaism*, 171, quoted in Finkelstein, *The Holocaust Industry*, 48.
12. The Israel lobby in any country includes *all* the domestic forces that work in diverse areas—and through diverse instruments—to advance the interests of Israel, most commonly as defined by the government of Israel. As a result, the Israel lobby is larger than the Jewish lobby, but the latter lies at its core, but, in addition, the major mainstream Jewish organizations generally lead and orchestrate the activities of the Jewish lobby.
13. Dror, "On the Uniqueness of Israel," 257.

CHAPTER 3

1. A Marxist historian, Isaac Deutscher (1907–67) was born in Poland in 1907, moved to England in 1939 where he worked for *The Economist* and *The Observer*. See Deutscher, "Israel's Spiritual Climate," 30.
2. Shatz, *Prophets Outcast*, 40.
3. As early as 1891, Ahad Ha'am, after a visit to Palestine, wrote that the Jewish settlers "treat the Arabs with hostility and cruelty, deprive them of their rights, offend them without cause, and even boast of these deeds; and nobody among us opposes this despicable and dangerous inclination." Rejwan, *Israel in Search of Identity*, 9.

4. Kushner and Solomon, *Wrestling Zion*, 18.
5. Horowitz, "Editor's Notes."
6. Shatz, *Prophets Outcast*, 51.
7. Rejwan, *Israel in Search of Identity*, 8–9. In 1929, in a letter to Chaim Weizmann, Judah Magnes complained that the "Palestine Arabs are unhappily still half savage, and their leaders are almost all small men." Kushner and Solomon, *Wrestling Zion*, 18.
8. Rejwan, *Israel in Search of Identity*, 7. Several Zionists—starting with Theodore Herzl—took this approach, trying to sway the Arabs or the Ottomans with sweet talk of the inestimable benefits that Zionism would bring to them, if only they would open up Palestine to Jewish colonization. It is the approach that adults take toward children when trying to foist a bad bargain on them. A fine example of this ostensibly naïve approach is provided by Yitzhak Epstein, even though he is aware of the risks of flouting Palestinian rights. "These two people," writes Epstein, "the Hebrew and Arab, can supply each other's deficiency, because what we can give to the Arabs they can get from no other people. Every nation that comes to Syria in the guise of an economic savior will seek to conquer, to subjugate, and to assimilate, which is not the case with us, the people without an army and without warships: we are guileless, we have no alien thought of subjugation and of diluting the national character of our neighbors; with a pure heart we come to settle among them in order to better them in all respects." As late as 1930, after the Arab revolt of 1929, Albert Einstein could write, "I am convinced that the devotion of the Jewish people to Palestine will benefit all the inhabitants of the country, not only materially, but also culturally and nationally." Shatz, *Prophets Outcast*, 48, 62.
9. Rejwan, *Israel in Search of Identity*, 14–20.
10. Rodinson, *Israel*, 54.
11. Shlaim, *The Iron Wall*, 13.
12. In 2005, Israel removed the Jewish settlers from Gaza, but, in collaboration with Egypt, continued to police its borders and shoreline, effectively placing the Gazans inside a cage.
13. Rejwan, *Israel in Search of Identity*, 11.

CHAPTER 4

1. Morris, *Righteous Victims*, 57; Fromkin, *A Peace to End All Peace*, 257; Rejwan, *Israel in Search of Identity*, 11, 12. Col. House was aide to President Wilson.
2. Khalidi, *From Haven to Conquest*, 89.
3. The central idea of this book—Zionism contained a destabilizing logic that would inevitably pit the West against the Islamicate—was first presented in Alam ("Israel and the Consequences of Uniqueness"); it is reprinted in Alam, *Challenging the New Orientalism*, 103–16.
4. In the preface to his plan for the creation of a Jewish state in Palestine, Herzl (*The Jewish State*, x, 28) used the metaphor of steam (where Anti-Semitism is the force of the steam) to define the (steam) power that will propel the creation of his proposed Jewish state. He writes, "Now I believe that this power [of Anti-Semitism], if rightly employed, is powerful enough to propel a large engine and to despatch passengers and goods: the engine having whatever form men may choose to give it." He also writes that the "governments of all countries scourged by Anti-Semitism will serve their own interests in assisting us to obtain the sovereignty we want."

5. This alliance appears improbable because of the strong differences between Judaism and Christianity. The Jews view Christianity as a Jewish heresy, and Christ as a false Messiah. On the other hand, the Christians view Judaism as a religion that was superseded by their own. More importantly, since Christianity gained power over Jews in Europe—and, for a while, in the Middle East—it relegated Jews to the margins of society, forced them to live in segregated communities, denied them a wide range of civil and religious rights, and, often, unleashed pogroms against them. Later, starting in the nineteenth century, when Jews were granted greater equality of rights, they began to prosper financially and professionally. The last decades of the nineteenth century, however, witnessed the rise of new forms of anti-Semitism, which combined old hatreds with envy of Jewish prosperity, and (especially in Eastern Europe) growing fears of economic competition from Jews arriving in the towns and cities.

6. Lozowick, *Right to Exist*, 306.

CHAPTER 5

1. Shatz, *Prophets Outcast*, 45; Lewis, "The New Anti-Semitism," 31; Goldman, *The Jewish Paradox*, 99.

2. Peters elaborated on this thesis in her book, *From Time Immemorial*. The book was a smashing hit in the United States. According to Finkelstein (*Image and Reality*, 21–22), "Virtually every important journal of opinion printed one or more reviews within weeks of the book's release. Harper & Row reported that, scarcely eight months after publication, *From Time Immemorial* went into its seventh printing. Author Joan Peters reportedly had 25 speaking engagements scheduled for the coming year." Even Saul Bellow joined the chorus of praise, predicting that "millions of people the world over, smothered by false history and propaganda, would be grateful for this clear account of the origins of the Palestinians." However, Finkelstein has shown that the book was also a monumental fraud. "The fraud in Peter's book," he writes, "is so pervasive and systematic that it is hard to pluck out a single thread without getting entangled in the whole unraveling fabric." When this book was published in Britain—where, according to Chomsky ("The Fate of an Honest Intellectual"), "you can't control the intellectual community quite as easily"—it received very different reviews. Chomsky had sent an early version of Norman Finkelstein's critique of Peter's book to some authors and some journalists he knew in Britain. "As soon as the book appeared," Noam Chomsky writes, "it was just demolished, it was blown out of the water. Every major journal, the *Times Literary Supplement*, the *London Review*, the *Observer*, everybody had a review saying, this doesn't even reach the level of nonsense, of idiocy."

3. Ye'or (*Dhimmi* and *Islam and Dhimmitude*) is the leading writer in this area. In these ranks also belong Julius ("Review of: Nathan Weinstock") and the French writer Weinstock (*Zionism*, *Histoires de Chiens*, and *Use si Longue Présence*), a former Trotskyite who repudiated his earlier anti-Zionist book of 1979 to argue, in 2004, that Palestinian nationalism was motivated by anti-Semitism. In his 2008 book, Weinstock argues that Jews in the Islamicate received only a marginally better treatment than in Europe. See Julius ("Review of: Nathan Weinstock") for a review of Weinstock's work.

4. For balanced accounts of the status of non-Muslim communities in the Islamic world, see Cohen (*Under Crescent and Cross* and "The Jews under Islam"), Lewis ("The New Anti-Semitism"), and Menocal (*The Ornament of the World*).

5. Karsh, "The Long Train." Also, see Israeli, *War, Peace and Terror*, 61–80; Dalin, *The Myth of Hitler's Pope*, 127–46; and Schoenfeld, *The Return of Anti-Semitism*, 7–56.
6. Lewis, "The New Anti-Semitism."
7. Some Islamicate states invoked this interpretation of Jihad, mostly in the medieval period, when waging wars against non-Muslim states; this did not preclude long periods of truce between Muslim and non-Muslim states. Over the past two centuries, however, Muslims have invoked Jihad almost exclusively in defensive wars, when resisting colonization of their lands by Western powers.
8. Lewis, "The Roots of Muslim Rage."
9. Huntington, *The Clash of Civilizations*.
10. Portis, "Zionism and the United States."
11. Davidson, "Christian Zionism." Some of the quotes in this paragraph are from the original article in *New York Times*.

CHAPTER 6

1. Hertzberg, *The Zionist Idea*, 39.
2. Eliezer Ben-Yehudah (1858–1923) played a leading role in the revival of the Hebrew language. He was "the first to state, and to incarnate in a significant career, a main 'messianic' theme of Zionism—the notion that the Jews must end their peculiar history by becoming a modern nation." Hertzberg, *The Zionist Idea*, 159.
3. At first, Peretz Smolenskin (1842–85) embraced the Jewish Enlightenment and saw the Jews as a "spiritual nation," but, later, he rejected the Enlightenment and assimilation, developed a nationalist doctrine, and argued that the Jews should preserve their identity by returning to Eretz Israel. Hertzberg, *The Zionist Idea*, 145.
4. Simon, *About Zionism*, quoted in Brenner, *51 Documents*, 29.
5. Hess, *Rome and Jerusalem*, 58.
6. Hertzberg, *The Zionist Idea*, 197.
7. Kessner, *The Other New York*, 39.
8. Jewish Virtual Library, *World Jewish Population*.
9. ProCon.Org, *Israeli-Palestinian*.
10. See Laqueur (*A History of Zionism*, 85) for the territories claimed by the World Zionist Organization; this included, in addition to the British mandate of Palestine, parts of the Sinai, southern Lebanon, a slice of Syria, and all of Jordan west of Amman.
11. Morris, *Righteous Victims*, 41; Laqueur, *A History of Zionism*, 100–101, 115–19.
12. Leo Pinsker was perhaps the only eminent Zionist leader who argued that the "goal of our present endeavors must be not the 'Holy Land' but a land of our own." Shimoni, *The Zionist Ideology*, 35. Theodore Herzl too was less rigid in his commitment to Eretz Israel.
13. Hertzberg, *The Zionist Idea*, 579.
14. Shimoni, *The Zionist Ideology*, 98–99, 335.
15. Brenner, *Zionism*, 113.
16. Herzl, *The Jewish State*, 12.
17. Ibid., 12.
18. Leon, *The Jewish Question*.
19. Hertzberg, *The Zionist Idea*, 518.
20. DellaPergola, *Demography in Israel/Palestine*.
21. Bell, *Jews in the Early Modern World*, 63.
22. Between 1881 and 1914, another 300,000 European Jews emigrated to the United Kingdom, 100,000 to Argentina, 80,000 to France, 60,000 to Canada, and 50,000

to South Africa. Alroey, *Mass Jewish Migration*. The data on migration to Israel are from Jewish Virtual Library, *World Jewish Population*.

23. Moses Hess had anticipated this problem in 1862, when he wrote, "Even after the establishment of a Jewish state the majority of the Jews who live at present in the civilized countries of the Occident will undoubtedly remain where they are." Hertzberg, *The Zionist Idea*, 138.

24. Some of the Zionist precursors had foreseen this difficulty. In 1881, Peretz Smolenskin wrote, "Not all Jews will go there—only those who are destitute or persecuted will look for a place to which to emigrate." Hertzberg, *The Zionist Idea*, 152.

25. Nordau and Gottheil, *Zionism and Anti-Semitism*, 17, 19, 20.

26. Hertzberg, *The Zionist Idea*, 24.

27. "Modern Zionism," writes Hertzberg (*The Zionist Idea*, 18–19), "agreed with the classical faith that the Jews had once been chosen to lead the world . . . Despite some remarks to the contrary, the weight of learned opinion in the authoritative religious writings and the whole of popular Jewish feeling had always been certain that the election of the Jew would persist to all eternity."

28. Grose, *Israel in the Mind*, 14, 20. In the 1820s, Mordecai Noah tried to establish an agricultural Jewish colony—he called it Ararat—on Grand Island in Niagara River in western New York. Noah wanted Ararat to be a "City of Refuge," a "New Jerusalem" for the world's persecuted Jews. Not many Jews anywhere took up his offer: and the plan was widely ridiculed in the American Jewish press. See Dalin, "Jacksonian Jew."

29. In 1845, Noah ("Restoration of the Jews") wrote, "The restoration is to be brought about by human agency, and can only be accomplished by and with the consent of the Christian powers, who, from their own active energies, and, if you please, spirit of conquest, now control, I may say, the whole world, civilized and barbarian. We can only be peaceably restored by and with their consent, and if so restored, we shall, beyond doubt, be secure and protected in all our national rights."

30. In 1862, Moses Hess wrote, "Judaism is not threatened, like Christianity, with danger from nationalistic and humanistic aspirations of our time, for, in reality, the spirit of the age is approaching ever closer to the essential Jewish emphasis on real life." Hertzberg, *The Zionist Idea*, 125.

31. In 1862, Moses Hess writes, "Through the industrial and commercial endeavors the Jews have become necessary to the civilized nations in whose midst they live, and they are an indispensable leaven to the future development of these peoples. I have even heard it said quite seriously that the Indo-Germanic race improve its quality by mingling with the Jewish race!" Hertzberg, *The Zionist Idea*, 127. Theodore Herzl (*The Jewish State*, 8) too wrote, "We have doubtless attained preeminence in finance, because medieval conditions drove us to it."

32. Hertzberg (*The Zionist Idea*, 35) writes, "[Rabbi] Alkalai is particularly aware of the new political possibilities that the Emancipation had opened to the Jew. The prominence of individual Jews in European society and the later formation in 1860 of the Alliance Israelite Universelle to conduct the political defense of Jewish rights all over the world were used by him as arguments for Zionism: the Jew has now learned to deal as an equal on the international scene; let him act, with all the political and economic power he has achieved in freedom, for the restoration of his people." Pasachoff and Littman (*A Concise History*, 212) also write that Rabbi Alkalai and Rabbi Kalischer viewed the emancipation of Jews and the unprecedented rise of a few Jews—like Rothschild and Montefiore—to leadership in finance as signs of the coming redemption. In the 1830s, Kalischer urged the head of the Rothschild family and Moses Montefiore to buy Palestine—or, at least, Jerusalem—from the Ottomans for Jewish settlement.

33. Hertzberg, *The Zionist Idea*, 133–34.
34. Herzl, *The Jewish State*, 12.
35. "We cannot assimilate," writes Samuel (*You Gentiles*, 209). "It is so humiliating to us that we become contemptible in submitting to this process: it is so exasperating to you that, even if we were willing to submit, it would avail us nothing."
36. Several prominent Jews in the United States, including Felix Warburg, worried that Zionism would encourage anti-Semites to question if American Jews owed their primary loyalty to the United States. Berman, *Nazism, the Jews*, 60.
37. Hertzberg, *The Zionist Idea*, 265.
38. Ibid., 15.
39. In June 1912, Portugal offered to create a "self-governing colony on the model of British South Africa or Canada" in Angola. This offer was made by the Portuguese government to Israel Zangwill in Lisbon. Telegraph, "Angola Is Offered," 8.
40. This could not have been as fantastic an idea in 1900 as it sounds today, given the dramatic changes in the relative populations of world Jewry and the population of the Arab Middle East. In 1900, the world Jewish population stood at 10.6 million. Most likely, the total population of the Ottoman provinces of Syria, Iraq, and the Hijaz at the time was much less than the world total for the Jews. Jewish Virtual Library, *World Jewish Population*.
41. Hertzberg, *The Zionist Idea*, 19.
42. Brown, "Iron and a King," 7.
43. Hertzberg, *The Zionist Idea*, 20.
44. Ibid., 145.

CHAPTER 7

1. Hess, *Rome and Jerusalem*, 49; Herzl, *The Jewish State*, 11; Shlaim, *The Iron Wall*, 101; Ottolenghi, "Anti-Zionism."
2. The slogan, "a land without a people for a people without a land," is often attributed to Israel Zangwill, but it was first used by the Earl of Shaftesbury, a leading Christian Zionist, in 1840s. Garfinkle, "On the Origins."
3. At the hearings of the Royal Commission on Alien Immigration in 1902, Herzl said, "A nation is, in my mind, a historical group of men of a recognizable cohesion held together by a common enemy. That is in my view a nation. Then if you add to that the word 'Jewish' you have what I understand to be the Jewish nation." Raisin, *A History of the Jews*, 411.
4. Hertzberg, *The Zionist Idea*, 183. In 1900, Karl Kraus, an early critic of Zionism, wrote, "After all, what common bond could unite the interests of the German, English, French, Slavic and Turkic Jews into one political entity?" Brenner, *Zionism*, 45.
5. In 1905, Max Nordau wrote, "Since the destruction of the second temple by Titus, since the dispersion of the Jewish nation in all countries, this people has not ceased to long intensely, and hope fervently, for the return to the lost land of their fathers." Nordau and Gottheil, *Zionism and Anti-Zionism*, 10–11.
6. As a result, in his negotiations with the Ottomans, Herzl (*The Jewish State*, 29–30) did not merely seek permission for the Jews to immigrate freely; he asked the Sultan to "give" Palestine to the Jews. "Suppose His Majesty the Sultan were to *give us* Palestine," Herzl wrote, "we could in return pledge ourselves to regulate the whole finances of Turkey" (emphasis added).
7. These ideas will be examined more extensively in Chapter 13 when we discuss the connections between Christian Zionism and the Zionist movement.

8. Sokolow, *History of Zionism*, 63.

9. Ould-Mey, "Geopolitical genesis," 4–5.

10. The rivalry between Britain and France for global domination had been settled quite decisively in Britain's favor with Napoleon's defeat in 1815. In 1840, the expansionist bid made by Muhammad Ali Pasha had also been decisively contained. Moreover, given the overwhelming superiority of their naval forces, French control over the Suez Canal was only a minor irritant to the British. In 1882, this irritant too was eliminated when the British occupied Egypt.

11. Shimoni, *The Zionist Ideology*, 34.

12. This was the common denominator of all Zionist movements: the belief that "Jews are a single, distinctive entity, possessing national, not just religious attributes. This understanding of the nature of the Jewish entity distinguished the adherents of Zionism sharply from those who abjured the national attributes of the Jewish entity and advocated the panacea of diasporic emancipation and integration." Shimoni, *The Zionist Ideology*, 85.

13. Herzl, *The Jewish State*, 2, 4.

14. Ibid., ix, 11.

15. In 1919, Sokolow (*History of Zionism*, 296) complains, "The *official* Jewish community [in Britain], with its rather parochial view, long looked askance at Zionism, and until quite recent years those who followed Herzl have been a minority struggling hard against a vast amount of prejudice and of indifference."

16. "The proper, the only remedy [for Jewish homelessness]," wrote Leo Pinsker, "would be the *creation of a Jewish nationality*, of a people living upon its own soil, the auto-emancipation of the Jews; their emancipation as a nation among nations by the acquisition of a home of their own" (emphasis added). Shimoni, *The Zionist Ideology*, 34.

17. "The question, from whom was the land 'liberated,' is difficult to answer," writes Hans Kohn. "From the British, whose administration had alone made possible the growth of the Jewish settlement against the will of the great majority of Palestinians? From its native inhabitants who, though ruled by foreign empires, had tilled and owned the soil for many centuries." Kohn, "Zion and the Jewish," 209.

18. Lindqvist, *Exterminate All the Brutes*. In its narrative approach to history, this book reveals the banality of racism and genocide in the Western encounter with the Other outside of Europe.

19. Hochschild, *King Leopold's Ghost*.

20. Meyer, "Editorial Notebook."

21. Just as Israel has refused to define its borders, the early Zionists too avoided defining the boundaries of their projected state. In private, different claims were made about the proposed borders of the Jewish state, some more ambitious than others. In 1918, David Ben-Gurion and Yitzhak Ben-Zvi, in a book written in Yiddish, described a Jewish state that (in the words of the Benny Morris) would stretch "from the Litani River in southern Lebanon, the Hermon Mountain foothills and Wadi A'waj (just south of Damascus) in the north, to the Gulf of Aqaba (Eilat) in the south. In the West it would reach as far as Al-'Arīsh in Sinai, and in the east it would stretch to a rough line between Aqaba and Amman." Morris, *Righteous Victims*, 75.

22. Superficially, the Zionists seem to have a point. How could Zionism not be a movement for liberation, given the armed struggle that Jews had to wage against a colonial power that was in occupation of Palestine? Isaac Deutscher, a Marxist historian, has offered a succinct response to the specious logic of this claim. "The fact that the Jewish community in Palestine," he writes, "afterward fought the British is no more evidence of its not being a colonial implantation than similar wars of British colonists

against the mother country from the American Revolution to Rhodesia. In the case of Palestine, as of other such struggles, the Mother Country was assailed because it showed more concern for the native majority than was palatable to the colonist minority." Kushner and Solomon, *Wrestling Zion*, 30.

23. Shlaim, "Why Zionism Today."
24. Rodinson, *Israel: A Colonial Settler State*, 30.
25. In a conversation with Nahum Goldmann in 1955, Ben-Gurion declared, "Why should the Arabs make peace? If I was an Arab leader I would never make terms with Israel. That is natural: we have taken their country. Sure God promised it to us, but what does that matter to them? Our God is not theirs. We come from Israel, but two thousand years ago, and what is that to them? There has been antisemitism, the Nazis, Hitler, Auschwitz, but was that their fault? They only see one thing: we have come here and stolen their country. Why should they accept that? They may perhaps forget in one or two generations' time, but for the moment there is no chance. So, it's simple: we have to stay strong and maintain a powerful army. Our whole policy is there. Otherwise the Arabs will wipe us out." Goldmann, *The Jewish Paradox*, 99.

CHAPTER 8

1. Masalha, *Expulsion of the Palestinians*, 9–10; Hirst, The Gun and the Olive Branch, 161; Morris, *The Birth of the Palestinian*, 50; Shavit, "Survival of the Fittest."
2. DellaPergola, *Demography in Israel/Palestine.*
3. Jewish Virtual Library, *Jewish and non-Jewish Population of Palestine-Israel.*
4. In 1994, Elia Zureik ("Palestinian Refugees," 11) surveyed the different estimates of the numbers of Palestinians expelled from Israel: these estimates range from 700,000 to 800,000; but Salman Abu-Sitta (*The Palestinian Nakba*, 14) maintains that the numbers expelled were 935,000.
5. Many Arabs who were forced to flee their homes in 1948 and 1949, but stayed inside Israel, were also prevented from returning to their homes; they became refugees inside Israel. Masalha, *Catastrophe Remembered.*
6. Avi Shlaim (*The Iron Wall*, xiii) identifies four works, all published in the late 1980s, with the beginning of revisionist history: Flapan, *The Birth of Israel*; Morris, *The Birth of the Palestinian Refugee Problem, 1947–49*; Pappé, *Britain and Arab-Israeli Conflict*; and Shlaim, *Collusion across the Jordan*. Since then, these books have been followed by others, notably Pappé, *The Ethnic Cleansing of Palestine*; and Morris, *1948: A History.*
7. Karsh, *Fabricating Israeli History.*
8. Finkelstein, *Image and Reality*, 8.
9. Hirst, *The Gun and the Olive Branch*, 161.
10. According to Herzl (*The Jewish State*, 10), the "immediate cause" of anti-Semitism "is our excessive production of mediocre intellects, who cannot find an outlet downwards or upwards—that is to say, no wholesome outlet in either direction. Whenever we sink, we become a revolutionary proletariat, the subordinate officers of the revolutionary party; when we rise, there arises the terrible power of our purse."
11. Israel Zangwill proposed to expel the Palestinians. As early as 1905, he declared, "[We] must be prepared either to drive out by the sword the [Arab] tribes in possession as our forefathers did or to grapple with the problem of a large alien population, mostly Mohammedan and accustomed for centuries to despise us." Masalha, *Expulsion of the Palestinians*, 10.
12. Ibid., 176.

13. Finkelstein, *Image and Reality*, 8–9.
14. Ibid., 9; Sternhell, *The Founding Myths*, ch. 2.
15. Colonial settler states come in at least three forms. In the first, the alien settlers in the colony end up displacing or exterminating all or nearly all the "natives"; this is the exclusive settler colony. In a second version, the settlers appropriate the best lands and use the displaced natives as a reserve of cheap labor; this is the mixed settler colony. In its third form, the settlers in the colony replace the extinct native populations—killed by diseases, the savagery of the colonists, or both—with imported slaves or indentured workers; this is the plantation settler colony. See Fieldhouse, *Colonial Empires*, 11–12.
16. Masalha, *Expulsion of the Palestinians*, 27.
17. "The Zionist public catechism, at the turn of the century, and well into the 1940s, remained that there was room enough in Palestine for both people; there need not be a displacement of Arabs to make room for the Zionist immigrants or the Jewish state. There was no need for a transfer of the Arabs and on no account must the idea be incorporated into the movement's ideological-political platform." Morris, *The Birth of the Palestinian Refugee Problem Revisited*, 43.
18. The mayor of Jerusalem had written to the chief rabbi of France, advising the Jews that they (in the words of Herzl) "would do better to go somewhere else." Khalidi, *From Haven to Conquest*, 91–92.
19. It may be worth noting that Herzl (*The Jewish State*, 11) displays an obsessive interest in working out all manner of details that he thinks will ensure the success of his plan for a Jewish state. He dedicates an entire paragraph on how to rid Palestine of "wild beasts." Instead of pursuing them with the primitive spear and lance, they should be exterminated with "melinite bombs." Yet there is no mention of the Arabs in the pages of *The Jewish State*: as if Palestine were truly empty.
20. Morris, *Righteous Victims*, 21–22.
21. Khalidi, "The Jewish-Ottoman Land Company," 44; Hirst, *The Gun and the Olive Branch*, 138–39.
22. Hirst, *The Gun and the Olive Branch*, 161.
23. Ibid., 171.
24. Elon (*The Israelis*, 149) attributes this phrase to Israel Zangwill. In 1903, Zangwill wrote, "Palestine is a ruined country and the Jews are a broken people. But neither is beyond recuperation. Palestine needs a people; Israel needs a country." See Simon, *Speeches, Articles*, 80.
25. Masalha, *Expulsion of the Palestinians*, 5–6.
26. Zangwill, *The Voice of Jerusalem*, 104, quoted in Masalha, *Expulsion of the Palestinians*, 6, 14.
27. Masalha, *Expulsion of the Palestinians*, 15.
28. Hirst, *The Gun and the Olive Branch*, 162–63.
29. Ibid., 184–85.
30. In 1937, when the members of *Hashomer Hatza'ir*—a *kibbutz* federation who advocated a binational state—objected that the creation of a "Hebrew state" would create barriers between Jews and Arabs, Yosef Baratz, a Mapai leader, answered: "Isn't such a barrier already existing and permanent in the country? Aren't we building *exclusive* train stations, an *exclusive* post service, *exclusive* government office, an *exclusive* sea port, *exclusive* roads, and an *exclusive* economy as far as possible?" (emphasis added). Masalha, *Expulsion of the Palestinians*, 75.
31. Morris, *The Birth of the Palestinian Refugee Problem*, 44.

32. The quotes in this paragraph are from Morris, *The Birth of the Palestinian Refugee Problem*, 44, 50.
33. Ibid., 47–48.
34. Ibid., 48, 50, 54.
35. Ibid., 50.
36. Pappe, *The Ethnic Cleansing of Palestine*, 48.
37. Ibid., 55–60.

CHAPTER 9

1. Grose, *Israel in the Mind*, 14; Slezkin, *The Jewish Century*, 50.
2. Lindemann (*Essau's Tears*, 14, 15) has argued that a Jewish historiography of victimization has focused excessively on anti-Semitic violence in the history of European Jews and on anti-Semitism as an ideology that has dominated Western thinking in medieval and modern times. He suggests that this historiography, in part, serves as an "ideology of revenge" against Gentiles. Its primary purpose, however, is to prevent Jewish suffering "largely by exposing the sinful or corrupt nature of Gentile society and its responsibility for Jewish suffering."
3. Ben-Sasson (*A History of the Jewish People*, 790) writes, "The Jewish rate of increase was twice as fast as that of the non-Jewish population, and several scholars have spoken of the 'demographic miracle' of the Jewish people in the nineteenth century." Based on new estimates of Jewish populations in Netherlands, the Polish province of Posen, and Germany, Straten and Snel ("The Jewish 'Demographic Miracle'") conclude that claims of a Jewish demographic miracle in the nineteenth century are exaggerated; the exaggeration is put down to underestimates of the Jewish population in 1800.
4. Dowty, *Israel/Palestine*, 27; Rottenberg, *Finding Our Fathers*, 43.
5. Roupp, *Teaching World History*, 121.
6. Dellapergolla, "An Overview," 62; Rottenberg, *Finding Our Fathers*, 43.
7. Dellapergolla, "An Overview," 62. According to earlier estimates by Ettinger ("Demographic Changes," 792), the share of Western and Central Europe in the world's Jewish population was only 11 percent.
8. Dellapergolla, "An Overview," 62. According to Ettinger ("Demographic Changes," 792), 37 percent of the world's Jews lived in the Islamic world; their share had declined to 10 percent in 1880.
9. Endelman, *The Jews of Britain*, 41, 130.
10. Jewish Virtual Library, *World Jewish Population*. The share of the Americas in the world's Jewish population increased dramatically from 0.3 percent in 1825 to 11 percent in 1900. On the contrary, the share of the world's Jewish population in Africa and Asia declined from 16.5 percent in 1825 to 6.7 percent in 1900. Engelman, *The Rise of the Jew*, 103.
11. Ettinger, "Demographic Changes," 793; Gelvin, *The Israeli-Palestinian Conflict*, 42.
12. Elazar and Cohen, *The Jewish Polity*, 242.
13. Katz, *Tradition and Crisis*, 44. In his assessment of European Jewish society from the sixteenth to the eighteenth century, Katz (*Tradition and Crisis*, 55) writes, "We have before us the classic example of a social minority whose very segregation and isolation ideally conditioned it for economic activity—and for that alone."
14. Lazare, *Anti-Semitism*, 108.

15. Lazare (ibid., 109) writes, "At the beginning of the great industrial development, after 1815, when canal, mine, and insurance companies were formed, the Jews were among the most active in promoting combination of capital."

16. Slezkin, *The Jewish Century*, 47–48; Ettinger, "Demographic Changes," 796.

17. "In 1912, 20 percent of all millionaires in Britain and Prussia . . . were Jews. In 1908–11, in Germany as a whole, Jews made up . . . 31 percent of the richest families . . . In 1930, about 70 percent of the richest Hungarian taxpayers . . . were Jews. And of course, the Rothschilds . . . were, by a large margin, the wealthiest family of the nineteenth century." Slezkin, *The Jewish Century*, 48.

18. Ibid., 50.

19. Beller, *Vienna and the Jews*, 40, quoted in Slezkin, *The Jewish Century*, 51.

20. Ettinger, "Demographic Changes," 797–8.

21. Endelman, *The Jews of Britain*, 81, 92.

22. The Gypsies were another transnational community in Europe, but their numbers were smaller, and, more importantly, they were unable to rise above their marginal existence in European societies.

23. In 1911, Lucien Wolf, an eminent Jewish activist, wrote, "So far from injuring the Jews, it [anti-Semitism] has really given Jewish racial separatism a new lease on life . . . Its agitation . . . has helped to transfer Jewish solidarity from a religious to a racial basis." Lindemann, *Essau's Tears*, 330.

24. Jewish activists were already an important force in the various non-Marxist but radical movements in Russia during the 1870s and 1880s. "In the peak years of 1886–89 [in the career of the People's Will party], the Jews accounted for between 25 and 30 percent of all activists, and between 35 and 40 percent of those in southern Russia." Moreover, with "the rise of Marxism, the role of Jews in the Russian revolutionary movements became still more prominent . . . The first group of 29 [exiles] that arrived with Lenin included 17 Jews (58.6 percent). At the Sixth (Bolshevik) party Congress of July–August 1917 . . . the Jewish share was about 16 percent overall, and 23.7 percent in the Central Committee." Slezkin, *The Jewish Century*, 151–52.

25. "A stream of about two and a half million Eastern European Jews gave the United States the largest Jewish community after World War I." Brenner, *Zionism: A Brief History*, 68.

26. Lindemann (*Essau's Tears*, 320) writes that Zionism "might also be considered corroboration, by eloquent Jewish leaders, of the charge made by anti-Semites that there was something deep in Jewish consciousness that finally could not accept absorption into a modern nationalist identity."

27. Theodore Herzl (*The Jewish State*, x) compared anti-Semitism to the power of steam that, "if rightly employed, is powerful enough to propel a large engine and to despatch passengers and goods: the engine having whatever form men may choose to give it."

28. "From the start of the mass migration in 1881," writes Hochberg ("The Repatriation of Eastern European Jews," 49–50), "repatriation was one of the pillars of communal policy for an Anglo-Jewish community opposed in principle to the settling of foreign Jews in Britain."

29. Slezkin, *The Jewish Century*, 166–70.

30. Ibid., 149–50.

31. Hertzberg, *The Zionist Idea*, 329–90; Shimoni, *The Zionist Ideology*, ch. 5.

32. Lacqueur, *A History of Zionism*, 84–135.

33. Ibid., 97–98

34. Ibid., 101.

35. Ibid., 109.

36. For example, Theodore Herzl gained access to the Ottoman Sultan through the services of Arminius Vambery, an Orientalist, traveler, and friend of the Sultan, who was of Hungarian-Jewish origin. Lacqueur, *A History of Zionism*, 111–12. In January 1915, Herbert Samuel, the postmaster general and a Jew, submitted "the first British proposal to conquer Palestine" in a detailed memorandum submitted to the British cabinet. Segev, *One Palestine Complete*, 33. In addition, two close associates of President Woodrow Wilson—Rabbi Stephen Wise and Louis Brandeis—were Jews.

CHAPTER 10

1. Hertzberg, *The Zionist Idea*, 109–110; Schuldiner and Kleinfeld, *The Selected Writings*, 126; Hertzberg, *The Zionist Idea*, 133; Sokolow, *History of Zionism*, 295; Hertzberg, *The Zionist Idea*, 576.

2. Herzl, *The Jewish State*, 12.

3. Grose, *Israel in the Mind*, 14.

4. Mordecai Noah wrote that since the Jews, on their own, cannot take possession of Syria, the Christian nations that "now control the destinies of the world, must be invoked in carrying out this most interesting project." Specifically, he expected the British to take up this task. Noah predicted that Britain will colonize Egypt to secure access to its possessions in India; once this happens, a Jewish state in Palestine could serve as a reliable buffer between the British in Egypt and the Russians. Moreover, the Jews are prepared—and they have the capability—to take on this great task. "The whole sect are . . . in a position," according to Mordecai Noah, "as far as intelligence, education, industry, undivided enterprise, variety of pursuits, science, a love of the arts, political economy, and wealth could desire, to adopt the initiatory steps for the organization of a free government in Syria." Schuldiner and Kleinfeld, *The Selected Writings*, 139, 141.

5. Hertzberg, *The Zionist Idea*, 133.

6. Pinsker, *Auto-Emancipation*, 96, quoted in Hirst, *The Gun and the Olive Branch*, 41.

7. Herzl, *The Jewish State*, 2, 6. In a letter written in 1899 to Zia Al-Khalidi, the mayor of Jerusalem, Theodore Herzl, had assured him that "the Jews have no belligerent Power behind them" and "there is absolutely nothing to fear from their immigration." Yet Theodore Herzl had spent the last few years in a frantic bid to secure the support of just such a "belligerent Power." Khalidi, *From Haven to Conquest*, 91–92. In addition, the draft of the charter for the Jewish-Ottoman Land Company (JOLC)—that Herzl wanted the Ottomans to endorse—included plans for setting up a Jewish army and navy under the control of the JOLC. Khalidi, "The Jewish-Ottoman Land Company," 46.

8. The endorsements of the following governments of the Balfour Declaration were entered into the record of the U.S. Congress in April 1922: France, Italy, Holland, Greece, Serbia, China, Siam, and Japan. Zionist Organization of America, *The American War Congress*, 151–54.

9. The territorial Zionists had a different list of "surrogates" that included smaller European powers, such as Portugal, with colonies in Africa.

10. In Poland, the victims of the new communist regime as well as ordinary members of the communist party saw Jews in the party as "servants of Stalin and betrayers of national communism." Naimark, "Revolution and Counter-Revolution," 76–77.

In the revolutionary movements that sought to capture power in the wake of the collapse of the Hohenzollern, Romanov, and Hapsburg empires after World War I, "Jews played important roles." Jews played a leading role in the Hungarian revolution of 1919, led by Bela Kun, a Transylvanian Jew; in addition, eighteen of the twenty-nine members of the Hungarian Soviet Revolutionary Council were Jewish. Jews also "played key roles in the revolutionary upheavals in Berlin and Munich." Brustein, *Roots of Hate*, 272.

11. It should be noted that not all Christians favored Zionism on religious grounds. "It is revolting," the special correspondent of a British newspaper, wrote, "that a Christian country such as Britain is should turn the Holy Land into the domain for freethinking Judaeo-Slavs. Our forefathers made the Crusades; but our statesmen . . . hand over the country of the Redeemer to infidels such as Richard Coeur de Lion knew." Kerekes, *Masked Ball*, 272.

12. Brenner, *Zionism in the Age* and *51 Documents*; Black, *The Transfer Agreement*; Hecht, *Perfidy*.

13. Czechoslovakia began to supply arms to Israel in January 1948, and by late summer of the same year they had supplied "84 fighter planes, 22 tanks, 16 artillery pieces, 60,000 light arms, and tens of millions of rounds of ammunition." Sachar, *Israel and Europe*, 56–57.

14. Lewan, "How West Germany Helped," 41–43. At the end of 2000, the total value of German reparations for its persecution of Jews amounted to 55 billion Euros, and of this amount, 40 percent went to Israel or recipients in Israel. Germany, *Israel.*

15. Safran, *Israel*, 376.

16. Kamrava, *The Modern Middle East*, 79.

17. Yaacobi, *Breakthrough*, 184.

CHAPTER 11

1. This is how Sir Mark Sykes, secretary to Britain's war cabinet in 1917, greeted Chaim Weizmann with news that the British cabinet had approved the statement of support for Zionism, known as the Balfour Declaration. Fromkin, *A Peace to End All Peace*, 297.

2. Morris, *Righteous Victims*, 15. In his speech to the first Zionist Congress, Theodore Herzl stated, "Asia is the diplomatic problem of the coming decade. Let us recall in all modesty that we Zionists . . . foresaw and proclaimed this development of the European contest [over Palestine] several years ago." Straus, *The Congress Addresses*, 13.

3. Hess, *Rome and Jerusalem*, 167.

4. Herzl, *The Jewish State*, 12. The second sentence in this quote is missing from the cited edition, but is present in other editions.

5. Stein, *The Balfour Declaration*, 8.

6. Kayyali, "Zionism and Imperialism," 100.

7. Jabbour, *Settler Colonialism*, 22–23.

8. Jeffries, "Analysis of the Balfour Declaration," 173.

9. Hirst, *The Gun and the Olive Branch*; Laqueur, *A History of Zionism*, 203; Levene, "The Balfour Declaration," 54.

10. Laqueur, *A History of Zionism*, 162.

11. Information in this and the previous paragraph is from British Embassy, Vienna, *Herzl in England: UK and Austria, Bilateral Relations*. http://www.britishebassy .gov.uk/servlet/Front?pagename=OpenMarket/Xcelerate/ShowPage&c=Page& cid=1107298483043

12. Fromkin, *A Peace to End All Peace*, 274.
13. Sidebotham, "British Interests in Palestine," 128–33.
14. Toward the end of 1914, when Lord Kitchener asked his Oriental Secretary in Cairo for his opinion on the significance of Palestine in relation to a French or Russian presence to the north, he wrote back, "A buffer State [in Palestine] is most desirable, but can one get one up?" A Jewish state in Palestine, he offered, was not feasible, since the Jews formed only one-sixth of the population. Instead, he proposed that Palestine should be incorporated into Egypt. Fromkin, *A Peace to End All Peace*, 142–43.
15. Ibid., 269–71.
16. Lloyd George, *Memoirs*, 721.
17. See note 15.
18. Lord Balfour—in a cabinet meeting in October 1917—expressed the British viewpoint very well: "The vast majority of Jews in Russia and America, as indeed all over the world, now appear to be favorable to Zionism. If we could make a declaration favorable to such an ideal, we should be able to carry on extremely useful propaganda both in Russia and America." Morris, *Righteous Victims*, 74.
19. Laqueur, *A History of Zionism*, 177.
20. Morris, *Righteous Victims*, 74.
21. "While [Dr. A] Hankte, [Kurt] Blumenfeld and [Richard] Lichtheim [leading Zionists in Germany] impressed on their Berlin contacts that England was about to make an important pro-Zionist declaration, Weizmann used the reverse argument in his dealings with the British cabinet and Foreign Office: unless the British hurried the central powers would come out first and secure an important advantage." Laqueur, *A History of Zionism*, 177.
22. Morris, *Righteous Victims*, 73.
23. Lloyd George, *Memoirs*, 724.
24. The three assistant secretaries in the war cabinet were Sir Mark Sykes, William Ormsby-Gore, and Leopold S. Amery. Morris, *Righteous Victims*, 72–73.
25. Laqueur, *A History of Zionism*, 456.
26. Smith, *Palestine*, 64.
27. Morris, *Righteous Victims*, 103.
28. Shlaim, *The Iron Wall*, 10; Morris, *Righteous Victims*, 103–4.
29. Smith, *Palestine*, 90–92.
30. Ibid., 103.
31. Ibid., 102–5.

CHAPTER 12

1. Avishai, *The Tragedy of Zionism*, 28; Patai, *The Complete Diaries*, quoted in Friedman, *Germany, Turkey, Zionism*, 55; Quigley, *Flight into the Maelstrom*, 167; Seidman, *Socialists and the Fight*, 26; and Chomsky, "Anti-Semitism, Zionism."
2. According to Katz ("The Jewish National Movement," 273), the early nationalist theories of Rabbi Alkalai (1798–1878) and Rabbi Kalischer (1795–1874) "were derived from reinterpretation of the old Messianic tradition in the light of new historic experiences. In view of later developments it is well to remember that *modern anti-Semitism was not amongst these experiences*" (emphasis added). The two rabbis developed their nationalist theories "during the flourishing period of Middle European Liberalism, i.e. between 1840–1875, when optimism as to the possible integration of

Jews into the life of European nations was almost universal." In addition, Katz writes that Rabbi Kalischer interpreted the emancipation of Jews in his youth "exclusively in terms derived from Jewish tradition. The emancipation and even more the ascendance of Jewish individuals, as, for instance, the Rothschilds, to unheard of economic and political influence appeared to him to be the fulfillment of the old prophecy of liberation which according to Jewish tradition was to terminate the exile."

3. On the "lachrymose" history constructed by Jews, see Liberles and Lyman (*Salo Wittmayer Baron*), Foa (*The Jews of Europe*, 219), and Kiener (*The Jewish Experience of Suffering*). Contrary to their Gentile colleagues, the Jewish scholars of Islam and the Middle East, during the height of Orientalism, were more generous in their recognition of Islamic and Islamicate achievements, as a snub to European claims of superiority. Once Zionism became the dominant discourse among the Jews, starting in the 1940s, a new generation of Jewish scholars began to practice a more predatory Orientalism that blamed Islam for all the problems of the Islamicate. Alam, "Bernard Lewis," reprinted in Alam, *Challenging the New Orientalism*, 3–23. A revisionist history of the Jews in the Islamicate has also been added to the arsenal of Zionism, described as neo-lachrymose by Cohen, "The Neo-Lachrymose Conception."

4. Frankfurter, "An Interview," 196.

5. Findley, *They Dare to Speak Out*; Finkelstein, *The Holocaust Industry*, 11–38; Alam, "A New Theology," reprinted in Cockburn and St. Clair, *The Politics of Anti-Semitism*, 73–77. For the attacks launched against Mearsheimer and Walt ("The Israel Lobby") for their article on the Israeli lobby, see Solomon, "The Lobby and the Bulldozer," and Cohen, "Yes, It's Anti-Semitic." See Finkelstein, "The Ludicrous Attacks," and Lipstadt, "Jimmy Carter's Jewish Problem," for the attacks on President Carter's book, *Palestine: Peace Not Apartheid*.

6. In 1894, Lazare (*Anti-Semitism*, 124) wrote, "If the anti-Semite reproaches the Jew for being part of a strange and base race, the Jew vaunts of belonging to an elect and superior race; to his nobility and antiquity he attaches the highest importance and even now he is the prey of patriotic pride. Though no longer a nation, though protesting against those who see in him the representative of a nation encamped among strange nations, he nevertheless harbors in the depth of his heart this absurdly vain conviction, and thus he is like the chauvinists of all lands."

7. Herzl, *The Jewish State*, x; Hirst, *The Gun and the Olive Branch*, 286.

8. Herzl, *The Jewish State*, x.

9. Hirst, *The Gun and the Olive Branch*, 285–86.

10. Lilienthal, *The Other Side*, 184, quoted in Hirst, *The Gun and the Olive Branch*, 286.

11. Zionist and Jewish organizations in the United State did very little to register their protest against the immigration restrictions during the 1930s when Nazi persecution of the Jews was common knowledge. Seidman (*Socialists and the Fight*, 30) concluded, "Leaders of Zionists and most Jewish organizations raised no significant protests against the policies of the Roosevelt administration that left hundreds of refugees, Jews and others, to die at the hands of the fascist and anti-Semites in Europe during the 1930s."

12. Khalidi, *From Haven to Conquest*, xxxi. In 1938, David Ben-Gurion wrote, "If Jews will have to choose between the refugees, saving Jews from concentration camps, and assisting a national museum in Palestine, mercy will have the upper hand and the whole energy of the people will be channeled into saving Jews from various countries. Zionism will be struck off the agenda not only in world opinion, in Britain and the USA, but elsewhere in Jewish public opinion. If we allow a separation between the

refugee problem and the Palestine problem, we are risking the existence of Zionism." Quigley, *Flight into the Maelstrom*, 167.

13. Quigley, *Flight into the Maelstrom*, 167. In an entry on the Evian Conference, Taylor ("Evian Conference," 213) writes, "The expectation that the Jewish organizations would present a stable immigration plan was unfulfilled when they proved unable to agree among themselves."

14. This is not the only example of Zionist resistance to various proposals and offers to rescue Europe's Jews. Miller, *Awake My Glory*, excerpted in Jews Against Zionism, *Words of the Rabbis*.

15. Ernst, *So Far So Good*, 172–76.

16. According to Feingold ("American Jewry," 6), "When news of the systematic killing of Jews leaked out of Switzerland in 1942, American Jews found the stories too grue-some to believe and hence were slow to urge the U. S. government to take action to stop the Nazi implementation of the Final Solution."

17. Rodinson, *Israel: A Colonial Settler State*, 45.

18. Brenner, *Zionism in the Age*, chs. 5, 14, and 19.

19. Khalidi, *From Haven to Conquest*, Appendix I.

20. Kerekes, *Masked Ball*, 271.

21. Lilienthal, *What Price Israel?*, 146.

22. Ibid., 148–50, 153–54.

23. Lilienthal, *The Other Side*, 47, quoted in Hirst, *The Gun and the Olive Branch*, 286.

24. Hirst, *The Gun and the Olive Branch*, 281–83, 288–89.

25. Shiblak, *Iraqi Jews*, reviewed in Al-Shawaf, "Review: Abbas Shiblak."

26. Prager and Telushkin, *Why the Jews*, 183.

CHAPTER 13

1. Strauss, *The Congress Addresses*, 12; Berle, *The World Significance*, 15; Jastrow, *Zionism and the Future of Palestine*, 16; Sokolow, *History of Zionism*, 54; Lazare, "The Chosen: Ideological Roots," 80; Pipes, "Israel's Ultimate Strategic Asset."

2. The most prominent of the Jewish thinkers of the nineteenth century, who advocated Jewish restoration, include Rabbi Yehuda Alkalai, Rabbi Zvi Hirsch Kalischer, Moses Hess, Peretz Smolenskin, and Leo Pinsker.

3. Vreté, "The Restoration of the Jews," 3.

4. The English Protestants, in particular, saw the Jews as allies against the Catholic Church and the Turks. Matar, *Islam in Britain*, 173–75.

5. The Protestant support for restoration was inspired in part by the belief that—some-how—they would gain victory over Islam and Catholicism *before* the restoration of Jews to Palestine. Moreover, the Jews would convert to Christianity before the resto-ration. Matar, "The Restoration of the Jews," 23–36.

6. In the middle of the seventeenth century, there were no Jews living in Spain, Portugal, England, France, and parts of Germany; by the end of the eighteenth century, there were 175,000 Jews in Germany, 40–50,000 in France, 70,000 in the Austrian Empire, 50,000 in Holland and 25,000 in Britain. Malino, "Jewish Christian Relations," 208.

7. Lazare, *Anti-Semitism*, 76. The Ebionites were an early Judaizing Christian sect in Palestine who retained Jewish Law and rituals as part of their practice.

8. "*Hebrew* was a favorite study with Puritan ministers, who dwelt much upon the Mes-sianic hopes and promises of the Scriptures and *Rabbinical* works." Sokolow, *History of Zionism*, 40.

9. Ould-Mey, "The Non-Jewish Origin of Zionism," 2.
10. Ould-Mey, "The Non-Jewish Origin of Zionism," 6.
11. Roth, *Essays and Portraits*, 13, quoted in Ingram, "Christian Zionism," 4.
12. Sokolow, *History of Zionism*, 40–46, 53.
13. Sharif, "Christians for Zion," 125.
14. Sharif, *Non-Jewish Zionism*, 36.
15. Snobelen, "The Mystery of this Restitution," 95–118.
16. Sharif, "Christians for Zion," 127.
17. Davidson, *America's Palestine*, 8.
18. King, "William Eugene Blackstone."
19. Prior, "Israel-Palestine," 69.
20. Merkley, *The Politics of Christian Zionism*, 89.
21. Sharif, "Christians for Zion," 123.
22. This connection was made as early as 1649 in a petition to the English sovereign, submitted by two English Puritans then living in Amsterdam. The petition stated, ". . . that this Nation of England, with the inhabitants of the Netherlands, shall be the first and the readiest to transport Israel's sons and daughters in their ships to the land promised to their forefathers, Abraham, Isaac and Jacob for an everlasting inheritance." Sharif, "Christians for Zion," 125.
23. Shimoni, *The Zionist Ideology*, 61, 64.
24. Merkley, *The Politics of Christian Zionism*, 100–106; Davidson, *America's Palestine*, 158–59.
25. Prior, *Zionism and the State of Israel*, 142; Stone, *Professor Reinhold Niebuhr*, 262.
26. Prior, *Zionism and the State of Israel*, 106.

CHAPTER 14

1. Vladimir Dubnow was one of the early Jewish colonists. Benny Morris, *Righteous Victims*, 49.
2. Nordau and Gottheil, *Zionism and Anti-Semitism*, 13.
3. If ethnic cleansing of Palestinians was not initially the goal of mainstream Zionists—although, there are strong indications to the contrary—they would start thinking in terms of this goal at the first signs of Palestinian resistance to their colonial project.
4. Gershon Gorenberg, an Israeli-American journalist, nicely sums up how Jews fit into the Christian Zionist narrative of end times. According to Gorenberg, the Christian Zionists "don't love real Jewish people. They love us as characters in their story, in their play, and that's not what we are . . . and the play is not one that ends up good for us." Clark, *Allies for Armageddon*, 228.
5. Theodore Herzl met several times with senior Ottoman officials, including the Sultan, offering to pay off their foreign debts in return for a charter to colonize Palestine. The Ottomans offered limited Jewish immigration to all provinces of the empire *except* Palestine, provided the Jewish immigrants became Ottoman subjects and did not concentrate in any one place. Laqueur, *A History of Zionism*, 100–101, 114–19.
6. Quite implausibly, Mordecai M. Noah, an early American Zionist, had raised this possibility in a speech in 1818. Jews, he said, "hold the purse strings, and can wield the sword: they can bring 100,000 men into the field." Grose, *Israel in the Mind of America*, 14.

CHAPTER 15

1. Johnson, *A History of the Jews*, 566.
2. Edward House, adviser and confidant to President Wilson, wrote this in a note to him. Davidson, *America's Palestine*, 16–17.
3. Rabbi Stephen Wise (1874–1949) founded the Federation of American Zionists in 1897. In 1918, he became the first president of the Zionist Organization of America and was the president of the American Jewish Congress from 1925 until he died in 1949. Davidson, *America's Palestine*, 21.
4. Christison, *Perceptions of Palestine*, 33.
5. de Novo, *American Interests and Policies*, 340.
6. Christison, *Perceptions of Palestine*, 34.
7. Chomsky, *Fateful Triangle*, 17.
8. In its report to President Wilson, the King-Crane Commission included a table summarizing a count of the petitions it had received from three geographical divisions in Syria (including present-day Syria, Lebanon, Jordan, and Israel) in favor of some form of the Zionist project and against it: only 19 petitions favored the Zionist project, while 1,350 petitions expressed opposition to the project. Khalidi, *From Haven to Conquest*, 213–14.
9. Khalidi, *From Haven to Conquest*, 197.
10. "Among all of its challenges around the globe," according to Donald Neff, "the State Department had little reason to devote much attention to Zionism or, when it did, to support Zionist goals. The aloof tone of the State Department's attitude was illustrated in 1912 when the Zionist Literary Society sought a public endorsement from President William Howard Taft. Secretary of State Philander C. Knox turned it down with the reply that "problems of Zionism involve certain matters primarily related to the interests of countries other than our own . . . and might lead to misconstructions." Neff, *Fallen Pillars*.
11. Paul, "Great Power Conflict."
12. Davidson, *America's Palestine*, 17–18.
13. Ibid., 19.
14. Christison, *Perceptions of Palestine*, 32–33; Davidson, *America's Palestine*, 20.
15. Christison, *Perceptions of Palestine*, 35.
16. Davidson, *America's Palestine*, 55; Christison, *Perceptions of Palestine*, 35.
17. Gaebelein, *The History of the Scofield Reference Bible*, 11.
18. Currie, "God's Little Errand Boy."
19. Davidson, *America's Palestine*, 8.
20. Prior, *Zionism and the State of Israel*, 140.
21. Davidson, *America's Palestine*, 9.
22. Ariel, "An Unexpected Alliance," 79, 80.
23. Stork and Rose, "Zionism and American Jewry," 41; Maisel, *Jews in American Politics*, 472–74.
24. Shapiro, *Leadership of the American Zionist Organization*, 24–29.
25. Laqueur, *A History of Zionism*, 160.
26. Laqueur, *A History of Zionism*, 159; Shapiro, *Leadership of the American Zionist Organization*, 24.
27. Stork and Rose, "Zionism and American Jewry," 41; Shapiro, *Leadership of the American Zionist Organization*, 180.
28. All the quotes in this paragraph are from Laqueur, *A History of Zionism*, 179.

29. The new leaders that Louis Brandeis brought into the Zionist movement "occupied positions of some prominence in American society, and all were reformers connected with different progressive causes. All were listed in *Who's Who in America*." Shapiro, *Leadership of the American Zionist Organization*, 54–55.

30. Louis Brandeis (1856–1941) was a Harvard Law graduate and one of the most respected progressive lawyers in the country. As head of the Provisional Executive Committee for Zionist Affairs, he was the leader of the American Zionist movement from 1914 to 1918. Brandeis was appointed to the Supreme Court in 1916 by President Woodrow Wilson, where he served until 1939.

31. Laqueur, *A History of Zionism*, 181.

32. Davidson, *America's Palestine*, 16–17.

33. Ibid., 49–51.

34. Laqueur, *A History of Zionism*, 194–95; Reinharz, "His Majesty's Zionist Emissary," 259–77.

35. In September 1936, forty-six senators wrote letters to the president asking him to use his influence with the British to keep Palestine open to unrestricted Jewish immigration. This was followed in August 1937 by a Senate resolution warning against any dilution in the terms of the British mandate. Again, in June 1939, two hundred congressmen and twenty-eight senators put their signatures to statements demanding the Jewish right to unlimited immigration into Palestine. Finally, in January 1944, despite the fact that the United States was at war, some members of the Congress introduced a resolution urging U.S. support for unlimited Jewish immigration into Palestine and the establishment of a Jewish state in Palestine. Only direct intervention from the president, and the State and War Departments, persuaded the Congress to shelve this resolution. Davidson, *America's Palestine*, 118, 124, 140, 142.

36. In June 1936, Cordell Hull, Secretary of State, instructed the U.S. ambassador in Britain to inform the British foreign secretary—informally and unofficially—of the concerns of Jewish Americans on the question of Palestine. Davidson, *America's Palestine*, 116.

37. Smith, *Palestine and the Arab-Israeli Conflict*, 105.

38. The Zionist policy during the war is best summed up by a slogan coined by David Ben-Gurion: "We will make war as though there were no White Paper, and we will fight the White Paper as though there were no war." Bar-Zohar, *Ben-Gurion*, 63.

39. Laqueur, *A History of Zionism*, 530.

40. Here is Moshe Shertok's evaluation in 1939 of the strength of the Jewish diaspora in the United States: "There are millions of active and well-organized Jews in America, and their position in life enables them to be most dynamic and influential. They live in the nerve-centers of the country, and hold important positions in politics, trade, journalism, the theatre and the radio. They could influence public opinion, but their strength is not felt since it is not harnessed and directed at the right target." Khalidi, *From Haven to Conquest*, li.

41. In 1939, David Ben-Gurion wrote, "For my part, I had no doubt that the center of gravity of our political efforts had shifted from Great Britain to America, who was making sure of being the world's leading power and where the greatest number of Jews, as well as the most influential, were to be found. All Europe was under Nazi domination. Hitler would be defeated in the end, but Europe would emerge from the war enfeebled and dependent for many years upon economic aid from the United States." Bar-Zohar, *Ben-Gurion*, 64.

42. Laqueur, *A History of Zionism*, 537.

43. Smith, *Palestine and the Arab-Israeli Conflict*, 117–8.

44. Libo and Skakun, *The Clash of the Titans*.
45. Laqueur, *A History of Zionism*, 549; Christison, *Perceptions of Palestine*, 73.
46. Laqueur, *A History of Zionism*, 549–50.
47. Smith, *Palestine and the Arab-Israeli Conflict*, 118; Laqueur, *A History of Zionism*, 118.
48. Laqueur, *A History of Zionism*, 556.
49. Ibid., 551.
50. Ibid., 554–55.
51. Christison, *Perceptions of Palestine*, 73.
52. Laqueur, *A History of Zionism*, 556.
53. Druks, *The Uncertain Friendship*, 39–41, 55–56.
54. Christison, *Perceptions of Palestine*, 49.
55. Bain, *The March to Zion*, 20; Davidson, *America's Palestine*, 150–2.
56. Davidson, *America's Palestine*, 172.
57. Ibid., 177, 180–81, 183.
58. Khalidi, *Palestine Reborn*, 60. "The British say," wrote James Forrestal, Secretary of Defense, "that they cannot do all they would like to do for the Arabs because of the pressure that we were able to exert in connection with the British loan." Sharabi, *Palestine and Israel*, 25.
59. Shlaim, "The Impact of U.S. Policy," 17.
60. Benson, *Harry S. Truman and the Founding of Israel*, 78.
61. "According to contingency war plans devised during the late 1940s by strategists in Washington and London, military bases in Arab states would prove essential to victory in any armed conflict with the Soviet Union. Possession of bases in Egypt would enable the Western allies to conduct a punishing aerial offensive against the Soviet industrial heartland, to concentrate armored forces for offensive ground action, and to position intelligence gathering, propaganda, and covert action operations close to the enemy's frontier. The Suez Canal, interregional air routes, and other communications facilities gave the Middle East additional security importance in peace and war." Hahn, *Caught in the Middle East*, 21.
62. Benson, *Harry S. Truman and the Founding of Israel*, 82, 84.
63. Davidson, *America's Palestine*, 176.
64. Benson, *Harry S. Truman and the Founding of Israel*, 80.
65. Davidson, *America's Palestine*, 188.
66. Benson, *Harry S. Truman and the Founding of Israel*, 196.
67. Christison, *Perceptions of Palestine*, 73.
68. "Some of Truman's assistants conducted a study of Palestine correspondence and drew up detailed statistics running from 1946 through 1951. From 1947 to 1948, Truman received 48,600 telegrams, 790,575 cards, and 81,200 pieces of other mail— far and away a record for unsolicited mail for any president until that time. In 1948, during one three-month period alone, Truman received 301,900 postcards." Benson, *Harry S. Truman and the Founding of Israel*, 94.
69. Benson, *Harry S. Truman and the Founding of Israel*, 95.
70. Miglietta, *American Alliance Policy*, 112.
71. Cohen, *Truman and Israel*, 70, 72–73.
72. Benson, *Harry S. Truman and the Founding of Israel*, 175.
73. Ibid., 156–57.
74. Millis, *The Forrestal Diaries*, 344, quoted in Sharabi, *Palestine and Israel*, 24–25.

CHAPTER 16

1. Davidson, *America's Palestine*, 184; Grose, *Israel in the Mind of America*, 258; Mansour, *Beyond Alliance*, 82. Loy Henderson was Office Director of the State Department's Office of Near East and African Affairs.

2. Davidson, *America's Palestine*, 19–20; Christison, *Perceptions of Palestine*, 32–33.

3. "Virtually every professional in the foreign affairs bureaucracy, including the secretaries of state and war (later, defense) and the Joint Chiefs of Staff, opposed the creation of Israel from the standpoint of U.S. national interests." Rubenberg, *Israel and the American National Interest*, 9–10.

4. "On all salient questions—partition, trusteeship, recognition of the state of Israel, arms embargo, and disposition of the Negev—Truman . . . took a consistently pro-Zionist line." Shlaim, "The Impact of U.S. Policy in the Middle East," 17.

5. Schweitzer, "Moshe Dayan," quoted in Beit-Hallahmi, *The Israeli Connection*, 5.

6. Crosbie, *A Tacit Alliance*, 16–20.

7. Sachar, *Israel and Europe*, 14–15, 18.

CHAPTER 17

1. Green, *Taking Sides*, 20; Morris, *Righteous Victims*, 276.

2. Green, *Taking Sides*, 20–21.

3. American air force and army experts knew in 1950 that Israel had "the preponderance of striking power" in the region. Indeed, they turned down Israeli demands for large weapons systems in May 1950—at least in part—because this "would increase Israel's offensive capabilities and give incentive to offensive planning." Hahn, *Caught in the Middle East*, 73.

4. On the continued ethnic cleansing of Palestinians, Jonathan Cook writes, "Regular, small-scale expulsions of Palestinians continued throughout the early years of the state. In 1950, for example, the remaining population of 2,700 Palestinians in the town of al-Majdal were transported over the border to the Gaza strip . . . As many as 7,000 Bedouins were expelled from the Negev, either to Jordanian or Egyptian territory, over the period of a year from November 1949. And more than 5,000 Palestinians were forced out of their villages in the Wadi Ara region and made to cross over into the West Bank in the summer of 1949." Further, under the cover of the 1956 Suez war, Israel was planning to expel 40,000 Arab citizens into Jordan. This plan backfired because of an Israeli massacre in Kafr Qassem, but they did expel 2,000 Palestinians from two villages in Galilee into Syria. Cook, *Blood and Religion*, 112–13.

5. Rubenberg, *Israel and the American National Interest*, 51.

6. Mearsheimer and Walt ("The Israel Lobby") write, "Prior to the Six-Day War . . . Israeli intelligence assessments painted a grim and frightening picture of Egyptian capabilities and intentions, which American intelligence officials believed was both incorrect and politically motivated."

7. Gazit, "Israeli Military Procurement," 89.

8. Mansour, *Beyond Alliance*, 73.

9. Ben-Zvi, *The United States and Israel*, 54.

10. Hahn, *Caught in the Middle East*, 28.

11. Walt, *The Origins of Alliances*, 61–62.

12. Mansour, *Beyond Alliance*, 79–81.

13. Burns, *Economic Aid and American Policy*, 21.

14. Tivnan, *The Lobby*, 36–38.

15. Morris, *Righteous Victims*, 299.
16. Sharabi, *Palestine and Israel*, 26.
17. Tivnan, *The Lobby*, 38, 41.
18. Ben-Zvi, *The U.S. and Israel*, 69, 73.
19. Tivnan, *The Lobby*, 52, 53, 56.
20. It is customary for studies of the special relationship to focus on these statistics. Organski, *The $36 Billion Bargain*, 15–24.
21. The timing of acceleration in U.S. aid to Israel does not change when we compare the aid flows over these two periods in terms of their share in total U.S. aid flows. Between 1950 and 1970, Israel received 1.14 percent of all U.S. aid; over the period of 1971 to 1983, this share had jumped a little more than eighteenfold to 20.7 percent. Laufer, "U.S. Aid to Israel," 126–27.
22. Aliya Bet & Machal Virtual Museum, *Pictorial History*.
23. In October 1958, the United States facilitated the sale of fifty-five British Centurian tanks to Israel; between 1962 and 1965, it pushed through the sale of 150 Patton tanks from German stocks; and in August 1956, it authorized Canada to transfer F-86 fighter planes to Israel even though they were originally scheduled for delivery to the United States. On yet another occasion, the United States set aside NATO priority for French Mystère planes in favor of Israel. Levey, "Israeli Foreign Policy," 42, 44; Mansour, *Beyond Alliance*, 77.
24. Mansour, *Beyond Alliance*, 72, 76–78, 81; Wenger, "Recipe for an Israeli Nuclear Arsenal," 11–12.
25. Mansour, *Beyond Alliance*, 75.
26. Ibid., 76.
27. According to Abba Eban, the United States established regular consultations with Israel during the late 1950s: "The U.S. was obviously coming to regard Israel not as a burden to be chivalrously sustained, but as an asset in the global and ideological balance." Mansour, *Beyond Alliance*, 79–80.
28. In the fall of 1964, West Germany entered into a secret deal with Israel to deliver fifty aircraft, 150 American tanks, two submarines, six speedboats, and several trucks, antiaircraft rockets, and antitank rockets. Israel did not have to pay for these weapons, estimated conservatively to be worth $250 million. Lewan, "How West Germany Helped to Build Israel," 56–57; Mansour, *Beyond Alliance*, 81–83.
29. Howard, "Israel: The Sorcerer's Apprentice," 16–17.
30. Bainerman, "End American Aid to Israel?"
31. Balabkins, *West German Reparations to Israel*.
32. Nahum Goldman also threatened Chancellor Adenauer with dire consequences if the Zionist demands for reparations were not met: "The violent reaction of the whole world, supported by wide circles of non-Jews, who have deep sympathy with the martyrdom of the Jewish people during the Nazi period, would be irresistible and completely justified." Lewan, "How West Germany Helped to Build Israel," 53–54.
33. Wyman and Rosenzveig, *The World Reacts to the Holocaust*, 866.
34. Sachar, *Israel and Europe*, 51. *Wiedergutmachung* refers to the reparations paid by West Germany to the direct survivors of the Holocaust.

CHAPTER 18

1. Morris, *Righteous Victims*, 329; Bregman, *A History of Israel*, 120; Morris, *Righteous Victims*, 329; Teger, "Coming Together, Falling Apart." Michael B. Oren is a senior fellow at the Shalem Center.
2. Mansour, *Beyond Alliance*, 86.
3. President Nasser knew of Egypt's military vulnerability in the 1960s. In 1963, at Port Said, he put it plainly, "I am not in a position to go to war; I tell you this frankly, and it is not shameful to say it publicly. To go to war without having the sufficient means would be to lead the country and the people to disaster." Sharabi, *Palestine and Israel*, 111.
4. Morris, *Righteous Victims*, 317–18.
5. Shlaim, *The Iron Wall*, 240–41.
6. In the days before the June War, the United States secretly moved its 38th Tactical Reconnaissance Squadron into the Negev Desert from where it provided vital surveillance data on the destruction of the Egyptian air force and the movements of the Egyptian land forces. Green, *Taking Sides*, 204–11.
7. In one specific formulation of this doctrine, Moshe Dayan stated in 1969, "Sharm el-Sheikh without peace is better than peace without Sharm el-Sheikh." Shlaim, *The Iron Wall*, 290.
8. Israel's terms for a peace settlement with Egypt included: freedom of navigation and overflight rights over the Straits of Tiran and the Gulf of Aqaba; rights of navigation through the Suez Canal; and demilitarization of the Sinai. Ibid., 253.
9. Ibid., 254.
10. Gerges, "The 1967 Arab-Israeli War," 195.
11. Sharabi, *Palestine and Israel*, 135.
12. Ibid., 136.
13. Ibid., 135.

CHAPTER 19

1. Burns, *Economic Aid and American Policy*, 20; Goldberg, *Jewish Power*, 225; Mearsheimer and Walt, *The Israel Lobby and U.S. Foreign Policy*, 146; Schwartz, *Is It Good for the Jews*, 121; Goldberg, "Real Insiders"; Reed, "No Happy Ending." Isaiah Kenen founded the American Zionist Committee for Public Affairs, the precursor to American Israeli Public Affairs Committee (AIPAC); J. J. Goldberg is director of foreign policy issues, AIPAC; and Douglas Bloomfield is AIPAC's former legislative director.
2. In response to Zionist offers to relinquish Palestine for offers of financial assistance, the Ottoman Sultan insisted, "He could never part with Jerusalem." In 1896, he told Theodore Herzl—through an intermediary—"My people have won this empire by fighting for it with their blood and have fertilized it with their blood. We will again cover it with our blood before we allow it to be wrested away from us . . . Let the Jews save their billions." Morris, *Righteous Victims*, 39, 41.
3. Jewish Virtual Library, *US Assistance to Israel, FY 1994–FY2006*.
4. Mearsheimer and Walt, *The Israel Lobby and U.S. Foreign Policy*, 26–28, 32; Mark, *Israel: U.S. Foreign Assistance*, 8–9.
5. Zunes, "US Aid to Israel."
6. Sharp, *U.S. Foreign Assistance*, 6–7; Mearsheimer and Walt, *The Israel Lobby and U.S. Foreign Policy*, 28–29.

7. Stauffer, "The Cost of Conflict in the Middle East," 45, 61.

8. Reich, *Securing the Covenant*, 43–45; Rabil, *Syria, the United States*, 80–82; Mearsheimer and Walt, *The Israel Lobby and U.S. Foreign Policy*, 31–36.

9. Mearsheimer and Walt, *The Israel Lobby and U.S. Foreign Policy*, 35; Thomas, *Gideon's Spies*, 93.

10. Cockburn and Cockburn, *Dangerous Liaison*, 78–81.

11. Pry, *Israel's Nuclear Arsenal*, 28–29.

12. On September 12, 1991, a frustrated President Bush went over the heads of the Congress to make a direct appeal to the American public; but this was a mistake. A few weeks later, the Israel lobby mobilized to defeat Richard Thornburgh, a close friend of the President, in his senatorial bid. Thornburgh had been leading the polls with a huge margin only a few weeks before President Bush's speech of September 1991. Goldberg, *Jewish Power*, xv–xvi, xxiv.

13. Mearsheimer and Walt, *The Israel Lobby and U.S. Foreign Policy*, 37.

14. Ibid., 40.

15. Lovett, Eckes, and Brinkman, *U.S. Trade Policy*, 95.

16. AFP, *Egypt, Israel Enhances Trade*.

17. "Virtually every professional in the foreign affairs bureaucracy, including the secretaries of state and war (later, defense) and the joint chiefs of staff, opposed the creation of Israel from the standpoint of US national interests." Rubenberg, *Israel and the American National Interest*, 9–10.

18. In 1952, the British controlled substantial military and economic assets in the Middle East; "80,000 troops manned the Suez Canal base complex; there were naval facilities in Aden; air squadrons in Iraq; the Arab Legion in Jordan; rear bases in Cyprus and Malta; they controlled Iranian oil production and owned the world's largest oil refinery in Abadan; and, finally, Britain was in charge of the defense and foreign policies of a string of protectorates along the Persian Gulf." Peterson, *The Decline of the Anglo-American Middle East*, 1.

19. At the same time, in violation of the arms embargo, the United States allowed Israel to import World War II surplus personnel carriers and to recruit American Jewish veterans of World War II to fight in Israel, the latter in violation of US citizenship laws. Aliya Bet & Machal Virtual Museum, *Pictorial History*.

20. "The Almighty placed massive oil deposits under Arab soil," an Israeli diplomat once told a State Department official [in the 1950s]. "It is our good fortune that God placed five million Jews in America." Bass, *Support Any Friend*, 6.

21. Chomsky (*Fateful Triangle*, 9–83) and Zunes (*Why the U.S. Supports Israel?*; "U.S. Aid to Israel") have been the leading exponents of this position. More recently, this position has been defended by Amin and Kenz (*Europe and the Arab World*, 39–41), Massad ("Blaming the Lobby"), and Abu-Manneh ("Israel in the U.S. Empire"). Zionist apologists who take this position are a legion, including Spiegel ("The Other Arab-Israeli Conflict"), Organski (*The $36 Billion Bargain*), and Kramer ("The American Interest"). For writers on the left who blame the Jewish lobby, see Petras (*The Power of Israel*, 168–81), Cockburn ("The Uproar over the Israel Lobby), and Blankfort ("The Israeli Lobby and the Left"; "Damage Control").

22. This assessment comes from a 1945 report of the State Department. Chomsky, *Fateful Triangle*, 17.

23. Ibid., 13.

24. Bacevich, *The New American Militarism*, 134.

25. Chomsky, *Fateful Triangle*, 17.

26. Indeed, the term is in some ways a misnomer. The online Merriam-Webster Dictionary defines a lobby as "a group of persons engaged in lobbying especially as representatives of a particular interest group." This speaks of a distinction between the "lobby" and "the interest group," the former acting as an agent for the latter. Largely, this distinction breaks down in the case of the Jewish "lobby" because of the diverse channels through which this lobby seeks to influence government officials, including the media, academia, voting, campaign contributions, political activism, rallies, and intimidation. As voters, donors, writers, academics, politicians, field workers, and activists, a large part of the Jewish community engages in lobbying activities on behalf of Israel. The activities of the American Jewish community in support of Israel are better described as a movement—part of the global Zionist movement.

27. Chomsky, *Fateful Triangle*, 17.

28. Ibid., 17.

29. Ibid., 17.

30. During the late 1950s and early 1960s, the British maintained a substantial military presence in the Arabian Peninsula. In a memorandum to Robert McNamara, Secretary of State, the Joint Chiefs of Staff wrote, "The UK forces in the Middle East can conduct effective military operations anywhere in the Arabian Peninsula. The combination of coordinated US and UK military capability represents a responsive and flexible force for stabilizing a credible deterrent." Peterson, *The Decline of the Anglo-American Middle East*, 38. In addition, in order to deter Egyptian attacks on Saudi Arabia, the United States stationed—between July 1963 and January 1964—a squadron of eight F-100 planes and five hundred troops on Saudi territory. Peterson, *The Decline of the Anglo-American Middle East*, 36.

31. Mearsheimer and Walt, *The Israel Lobby and U.S. Foreign Policy*, 143.

32. Ibid., 145.

33. Goldberg, *Jewish Power*, 112.

34. Ginsberg, *The Fatal Embrace*, 1.

35. Goldberg, *Jewish Power*, 280.

36. Ginsberg, *The Fatal Embrace*, 1.

37. Lipset and Raab, *Jews and the New American Scene*, 26–27.

38. Ginsberg, *The Fatal Embrace*, 1, 103.

39. One book lists seventeen Jewish holidays in its table of contents; some of them commemorate pivotal events in Jewish history; some date back to the Torah, others were instituted later. Goodman, *Teaching Jewish Holidays*.

40. Some American Jews prefer to see the roots of their liberalism in Jewish tradition. However, according to Goldberg (*Jewish Power*, 27), "Many non-Jewish activists who came in contact with the organized Jewish community see Jewish liberalism in much more straightforward terms: as a simple matter of self-interest."

41. Ibid., 23.

42. Laqueur, *A History of Zionism*, 549–50.

43. Bass, *Support My Friend*, 6.

44. The Jewish lobby continued to exert pressure on President Eisenhower to provide military assistance to Israel. In the fall of 1955, it organized public rallies, attended by such luminaries as Harry Truman and Eleanor Roosevelt, "to demonstrate the strength of American sympathy for Israel." It also sponsored a congressional petition, signed by 40 Republican congressmen in support of U.S. military assistance. The lobby met with greater success in mobilizing the Senate and House against American support for the Aswan Dam project. Burns, *Economic Aid and Foreign Policy*, 21, 49.

45. The turning point in President Eisenhower's approach to Egypt can be dated to early 1956, when it was becoming clear that he could not persuade Gamal Nasser to accept Israel or give up his growing friendship with the Soviet Union. The new approach, spelled out in the *Omega Memorandum*, spelled out the need to undermine Egypt and the nationalists in Syria, to shelve assistance for the Aswan Dam, and continue to block military supplies to Egypt. Burns, *Economic Aid and American Policy*, 77–70.

46. Ben-Zvi, *Lyndon B. Johnson and the Politics of Arms Sales*, 70.

47. Goldberg, *Jewish Power*, 149.

48. Ibid., 146–47.

49. Ibid., 147, 149.

50. Ibid., 171, 174.

51. Timothy Weber, former president of the Memphis Theological Seminary, writes, "Before the Six Day War, dispensationalists were content to sit in the bleachers of history, explaining the End-Time game on the field below . . . But after [the] expansion of Israel into the West Bank and Gaza, they began to get down on the field and be sure the teams lined up right, becoming involved in political, financial, and religious ways they never had before." Mearsheimer and Walt, *The Israel Lobby and U.S. Foreign Policy*, 133.

52. Pipes, "Israel's Ultimate Strategic Asset."

53. Ginsberg (*The Fatal Embrace*, 231) writes that the neoconservatives moved to the right primarily because of "their attachment to Israel and their growing frustration during the 1960s with a Democratic party that was becoming increasingly opposed to American military preparedness and increasingly enamored of Third World causes."

54. The neoconservatives Jews kept predicting, during the 1970s, "that the Jews were done with liberalism and would now switch their allegiance to the Republican column." Goldberg, *Jewish Power*, 161.

55. Chomsky, *Fateful Triangle*, 455–63.

56. Mearsheimer and Walt, *The Israel Lobby and U.S. Foreign Policy*, 128–32.

57. "Further, the process of transformation [to new technologies that will 'preserve American military preeminence in the coming decades'], even if it brings revolutionary change, is likely to be a long one, absent some catastrophic and catalyzing event—like a New Pearl Harbor." Project for the New American Century, *Rebuilding America's Defenses*, 51.

58. Schwartz, *Is It Good for the Jews*, 121.

59. Goldberg, *Jewish Power*, 15.

60. In the Zionist worldview, writes Goldberg (*Jewish Power*, 18), it was the Jewish state that "would give a voice to the voiceless people and return Jews to the stage of history after centuries of helplessness. American Jewish power has turned the Zionist idea on its head."

CHAPTER 20

1. Ahad Ha'am wrote this upon hearing a rumor that the Jews of Jaffa, in an act of revenge, had killed an Arab boy. Khalidi, *From Haven to Conquest*, 831.

2. Laskier, "Israel and Algeria," 7; Rodinson, *Israel and the Arabs*, 92.

BIBLIOGRAPHY

Abu-Manneh, Bashir. "Israel in the U.S. Empire." *Monthly Review* 58, no. 10 (March 2007): 1–25.

Abu-Sitta, Salman H. *The Palestinian Nakba, 1948: The Register of Depopulated Localities in Palestine.* London: Palestine Return Center, 1998.

AFP. "Egypt, Israel Enhances Free-Trade Accord." Bilaterals.org, October 31, 2005, http://www.bilaterals.org/article.php3?id_article=3019.

Alam, M. Shahid. "Bernard Lewis: Scholarship or Sophistry." *Studies in Contemporary Islam* 4, no. 1 (Spring 2002): 53–80.

———. "A New Theology of Power." *CounterPunch*, September 16, 2002, http://www.counterpunch.org/alam0916.html.

———. "Israel and the Consequences of Uniqueness." *CounterPunch*, October 29–30, 2005, http://www.counterpunch.org/shahid10292005.html.

———. *Challenging the New Orientalism: Dissenting Essays on the "War Against Islam."* North Haledon, NJ: Islamic Publications International, 2006.

Aliya Bet & Machal Virtual Museum. *Pictorial History: Acquiring Arms and Personnel.* http://israelvets.com/pictorialhist_acquiring_arms.html.

Alroey, Gur. *Mass Jewish Migration Database.* Haifa, Israel: University of Haifa, 2005. http://mjmd.haifa.ac.il/index.php?link=history1.

Al-Shawaf, Rayyan. "Review: Abbas Shiblak, *Iraqi Jews: A History of Mass Exodus* (London: Saqi Books, 2005)." *Democratiya*, Winter 2006, http://www.democratiya.com/review.asp?reviews_id=55.

Amin, Samir, and Ali El Kenz. *Europe and the Arab World: Problems and Prospects for the New Relationship.* London: Zed Books, 2005.

Ariel, Yaakov. "An Unexpected Alliance: Christian Zionism and Its Historical Significance." *Modern Judaism* 26, no. 1 (2006): 74–100.

Avishai, Bernard. *The Tragedy of Zionism: How Its Revolutionary Past Haunts Israeli Democracy.* New York: Allworth Press, 2003.

Avnery, Uri. "Israel's Missed Opportunities for Peace (Partial List)." *Redress*, May 28, 2006, http://www.redress.cc/palestine/uavnery20060528.

Bacevich, A. J. *The New American Militarism: How Americans Are Seduced by War.* New York: Oxford University Press, 2005.

Badi, Joseph, ed. *Fundamental Laws of the State of Israel.* New York: Twayne, 1960.

Bain, Kenneth Ray. *The March to Zion: United States Policy and the Founding of Israel.* College Station, TX: Texas A&M University Press, 1979.

Bainerman, Joel. "End American Aid to Israel?: Yes, It Does Harm." *The Middle East Quarterly* 2, no. 3 (September 1995), http://www.meforum.org/article/258.

Balabkins, Nicholas. *West German Reparations to Israel.* New Brunswick, NJ: Rutgers University Press, 1971.

Bar-Zohar, Michael. *Ben-Gurion: The Armed Prophet.* Englewood Cliffs, NJ: Prentice Hall, 1968.

Bass, Warren. *Support Any Friend: Kennedy's Middle East and the Making of U.S.-Israel Alliance.* New York: Oxford University Press, 2003.

Beit-Hallahmi, Benjamin. *The Israeli Connection: Whom Israel Arms and Why.* London: I. B. Tauris, 1988.

Bell, Dean Phillip. *Jews in the Early Modern World: Continuity and Transformation.* Boston: Rowman & Littlefield, 2008.

Beller, Steven. *Vienna and the Jews, 1867–1938: A Cultural History.* Cambridge: Cambridge University Press, 1989.

Benbassa, Esther. *La Souffrance Comme Identité.* Paris: Fayard, 2007. http://www.estherbenbassa .net/ATB_EB_actualite2.php.

Ben-Gurion, David. *Ben-Gurion Looks at the Bible.* Translated by Jonathan Kolatch. Middle Village, NY: Jonathan David, 1972.

Ben-Sasson, Haim, ed. *A History of the Jewish People.* Cambridge: Harvard University Press, 1976.

Benson, Michael T. *Harry S. Truman and the Founding of Israel.* Westport, CT: Praeger, 1997.

Ben-Zvi, Abraham. *The United States and Israel: The Limits of the Special Relationship.* New York: Columbia University Press, 1993.

———. *Lyndon B. Johnson and the Politics of Arms Sales to Israel.* London: Routledge, 2004.

Berle, A. A. *The World Significance of a Jewish State.* New York: Mitchell Kennerley, 1918.

Berlin, Adele, and Marc Zvi Brettler, eds. *The Jewish Study Bible.* Oxford: Oxford University Press, 2004.

Berman, Aaron. *Nazism, the Jews, and American Zionism, 1933–1988.* Detroit, MI: Wayne State University, 1992.

Black, Edwin. *The Transfer Agreement: The Dramatic Story of the Agreement Between the Third Reich and Jewish Palestine.* New York: Carroll and Graf, 2001.

Blankfort, Jeffrey. "Damage Control: Noam Chomsky and the Israeli-Palestine Conflict." *Dissident Voice,* May 25, 2005, http://www.dissidentvoice.org/May05/Blankfort0525 .htm.

Bregman, Ahron. *A History of Israel.* Houndmills, UK: Macmillan, 2003.

Brenner, Lenni. *Zionism in the Age of Dictators.* Highland Park, NJ: Lawrence Hill, 1983.

———, ed. *51 Documents: Zionist Collaboration with the Nazis.* Fort Lee, NJ: Barricade Books, 2002.

Brenner, Michael. *Zionism: A Brief History.* Translated by Shelley L. Frisch. Princeton, NJ: Markus Wiener, 2006.

Brown, Kenneth. "Iron and a King: Likud and the Oriental Jews." *MERIP Reports* 114 (May 1983): 3–13.

Brownfeld, Allan. "Judaism and the Jewish State." *Journal of Palestine Studies* 3, no. 2 (Winter 1974): 194–95.

Brustein, William I. *Roots of Hate: Anti-Semitism in Europe Before the Holocaust.* Cambridge: Cambridge University Press, 2003.

Burns, William J. *Economic Aid and American Policy Towards Egypt, 1955–1981.* Albany: State University of New York Press, 1985.

Carter, Jimmy. *Palestine: Peace Not Apartheid.* New York: Simon and Schuster, 2006.

Chomsky, Noam. *Fateful Triangle: The United States, Israel and the Palestinians.* 1983. Cambridge: South End, 1999.

———. "Anti-Semitism, Zionism and the Palestinians." *From Occupied Palestine,* October 2002, http://www.fromoccupiedpalestine.org/node/116.

———. "The Fate of an Honest Intellectual." In *Understanding Power,* edited by Peter R. Mitchell and John Schoeffel. New York: New Press, 2002. http://www.chomsky .info/books/power01.htm.

Christison, Kathleen. *Perceptions of Palestine: Their Influence on U.S. Middle East Policy.* Berkeley: University of California, 1999.

Clark, Harry. "How It All Began: Truman and Israel." *CounterPunch,* June 3–4, 2006, http://www.counterpunch.org/clark06032006.html.

Clark, Victoria. *Allies for Armageddon.* New Haven, CT: Yale University Press, 2007.

Cockburn, Alexander. "The Uproar Over the Israel Lobby." *The Free Press,* May 5, 2006, http://www.freepress.org/columns/display/2/2006/1368.

Cockburn, Alexander, and Jeffrey St. Clair, eds. *The Politics of Anti-Semitism.* Petrolia, CA: AK Press and CounterPunch, 2003.

Cockburn, Andrew, and Leslie Cockburn. *Dangerous Liaison: The Inside Story of the U.S.-Israeli Covert Relationship.* New York: HarperCollins, 1991.

Cohen, Eliot A. "Yes, It's Anti-Semitic." *Washington Post,* April 5, 2006, http://washingtonpost.com/wp-dyn/content/article/2006/04/04/AR2006040401282.html.

Cohen, Mark R. "The Neo-Lachrymose Conception of Jewish-Arab History." *Tikkun,* 6, no. 3 (May–June 1991): 55–60.

———. "The Jews under Islam: From the Rise of Islam to Sabbatai Zevi: A Bibliographical Essay." In *Sephardic Studies in the University,* edited by Jane S. Gerber. Madison, NJ: Fairleigh Dickinson University Press, 1995.

———. *Under Crescent and Cross: The Jews in the Middle Ages.* Princeton, NJ: Princeton University Press, 1995.

Cohen, Michael J. *Truman and Israel.* Berkeley: University of California Press, 1990.

Committee on Foreign Affairs, House of Representatives. *Establishment of a National Home in Palestine: Hearings before the Committee on Foreign Affairs, Sixty-Seventh Congress.* Washington, DC: Government Printing Press, 1922.

Cook, Jonathan. *Blood and Religion: The Unmasking of the Jewish and Democratic State.* London: Pluto Press, 2006.

Corcos, Alain F. *The Myth of the Jewish Race: A Biologist's Point of View.* Bethlehem, PA: Lehigh University Press, 2005.

Crosbie, Sylvia K. *A Tacit Alliance: France and Israel from Suez to the Six Day War.* Princeton, NJ: Princeton University Press, 1974.

Currie, William E. "God's Little Errand Boy," *Life in Messiah,* originally published in 1987, http://www.lifeinmessiah.org/gleb.php.

Dalin, David G. "*Jacksonian Jew: The Two Worlds of Mordecai Noah* by Jonathan D. Sarna." *AJS Review* 10, no. 1 (Spring 1985): 122–23.

———. *The Myth of Hitler's Pope: How Pope Pius XII Rescued Jews from the Nazis.* Washington, DC: Regnery, 2005.

Davidson, Lawrence. *America's Palestine: Popular and Official Perceptions from Balfour to Israeli Statehood.* Gainesville: University of Florida Press, 2001.

———. "Christian Zionism and American Foreign Policy: Paving the Road to Hell in Palestine." *Logos* 4, no. 1 (Winter 2005), http://www.logosjournal.com/issue_4.1/davidson.htm.

Davis, Moshe. *Zionism in Transition.* New York: Arno, 1980.

DellaPergola, Sergio. "An Overview of the Demographic Trends of European Jewry." In *Jewish Identities in the New Europe,* edited by Jonathan Webber. London: Littman Library of Jewish Civilization, 1994.

———. *Demography in Israel/Palestine: Trends, Prospects, Policy Implications.* Jerusalem: Hebrew University of Jerusalem, August 2001. http://www.iussp.org/Brazil2001/s60/S64_02_dellapergola.pdf.

de Novo, John A. *American Interests and Policies in the Middle East, 1900–1939.* Minneapolis: University of Minnesota Press, 1963.

Deutscher, Isaac. "Israel's Spiritual Climate." In *Wrestling with Zion*, edited by Tony Kushner and Alisa Solomon. New York: Grove, 2003.

Dowty, Alan. *Israel/Palestine*. London: Polity, 2008.

Dror, Yehezkel. "On the Uniqueness of Israel: Multiple Readings." In *Israel in Comparative Perspective: Challenging the Conventional Wisdom*, edited by Michael N. Barnett. Albany: State University of New York Press, 1996.

Druks, Herbert. *The Uncertain Friendship: The U.S. and Israel from Roosevelt to Kennedy*. Westport, CT: Greenwood, 2001.

Einstein, Albert. "Our Debt to Zionism." In *Prophets Outcast*, edited by Adam Shtaz. New York: Nation Books, 2004.

Elazar, Daniel J. *World Jewry as a Polity*. Jerusalem: Jerusalem Center for Public Affairs, 1992. http://www.jcpa.org/dje/articles2/worldjewry-pol.htm.

Elazar, Daniel Judah, and Stuart Cohen. *The Jewish Polity: Jewish Political Organization from Biblical Times to the Present*. Bloomington: Indiana University Press, 1984.

Elon, Amos. *The Israelis: Founders and Sons*. New York: Holt, Rinehart and Winston, 1971.

Endelman, Todd M. *The Jews of Britain: 1656–2000*. Berkeley: University of California Press, 2002.

Engelman, Uriah Zevi. *The Rise of the Jew in the Western World: A Social and Economic History of the Jewish People of Europe*. New York: Behrman's Jewish Book House, 1944.

Ernst, Morris L. *So Far So Good*. New York: Harper and Brothers, 1948.

Ettinger, Shmuel. "Demographic Changes and Economic Activity in the Nineteenth Century." In *A History of the Jewish People*, edited by H. H. Ben-Sasson. Cambridge: Harvard University Press, 1976.

Falk, Avner. *Fratricide in the Holy Land: A Psycho-Analytic View of the Arab-Israeli Conflict*. Madison: University of Wisconsin Press, 2004.

Farsoun, Samih K., and Naseer H. Aruri. *Palestine and the Palestinians: A Social and Political History*. Boulder, CO: Westview, 2006.

Feingold, Henry L. "American Jewry." In *The Holocaust Encyclopedia*, edited by Judith Tydor Baumel. New Haven, CT: Yale University Press, 2001.

Feldman, Seymour. *Philosophy in a Time of Crisis: Don Isaac Abravanel, Defender of the Faith*. London: Routledge/Curzon, 2003.

Fieldhouse, David K. *Colonial Empires: A Comparative Study from the Eighteenth Century*. New York: Delacorte, 1965.

Findley, Paul. *They Dare to Speak Out: People and Institutions Confront Israel's Lobby*. Westport, CT: Lawrence Hill, 1985.

Finkelstein, Norman G. *The Holocaust Industry: Reflections on the Exploitation of Jewish Suffering*. London: Verso, 2001.

———. *Image and Reality of the Israeli-Palestine Conflict*. 1995. London: Verso, 2003.

———. "The Ludicrous Attacks on Jimmy Carter's Book." *CounterPunch*, December 28, 2006, http://www.counterpunch.org/finkelstein12282006.html.

Flapan, Simha. *The Birth of Israel: Myths and Realities*. New York: Pantheon, 1987.

Foa, Anna. *The Jews of Europe After the Dark Ages*. Berkeley: University of California Press, 2000.

Frankfurter, Felix. "An Interview in Mr. Balfour's Apartment, 23 Rue Nitot, Paris." In *From Haven to Conquest: Readings in Zionism and the Palestine Problem until 1948*, edited by Walid Khalidi. Beirut: Institute for Palestine Studies, 1971.

Friedman, Isaiah. *Germany, Turkey, Zionism, 1897–1918*. Oxford: Clarendon, 1977.

Fromkin, David. *A Peace to End All Peace*. New York: Henry Holt, 1989.

Gaebelein, Arno C. *The History of the Scofield Reference Bible*. New York: Our Hope, 1943.

Garfinkle, Adam M. "On the Origin, Meaning, Use and Abuse of a Phrase." *Middle Eastern Studies*, 27 (October 1991): 539–50.

Gazit, Mordechai. "Israeli Military Procurement from the United States." In *Dynamics of Dependence: U.S.-Israeli Relations*, edited by Gabriel Sheffer. Boulder: Westview, 1987.

Gelvin, James L. *The Israeli-Palestinian Conflict: One Hundred Years of War*. Cambridge: Cambridge University Press, 2005.

Gerges, Fawaz A. "The 1967 Arab-Israeli War: U.S. Actions and Arab Perceptions." In *The ME and the United States: A Historical and Political Assessment*, edited by David B. Lesch. Boulder, CO: Westview, 1996.

Germany, Federal Foreign Office. *Israel*. http://auswaertiges-mt.de/diplo/en/Laender/Israel.html (accessed December 26, 2006).

Ginsberg, Benjamin. *The Fatal Embrace: Jews and the State*. Chicago: University of Chicago Press, 1993.

Glazer, Nathan. *American Judaism*. Chicago: University of Chicago Press, 1972.

Goldberg, J. J. *Jewish Power: Inside the American Jewish Establishment*. New York: Basic Books, 1996.

Goldberg, Jeffrey. "Real Insiders." *New Yorker*, July 4, 2005, http://www.newyorker.com/archive/2005/07/04/050704fa_fact.

Goldmann, Nahum. *The Jewish Paradox*. Translated by Steve Cox. New York: Grosset and Dunlap, 1978.

———. "Zionist Ideology and the Reality of Israel." *Foreign Affairs* 57, no. 1 (Fall 1978): 70–82.

Goodman, Robert. *Teaching Jewish Holidays: History, Values and Activities*. Denver, CO: A. R. E., 1997.

Green, Stephen. *Taking Sides: America's Secret Relations with a Militant Israel*. New York: William Morrow, 1984.

Grose, Peter. *Israel in the Mind of America*. New York: Alfred A. Knopf, 1983.

Ha'am, Ahad. "A Truth from Eretz Israel." In *Wrestling with Zion: Progressive Jewish-American Responses to the Israeli-Palestinian Conflict*, edited by Tony Kushner and Alisa Solomon. New York: Grove, 2003.

Hahn, Peter L. *Caught in the Middle East: U.S. Policy Towards the Arab-Israeli Conflict, 1945–61*. Chapel Hill: University of North Carolina, 2004.

Hecht, Ben. *Perfidy*. 1962. Jerusalem: Milah, 1997.

Hertzberg, Arthur, ed. *The Zionist Idea: A Historical Analysis and Reader*. 1959. Philadelphia: Jewish Publication Society, 1997.

———. *The Fate of Zionism: A Secular Future for Israel and Palestine*. New York: HarperSanFrancisco, 2003.

Hertzberg, Arthur, and Aron Hirt-Manheimer. *Jews: The Essence and Character of a People*. New York: HarperSanFrancisco, 1998.

Herzl, Theodore. *The Jewish State: An Attempt at a Modern Solution of the Jewish Question*. 1896. Translated by Sylvie D'Avigdor. New York: Federation of American Zionists, 1917.

———. *Old-New Land (Altneuland)*. 1902. Translated by Lotta Levensohn. New York: Block, 1960.

Hess, Moses. *Rome and Jerusalem: A Study in Jewish Nationalism*. 1862. Translated by Meyer Waxman. New York: Block, 1918.

Hirst, David. *The Gun and the Olive Branch: The Roots of Violence in the Middle East*. New York: Thunder's Mouth, 2003.

Hochberg, Severin Adam. "The Repatriation of Eastern European Jews from Great Britain: 1881–1914." *Jewish Social Studies 50*, no. 1/2 (Winter 1988–Spring 1992): 49–62.

Hochschild, Adam. *King Leopold's Ghost: A Story of Greed, Terror and Heroism in Colonial Africa*. New York: Houghton Mifflin, 1999.

Hodgson, Marshall. *The Venture of Islam, volume 1: The Classical Age of Islam*. Chicago: University of Chicago Press, 1974.

Horowitz, David. "Editor's Notes: It Was Always Jihad." *Jerusalem Post*, April 10, 2008, http://www.jpost.com/servlet/Satellite?cid=1207649985946&pagename=JPost%2FJPArticle%2FPrinter.

Howard, Esther. "Israel: The Sorcerer's Apprentice." *MERIP Reports*, no. 112 (February 1983): 16–25.

Huntington, Samuel. *The Clash of Civilizations: Remaking of World Order*. New York: Simon and Schuster, 1997.

Ingram, O. Kelly. "Christian Zionism." *The Link*, 16, no. 4 (November 1983): 1–13, http://www.ameu.org/summary1.asp?iid=74.

Ingrams, Doreen. *Palestine Papers, 1917–1922: Seeds of Conflict*. London: John Murray, 1972.

Israel, Ministry of Foreign Affairs. "PM Rabin Response to Alleged Killing of Egyptian POWs." August 16, 1995, http://www.mfa.gov.il/MFA/.

———. "Address by Prime Minister Netanyahu to the American Jewish Committee, Washington, 14 May 1998." May 14, 1998, http://www.mfa.gov.il/MFA/.

Israeli, Raphael. *War, Peace and Terror in the Middle East*. New York: Routledge, 2003.

Jabbour, George. *Settler Colonialism in Southern Africa and the Middle East*. Khartoum: University of Khartoum, 1970.

Jastrow, Morris. *Zionism and the Future of Palestine*. New York: Macmillan, 1919.

Jeffries, J. M. N. "Analysis of the Balfour Declaration." In *From Haven to Conquest*, edited by Walid Khalidi. Beirut: Institute for Palestine Studies, 1971.

Jewishencylopedia.com. "Zionism: Rejected by Reform Judaism." 2008, http://jewishencyclopedia.com/view.jsp?artid=132&letter=Z&search=.

Jewish Virtual Library. *Immigration*. http://jewishvirtuallibrary.org/jsource/Immigration/immigtoc.html.

———. *Jewish and Non-Jewish Population of Palestine-Israel*. http://jewishvirtuallibrary.org/jsource/Society_&_Culture/israel_palestine_pop.html.

———. *US Assistance to Israel, FY-1949-FY2006*. http://jewishvirtuallibrary.org/jsource/US-Israel/U.S._Assistance_to_Israel1.html.

———. *World Jewish Population*. (1882–2000). http://jewishvirtuallibrary.org/jsource/History/worldpop.html.

Jews Against Zionism. *Words of the Rabbis: Rabbi Avigdor Miller, 1908–2001*. http://www.jewsagainstzionism.com/Rabbi_quotes/miller.cf.

Johnson, Paul. *A History of the Jews*. New York: Harper & Row, 1987.

———. "The Miracle." *Commentary* 105, no. 5 (May 1998): 21–27.

Julius, Lyn. "Dilemmas of Dhimmitude." *Jewish Quarterly Review* 197 (Spring 2005), http://www.jewishquarterly.org/article.asp?articleid=73.

———. "Review of: Nathan Weinstock. *Une si longue presence: comment le monde arabe a perdu ses juifs 1947–1967*." *Democratiya*, Winter 2008, http://www.democratiya.com/review.asp?reviews_id=219.

Kamrava, Mehran. *The Modern Middle East: A Political History Since the First World War*. Berkeley: University of California Press, 2005.

Karsh, Ephraim. *Fabricating Israeli History: The 'New Historians.'* New York: Frank Cass, 1997.

———. "The Long Train of Islamic Anti-Semitism," *Israel Affairs* 12, no. 1 (January 2006): 1–12.

————. *Islamic Imperialism: A History.* New Haven, CT: Yale University Press, 2007.

Katz, Jacob. "The Jewish National Movement: A Sociological Analysis." In *Jewish Society Through the Ages*, edited by H. H. Ben-Sasson and S. Ettinger. New York: Schocken Books, 1971.

————. *Tradition and Crisis: Jewish Society at the End of the Middle Ages.* New York: Schocken Books, 1971.

Kayyali, Abdul-Wahab. "Zionism and Imperialism: The Historical Origins." *Journal of Palestine Studies* 6, no. 3 (Spring 1977): 98–112.

Kerekes, Janet Elizabeth. *Masked Ball at the White Cross Café: The Failure of Jewish Assimilation.* Lanham, MD: University Press of America, 2005.

Kessner, Carole S., ed. *The Other New York Jewish Intellectuals.* New York: New York University Press, 1994.

Khalidi, Walid. *From Haven to Conquest: Readings in Zionism and the Palestine Problem until 1948.* Beirut: Institute for Palestine Studies, 1971.

————. *Palestine Reborn.* London: I. B. Tauris, 1992.

————. "The Jewish-Ottoman Land Company: Herzl's Blueprint for the Colonization of Palestine." *Journal of Palestine Studies* 22, no. 2 (Winter 1993): 30–47.

Kiener, Ronald C. *The Jewish Experience of Suffering.* Wisdom House, 2002. http://shakti.trincoll.edu/~kiener/Suffering_talk.htm.

King, Ruth. "William Eugene Blackstone, October 6, 1841–November 7, 1935." *Mideast Outpost*, February 25, 2008, http://mideastoutpost.com/archives/000437.html.

Kohn, Hans. "Zion and the Jewish National Idea." In *Zionism Reconsidered: The Rejection of Jewish Normalcy*, edited by Michael Selzer. London: Macmillan, 1970.

Kook, Rabbi Isaac Hakohen. "The Rebirth of Israel." In *The Zionist Idea: A Historical Analysis and Reader*, edited by Arthur Hertzberg. Philadelphia: Jewish Publication Society, 1997.

————. *When God Becomes History: Historical Essays of Rabbi Abraham Isaac Hakohen Kook.* Translated by Bazalel Naor. Spring Valley, NY: Orot, 2003. http://www.orot.com/history2.html.

Kovel, Joel. "Zionism's Bad Conscience." *Tikkun*, September–October 2002, http://www.joelkovel.org/zionism.html.

————. *Overcoming Zionism: Creating a Single Democratic State in Israel/Palestine.* London: Pluto, 2007.

Kramer, Martin. "The American Interest." *Azure*, no. 26 (Fall 2006): 21–33.

Kushner, Tony, and Alisa Solomon, eds. *Wrestling Zion: Progressive Jewish-American Responses to the Israeli-Palestinian Conflict.* New York: Grove, 2003.

Laqueur, Walter. *A History of Zionism.* New York: MJF Books, 1972.

Laskier, Michael M. "Israel and Algeria Amid French Colonialism and the Arab-Israeli Conflict, 1954–1978." *Israel Studies* 6, no. 2 (Summer 2001): 1–32.

Laufer, Leopold Yehuda. "U.S. Aid to Israel: Problems and Perspectives." In *Dynamics of Dependence: U.S.-Israeli relations*, edited by Gabriel Sheffer. Boulder, CO: Westview, 1987.

Lazare, Bernard. *Anti-Semitism: Its History and Causes.* 1894. Lincoln: University of Nebraska Press, 1995.

Lazare, Daniel. "The Chosen: Ideological Roots of the U.S.-Israeli Relationship." In *Wrestling Zionism: Progressive Jewish-American Responses to the Israeli–Palestinian Conflict*, edited by Tony Kushner and Alisa Solomon. New York: Grove, 2003.

Leon, Abram. *The Jewish Question: A Marxist Interpretation.* Mexico City: Ediciones Pioneras, 1950. http://www.marxists.de/religion/leon/index.htm.

Levene, Mark. "The Balfour Declaration: A Case of Mistaken Identity." *English Historical Review*, January 1992, 54–77.

Levey, Zach. "Israeli Foreign Policy and the Arms Race in the Middle East 1950–1960." *Journal of Strategic Studies* 24, no. 1 (March 2001): 29–48.

Lewan, Kenneth M. "How West Germany Helped to Build Israel." *Journal of Palestine Studies* 4, no. 4 (Summer 1995): 41–64.

Lewis, Bernard. *Semites and Anti-Semites.* New York: Norton, 1986.

———. *The Jews of Islam.* Princeton, NJ: Princeton University Press, 1987.

———. "The Roots of Muslim Rage." *The Atlantic*, September 1990, http://www.theatlantic.com.

———. "The New Anti-Semitism." *American Scholar* 75, no. 1 (Winter 2006): 25–36.

Liberles, Robert, and Stanford M. Lyman. *Salo Wittmayer Baron: Architect of Jewish History.* New York: New York University Press, 1995.

Libo, Kenneth, and Michael Skakun. *The Clash of the Titans: Stephen S. Wise vs Abba Hillel.* Part IV. New York: Center for Jewish History, 2004. http://www.cjh.org/education/essays.php?action=show&id=24.

Lilienthal, Alfred. *What Price Israel?* 1953. Haverford, PA: Infinity, 2003.

———. *The Other Side of the Coin.* New York: Devin-Adair, 1965.

Lindemann, Albert S. *Esau's Tears: Modern Anti-Semitism and the Rise of the Jews.* Cambridge: Cambridge University Press, 1998.

Lindqvist, Sven. *Exterminate All the Brutes.* New York: New Press, 1996.

Lipset, Seymour Martin, and Earl Raab. *Jews and the New American Scene.* Cambridge, MA: Harvard University Press, 1995.

Lipstadt, Deborah. "Jimmy Carter's Jewish Problem." *Washington Post*, January 20, 2007, http://www.washingtonpost.com/wp-dyn/content/article/2007/01/19/AR2007011901541.html.

Lloyd George, David. *Memoirs of the Peace Conference, Volume II.* New Haven, CT: Yale University Press, 1939.

Lovett, William Anthony, Alfred E. Eckes, and Richard L. Brinkman. *U.S. Trade Policy: History, Theory and the WTO.* Armonk, NY: M. E. Sharpe, 1999.

Lozowick, Yaacov. *Right to Exist: A Moral Defense of Israel's Wars.* New York: Doubleday, 2003.

Maisel, L. Sandy, ed. *Jews in American Politics.* Lanham, MA: Rowman & Littlefield, 2001.

Malino, Frances. "Jewish-Christian Relations." In *Christianity: Enlightenment, Reawakening and Revolution, 1600–1815*, edited by Stewart J. Brown and Timothy Tackett. Cambridge: Cambridge University Press, 2006.

Mansour, Camille. *Beyond Alliance: Israel in U.S. Foreign Policy.* New York: Columbia University Press, 1994.

Mark, Clyde R. *Israel: U.S. Foreign Assistance.* Washington, DC: Library of Congress, Congressional Research Service, October 17, 2002. http://www.adc.org/IB85066.pdf.

Masalha, Nur. *Imperial Israel and the Palestinians: The Politics of Expansion.* London: Pluto, 2000.

———. *Expulsion of the Palestinians: The Concept of "Transfer" in Zionist Political Thought, 1882–1948.* Washington, DC: Institute for Palestine Studies, 2001.

———. *Catastrophe Remembered: Palestine, Israel and the Internal Refugees.* New York: Zed Books, 2005.

Massad, Joseph. "Blaming the Lobby." *Al-Ahram Weekly* 787 (March 23–29, 2006), http://weekly.ahram.org.eg/2006/787/op35.htm.

Matar, N. I. "The Restoration of the Jews in English Protestant Thought: Between the Reformation and 1660." *Durham University Journal*, December 1985, 23–36.

———. *Islam in Britain: 1558–1685.* Cambridge, UK: Cambridge University Press, 1998.

Mearsheimer, John, and Stephen Walt. "The Israel Lobby." *London Review of Books*, March 23, 2006, http://www.lrb.co.uk/v28/n06/mear01_.html.

———. *The Israel lobby and US foreign policy*. New York: Farrar, Straus and Giroux, 2007.

Menocal, María Rose. *The Ornament of the World: How Muslims, Jews, and Christians Created a Culture of Tolerance in Medieval Spain*. Boston: Little, Brown & Company, 2003.

Merkley, Paul C. *The Politics of Christian Zionism, 1891–1948*. London: Frank Cass, 1998.

Merom, Gil. "Israel's National Security and the Myth of Exceptionalism." *Political Science Quarterly* 114, no. 3 (Autumn 1999): 409–34.

Meyer, Karl E. "Editorial Notebook: Woodrow Wilson's Dynamite." *New York Times*, August 14, 1991, http://query.nytimes.com/gst/fullpage.html?res=9D0CE0DC173F F937A2575BC0A967958260.

Miglietta, John P. *American Alliance Policy in the Middle East, 1945–1992: Iran, Israel and Saudi Arabia*. Lanham, MD: Rowman & Littlefield, 2002.

Miller, Rabbi Avigdor. *Awake My Glory: Aspects of Jewish Ideology*. Brooklyn, NY: Bais Yisroel of Rugby, 1980.

Millis, Walter, ed. *The Forrestal Diaries*. New York: Viking, 1951.

Morris, Benny. *The Birth of the Palestinian Refugee Problem, 1947–49*. Cambridge, UK: Cambridge University Press, 1987.

———. *Righteous Victims: A History of the Zionist-Arab Conflict, 1881–2001*. New York: Vintage Books, 2001.

———. *The Birth of the Palestinian Refugee Problem Revisited*. Cambridge, UK: Cambridge University Press, 2004.

———. *1948: A History of the Arab-Israeli War*. New Haven, CT: Yale University Press, 2008.

Naimark, Norman M. "Revolution and Counter-Revolution in Eastern Europe." In *The Crisis of Socialism in Europe*, edited by Christiane Lemke and Gary Marks. Durham, NC: Duke University Press, 1992.

Neff, Donald. *Fallen Pillars: U.S. Policy Towards Israel and Palestine Since 1945*. Washington, DC: Institute for Palestine Studies, 2002. http://www.washingtonpost.com/wp-srv/style/longterm/books/chap1/fallenpillars.htm.

Neusner, Jacob. "A 'Holocaust' Primer." *National Review*, August 3, 1979.

———. *The Comparative Hermeneutics of Rabbinic Judaism*. Vol. 1. Binghamton, NY: Global Academic Publishing, 2000.

Neusner, Jacob, and Alan Jeffery Avery-Peck. *The Routledge Dictionary of Judaism*. New York: Routledge, 2003.

Noah, Mordecai. "Restoration of the Jews," *The Occident and American Jewish Advocate* 3, no. 1 (April 1845), http://www.jewish-history.com/Occident/volume3/apr1845/restoration.html.

Nordau, Max, and Gustav Gottheil. *Zionism and Anti-Semitism*. New York: Fox, Duffield, 1905.

Organski, A. F. K. *The $36 Billion Bargain: Strategy and Politics in U.S. Assistance to Israel*. New York: Columbia University Press, 1990.

Ottolenghi, Emanuele. "Anti-Zionism is Anti-Semitism." *Guardian*, November 29, 2003, http://www.guardian.co.uk/world/2003/nov/29/comment.

Ould-Mey, Mohameden. "The Non-Jewish Origin of Zionism." *The Arab World Geographer* 5, no. 1 (2002): 34–52, http://mama.indstate.edu/users/mouldmey/The%20Non-Jewish%20Origin%20of%20Zionism.PDF.

———. "Geopolitical Genesis and Prospect of Zionism." *Journal of Political Geography* (2003): 1–29, http://mama.indstate.edu/users/mouldmey/Geopolitical%20Genesis %20and%20Prospect%20of%20Zionism.PDF.

Pappe, Ilan. *Britain and Arab-Israeli Conflict, 1948–51*. London: Macmillan, 1988.
———. *The Ethnic Cleansing of Palestine*. Oxford: One World, 2006.
Pasachoff, Naomi, and Robert J. Littman. *A Concise History of the Jewish People*. Lanham, MD: Rowman & Littlefield, 2005.
Patai, Raphael. *The Complete Diaries of Theodore Herzl*. Translated by Harry Zohn. New York: Herzl Press and Thomas Yoseloff, 1960.
Patai, Raphael, and Jennifer P. Wing. *The Myth of the Jewish Race*. New York: Charles Scribner's, 1975.
Paul, James A. "Great Power Conflict over Iraqi Oil: The World War One Era." *Global Policy Forum*, October 2002, http://globalpolicy.org/security/oil/2002/1000history.htm.
Peters, Joan. *From Time Immemorial: The Origins of Arab-Jewish Conflict Over Palestine*. New York: Harper & Row, 1984.
Peterson, Tore T. *The Decline of the Anglo-American Middle East, 1961–1969: A Willing Retreat*. Brighton, UK: Sussex Academic Press, 2006.
Petras, James. *The Power of Israel in the United States*. Atlanta: Clarity, 2006.
Pinsker, Leo. *Auto-Emancipation*. Translated by J. Schulsinger. 1882. Cairo-Alexandria: 1944.
Pipes, Daniel. "[Michael Oren's] Six Days of War." *New York Post*, June 4, 2002, http://www.danielpipes.org.
———. "Israel's Ultimate Strategic Asset." *Jerusalem Post*, July 16, 2003, http://jewishpoliticalchronicle.org/oct03/Israel%20s%20ultimate.pdf.
Portis, Larry. "Zionism and the United States." *CounterPunch*, February 24–25, 2007, http://www.counterpunch.org/portis02242007.html.
Prager, Dennis, and Joseph Telushkin. *Why the Jews? The Reason for Anti-Semitism*. New York: Touchstone, 2003.
Prior, Michael. *Zionism and the State of Israel: A Moral Inquiry*. London: Routledge, 1999.
———. "Israel-Palestine: A Challenge to Theology." In *Faith in the Millennium*, edited by Stanley E. Porter, Michael A. Hayes, and David Tombs. London: Continuum International Publishing Group, 2001.
ProCon.Org. *Israeli-Palestinian: Population Statistics*. http://israelipalestinian.procon.org/viewresource.asp?resourceID=000636.
Project for the New American Century. *Rebuilding America's Defenses: Strategy, Forces, Resources For a New Century*. Washington, DC: September 2000. http://www.newamericancentury.org/RebuildingAmericasDefenses.pdf.
Pry, Peter. *Israel's Nuclear Arsenal*. Boulder, CO: Westview, 1984.
Quigley, John. *Flight into the Maelstrom: Soviet Immigration to Israel and the Middle East Peace*. Ithaca, NY: Ithaca Press, 1997.
Qumsiyeh, Mazin B. *Sharing the Land of Canaan: Human Rights and the Israeli-Palestinian Struggle*. London: Pluto, 2004.
Rabil, Robert G. *Syria, the United States, and the War on Terror in the Middle East*. Westport, CT: Greenwood, 2006.
Rabkin, Yakov M. *A Threat from Within: A History of Jewish Opposition to Zionism*. London: Zed Books, 2006.
Raisin, Max, *A History of the Jews in Modern Times*. New York: Hebrew, 1919.
Reed, Fred. "No Happy Ending." *LewRockwell.com*, January 30, 2009, http://www.lewrockwell.com/reed/reed154.html.
Reich, Bernard. *Securing the Covenant: United States-Israel Relations after the Cold War*. Westport, CT: Greenwood, 1995.
Reinharz, Jehuda. "His Majesty's Zionist Emissary: Chaim Weizmann's Mission to Gibraltar in 1917." *Journal of Contemporary History* 27, no. 2 (April 1992): 259–77.

Rejwan, Nissim. *Israel in Search of Identity: Reading the Formative Years.* Gainesville: University of Florida Press, 1999.

Rodinson, Maxime. *Israel: A Colonial-Settler State?* New York: Monad, 1973.

———. *Israel and the Arabs.* Harmondsworth, UK: Penguin, 1982.

Rose, Jacqueline. *The Question of Zion.* Princeton, NJ: Princeton University Press, 2005.

Rose, John. *The Myth of Zionism.* London: Pluto, 2004.

Roth, Cecil. *Essays and Portraits in Anglo-Jewish History.* Philadelphia: Jewish Publication Society of America, 1962.

Rottenberg, Dan. *Finding our Fathers: A Guidebook to Jewish Genealogy.* Baltimore: Genealogical Publishing, 1986.

Roupp, Heidi, ed. *Teaching World History: A Resource Book.* Armonk, NY: M. E. Sharpe, 1996.

Rubenberg, Cheryl A. *Israel and the American National Interest: A Critical Examination.* Urbana: University of Illinois Press, 1986.

Sachar, Howard. *Israel and Europe: An Appraisal in History.* New York: Alfred A. Knopf, 1999.

Safran, Nadav, *Israel: The Embattled Ally.* Cambridge: Belknap Press of Harvard University Press, 1982.

Said, Edward. "An Ideology of Difference." *Critical Inquiry* 12, no. 1 (Autumn 1985): 38–58.

———. "Foreword." In *Jewish History, Jewish Religion*, by Israel Shahak. London: Pluto, 1994.

Samuel, Maurice. *You Gentiles.* Boring, OR: CPA, 1924.

Sand, Shlomo. "Israel Deliberately Forgets Its History." *Le Monde Diplomatique*, September 2008, http://mondediplo.com/2008/09/07israel.

———. *The Invention of the Jewish People.* London: Verso, 2009.

Schnall, David J. "Review of Raphael Patai and Jennifer P. Wing, *The Myth of the Jewish Race.*" *Review of Jewish Quarterly* 66, no. 3 (January 1976): 181–85.

Schoenfeld, Gabriel. *The Return of Anti-Semitism.* San Francisco: Encounter Books, 2004.

Schuldiner, Michael J., and Daniel J. Kleinfeld, eds. *The Selected Writings of Mordecai Noah.* Westport, CT: Greenwood, 1999.

Schwartz, Stephen. *Is It Good for the Jews? The Crisis of America's Israel Lobby.* New York: Doubleday, 2006.

Schweitzer, A. "Moshe Dayan: Between Leadership and Loneliness." *Haaretz*, December 12, 1958.

Scult, Mel. *Millennial Expectations and Jewish Liberties: A Study of the Efforts to Convert the Jews in Britain, Up to the Mid-Nineteenth Century.* Leiden, the Netherlands: E. J. Brill, 1978.

Secretary of State for Colonies. *British White Paper of June 1922.* Yale Law School: Avalon Project. http://www.yale.edu/lawweb/avalon/mideast/brwh1922.htm.

Segev, Tom. *One Palestine Complete: Jews and Arabs Under the British Mandate.* New York: Henry Holt and Co., 2000.

Seidman, Peter. *Socialists and the Fight Against Anti-Semitism: An Answer to the B'nai B'rith Anti-Defamation League.* 1973. New York: Pathfinder, 2002.

Shahak, Israel. *Jewish History, Jewish Religion: The Weight of Three Thousand Years.* London: Pluto, 1994.

Shapira, Anita. *Land and Power: The Zionist Resort to Force, 1881–1948*, 40–41. New York: Oxford University Press, 1992.

Shapiro, Yonathan. *Leadership of the American Zionist Organization, 1897–1930.* Urbana: University of Illinois Press, 1971.

Sharabi, Hisham. *Palestine and Israel: The Lethal Dilemma*. New York: Pegasus, 1969.

Sharif, Regina. "Christians for Zion, 1600–1919." *Journal of Palestine Studies* 5, no. 3/4 (Spring–Summer 1976): 123–41.

———. *Non-Jewish Zionism: Its Roots in Western History*. London: Zed, 1983.

Sharp, Jeremy M. *U.S. Foreign Assistance to the Middle East: Historical Background, Recent Trends, and the FY2006 request*. Washington, DC: Library of Congress, Congressional Research Service, June 13, 2005. http://fpc.state.gov/documents/organization/50383.pdf.

Shatz, Adam, ed. *Prophets Outcast: A Century of Dissident Jewish Writing about Zionism and Israel*. New York: Nation Books, 2004.

Shavit, Ari. "Survival of the Fittest: An Interview with Benny Morris," *Logos* 3, no. 1 (Winter 2004), http://www.logosjournal.com/morris.htm.

Shiblak, Abbas. *Iraqi Jews: A History of Mass Exodus*. London: Saqi Books, 2005.

Shimoni, Gideon. *The Zionist Ideology*. Hanover, NH: University Press of New England/Brandeis University Press, 1995.

Shlaim, Avi. *Collusion Across the Jordan: King Abdullah, the Zionist Movement, and the Partition of Palestine*. Oxford: Clarendon, 1988.

———. "The Impact of U.S. Policy in the Middle East." *Journal of Palestine Studies* 17, no. 1 (Winter 1988): 15–28.

———. "The Protocol of Sèvres, 1956: Anatomy of a War Plot." *International Affairs* 73, no. 3 (1997): 509–30, http://users.ox.ac.uk/~ssfc0005/The%20Protocol%20of%20Sevres%201956%20Anatomy%20of%20a%20War%20Plot.html.

———. *The Iron Wall: Israel and the Arab World*. New York: W. W. Norton, 2001.

———. "Why Zionism Today Is the Real Enemy of the Jews." *Electronic Intifada*, February 4, 2005, http://www.electronicintifada.net/v2/article3599.shtml.

Sidebotham, Herbert. "British Interests in Palestine, 1917." In *From Haven to Conquest: Readings in Zionism and the Palestine Problem until 1948*, edited by Walid Khalidi. Beirut: Institute for Palestine Studies, 1971.

Simon, Leon, ed. *About Zionism: Speeches and Letters by Professor Albert Einstein*. London: Soncino, 1930.

Simon, Maurice, ed. *Speeches, Articles and Letters of Israel Zangwill*. London: Soncino, 1937.

Slezkin, Yuri. *The Jewish Century*. Princeton, NJ: Princeton University Press, 2004.

Smith, Charles D. *Palestine and the Arab-Israeli Conflict*. New York: St. Martin's, 1988.

Snobelen, S. "'The Mystery of this Restitution of All Things': Isaac Newton on the Return of the Jews." In *Millenarianism and Messianism in Early Modern European Culture: The Millenarian Turn*, edited by J. E. Force and R. H. Popkin. Dordrecht: Kluwer Academic, 2001.

Sokolow, Nahum. *History of Zionism: 1600–1918*. Vol. 1. London: Longmans, Green, 1919.

Solomon, Norman. "The Lobby and the Bulldozer: Mearsheimer, Walt and Corrie." *Huffington Post*, April 13, 2006, http://www.huffingtonpost.com/norman-solomon/the-lobby-and-the-bulldoz_b_19028.html.

Spiegel, Steven L. *The Other Arab-Israeli Conflict: Making America's Middle East Policy from Truman to Reagan*. Chicago: University of Chicago Press, 1985.

Stannard, David. "The Politics of Genocide Scholarship." In *Is the Holocaust Unique? Perspectives on Comparative Genocide*, edited by Alan S. Rosenbaum. Boulder, CO: Westview, 2001.

Stauffer, Thomas R. "The Cost of Conflict in the Middle East, 1956–2002: What the U.S. Has Spent." *Middle East Policy* 10, no. 1 (March 2003): 45–102.

Stein, Leonard. *The Balfour Declaration*. New York: Simon and Schuster, 1961.

Sternhell, Zeev. *The Founding Myths of Israel*. Translated by David Maisel. Princeton, NJ: Princeton University Press, 1998.

Stone, Ronald H. *Professor Reinhold Niebuhr: A Mentor to the Twentieth Century*. Louisville, KY: Westminster John Knox, 1992.

Stork, Joe, and Sharon Rose. "Zionism and American Jewry." *Journal of Palestine Studies* 3, no. 3 (Spring 1974): 39–57.

Straten, Jits Van, and Harmen Snel. "The Jewish 'Demographic Miracle' in Nineteenth-Century Europe: Fact or Fiction." *Historical Methods: A Journal of Quantitative and Interdisciplinary History* 39, no. 3 (Summer 2006): 123–31.

Straus, Nellie. *The Congress Addresses of Theodore Herzl*. Translated by Nellie Straus. New York: Federation of American Zionists, 1917.

Taylor, Melissa Jane. "Evian Conference." In *Anti-Semitism: A Historical Encyclopedia of Prejudice and Persecution*, edited by Richard S. Levy. Santa Barbara, CA: ABC-CLIO, 2005.

Teger, Shira. "Coming Together, Falling Apart." *Jerusalem Post*, April 23, 2007, http://www.jpost.com/servlet/Satellite?apage=1&cid=1177251151218&pagename=JPost%2FJPArticle%2FShowFull.

Telegraph (Marconi Transatlantic Wire Telegraph). "Angola Is Offered for Zionist Colony." *New York Times*, June 28, 1912.

Thomas, Gordon. *Gideon's Spies: The Secret History of the Mossad*. Houndmills, UK: Macmillan, 2007.

Tivnan, Edward. *The Lobby: Jewish Political Power and American Foreign Policy*. New York: Simon and Schuster, 1987.

van Straten, Jits, and Harmen Snel. "The Jewish 'Demographic Miracle' in Nineteenth Century Europe." *Historical Methods* 39, no. 3 (Summer 2006): 123–31.

Vital, David. *The Origins of Zionism*. New York: Oxford University Press, 1975.

———. *A People Apart: The Jews in History*. New York: Oxford University Press, 1999.

Vreté, Mayir. "The Restoration of the Jews in English Protestant Thought 1790–1840." *Middle Eastern Studies* 8, no. 1 (January 1972): 3–50.

Walt, Stephen M. *The Origins of Alliances*. Cornell, NY: Cornell University Press, 1990.

Weinstock, Nathan. *Zionism: False Messiah*. Translated by Alan Adler. London: Ink Links, 1979.

———. *Histoires de chiens*. Paris: Mille et Une Nuits, 2004.

———. *Use si longue présence: comment le monde arabe a perdu ses juifs 1947–1967*. Plon, 2008.

Wenger, Martha. "Recipe for an Israeli Nuclear Arsenal." *MERIP Middle East Report*, no. 143 (November–December 1986): 8–12, 14–15.

Wexler, Paul. *The Non-Jewish Origins of the Sephardic Jews*. Albany: SUNY Press, 1996.

Wyman, David S., and Charles H. Rosenzveig. *The World Reacts to the Holocaust*. Baltimore: Johns Hopkins University Press, 1996.

Yaacobi, Gad. *Breakthrough: Israel in a Changing World*. New York: Cornwall Books, 1996.

Ye'or, Bat. *The Dhimmi: Jews and Christians under Islam*. Madison, NJ: Dickinson University Press, 1985.

———. *The Decline of Eastern Christianity under Islam: From Jihad to Dhimmitude*. Madison, NJ: Dickinson University Press, 1996.

———. *Islam and Dhimmitude: Where Civilizations Collide*. Madison, NJ: Dickinson University Press: 2002.

Young, James E. "Bad for the Jews: Review of David Vital, *A People Apart*." *New York Times*, November 7, 1999, http://query.nytimes.com/gst/fullpage.html?res=9C02E6DA1138F934A35752C1A96F958260.

Zangwill, Israel. *The Voice of Jerusalem*. London: William Heinemann, 1920.

Zionist Organization of America, *The American War Congress and Zionism: Statements by Members of the American War Congress on the Jewish National Movement*. New York: Zionist Organization of America, 1919. http://ia360919.us.archive.org/1/items/americanwarcongr00zion/americanwarcongr00zion.pdf.

Zunes, Stephen. "U.S. Aid to Israel: Interpreting the 'Strategic Relationship.'" *Washington Report on Middle East Affairs*, http://www.wrmea.com/html/us_aid_to_israel.htm.

————. *Why the U.S. Supports Israel*. Washington, DC: Foreign Policy in Focus, May 1, 2002. http://www.fpif.org/fpiftxt/1545.

Zureik, Elia. "Palestinian Refugees and Peace." *Journal of Palestine Studies* 24, no. 1 (Summer 1994): 5–17.

INDEX

al-Beruni, xi
Alkali, Rabbi, 20
Al-Khalidi, Youssuf Zia, 76, 236
American Israel Public Affairs Committee (AIPAC). *See* Zionist organizations
American Jewish Committee. *See* Zionist organizations
American Palestine Committee, 134, 158
anti-Semitism, 12, 50, 85, 87, 119, 227
  accusations of Arab/Islamic, 13, 39, 40, 41
  catalyzed into dispensationalism, 127
  causes of, 65, 74, 84, 85, 227, 232
  complementarities (after 1948) between Zionism and, 45, 100, 119, 122, 123, 125, 127
  complementarities (before 1948) between Zionism and, 35, 82, 98, 117–27, 139, 142
  in Eastern Europe, 65, 98
  new (in Europe), 13, 85, 87, 89, 227
  not only cause of Zionism, 53
  socialist revolution, as solution to, 87
  unique hatred, 12, 13
  in the United States, 117, 127
  in Western Europe, 47, 84, 98
  Zionist provocation of, 121, 126
apartheid (South Africa), 30, 75. *See also* Israel: apartheid society
Arab-Israeli Wars. *See* June War of 1967; Suez War (1956); War of 1948; Yom Kippur War

Arab nationalism, 11, 28, 125, 147, 163, 169, 170, 175, 176, 180, 192
  approach to Jewish colonial settler state, 184–85
  Arab Christians and, 184
  British invoke, 184
  class character of, 184
  Emir Faisal and, 27
  weakness and failures of, 184, 185
  without Zionism, 168–69
Azouri, Najib, 31

Balfour, Lord, 77, 103, 112, 119, 150, 238
Balfour Declaration, 71, 76, 77, 103, 134, 138, 149, 150, 154, 155, 156, 165, 176, 199, 204, 236, 237
  Britain's strategic interests and, 106–10, 113
  as British policy offering, 106
  British retreat from, 115, 116, 113–15, 148, 181 (*see also* White Paper: 1939)
  Christian Zionists in David Lloyd George's cabinet, 112, 217
  David Lloyd George on, 106–7
  great power competition for support of Jews during WWI, 111, 112, 113, 142
  Jewish power and, 106, 107, 176
  WW I and, 110–11, 112
Basel Program, 31, 32, 221
Ben-Gurion, David, 90, 117, 156, 157, 177, 214, 231, 232, 239, 243

9 780230 619982